PROSPECTS FOR A
COMMON MORALITY

PROSPECTS FOR A COMMON MORALITY

GENE OUTKA AND
JOHN P. REEDER, JR.,
EDITORS

PRINCETON UNIVERSITY PRESS

PRINCETON, NEW JERSEY

Copyright © 1993 by Princeton University Press

Published by Princeton University Press, 41 William Street,

Princeton, New Jersey 08540

In the United Kingdom: Princeton University Press,

Chichester, West Sussex

All Rights Reserved

Library of Congress Cataloging-in-Publication Data

Prospects for a common morality / Gene Outka and John P. Reeder,
editors.

p.   cm.

Includes index.

ISBN 0-691-07418-6 — ISBN 0-691-02093-0

1. Ethics. I. Outka, Gene H. II. Reeder, John P., 1937– .

BJ1012.P76   1992

170′.44—dc20   92-5681

This book has been composed in Linotron Sabon

Princeton University Press books are printed
on acid-free paper and meet the guidelines for
permanence and durability of the Committee on
Production Guidelines for Book Longevity
of the Council on Library Resources

Printed in the United States of America

10 9 8 7 6 5 4 3 2 1

10 9 8 7 6 5 4 3 2 1

(pbk)

CONTENTS

ACKNOWLEDGMENTS

O
UR EARLY EFFORTS were aided significantly by a workshop that explored this vast subject, held in October 1984 at the Woodrow Wilson International Center for Scholars in Washington, D.C. We are grateful to those at the Center, especially Prosser Gifford and Ann Sheffield, who brought together fellows at the Center and outside participants to discuss approaches and identify pitfalls. The stimulus of those sessions proved decisive for our subsequent work. The Center, which does so many things well, was exemplary in its support of this undertaking.

The expenses incurred in preparing the index and for other editorial matters were defrayed by a Griswold Award and a Divinity School faculty research grant from Yale University, and by a Faculty Development Fund grant from Brown University. We thank also Gerhard Böwering, Dan Brock, Cathleen Kaveny, Thomas Lewis, Gordon Marino, and David Wills for editorial counsel at critical stages. David Little and Jeffrey Stout offered helpful suggestions for the introduction and organization of the volume. James Gubbins and Zachary Lesser assisted with editorial details. Susan Lundgren prepared the index. Finally, we thank anonymous reviewers of the volume, our editor at Princeton University Press, Ann Himmelberger Wald, and our copyeditor, Megan Benton.

"The Priority of Democracy to Philosophy" was published first in *The Virginia Statute of Religious Freedom*, ed. Merrill Peterson and Robert Vaughn (Cambridge: Cambridge University Press, 1988), pp. 257–82. It also appeared in Richard Rorty, *Objectivity, Relativism and Truth*, Philosophical Papers, vol. 1 (Cambridge: Cambridge University Press, 1991), pp. 175–96. Copyright 1988 and 1991 by Cambridge University Press and reprinted here with the permission of the author and Cambridge University Press. "Truth and Freedom: A Reply to McCarthy" appeared in *Critical Inquiry* 16 (Spring 1990): 633–43. Copyright 1990 by The University of Chicago Press and reprinted here with the permission of the author and The University of Chicago Press.

PROSPECTS FOR A
COMMON MORALITY

INTRODUCTION

GENE OUTKA AND JOHN P. REEDER, JR.

RECENT MORAL and political thought seems Janus-faced. We find on the one side a remarkable kind of cross-cultural moral agreement about human rights. The Universal Declaration of Human Rights, announced in the United Nations in 1948, proves to be far more than an isolated episode of idealistic recoil from the horrors of World War II. Such rights have been reaffirmed and elaborated in numerous international instruments and agreements; as a result, the policies of some governments have changed, and people in many parts of the world have risen against repression. For example, many people take the work of Amnesty International to be the exercise of the conscience of the world. The verdicts rendered about how various societies treat their members assume moral criteria that transcend "Western" values. Assumed, in short, is the nonrelative validity of certain moral claims that protect and promote the freedom and welfare of persons *as such*. A cross-cultural consensus about these claims would seem to provide us with a "common morality."

We find on the other side an apparent loss of confidence in any such consensus. A host of modern and postmodern developments stress the distinctive historicity of every person and every moral claim. These developments include mounting unhappiness with the ahistorical aspirations of the Enlightenment and the liberalism it inspired, the full arrival of feminist, African-American, and other hitherto-neglected sources of distinctive moral experience, the insistence—fueled by Wittgensteinian insights—that moral standards retain their intelligibility and point only within the traditions that articulate them, the resources of Marxist criticism, Nietzschean skepticism, Foucault's historical labors, and Derridean literary theory. Called into question are not only universal human rights but any notion of a common morality that applies and can be justified to persons as such.

It is important to reckon with both sides if we are to understand what considerations govern current discussion. The notion of a common morality known to all human beings has a long history in Western thought. Concepts of "natural law," blending Stoic and Aristotelian ideas, have been influential for centuries. Since the Enlightenment, but reflecting earlier traditions, "natural" or human rights (Locke) or duties based on universal reason (Kant) have often served as a common moral currency, endorsed by philosophers and theologians alike. Of late, however, both the rationale and the content of notions of a common morality have come under severe attack. Alasdair MacIntyre, for example, argues that Alan Gewirth's justification of human rights fails; one cannot find an objective basis for rights in general facts about human beings.[1] Moreover, whereas earlier critics generally wanted to retain the substance of the morality whose basis they undermined, recent critics also call into question the content of natural rights or Kantian duties. Sharon Welch, for example, drawing on Foucault, suggests that Western notions of equality have functioned in part as the morality of a dominant gender and class that masks oppression.[2] Thus critics not only reject the effort to find a foundation in common features of human nature but propose alternatives to the reigning paradigms of rights or rational duty.

These criticisms arise in both philosophical and theological circles. MacIntyre announces that human rights do not exist, and others claim that the notion of a common morality is an illusion. They offer a historicist (sometimes called pragmatist or coherentist) understanding of how moralities are legitimated in particular contexts, in contrast to the search for an ahistorical foundation, and they turn away from the rights or duties of Enlightenment traditions, urging for example a return to an Aristotelian conception of ethics.

This volume assembles essays that reflect such current debates.[3] The essays attempt to clarify senses of common morality and to furnish readers with a spectrum of estimates about its prospects. We have sought to avoid any party line. Some essays defend and others attack the prospects, in varying though representative ways; they exhibit a plurality of concerns and issues that fuel the debate. Taken together the essays provide a succinct and accessible overview. They also, we believe, advance the debate. Thus we hope the volume will prove widely useful to specialists and to students.

The volume is also distinctive at two points. First, the authors in the volume—regardless of the traditions from which they work—all address the issue of cross-cultural, cross-traditional moral agreement; they are concerned with the possibility of a "common morality" in the sense of moral judgments that not only apply, but could be justified, to persons in a variety of cultures. Some address the particular question of what role, if any, religious communities play in the pursuit of a common morality. Second, the volume does not focus directly on standard philosophical questions about moral realism, or about various senses of relativism. Certainly many of our authors discuss general issues in moral epistemology, and many eschew relativism in one sense or the other. Yet the volume overall has a more historically attuned connection to an inherited paradigm that has shaped both popular culture and intellectual discourse in the West. The paradigm is an Enlightenment interpretation of a common or universal morality. We believe the essays in this volume may be intelligibly seen as exhibiting a variety of responses to this paradigm.

The paradigm—operative in the constitutions of many democratic states and given various theoretical interpretations by philosophers and theologians—has three major focuses:

1. certain moral beliefs are required by the structure of human reason; these are universal, at least implicitly, in the conscience of humankind, and they serve as the foundation of morality;[4]

2. these basic beliefs are not derived from a vision of the good, but they regulate how we should seek human flourishing or eudaimonia;[5]

3. the content and justification of these moral beliefs are independent of religious conceptions of transcendent powers or states and their relation to human beings; these core moral beliefs provide the normative glue that protects religious and other liberties in the democratic tradition; religious communities, however, can interpret this morality in terms of a larger conception of human existence, and can serve as vehicles for moral education and training.[6]

One could loosely place our authors into three groups: those who retain, yet perhaps also modify, the central tenets of the paradigm; those who reject one or more of those tenets, yet do not depart from its central impulse to address a universal audience; and those who not only want to reject elements of the paradigm but give up any appeal to a universal audience. Much depends, however, on how one reads our authors, and in any case there are important overlaps, as we note, even between authors predominantly on the "right" and on the "left." Although their voices often seem entirely disparate, we believe we can locate fruitful points of comparison and contrast that provide resources to shape the next stages of the debate.

Let us now sketch our authors' views, and then offer our own interpretation of where they agree and disagree.

THE ESSAYS

Alan Gewirth characterizes morality "as a set of rules or directives for actions and institutions" that bear especially on the interests of those other than the agent and that override all other claims. He distinguishes, on the metaethical level, between positive and normative conceptions of morality. The former is a morality that is, in fact, upheld by persons; the latter is a morality in which moral precepts or rules are valid "and thus ought to be upheld." He then distinguishes between a common morality that is an "ethical universalism" and various particularist moralities that prefer certain groups to others. He devotes the remainder of the paper to establishing human rights as the basis for a common morality that is normative at the metaethical level and universal in its range. He argues (1) that rights protect interests all persons have in common; (2) that commonly distributed interests are more fundamental than divergent interests; and (3) that the status of these protected interests as rights is susceptible to rational proof.

Gewirth does not repeat here in detail his well-known argument that freedom and well-being are necessary goods and that the requirement of consistency establishes basic rights; nor does he repeat his replies to critics of the premises or reasoning in his argument. Rather he considers objections (raised by feminists, for example) that attack the putative universality of human rights and their moral content. The first is the ethnocentric objection, which holds that rights are unique to an individualist, post-Enlightenment culture. He answers that the idea of equal human rights is found in ancient and medieval sources as well as non-Western cultures; that the fact that different cultures did not espouse this view does not thereby invalidate it; and that the tendency of political systems toward democracy exhibits a normative dynamic supporting the recognition of rights as protective of human dignity. The second is the egoistic objection, which holds that rights presuppose a self that is "purely self-interested, self-centered, and amoral." Gewirth answers that human rights can serve as the basis of social solidarity in units larger and more distant than family and friends; that rights are essentially social, since they require a mutual sharing of benefits and burdens, as well as reciprocal respect; and that a community of rights is nonutopian.

Finally, Gewirth considers further substantive challenges. The community of rights must resolve conflicts, and it does this by ranking rights. Furthermore, human rights must become accepted as a positive conception. To satisfy the latter challenge, one can say that the community of rights does not require that human beings be portrayed as exclusively rational; that the right institutions (a constitutional democracy) facilitate acceptance; and that religion's proper role is—in a subordinate position—to support morality. Religion is neither necessary nor sufficient, however, to ensure the "positive effectuation" of normative morality.

Alan Donagan, we note with sadness, died on May 29, 1991. We are pleased, however, to include the essay he prepared for this volume. Here he both elucidates morality as he believes Kant presented it and defends it against standard objections. Such morality ("traditional Christian morality demystified and universalized") Christianity presupposes as true, though it does not presuppose Christianity as true.

Kant's Enlightenment project assumes that something universally human "underlies the *mores* of any religious or socio-political community" and that there are requirements "on human beings simply as human." Kant accepts, with other Enlightenment philosophers, Plato's case against identifying morality with divine positive law (*Euthyphro* 10a–11a), but Kant also breaks with the empiricist tradition in refusing to say that requirements on human beings arise from some capacity for feeling or some moral sense. Such requirements arise instead from reason. In this claim Kant is anticipated by Aquinas and other medieval scholastics as well as by Protestants like John Calvin. Perhaps Kant's most important contribution to the theory of practical reason is to distinguish between producible and self-existent ends. Each producible end presupposes an existing being—a self-existent end—for whose sake it is produced. And "each human being necessarily regards himself or herself as a 'self-existent end, and can recognize that all others necessarily so regard themselves, on the same rational ground.'"

Donagan considers two sorts of objections to the doctrine that persons should think of themselves as ends in themselves. The first sort are skeptical. Some hold that it is logically possible to assent to Kant's theses about human beings and still deny the doctrine. Donagan regards this as a "skeptical cavil" of the kind rightly dismissed in other fields. Kant's reasoning to justify the doctrine is "dialectical," "practical," and "holistic." A variant of the skeptical objection is that Enlightenment moralists themselves fail to accept one another's conclusions. Donagan replies that the differences among such moralists are to be expected among "philosophers who are in substantial agreement about morality, but who differ in intellectual formation and temperament."

The second sort of objection can be traced to Hegel. To ground morality in rationality serves to "homogenize" human beings, and thus to undermine communal bonds without putting anything else in their place. Donagan finds this sort of objection to derive "from an error that pervades much Hegelian criticism of non-Hegelian philosophy: the error that abstracting a property of something, and examining what follows from having that property, implies that that thing has no other properties." Kant assumes that human beings are community-forming creatures who cannot be homogenized, and that they possess characteristics that they share with only some others and that influence the communities they join. What Kant rejects is the move to make such characteristics grounds for morality. He imposes rational limits on what kinds of communities people should join. He disallows any community, for example, that claims to determine the producible *tele* or ends of its members. And he claims that "every human being is a *viator*" who cannot be completely at home in any actual earthly community.

Donagan also considers two other related objections to the way Kant determines the structure or content of morality. The first objection goes to the deductive character of the structure. Donagan replies that Kantian

morality deduces specific requirements from a single moral principle—
"that it is irrational of possessors of practical reason not to treat themselves and each other as self-existent ends"—but it does so by attending
to "an indefinite number of nonmoral specifications of kinds of failure"
to honor the principle. The principle is *systemically* fundamental, but not
epistemically fundamental. Epistemically, the principles of deductive systems are accepted on holistic grounds and can be queried in light of new
evidence. And "the propositions by which Kant arrived at his fundamental moral principle" are presented not as self-evident but as "inseparable
from a variety of beliefs most of us share or can be brought to share."

The second objection is that Kant's moral theory is universal, abstract,
and unhistorical. Donagan replies that universal moral standards are required for any community to judge when its life has gone rotten. Kant
thought that nationalist and imperialist wars jeopardized the mutual recognition of human dignity. In general, "to deny content to a morality of
humanity, as distinct from the *Sittlichkeit* of this particular *Volk*, . . . is as
blind in theory as it is pernicious in practice."

David Little identifies two sets of claims and beliefs that purport to
describe "our contemporary spiritual and intellectual condition." The
first "postmodern" set denies that we have access to standards of morality we can justify and apply independently of our particular cultures and
religious traditions. The second set affirms such access, above all in the
case of human rights. These rights possess cross-cultural validity; to understand them and see them as binding does not require immersion in
European culture. Little adheres "unflinchingly" to the second set.

He offers here a rationale for his adherence. The rationale goes
through two stages. First, at a sociological or descriptive level, those who
neglect the movement toward "the internationalization of human rights"
ignore their own newspapers. Human rights constitute a moral language
to which appeal is increasingly made from diverse cultural quarters. A
normative vocabulary that is nowadays so widely employed confounds
MacIntyre's influential thesis that our moral discourse has degenerated
into incoherent fragments.

Little's second stage apparently involves the unfashionable attempt to
rehabilitate a version of rational intuitionism. He differs from earlier intuitionists in restricting the basic moral intuitions at stake to a more modest number and range, and in being less confident that his procedure can
resolve moral dilemmas. Even so, he thinks that something of what intuitionists were after illuminates our moral responses. Our revulsion to torture—to amuse or to intimidate—requires no further explanation or justification. To demonstrate the wrongness of such acts we simply describe,
graphically, their nature and circumstances. Moreover, responses like
these establish a prior standard for appraising moral theories. To the extent that any theory proves to dilute or enfeeble our basic moral intui-

tions, it refutes itself. Little judges that a number of historicist theories do serve to undermine our intuitions, and that other appeals, such as those to the Golden Rule and to utilitarian maximization, threaten to trivialize them. The moral authority of human rights, including the right against torture, rests finally then on our intuition or recognition that certain acts are transparently wrong: "Deliberately to inflict severe suffering upon defenseless individuals like children for some self-regarding purpose such as amusement or protection from political criticism is an important part of what the concept of 'moral wrongness' *has* to mean."

The specific characteristics of human rights are five: (1) a human right is a moral right that should serve as a standard for legal arrangements, governmental conduct, and the use of force; (2) it protects "something of indispensable human importance"; (3) it is neither earned nor achieved but is "natural" to us, and must not be "disallowed by virtue of race, creed, ethnic origin or gender"; (4) while some rights can be forfeited, others are indefeasible, whatever the circumstances; and (5) a human right is "universally claimable."

Little adds that the contemporary international consensus on human rights, which has grown rapidly, gained strength from the struggle against colonialism and fascism. Thus, "after World War II, no more convincing refutation of any set of beliefs could be given than by observing that it approved of (or led to, or trivialized) arbitrary suffering of the sort practiced during that period." Confronting colonial and fascist practices did not lead people for the first time to denounce discriminatory practices. Rather, "the overall moral effect of these movements" clarified the dimensions of our intuitions.

Robert Merrihew Adams argues that a shared morality is something every society must and will have, but that such a common morality does not require a shared ethical theory. And we are fortunate a shared ethical theory is not required, for we are unlikely to see it achieved anywhere, at least not in any modern society that permits free inquiry. He views common morality as "a set of agreements among people who typically also hold other, less widely shared ethical beliefs." These agreements constitute a large area of overlap among diverse moralities; they are "loosely recognizable" but remain an "untheoretical jumble" or an "unsystematic plurality." Indeed, what counts as common morality "is not only imprecise but variable and relative to one's historical and cultural context." Common morality encompasses as well principles we learn "that tell us not so much which actions to perform as how to judge which actions to perform." These principles include the Golden Rule or universalizability, fairness as the consistent application of rules, and beneficence.

Pretheoretical agreements in morals have their limits. We condemn killing and violent assault, for example, but we disagree about the morality of warfare, capital punishment, and euthanasia. Such controversies and uncertainties provide an impetus for the development of ethical theory. But the history of modern debate leads us to conclude that we will never agree on a single comprehensive ethical theory. Two points prove most important: (1) common morality persists without ethical theory or when theory is in disarray, and (2) any ethical theory is assessed by how well it accords with central precepts of common morality ("if an ethical theory were to imply that lying, cheating, stealing, and killing people are not generally wrong—so much the worse for the theory").

What occurs when we introduce religious theses into ethical theory? Certainly not all such theses are morally neutral: some have had horrendous moral consequences, and others have proven superior to and prophetic within the common morality of a given time and place. We may reasonably expect overall that a religious ethic will support the precepts of common morality and will add demands of its own. The most difficult questions remain epistemological. Adams employs the notion of general revelation to explain "principles that have wide enough acceptance to be genuinely a part of common morality." Thus general revelation does not jeopardize common morality. Special revelation (for example, solely in the Bible) may pose more problems, yet those who claim it demonstrate appreciable overlap with nonbelievers both in their patterns of reasoning and in their moral judgments.

Adams turns next to a rationale for democracy broadly inspired by Reinhold Niebuhr. Theorists like Rawls and MacIntyre suppose that more intellectual agreement is required for a good social order than Adams thinks possible. He contends that we need, in addition to common morality, agreement on some principles of constitutional law. Conflict is then accepted rather than eradicated, but within agreed limits. Democracy is a nonviolent process for working through social conflicts, in which compromise rather than agreement through reason is the chief alternative to violence.

Finally, Adams treats sympathetically the contention that religion must be practiced in a total form of life rather than in a pluralistic society. We do well to remember, however, that Christianity assumed shape in a pluralistic empire. It is committed to a characteristic distinction between church and state. He does not deplore Constantinianism, but thinks that it is not the only option. Christianity's stress on conversion and pilgrimage makes a pluralistic society as favorable as a homogeneous one.

Gene Outka concentrates on a particular standpoint and tradition, that of Augustinian Christianity. He locates its account of morality between the extremes usually associated with the Enlightenment and sectarianism. The tradition is constituted by determinate convictions about God as the supreme good. Believers depend on particular sources, the Bible above all, for awareness of our total situation. We cannot reverse this order of knowledge, though its circularity proves virtuous. Convictions internal to the tradition are never rendered redundant; they pervade the account in both obvious and subtle ways. Within its own web of belief, the tradition claims that creation is never replaced by the Fall, and that we remain morally capable creatures. The tradition recognizes, moreover, that there are certain "generally negotiable" moral appeals. Such appeals do not form a layer separate unto itself, unrelated to what the tradition holds about God as the supreme good. The appeals are interpreted in light of the larger convictions, and they confirm and reinforce data internal to the tradition.

Outka examines three kinds of interplay between determinate convictions and general moral appeals: the Golden Rule as an instance of the appeals to justice that all should acknowledge, the prohibition against lying, and two far-reaching generalizations about human beings summarized in Augustine's observation that "there is nothing so social by nature, so unsocial by its corruption as this race."

The Golden Rule attests to our status as morally capable creatures and displays Augustine's confidence that what persons normally want for themselves does not vary totally across cultures. It articulates something essential in the moral life. Yet determinate convictions influence his interpretation of the rule as well. They inform his replies to standard objections to the rule; they are linked to moral considerations the rule does not address; they dispose him to bring the rule into close interpretive proximity with the love commandment; and they sensitize him to violations so that the rule serves to disclose unwelcome truths about ourselves. The prohibition against lying is defended in the first instance to the particular religious community. Yet Augustine is also not content here to speak only esoterically. He adduces reasons against lying that he thinks merit acknowledgment by those outside the community. The two generalizations about human beings show the interplay on a more sweeping scale. Each generalization epitomizes a set of religious claims. The second generalization, for example, is connected to sin, an irreducibly religious notion. Nonetheless, Augustine thinks that nonbelievers can recognize the deep tendency of human beings to moral evil. A modern Augustinian, Reinhold Niebuhr, tries to show the general force and ongoing relevance of the notion. It is more than a dispensable picture, lacking all claims to permanence. Yet once again one cannot disentangle the political importance Niebuhr ascribes to the notion from the etiology he defends. There is a religious increment to his pessimism in arguing that sin sets upper limits to our malleability, a pessimism that differs from both moral cynicism and moral skepticism. In short, the interplay is too continuous to warrant a "two-level" morality with a floor of general appeals that exists independently of all determinate convictions. Rather, such appeals are integrated into a broader depiction of human good and human destiny.

Annette Baier argues that humans as social beings engage in a variety of cooperative enterprises, including speech, that protect and promote our vital interests. As speakers, we claim a right to a fair hearing regarding the production and distribution of goods in cooperative enterprises. We use disagreement and agreement as a substitute for the conflict and accord of nonspeaking animals.

We adduce our rights in particular as a way to resist dominance and to avoid begging. Historically rights have been used by oppressed groups, but their extension has been limited. For example, the white males who wrote the American Declaration of Independence opposed English tyranny but restricted its provisions. It took reformers, abolitionists, and feminists to expand the pool of rights-claimants beyond what American revolutionaries had in mind. Occasionally a universal right emerges, like Ann Lee's notion of a sex- and race-blind right to participate in the governance of the Shaker community.

Rights become the primary language of moral debate when individuals acquire consciousness of themselves as having claims to a due share of the fruits of cooperation. Rights belong to individuals, while obligations can be possessed collectively as well as individually. But individual rights are the tip of the moral iceberg, Baier argues, for they rest on cooperatively discharged responsibilities. Rights are parasitic on collective responsibilities, not vice versa.

Beyond our right to free speech, we debate other universal rights. We disagree about the vital interests that rights protect. We have always traded off rights. In American society we exchange welfare rights for individual liberties; we choose freedom of speech over the welfare of children, for example, or the free pursuit of economic well-being over a right to food, clothing, shelter, or job. Rights can be reduced as well as extended because they tend to conflict and because we not only claim and contest but also plea bargain, compromise, and adjust. But if rights are a way to offset dominance without begging, we should stress welfare rights more than we do, in particular the right not to be tortured, the violation of which is less the violation of a particular right than an escape from morality itself. Today we still need rights to protect interests, but the language of vital interests could come to replace the language of rights.

Margaret Farley endorses recent feminist criticisms of traditional notions of universal morality. Nonetheless, she sees a need to develop a new notion of common morality (action guides and character). She is not content with "liberal feminism"; the extension of equal rights to women does not "take account of the particular historical situations of women," for it appears to leave unchallenged the gendered division of labor inherent in the distinction between private and public spheres of life. "Marxist feminism" believes that liberal feminism rests on the false notion of a solitary self possessed of a universal and ahistorical faculty of reason. But Marxist feminism roots all oppression in class and does not sufficiently attend to gender or race. For "radical" feminists, patriarchy is the "most basic form of all oppression"; radical feminists want to recover women's experience: "emotion in relation to reason, embodiment in relation to transcendent mind, caring in relation to ahistorical principles of justice." Farley seeks a version of feminist theory that combines an emphasis on gender and class (and race and age as well) while finding connections across these barriers. Thus she recognizes that previous conceptions of universal morality have often masked the interests of particular groups, but she believes that feminists should be committed to conversation and provisional agreements across borders of nation, race, class, and gender. She sees two major obstacles to a universal morality: feminist theory's emphasis on the particular and contingent, and its recent doubts that even "women's experience" furnishes any true commonalities. Do all efforts to identify commonalities suppress difference and mistake the contingent for the essential? Despite these doubts Farley continues to believe in common features of human experience and thus in the possibility of moral agreements between diverse cultures. She apparently believes that appeals can and should be made to features of experience, such as capacities for suffering and joy, that are commonly recognizable in spite of differences in gender, class, race, and culture; working by analogy, we can recognize similarity as well as difference. She wants to avoid relativism (the view that all views are equally true) as well as foundationalistic claims to finality.

Substantively Farley wants an understanding of the person that overcomes the dichotomy between separation and relation. Not satisfied with the postmodern diffusion of the self, she defends a notion of the self that includes individual identity as well as sociality; she affirms "relation," but not at the expense of "autonomy." She also proposes a notion of just caring that does not divide these elements conceptually or along lines of gender. She seeks to break down the dichotomy, suggesting that while we act out of love (of something or someone), love needs the structure of justice. Her endorsement of a just love builds on the ideal of human well-being, and thus she anchors her morality in a conception of human good. She offers an account of common morality that would embrace and not deny cultural and gender difference, and that would thus provide for moral and religious pluralism.

John Reeder constructs a model of current neopragmatist moral epistemology that tries to negotiate between "foundationalism" and "relativism." On this model justification is nondeductive, consisting in specific judgments and inductive generalizations modified by their application to new cases. The neopragmatist also denies that moralities are conceptual schemes that may turn out to be mutually untranslatable. And although this neopragmatist allows for overlaps in issues and even in judgments, there is always the possibility of intractable moral disagreement; the neopragmatist does not propose a universal morality.

Reeder revises this model. He first argues that standards or criteria often have an independent justification; he then claims that a neopragmatist epistemology should not in principle rule out appeals to the nature of things, such as the nature of the self or transcendent reality. Reeder agrees with the neopragmatists that understanding is always possible, although it can require a "second first language" or "hermeneutical enrichment." He argues as well that understanding can take place analogically on the basis of "concrete universals," which refer to fundamental capacities such as compassion. Lastly, Reeder takes up the thesis that not only do we not have any assurance of moral agreement, but that we should not even search for a normative standpoint that all persons should hold in common. He notes that for John Rawls the theory of justice is a systematization of moral beliefs of a particular culture (liberal democracy) and hence is not addressed to all humankind. Moreover, Rawls's view of justice does not supplant or replace diverse moral traditions; rather, it regulates them. Reeder argues that a regulative conception of justice or, more broadly, a moral framework in the liberal tradition could be extended universally. He suggests that in contrast to the idea of a consensus that rests on culturally dissimilar grounds, or one that is accepted for its own sake without grounding, a consensus might be supported by appeals to analogous conceptions of human capacities such as compassion; thus views of the self could play a role in establishing a wide consensus.

Jeffrey Stout rejects nihilism (the view that there are no moral truths), skepticism (the view that moral beliefs have no justification), and radical relativism (the view that one's moral beliefs are not applicable outside of one's culture). But is there a set of "uniformities" (strong similarities) with which to settle moral conflicts? Stout thinks that this sense of a common morality is possible, but not likely; he recommends proceeding on an ad hoc basis, looking for local, not global, overlaps.

Stout does not think that anyone has established a "set of (nontrivial) moral beliefs that any human being or rational agent regardless of context, would be justified in accepting." Because epistemic contexts vary, "not everyone is justified in believing the same propositions." Since moral vocabularies, patterns of moral reasoning, and evidence differ, so do the beliefs people can accept. It is possible but not likely, therefore, that there are some beliefs everyone is justified in believing.

To be justified in believing a proposition one does not have to justify it, or even to be able to justify it. We can justifiably hold culturally acquired beliefs so long as we have no adequate reason to doubt them and we have not committed some epistemic fault, such as a neglect of evidence. We do not always need justifying *arguments*. Context will determine the relevant reasons for doubt and what suffices to eliminate it. We should not seek an abstract universal list of the "conditions a successful justification of moral propositions ought to satisfy." Thus while we can address ourselves to all moral agents, it would be foolish to do so. We can condemn the Nazis while realizing that their reasons for their morality are not relevant in our epistemic context. Our contexts can change, through education, for example, but they will likely continue to be limited. Hence on this "contextual account of justification" we do not need and should not seek a universal audience.

Thus for Stout justification is relative, but truth is not. When people disagree morally they entertain the same proposition, one believing it to be true and the other false. A relativist account of moral truth, which says that the two views are "right simultaneously" and that neither entails rejection of the other, cannot be correct: it is impossible for a proposition (for example, that a certain practice is unjust) and its negation to be true simultaneously. There could be an infinitely large set consisting of all the true moral propositions, but as finite beings we do not possess this "common morality." Since we cannot dismiss the possibility of having to revise our beliefs, we would not be justified in believing we had found the ideal set of axiomatic principles even if we had. We can believe that moral truth is one, but not that we have access to it.

Lee Yearley distinguishes between types of conflicts among ideals of human flourishing. First, there are conflicts in which one disagrees with someone else's ideals, even if one is not able to convince the other; this is an "external" conflict between "obviously better" lives, as when fame, sensory pleasure, and material gain are considered less good than friendship, complex pleasures, and sacrificial actions. Second, there are conflicts in which we approve of various ideals but only some of them fit in the context of our particular lives; this is an "internal" conflict between "obviously good" lives, such as that between a life of meditation and an active life.

Both of these sorts of conflicts render problematic for Yearley the historically important notion of a single ideal or a harmony of ideals. Indeed, in regard to external conflicts, Yearley thinks there are limits on convincing others; their conditioning is too deep. We use a good person criterion to make judgments about human flourishing; this is admittedly circular but virtuous. Ideals are imprecise and accepted only by those who are inclined to do so. But if there is disagreement, we ask how deeply the person grasps the human situation; abstract ideal and particular judgments go together. The ideal is a view of the human condition and human flourishing generally. But ideals are contextual; we have no access to an ideal that is "disengaged from the vagaries of self-understanding." Help from the transcendent is not ruled out, but good judgment depends on human training and effort. Habituation alone inclines people to take pleasure in good actions and states; judgments rest on what one is disposed to love. Hence we cannot persuade everyone, for their dispositions remain too dissimilar.

Internal conflicts are different. We discuss, but we do not try to dissuade; we are tempted; we do not condemn. We worry only whether the ideal fits. Our first-order desires rest on second-order "strong evaluations" that determine what fits for us. We recognize our limits and feel regret at good lives that do not fit us. This is not regret about morally wrong choices or even bad consequences that result from good actions; it is "spiritual" regret. We can see ideals in the past or in other cultures that we admire but cannot encompass. Communities of memory limit our choices; we can change, but only within limits. We cannot exhibit all the ideals we admire, but we can take joy in the variety.

Richard Rorty argues that the Enlightenment idea of a common moral reason that overrides privately held religious beliefs has been largely abandoned. Thus Rorty supports liberal democracy but only as the consensus of a particular culture. He argues that liberal democracy does not need a philosophical justification, in particular a justification based on a notion of the self or human nature. But a theory that makes the community "constitutive" of the self fits liberal democracy better than the Enlightenment notion of an ahistorical centered self.

Rawls has the right sort of view, Rorty argues. Justice as fairness does not rest on contested theological or philosophical ideas but on "intuitions" in a political tradition supported by an " 'overlapping consensus.' " Rawls is "historicist and antiuniversalist." Rawls does not and need not posit (against Michael Sandel) an "essence" of human nature on which rights rest.[7] He does not have to assume an essential self that is distinct from a contingent web of beliefs and desires; *we* simply put "liberty ahead of perfection" in our historical tradition. Rawls is trying, says Rorty, to seek out a middle ground between the ahistorical self and relativism. For Rawls there is no need to distinguish the self from its attributes, essence from accident. Rawls sees the self as radically situated in the liberal tradition. The point is not to "explain why we should give justice priority over our conception of the good," but to fill out the consequences of that commitment.

Thus Rorty does not think "that a single moral vocabulary and a single set of moral beliefs are appropriate for every human being and community everywhere." He sees no guarantee of universal moral agreement, and indeed he does not look for it. One looks only for the agreement that intersubjective reflective equilibrium can produce. One does not seek to justify moral convictions by appealing to a notion of the self that all can share; one simply uses the moral criteria in one's tradition along with common sense and social science. All one needs is a commitment to the moral identity of the citizen of a liberal democratic state.

Against Thomas McCarthy, moreover, Rorty argues that once one has given up the "aspiration toward something transcendent, beyond historical and cultural change," as Rorty assumes McCarthy has, one should give up the notion of truth as an "idea of reason," a regulative ideal, a sense of unconditional or transcultural validity. Rather, the notion of truth should function only to "commend fallibilism, to remind us that lots of people have been as certain of, and as justified in believing, things that turned out to be false as we are certain of, and justified in holding, our present views." For Rorty, not only must one admit that we justify our moral convictions by their coherence with a wider set of beliefs and desires but, when making truth claims, one should let go of the idea that we are trying to bring our beliefs into correspondence with some transcendent standard. Thus we should wean ourselves of the idea of truth as unconditional or transcendent validity.

COMPARISONS

The essays indicate a spectrum of voices heard nowadays in debates about common morality. These voices do not always directly engage each other, and our volume would be less than representative if we sought to disguise this absence of cohesion. We must not impose an artificial order on a volatile discussion. If recent moral and political thought is Janus-faced, so be it. We do better to face this state of affairs soberly and try to understand the variety of preoccupations, agendas, and fears that animate those who address this topic. Moreover, we certainly acknowledge that the essays by no means include all of the voices that should be heard. The present volume focuses on epistemic and normative debates about the continued viability of Enlightenment or liberal moral traditions. Such debates are unavoidably Eurocentric to a degree. Even within this focus, we have been unable to secure all the voices we had hoped to include—for example, other heirs of the natural law and Enlightenment traditions and a variety of critics from African-American, radical theological, and other communities. As it happens, the contributors to the present volume do not turn away entirely from the moral content of the liberal tradition; there are other voices that would demand a total break.

We have also realized from the beginning that another kind of volume would be required—namely, one that overlaps in part with the present volume's theoretical focus but that also presents a variety of voices speaking about more specific contexts of moral conflict and moral agreement. This latter kind of volume would surely include studies of how different religious traditions historically and currently view the "outsider," how persons involved in concrete social struggle understand their distance from and possible connections with those who oppose them (for instance, how African-Americans view their conflicts with other communities within the surrounding culture),[8] how those outside North Atlantic societies see their role historically and in the present, and how women in diverse cultural settings experience the formation of their moral identity over against misogynist traditions.

Let us now proceed to offer comparisons among the discussants assembled here (granting, of course, that we may err in interpreting particular essays) and to identify key questions that tend to recur. And we think the Enlightenment paradigm proves useful in this attempt. We will endeavor then to sort out where our authors stand on the crucial issues raised by the paradigm. In this way we may see more clearly the shape of contemporary and future debate.

1. Gewirth, Donagan, and Little remain closest to the first part of the paradigm. They find unconvincing the recent attacks on it. Their views of justification differ, however. Gewirth appeals to interests and modes of reasoning that all agents in any culture will share, at least upon reflection. Donagan endorses a holistic and dialectical mode of justification, which argues that human beings recognize each other as "self-existent ends" because they see themselves as a unique sort of social creature. He characterizes such beliefs as those one "necessarily" has, but he does not appeal to "self-evident" foundations. Little cites intuitions of the normal human psyche. While he may well view these intuitions as insights humans possess independent of their historical contexts, we might also read them as common moral agreements expressed in culturally distinctive ways. Note therefore that neither Gewirth, Donagan, nor even perhaps Little may be a "foundationalist" in the sense of claiming to have identified some culturally uninterpreted or unmediated basis of moral knowledge; all three, however, believe that our rational capacities, coupled with inescapable valuations, impose on human beings universal and unchanging moral requirements.

Baier and Farley also rely on appeals to human nature, but they attempt first to historicize our conception of how notions of moral reason or rights have developed, and they try to expand our notion of the capacities in virtue of which putatively universal moral claims are advanced. They depart from Donagan's Kantian claim that "reason" is essential to human nature, whereas capacities for certain emotions, such as compassion, are not. Baier, like Gewirth, has a notion of vital interests, which rights protect, but she believes that rights presuppose an underlying layer of responsibilities. Farley does not disparage the role of reason, but she stresses the place of love in an ethic influenced by insights from feminist theory. Reeder also wants to retain the possibility of cross-cultural appeals to motivational capacities such as sympathy, coupled with overlapping valuations and modes of reasoning; like Donagan, he insists that a principle can be holistically justified but systemically fundamental.

Rorty, Stout, and Yearley depart more dramatically from the first part of the paradigm. Rorty protests any argument based on human nature as such and hence any appeal to a universal audience. Little and Rorty are both prepared to label those who hold abhorrent views "mad" or "pathological," for instance; but Little is prepared to address his claim to all humanity, while Rorty is not. Rorty believes that any attempt to locate beliefs that persons should hold regardless of their cultural context continues the fruitless effort to find an ahistorical standpoint. Thus we should not seek grand philosophical models of human nature and society; we should leave politics to piecemeal reform. The philosopher's role, along with that of novelists and others, is to provide alternative descriptions of concrete utopias for which we might strive.

Stout argues that epistemic contexts vary, and that there is little likelihood therefore of beliefs everyone should adopt. Given the diversity of epistemic contexts, Stout thinks it is very unlikely that appeals addressed to everyone regardless of context will be effective. His point appears to be *empirical*: there is too much diversity to expect appeals to human nature as such to be widely, much less universally, successful. We can *apply* our judgments to the Nazis (that is, condemn them), but we should not think we can *justify* our beliefs to them (that is, give them reasons they can accept). Hence a "contextualist account of justification" coupled with the empirical judgment that contexts vary significantly results in pessimism about universal appeals.

Does Stout, who agrees with Rorty that justification is relative to historical context, depart from Rorty on truth? Stout says that when we claim that no one should do what the Nazis did to the Jews we are claiming this is true—not just "for us" but in all times and places, no matter what others did or will believe. He also seems to allow the notion of all the moral truths to serve as a regulative ideal. Compare McCarthy's view:

> Any adequate account of our practices of truth will have to attend not only to the situated, socially conditioned character of concrete truth claims and of the warrants offered for them, but to the situation-transcending import of the claims themselves. . . . We can and typically do make contextually conditioned and fallible claims to unconditional truth . . . ; and it is this moment of unconditionality that opens us up to criticism from other points of view. . . . It is precisely this context-transcendent, "regulative" surplus of meaning in our notion of truth that keeps us from being locked into what we happen to agree on at any particular time and place, that opens us up to the alternative possibilities lodged in otherness and difference that have been effectively invoked by poststructuralist thinkers.[9]

Where is the disagreement here? Rorty clearly is prepared to let us make judgments of the sort Stout makes about the Nazis. Rorty disagrees with McCarthy about how to understand what we are doing when we make that sort of truth claim. Rorty would say we should not adopt a notion of truth as unconditional validity, for such a notion still suggests we are trying to find an ahistorical standard. Stout would no doubt be sympathetic with McCarthy's point that truth is not relative as justification is, but he too would resist a *theory* of truth as unconditional validity; we simply retain the ability to say what we believe is true or correct.

Yearley's views on justification and truth seem close to Stout's. Yearley expects that defenses of ideals of flourishing will be backed with views of the human condition. But these appeals will not be addressed to persons regardless of context. Ideals are embedded in historical contexts and "the vagaries of self-understanding." Thus Yearley doubts the efficacy of appeals across traditions that exceed a minimal set of abstract injunctions. We cannot persuade everyone, for their dispositions may differ too greatly. We may perhaps argue cross-culturally that, for example, friendship is better than fame; what he doubts is whether we can persuade. Some goals are "errant"; we make a truth claim, but our justifications may not take hold with others. This type of conflict leads Yearley to suggest that we are unlikely ever to agree on a single ideal or harmony of ideals.

2. The second part of the paradigm is treated less explicitly by some of our authors than the first or the third parts, but it is an important strand of the debate that surfaces even when not directly addressed. Gewirth, Donagan, and Little seem to agree that common morality consists of rights or duties that regulate the pursuit of human good. As Gewirth argues, all human beings have certain basic interests or values that rights protect and promote, but these rights are not simply given as part of such values or interests; they are derived from reason's requirement of consistency. Once established, these rights will govern how humans pursue basic goods and their diverse views of human fulfillment.

Yearley and Farley, however, apparently take a neo-Aristotelian turn and insist that whatever set of requirements we accept will be grounded in our "thick" vision of the good. Farley, in continuity perhaps with Thomistic tradition, seems to assume that conceptions of morality are rooted in visions of human (and broader than human) well-being. And Yearley clearly locates the problem of moral disagreements in rival conceptions of human flourishing. Interestingly enough, however, these authors do not expressly jettison the core of rights to freedom and well-being that Gewirth, Donagan, and Little uphold.

Do any of our authors point to a way beyond the debate about whether the right is prior to the good, a debate at the heart of contemporary discussions of "liberalism" and "communitarianism"? Rorty and Adams might well be said to agreeon the following thesis: we need not, and probably will not, agree on a moral *theory* that settles the issue (in either a Kantian or an Aristotelian direction), but we can hope to find agreement on political values; that is, we can hope to agree for the purposes of public policy to establish a framework of freedom and well-being. Rorty, for example, in his endorsement of Rawls, wants to perpetuate the traditional liberal view of a set of public moral requirements that preserve the largest space possible for the private pursuit of plans of the good. But Rorty, noting Rawls's own attempt to separate philosophical theory from the systematization of political values, seems close to Adams's view that ad hoc moral agreement is both more available and more important than agreement in ethical theory. Rorty wants to give justice priority over plans of the good, "liberty" priority over "perfection," but he does not want to explain this priority as part of a moral theory. Baier may point to a way between the current theoretical options, moreover, when she suggests that a layer of relational responsibilities may go deeper than either goods or rights.[10]

3. On the issue of the independence or autonomy of morality, and hence its role at the core of a liberal polity, some of our authors clearly endorse the third part of the paradigm. Gewirth and Donagan argue that the content and justification of basic moral requirements are independent of religious convictions. Adams also distinguishes between the requirements and appeals that can be made to humans generally and those that rest on specific webs of religious belief. Adams notes that since believers and nonbelievers agree about much of the "meaning" of moral conceptions (which include both judgments and justifying principles), their views on moral epistemology—namely, whether they acknowledge an appeal to special revelation—will probably not matter materially, and their views on the metaphysics of morals (on ways of explaining the origin and nature of moral requirement) will certainly not get in the way of agreement. Note that Rorty also preserves this part of the paradigm: just as the liberal tradition was supposed to function independently of theological beliefs, so it can subsist apart from philosophical speculation about human nature. Rorty preserves in historicized form the notion of a public sphere separate from a private zone of beliefs about the self.

Some contemporary thinkers, however, oppose the thesis that the content and rationale of basic requirements are "autonomous." They claim that no vision of the good or the right stands independent of fundamental beliefs. There is no viable distinction, such as the paradigm claims to make, between the moral core and the framework of religious belief. They presumably would not deny the claim that moral belief can be independent of *theistic* belief or, even more generally, belief in the supernatural. Rather, they argue that moral beliefs are not independent of one's views of the ultimately real and the ultimately good; moral views are *holistically* embedded in webs of belief that involve a thick view of the human condition. Thus for the Christian, for example, as it is said in some influential circles today, moral beliefs are related to a network of religious conceptions—that is, morality is a matter of being a "Christian," not of being a "person." And some—let us call them "sectarians"—insist that Jews, Christians, humanists, or whoever, are utterly different, or only trivially similar.

Some of our authors reject the independent core model and insist on holistic justification, but they also refuse to say we are utterly different or only trivially similar. Stout thinks that we have a local overlap of moral views that can serve functionally as a framework for diversity. Outka finds a somewhat more ambitious overlap in the Augustinian tradition as he interprets it—across communities and historical periods humans normally agree on certain basic goods and the Golden Rule; appeals to these goods and this rule are therefore genuinely shared. But the goods and the rule are set within larger webs of determinate convictions; thus in each culture the goods and the rule do not stand alone as an independent layer of morality. In wider encounters, however, there is sufficient overlap to produce limited agreements on what normative appeals to invoke, appeals that conduce to earthly peace.

Another similar approach insists that even the meaning of capacities such as compassion have culturally specific senses that can be understood only in context. At the same time, their content is roughly analogous. While there is always difference, there is still always connection. Farley and Reeder take this last option. More than an overlap of judgment, these analogies point to major convergences in moral categories. The holist's overlap model, in Stout's vocabulary, suggests "local" agreements, whereas the notion of analogies suggests "global" convergences.

A related issue emerges in several essays. Gewirth, Donagan, and Little would agree that constitutional democracy (and even norms of international conduct) rests on an independent moral core. Rorty also affirms a layer of "intuitions" that are independent of religion and that require democracy. Adams and Outka, however, note the possible role of religious premises for building a case for constitutional democracy. They invoke Reinhold Niebuhr's view (based on Augustine) that we are capable of social order and yet "sin" makes it impossible for us to achieve more than precarious approximations to a more perfect justice. Thus Adams argues for constitutionalism and majority vote as a policy for compromise where interests continue to conflict, and Outka counsels a perpetual awareness of moral imperfection. These insights about human nature are ones that unbelievers can share to some extent, but the religious dimension remains distinctive.

FUTURE DEBATE

Though we do not presume to predict what later discussants will say, we find in the essays canvassed and comparisons offered that certain questions recur that deserve to figure prominently. Once more, we gather these questions under the three parts of the paradigm.

1. Can we accept the claim that there are certain universal and rationally required moral beliefs, and that they serve as person-time-place-invariant foundations of morality? Those who come closest to the claim differ among themselves in the patterns of justification put forward. Candidates include a supreme normative principle derived necessarily from other, immediately knowable, generic features of action that any prospective agent must accept; a recognition of ourselves and all others as self-existent ends, holistically justified, yet which we can bring virtually all persons to share; and immediately justified intuitions about the rightness and wrongness of certain actions. Proponents must account for these differences in a way that does not jeopardize their own lines of argument. And they must show that the normative force of their arguments breaks free of historically Western moorings.

If these several arguments (and others not discussed with a similar status) look less than compelling, what, if anything, can we put in their place? Two possible substitutes present themselves: (a) we hope still to make certain moral appeals that all persons can recognize, yet not to insulate such appeals systematically from larger, determinate views of human life or from surrounding, particular practices; and (b) we offer moral judgments that apply to all in the sense that we take the judgments as true, but we draw back from universal justification of any sort. Different lines of argument surface here again.

In the case of (a), candidates include a culturally modulated set of pre-theoretical agreements, variable and untidy much of the way yet within an area of overlap among diverse moralities; appeals like the Golden Rule that tell us not which actions to perform but that provide one way to judge actions, and for whose operations we seem to have a natural affinity; and an enlarged account of shared human capacities that incorporates affective as well as rational features and supports efforts to establish links by analogies between communities.

In the case of (b), candidates include our readiness simply to make the most effective use we can of local agreements; our sensitivity to and celebration of the variety of ideals of human flourishing, despite the limits they impose on our powers to convince those separate from us in time and space; and our liberated awareness that we are historical beings through and through, that an overlapping consensus is all our condition permits and enough for democracy to be viable.

Difficulties arise for both (*a*) and (*b*). Those proposing versions of (*a*) are liable to attacks from conservative and radical critics of their efforts to secure some middle ground. Such critics pose our alternatives starkly: any appeals that all persons can allegedly recognize as pertaining to themselves are either a vestige of foundationalism (and stand or fall with it) or are trivial, in that whatever interpretations they receive in given cultural contexts do the actual, and particularizing, normative work. To hold together generally negotiable appeals and tradition-specific beliefs requires therefore the execution of two tasks. One must show how such appeals do not yield the whole of the determinate morality commended. And one must show how something like the Golden Rule operates nevertheless in a way that can take hold on all of us.

Those proposing versions of (*b*) are liable to attacks at two points. First, the most proponents say is that a particular culture can claim to speak universally (that is, its moral judgments apply to all in that the judgments are taken as true ones), and that local overlaps are welcome. Yet these allowances by themselves furnish little normative guidance in cross-cultural encounters. We still must ask if we find concepts requisitely similar to establish links between particular cultures and, furthermore, if we can establish such links without assuming features of human nature common to all traditions. If it does not follow that to reject epistemic foundationalism is ipso facto to reject a self whose center inheres, for example, in a relation to God or in certain fundamental human capacities, then neopragmatism need not in principle disestablish possible cross-cultural links that assume common features. Second, if the case against the efficacy of universal appeals is indeed empirically based, it remains tentative and subject to revision. And it commits us to acknowledge in advance that the question of important cross-cultural similarities in human beings is a matter we can determine through empirical-theoretical investigation.[11]

We remarked as we began our comparisons in the previous section that debates about common morality reflect preoccupations, agendas, and fears we should try to understand. On the matter of whether we can found morality in common features of human beings, it is illuminating to ask, what do the discussants fear? Two fears seem to go deep, and to cut against each other. The first fear is the tyranny of particular communities. To allow such communities to define for us everything that can possibly matter in human life removes a sense of *homo viator* that many philosophers and religious thinkers identify. And to do so would foreclose ultimate tests or limits on the communities people should join, or in which they should remain or continue to support. By contrast, "a morality of humanity" prevents our concluding that the winners—of given cultural conversations, of historical struggles for economic or political power— take everything there is to have. The second fear is epistemic hubris. To aspire to a "God's eye" vantage point, or to suppose that our certainties will survive later scrutiny when so many of our forebears' certainties look quaint or false to us now, arrogates arbitrarily to ourselves a sense of validity no mortals enjoy. By contrast, "a morality for us," in our time and space, witnesses best to the virtue of fallibilism.

Conversation should then be promoted between two major camps. On one hand are those who wish to avoid either a totalizing, contingent community that governs all moral judgments or the conclusion that to understand all the factors that form our views is to forgive all. On the other hand are those who wish to renounce an ahistorical rationalism that seeks an Archimedean point available only to God, to eliminate epistemic doctrines that blind us to the conditioned restrictions on our power to convince across borders.

2. Shall we construe morality in terms of "deontological" rights or duties that constrain the pursuit of visions of the good? Or shall we revive an Aristotelian emphasis on the good; shall we appeal to relations of sympathy and love? Is there a way to undercut these traditional theoretical alternatives?

Two areas of debate pertaining to this part of the paradigm warrant particular elaboration. One concerns the assessment of rights. Some regard rights as the basic category of morality. Others regard them as historically evolved instruments for making claims that rest on other, more fundamental categories. In addition, we find either that freedom and well-being are taken to form a structural unity or that they must be continually traded off. These conflicting estimates extend to denying or affirming that different societies make adjustments differently, and that conceptions of vital interests vary across cultures.

A second area concerns the importance of ethical theory itself. Here expected alignments partly shift. Those who view theory as indispensable fall on both sides of the standard divide on the issue of the primacy of the right or the good. They maintain that something crucial hangs on our arriving at intellectual agreements about requirements that are not a function of some set of desires, or about a materially "thick" vision of the good, or about a starting point in sympathy and benevolence. Theory is not separate from practice; social change always involves a revision in an overall way of conceiving morality. Those who ascribe less significance to theory issue a variety of cautionary notes. The following four such notes need to be examined further. First, it is sophistical to think we must "justify" our revulsion to certain actions. Theorizing about both epistemic and normative questions proves pernicious when it weakens our immediately justified intuitions. Second, we should count ourselves fortunate that our pretheoretical moral agreements do not depend on consensus in ethical theory, for we cannot attain the latter in pluralistic societies. Third, we mislead ourselves about the depth of the challenges we face if we suppose that intellectual agreement assures exemplary moral performance. Massive injustices occurred and still occur in societies that share a material vision of the good. The tendency to make arbitrary exceptions on our own and our group's behalf is too powerful to warrant relying wholly in practice on theoretical persuasion. Moral change and progress remain genuine prospects, but they are always precarious and imperfect achievements. And they require that we turn to messy social and political details, to actual centers of power, to disputes moralists often neglect—disputes about land, natural resources, long-standing grievances, and histories of oppression. Fourth, the sort of theories Aristotelians and Kantians propose are not necessary and probably are not helpful. We do better to go at once to the question whether to continue to defend liberal democracy and, if we answer yes, to consider what beliefs and institutional arrangements are fitting.

3. Does morality possess an independent content and rationale? Or are meaning and justification holistic, so that the privatization of religion in the liberal tradition is suspect? Responses to the first two parts of the paradigm obviously bear decisively on what is said here. Yet two points again merit further discussion.

First, although we can expect that unqualified defenses and critiques of autonomy will persist, we should also allow for currents that pull certain discussants back and forth. The Enlightenment position seems to offer both too little and too much, or sometimes one and sometimes the other. It seems too little when it relegates to the periphery a plurality of substantive moral views. What many people care primarily about are the views themselves, total ways of life in which we live and move and find our identities. It seems too much when it aims to adjudicate among ways of life. Many are at a loss to see how the core or overlap in moral views can be overriding when total views vary so much and are cared about so deeply. There are those who welcome holistic accounts that provide philosophical backup to religious communities whose substantive convictions are incompatible with any strict private/public dichotomy. Insofar as holistic accounts also encourage those who feel marginalized from mainstream patterns of thought to articulate alternative conceptions, so much the better. Still, ambivalences abound. Even the welcomers of holistic accounts may confess to experiencing an "Enlightenment moment" when they view societies and regions where seemingly intractable conflicts are aided and abetted by rival religious and other "thick" conceptions of the good, and where the claims of the powerless are routinely suppressed. Enlightenment-inspired societal ground rules appear attractive by comparison.

Second, these currents help to explain why positions in the "middle" are variously sought. On the one hand, conceptions of the human condition are not adventitious. And they are organically related to everyday moral concepts, such as concern for others or self-interest. A strict private/public dichotomy not only falsely theorizes the role of religious convictions, but it embodies a host of other contestable normative assumptions about human nature, including gender roles. On the other hand, to eschew the notion of an independently justifiable core but still to want a liberal polity requires a strong commitment to tolerance. One must specify to what degree and in what respects a polity is endorsed that overrides important religious and moral convictions. At some point a case for compromise as well as consensus must come into play, provided the players are similar enough to work out a compromise in an area in which they have vital interests.

In sum, it seems our authors as a whole try to retain what is valuable in the Enlightenment moral paradigm and to discard what is not. Those who reaffirm all or most of the paradigm attempt to address criticisms, including the charges that there are no features of our condition or general principles that all human beings can be expected to recognize, or that appeals to common morality weaken bonds of particular communities. Those who revise the paradigm accept certain criticisms of it, yet they do not simply abandon the appeal to human beings as such. Those who depart most substantially from the paradigm give up the appeal to a universal audience yet retain some of the moral substance of the human rights tradition. At the end of the day, there is more normative than theoretical agreement, a fact that is significant in itself.

NOTES

1. Alasdair MacIntyre, *After Virtue*, 2d ed. (Notre Dame, Ind.: University of Notre Dame Press, 1984). Gewirth replies in "Rights and Virtues," *Review of Metaphysics* 38 no. 4 (June 1985): 739–62.

2. Sharon Welch, *Communities of Resistance and Solidarity: A Feminist Theology of Liberation* (Maryknoll, N.Y.: Orbis Books, 1985).

3. All of the essays except Rorty's were written expressly for this volume. We have included Rorty's reply to Thomas McCarthy as a way to update and clarify his views since "Priority." See McCarthy, "Private Irony and Public Decency: Richard Rorty's New Pragmatism," *Critical Inquiry* 16 (Winter 1990): 355–70. See also Richard Bernstein, "One Step Forward and Two Steps Backward: Rich-

ard Rorty on Liberal Democracy," *Political Theory* 15 (November 1987): 538–63; Rorty replies in "Thugs and Theorists: A Reply to Bernstein," *Political Theory* 15 (November 1987): 564–80.

4. Our paradigm overlaps in part one with Jane Flax's in "Postmodernism and Gender Relations in Feminist Theory," *Signs* 12 no. 4 (Summer 1987): 624–25. See her elaboration of the model of a centered self whose "transcendental" reason represents "the real."

5. Some of our authors, notably Gewirth and Donagan, are well-known opponents of utilitarianism, but neither their normative views, which seek to protect the individual from assimilation into the general good, nor utilitarianism are traditionally thought to be grounded in a vision of human good. The disagreement, for example, between R. M. Hare and Peter Singer, on the one hand, and Donagan and Gewirth, on the other, is about the normative implications of reason's universalizing demand. This debate has received considerable attention in the past and will not be emphasized here.

6. Our earlier volume (Outka and Reeder, eds., *Religion and Morality* [Garden City, N.Y.: Doubleday, 1973]) was focused in large part on the issue of the independence or autonomy of morality; the debates there were couched largely in terms of questions about the "meaning" or "definition" of moral terms. In this present volume issues about how morality is "grounded" (or whether that metaphor is even appropriate, as Rorty would ask) tend not to be presented as questions about meaning but as issues about moral reasoning or justification. This shift reflects a general turn in "metaethics" from "moral discourse" to "moral epistemology." But the same general concerns about the nature of moral convictions remain; for example, *do* moral propositions make truth claims? *Can* one give reasons for fundamental moral commitments? And particular concerns about the relations of religious beliefs to morality also carry over.

7. Michael Sandel, *Liberalism and the Limits of Justice* (Cambridge, Mass.: Harvard University Press, 1982).

8. On two pivotal figures, see James H. Cone, *Martin and Malcolm and America: A Dream or a Nightmare* (Maryknoll, N.Y.: Orbis Books, 1990). Among the specific complexities that require attention, see the brief but perceptive remarks by Cornel West, "Black-Jewish Dialogue: Beyond Rootless Universalism and Ethnic Chauvinism," *Tikkun* 4, no. 3 (July/August 1989): 95–97.

9. McCarthy, "Private Irony and Public Decency," pp. 369–70.

10. This move is reminiscent of H. Richard Niebuhr's suggestive but undeveloped theory in *The Responsible Self* (New York: Harper and Row, 1963).

11. Thomas McCarthy, "Ironist Theory as a Vocation: A Response to Rorty's Reply," *Critical Inquiry* 16 (Spring 1990): 645, 649–51.

Chapter 1

COMMON MORALITY AND THE COMMUNITY
OF RIGHTS

ALAN GEWIRTH

THE IDEA of a common morality has been central to many phases of the history of philosophy. It also figures prominently in recent moral, legal, and political thought and action. The Universal Declaration of Human Rights promulgated by the United Nations in 1948 assumed the existence, in some sense, of common moral standards for judging nations and governments; a common morality is also invoked not only in contemporary appeals for human rights but also in the agonized concern over such ongoing problems as homelessness, poverty, drug addiction, AIDS, and other human afflictions.

At the same time, however, the idea that there is a common morality seems to be refuted by the sharp disagreements over these and similar problems. We are all familiar with the thesis that the modern world exhibits such a plurality of ideas and values, such a loss of community and social solidarity, that the reality is one not of a common morality but of a divergence of warring, mutually incompatible moralities. A dramatic recent example of this divergence is the threat of assassination, purportedly based on Islamic morality, that Ayatollah Khomeini directed against Salman Rushdie; but we can also find examples much nearer to home in the vehement disagreements over such issues as abortion, affirmative action, and immigration policy.

We seem, then, to be confronted with conflicting assumptions about morality: on the one hand there is thought to be, in some sense, a common morality with common moral standards; on the other hand, moral standards are involved in irreconcilable disagreements. One way to deal with this conflict might be trying to show that the agreements and disagreements pertain to different objects or levels. For example, one might contend that there is agreement on very general principles, such as the Golden Rule, and disagreement over more specific precepts, or that there is agreement over general moral ends and disagreement over particular means or purely factual considerations. This solution would not be very helpful, however, if it turned out that the general principles or ends on which there was agreement were so general and vague that they gave little or no concrete guidance for human actions and social policies and institutions, or if the facts in dispute (such as the personhood of the fetus or the effects of affirmative action) were themselves inextricably involved in moral issues.

In this essay I examine the sense or senses in which there can correctly be said to be a common morality, and I try to indicate what sort of contents can be validly attributed to such a morality.

"COMMON MORALITY": TWO DISTINCTIONS

Let us first look at the general idea of a morality. In an initial characterization, a morality may be defined as a set of rules or directives for actions and institutions, especially as these are held to support or uphold what are taken to be the most important values or interests of persons other than or in addition to the agent. The rules purport to be categorically obligatory in that compliance with them is held to be mandatory regardless of one's personal inclinations or institutional affiliations. Thus, in contrast to municipal or statute laws, the obligatoriness of a morality is not held to be contingent on institutional enactments but is held to obtain independently of such enactments, and indeed to provide a criterion for judging the obligatoriness of laws and other institutions themselves.

Given this initial characterization, the phrase "a common morality" may have several different meanings. Two distinctions are especially pertinent. One is the distinction between *positive* and *normative* conceptions of morality. The positive conception consists in rules or directives that are in fact upheld as categorically obligatory; this upholding, in turn, may be a matter of words alone, of beliefs, or of actions, depending upon whether the rules or directives are those that persons *say* ought to be upheld, *believe* ought to be upheld, or *do* in fact uphold in their own actions as right or obligatory. In addition to such positive conceptions that incorporate the idea of "ought," a positive morality may also be construed as existing independently of this incorporation, as consisting simply in mores, habitual ways of thinking and acting with no reference to any ideas of what *ought* to be done. But without such a deontic component, mores are not moralities.

In the positive conception, then, a "common morality" would be a set of rules or directives for action that are upheld as categorically obligatory by all persons in their words or beliefs or actions. Now if "all" is taken literally, it is very doubtful that there has ever been such a common morality. Nostalgic references to eras in which one or another morality has been thus commonly maintained usually rest on implicitly restricted understandings of the assumed reference group. But there have been, and indeed still are, common positive moralities within such restricted groups, ranging from Communist, Nazi, and Afrikaner collectivities to Middletowners, Mormons, Catholics, Moslems, and other religious groups both in the United States and elsewhere. But even within each of these groups there are also many disagreements.

Contrasted with all such positive conceptions of morality is a normative conception. This consists in the moral precepts or rules or principles that are valid and thus ought to be upheld as categorically obligatory. For there to be a common morality in this normative sense its norms—its rules or principles—must be valid or justified for and incumbent upon all persons, so that, whether or not the norms are in fact universally upheld as valid, they ought to be thus upheld. The positive conceptions are appropriately studied by empirical disciplines like sociology or social psychology, but they raise questions that insistently show the need for the normative conception. For one thing, as we have seen, their contents may conflict with one another. This raises the normative question, which goes back at least to the Hebrew Bible and to Socrates: Which of these positive moralities, if any, is valid or justified, as against its various rivals? Even without the consideration of such conflicts, this question also arises from the conviction that many positive moralities, such as those of Nazis and Maoists, are morally wrong, so that they are opposed, at least implicitly, to a normative criterion or principle of what is morally right. And this, of course, raises the further questions of what it means for there to be a morally right criterion or principle and how, if at all, its proof or justification can be successfully established.

My reason for rehearsing these familiar points is that many discussions of the question whether there is now, or ever has been, a "common morality" seem to ignore important aspects of the distinction between positive and normative conceptions of morality. Negative answers to the question in any of the various positive senses do not entail a negative answer to the question taken in the normative sense. But negative answers to the positive question may pose a severe challenge to any affirmative answer to the normative question. For if persons, groups, or whole societies disagree in their words, beliefs, or actions about what is morally right, then what kind of justification can be given for a normative thesis about what moral rules or principles are in fact morally right?

The difficulties raised by this question are exacerbated when one juxtaposes the distinction between positive and normative conceptions of morality with a second important distinction. This bears not on the metaethical, second-order, or judgmental level of the source or basis of judgments about what is morally right, but on the substantive first-order contents of such judgments, especially regarding the persons whose interests or values are affected by the judgments. In this substantive focus, a "common morality" means that the goods and evils, benefits and burdens upheld in its precepts ought to be common to—that is, universally and also equally and impartially distributed among—all persons. A common morality in this substantive-distributive sense would thus be an ethical *universalism*, as distinguished from various *particularist* moralities that accord preferential status or treatment to certain groups of nations, races, classes, sexes, religions, families, local communities, and so forth.

There is no necessary correlation between the metaethical or judgmental distinction of positive and normative conceptions of morality and the substantive-distributive distinction of universalist and particularist moralities. A positive morality may be universalist or particularist, and it is at least logically possible that the normative conception of morality too is either universalist or particularist. If one is concerned with the normative conception of a common morality, the distinction between ethical universalism and ethical particularism poses an important set of normative alternatives. Suppose we begin with ethical universalism: the idea that the rights or important interests of all persons ought to be protected or promoted equally and impartially. This idea at once confronts us not only with the problem of conflicts between different persons' interests but also with the apparent moral invalidation or delegitimization of particularist moralities that uphold preferential concern for the members of one's own family or friendship circle or country, and so forth. Some parts of this problem could be dealt with by distinguishing between individual action and social policy; for example, whereas it is morally right for each person to give preferential consideration to the interests of her or his own family, social policy ought to support the interests of all families equally. But this solution would not apply, at least not so directly, when the interests at stake are those of countries rather than families and when, within each country, the interests of some groups are in severe opposition to the interests of other groups.

In such references to conflicts of interests, there is a distinction between positive and normative conceptions of "interests" that is parallel to the distinction among moralities. In the positive conception, a person's interests are the goals or purposes he or she tends to pursue (and these may, of course, have different levels of generality and of explicit awareness). In the normative conception, a person's interests are those conditions that are genuinely for his or her good. Specifying the content of such a normative conception incurs difficulties similar to those involved in providing a justification or proof of a valid morality. But at some points the positive and normative conceptions of interests readily coincide; an obvious example is the avoidance of nuclear war.

CONFLICTS OF PERCEIVED INTERESTS

Let us begin, then, with positive conceptions of interests (with levels unspecified) in relation to a normative conception of a common universalist morality. If persons differ radically in their perceived interests, then how can there be a common morality in the normative and universalist senses of moral precepts that are both valid for and in the interest of all persons? Suppose Marx is right, that there are basic conflicts of interests between capitalists and laborers in that the former exploit the latter by expropriating the surplus value produced by the workers. Even apart from this disputed issue, there are obvious conflicts of interests between political dictators and their victims, between rival business entrepreneurs, and so on. Perhaps less obvious but also deeply ingrained are the conflicts of perceived interests within American society between the homeless, the medically indigent, the inveterate poor, the ghetto dwellers, and other unfortunates, on the one hand, and, on the other, the more affluent segments of American society who oppose increased taxes and other means of helping the former groups because they think they are unworthy of help and/or because they want to maintain their own standards of living— that is, they want to pay their mortgages, save for their old age, and help their children to attain a college education.

These conflicts of interests can be analyzed in various ways. One side may be directly characterized as wrong and the other side as right, as in Marx's distinction between exploiters and exploited. In other cases the conflict may be regarded as between right and right or between varying degrees of right. Prescriptions for resolving the conflicts may likewise range from war and revolution to negotiation and compromise. But in all cases the conflicts at least initially call into question the idea that there can be a common morality in the normative and universalist senses: a morality that is valid for and in the interest of all persons who are on the opposing sides of such conflicts. How can there be directives for action that are in the interest of all persons equally when their perceived interests are so greatly opposed to one another?

There are two preliminary answers to this question. First, it is not the case that a normative morality's relation to perceived interests is simply one of indiscriminately promoting them. On such a view the conflicts of perceived interests would simply carry over into conflicts of morality. On the contrary, a normative morality adjudicates between interests, showing which are right, which are wrong, and why. Second, even when a morality cannot provide such adjudication, it still gives norms for regulating the conflicts, showing which means and methods are legitimate and which are not. The challenge faced by a normative and universalist morality is how it can successfully accomplish these tasks of adjudication and regulation.

HUMAN RIGHTS AND THE PROBLEM OF COMMON INTERESTS

Thus far I have presented what I take to be the main problem areas in the idea of a common morality. I now want to indicate how I think these problems are to be dealt with. My main suggestion is that the conceptual basis for dealing with these normative problems is to be found in the concept of *human rights*. There are three main steps here. First, the concept of rights is directly tied to the idea of justified interests. If some person A has a right (in the sense of a claim-right) to some object X, he or she ought to be protected in having or doing X for his or her own sake, as a matter of his or her personal due or entitlement, and not because such protection adds to overall social utility. Hence, having or doing X is a justified interest of A in a strong personal sense, which serves to ground other persons' duties toward A. The same point applies if A is a group of persons rather than a single individual.

Second, the concept of *human* rights implies that the justified interests in question are distributively common to all human beings. For human rights are rights that belong equally to all humans, so that every human ought to be protected equally in the interests that are the objects of his or her rights. And since the human rights apply equally to all humans, the interests in question likewise belong equally to all humans.

These first two steps are conceptual; they focus on the concepts of rights and of human rights. But now we face the challenge of connecting these concepts with reality, of showing that there really are human rights in the sense just indicated. This brings us to the third step. The concept of human rights implies that there are distributively common justified interests of all persons, but where should one look in reality for such interests amid the manifold perceived conflicts of interests among diverse persons? It must be emphasized that the interests here referred to as "common" are *distributively* common in that they belong to each person severally or individually. Thus interest X_A and interest X_B are "common" in that they are both instances of X, but they are distributively common in that interest X_A belongs to person A and interest X_B belongs to person B. It is not the case, as such, that A's achieving or fulfilling X is an interest of B, nor that B's achieving or fulfilling X is an interest of A. Hence there remains the problem of how to relate A's and B's respective interests in achieving or fulfilling X. This problem is exacerbated when X is not only a kind of interest or object, as in this discussion, but a particular object that both A and B want but that both cannot have, as in Marx's doctrine of surplus value, so that the conflict is of the zero-sum type.

But even the idea that there are kinds of common interests may be disputed. As I suggested earlier, persons pursue such a vast variety of ends or goals, and in such a vast variety of different ways, that it may seem impossible to reduce them to a common denominator. Consider, for example, the differences between religious interests and secular interests; between pacific goals or methods and bellicose or militaristic ones; between theoretical or intellectual interests and activist or political ones; between all of these and romantic or aesthetic interests; between narrowly biological, economic, or monetary interests and more spiritual ones; between sensual pleasure or happiness and duty, dignity, equality, or social solidarity; between freedom and security or order, and so forth.

In view of these great diversities of interests and values, three conditions must be fulfilled before one might hold that human rights provide the normative and universal basis for a common morality. First, it must be shown that, amid and despite these diversities, there are also interests that all humans have severally in common. Second, it must be shown that these commonly distributed interests are, in some relevant sense, prior to or more fundamental than the various diverse interests, so that the former have a kind of normative priority over the latter. Third, a rational proof or justification that these common interests are objects of equal and universal rights, and thus of human rights, must be given, so that their protection or fulfillment is in some way obligatory for all persons, and that they can serve as the grounds of a normatively and substantively common morality based on the moral principle of human rights.

THE NORMATIVE PRIORITY OF ACTION

Since I have tried to fulfill these conditions in considerable detail elsewhere,[1] I shall here be brief with regard to each of them. The first two conditions can be dealt with as follows. All the various interests pursued by persons are objects of purposive pursuit, that is, of action. Hence, each person's interests in being able to act in pursuit of his or her interests or purposes, and to act successfully in that pursuit, are for that person both logically and valuationally prior to his or her divergent and specific interests. Even if the objects of the latter interests include quiescence or passivity or contemplation, the fact that persons have an interest in it involves that they want to have or maintain it, and hence, in some relevant way, that they are committed to engaging in the corresponding actions even if, in the limiting case, these are only actions of demanding or requesting action by other persons. The nature of all such "actions" will be more fully indicated below.

A further, related reason for giving such pride of place to action as the common denominator of all particular interests is that all moralities and other practical precepts, amid their vast differences of specific contents, are concerned, directly or indirectly, with telling persons how they ought to act, especially toward one another. Hence in this concern with a common morality it is action that provides the necessary content or subject matter common to all moralities.

What this comes down to, then, is that all persons, amid their different particular interests, logically must acknowledge, as necessary goods or interests, the generic features and necessary conditions of their action and their generally successful action. It is these features and conditions that take normative priority over the various particular interests or goods that they want to pursue or maintain by action.

Now when moral and other practical precepts are addressed to persons, two main assumptions are made about their required actions, and these assumptions indicate the generic features and necessary conditions of all action in the relevant sense. The first generic feature is voluntariness or freedom; the second is purposiveness or well-being. Freedom is the *procedural* necessary condition of action; it consists in controlling one's behavior by one's unforced choice while having knowledge of relevant circumstances. Well-being is the *substantive* necessary condition of action; it consists in having the general abilities and conditions needed for achieving one's purposes. Such well-being falls into a hierarchy of three levels that are progressively less needed for action. Basic well-being consists in having the essential preconditions of action; it includes life, physical integrity, mental equilibrium. Nonsubtractive well-being consists in having the abilities and conditions needed for maintaining undiminished one's general level of purpose-fulfillment and one's capabilities for action; it includes not being lied to, not being cheated, not being robbed, and so forth. Additive well-being consists in having the abilities and conditions needed for increasing one's level of purpose-fulfillment and one's capabilities for action; it includes self-esteem, education, and opportunities for earning wealth and income.

In deriving freedom and well-being as the generic features of action and generally successful action from the assumptions of moral and other practical precepts addressed to persons, I am not implying that freedom and well-being are such features only under these assumptions. It is rather that the assumptions made by persons who address practical precepts to other persons provide clues to the generic features of action. But that freedom and well-being are such generic features is a truth that obtains independently of those assumptions.

The Moral Principle of Human Rights

Thus far, freedom and well-being have emerged as distributively common fundamental interests of all agents, and thus of all humans, since all humans are actual, prospective, or potential agents. But such distributive community of interests is not yet a sufficient basis for morality. For morality requires interpersonal consideration, whereby each person must be concerned for the important interests of other persons besides himself or herself. That freedom and well-being are necessary goods for A involves that A is concerned to have and maintain them for himself or herself, but not yet that A is, let alone categorically ought to be, concerned for the freedom and well-being of B, C, and other persons. Hence the normative requirements of a common substantive morality are not yet fulfilled.

How, then, can it be shown that each person ought to be concerned for the fundamental interests, the freedom and well-being, of all other persons? This question asks whether a rational proof or justification can be given of a normative moral principle that is thereby shown to be valid for all persons as the basis of a normatively and substantively common morality. A utilitarian principle, if it could be established or justified, might show that each person ought to be concerned to maximize the total or average amount of freedom and well-being. But such maximization could result in losing the distributively common character of freedom and well-being as common interests because the utilitarian principle could justify that the freedom and well-being of some persons should be diminished or removed if this would result in more freedom and well-being on the whole or on the average than would result from alternative actions or policies. Hence the requirements of a common substantive morality concerned with fulfilling each person's fundamental interests for his or her own sake would not be satisfied.

The case is different, however, if it can be shown that each person has rights to freedom and well-being. For the rights (in the sense of claim-rights) of any one person entail correlative duties of other persons at least not to interfere with the right-holder's having the objects of her or his rights, so that these other persons must take at least this negative favorable account of the right-holder's interests. In some cases, moreover, there must also be an affirmative concern, when the rights in question entail affirmative duties to help the right-holder have the objects of her rights.

I have tried elsewhere to show in considerable detail that the principle of human rights can be given a rational justification that establishes the principle as valid for all persons. The justification proceeds dialectically, through what every agent logically must accept on the basis of his or her need for the necessary conditions of action. From the fact that each actual or prospective agent logically must hold that freedom and well-being are necessary goods for him, it follows that he logically must also hold both that he has rights to freedom and well-being and that all other actual or prospective agents also have these rights equally with himself. Because these rights are thus universally distributed among all humans as actual, prospective, or potential agents, it follows that they are human rights. And because they are human rights, they are rights of all persons against all persons, so that each person not only is a right-holder but also has duties to all other persons to respect or promote their rights. In this way, the principle of human rights is shown to provide the basis of a common normative and substantive morality.

Since I have elsewhere presented in considerable detail this argument for the principle of human rights,[2] I shall give only the barest summary here. The argument may be put succinctly in two main parts. In the first part, it is argued that every agent logically must hold or accept that he or she has rights to freedom and well-being. The argument goes as follows. Since freedom and well-being are necessary goods for each person as an actual or prospective agent, one must accept such a statement as "I must have freedom and well-being," in which "must" is practical-prescriptive, indicating one's implicit or explicit advocacy of having the necessary conditions of one's action. Hence each person must also accept both that all other persons ought to refrain from interfering with his or her freedom and well-being and that, where one cannot have these necessary goods by one's own efforts, other persons ought to help him or her to have freedom and well-being. Those who reject these prudential "oughts" are logically committed to holding that they *may not* have what, as actual or prospective agents, they have previously accepted that they *must* have. These "oughts" entail correlative prudential rights on one's own part, since the "oughts" are intended by the agent to protect his or her own fundamental and necessary personal interests. In this way I have argued that every agent logically must hold or accept that he or she has rights to freedom and well-being as the generic features and necessary conditions of his or her action. I also call them *generic rights* because they are rights to have the generic features of action characterize one's behavior.

I now turn to the second main part of the argument. Here it is shown that each agent logically must accept that all other actual or prospective agents have the generic rights equally with his or her own. This part of the argument proceeds through the logical principle of universalization. If some predicate P belongs to some subject S because S has some quality Q (where this "because" is that of sufficient reason or condition), then P must also belong to all other subjects S1, S2, . . . Sn that also have the quality Q. Now the sufficient reason or ground on which the agent must hold that she has the generic rights is that she is a prospective purposive agent. If the agent were to claim the rights on some more restrictive ground, such as that she is white or American or a worker or a capitalist, and so forth, then she would contradict herself. The agent would then have to accept that if she were to lack such restrictive characteristics she would not have the generic rights. But we have already seen that every agent logically must hold that he or she has these rights. Hence the agent logically must accept that she has the generic rights simply by virtue of being, or for the sufficient reason that she is, an actual or prospective purposive agent. By universalization it follows that the agent logically must also accept that all actual or prospective purposive agents have rights to freedom and well-being. This completes the second main part of the argument.

In this way, then, I have argued that because the rights to freedom and well-being must be acknowledged to belong equally to all persons as actual or prospective agents, the rights in question are human rights, and every actual or prospective agent logically must accept as valid the moral principle of human rights: that all persons have equal rights to freedom and well-being. I have called this the Principle of Generic Consistency because the argument that proves it combines the formally necessary consideration of *consistency* or noncontradiction with the materially necessary consideration of the *generic* features and rights of action. Because of this universality that has been established for rights, the rational basis of the argument for human rights also includes the important quality of reasonableness, for each person must recognize that all other persons have against him the same fundamental rights he claims against them.

Many questions may be and have been raised about this argument for the principle of human rights. I have dealt with them elsewhere,[3] but I shall advert to some of them in my concluding sections.

I have tried to show, then, that amid the perceived conflicts of interests among persons and their diverse positive conceptions of morality, a normative moral conception—the principle of human rights, or the Principle of Generic Consistency—can be rationally established as valid for all persons. It is this principle that serves as the basis of a common normative morality in both the substantive-distributive and the metaethical or judgmental ways distinguished earlier. On the one hand, substantively, the justified interests in freedom and well-being that the principle of human rights upholds are distributively common to all persons and thus are universal. On the other hand, metaethically, the principle of human rights is normatively common to all persons because they rationally have to accept it as valid both in itself and as the basis of all the more specific moral judgments they are required to uphold.

THE ETHNOCENTRIC OBJECTION

There are two main kinds of objection to the thesis that human rights provide the normative and substantive basis of a common morality. One objection emphasizes the "common" aspect; the other emphasizes the "morality" aspect. The first objection is the *ethnocentric*. It holds that the "human" or "natural" rights that have been upheld in Western culture, at least from Hobbes to the Universal Declaration of Human Rights issued by the United Nations in 1948, have reflected a conception of the self that is unique to that culture, not universal or common to all humans. In this conception the self is a rational, calculating, autonomous, self-seeking individual, and its corresponding institutions are those of industrial or postindustrial capitalism and, for the most part, political democracy. But such an individualistic conception is foreign to much of the world; it is not found in Chinese or Hindu cultures, and even in parts of the world influenced by Catholicism the emphasis is far more on cooperation and community than on competitiveness and individuality. Hence the pretensions of Western doctrines of human rights to universality and impartiality, including the normative conception I have presented here, reflect at best sheer ignorance of how selves are conceived and maintained in other parts of the world and at worst a sinister kind of cultural imperialism.[4]

This ethnocentric objection may also be viewed as a species of a more general *particularistic* objection. It contends that the idea of a common universalist morality is mistaken because different moral requirements are appropriate for different groups. For example, the moral relations between parents and children and other family members should be different from the moral relations between business competitors; and, more generally, some moral relations require a partial, preferential status for their participants, such as the members of one's own community, rather than the kind of complete impartiality that is upheld in universalist moralities.

The ethnocentric objection is also put into a more specific historical frame. It contends that even within Western culture the idea of universal human rights as the normative property of distinct individuals is a relatively recent development, that it is far from having the universal, transhistorical validity that is claimed for it. The idea is not found among the ancient Greeks or Romans, nor in Roman law or in medieval thought before William of Ockham in the fourteenth century; and even with Ockham the idea of rights is not extended to any universal *human* rights. During this vast era the dominant conception of the self was organic or communitarian rather than individualistic; it viewed humans as constituted by the communities to which they belonged, and thus as organically interrelated members of societies, either small scale, as with the Greeks, or universal, as with the Romans and medievals.[5]

In answer to this objection, it must first be denied that the idea of human rights is exclusively a modern Western construct. As I have shown elsewhere,[6] the idea can also be found in ancient and medieval sources as well as in non-Western cultures. This is not surprising, in view of the universality of the generic features of action on which human rights are based. Thus Aristotle's analysis of human action, which focuses on these features, is just as applicable today as it was in ancient Greece or in the late medieval period when Thomas Aquinas took it over with certain qualifications.[7] This does not mean, of course, that the idea of human rights had the same degree of positive support in all eras or climes; historical factors strongly influenced the idea's acceptance.

There is another respect in which the historical and ethnocentric objections should be considerably discounted. This bears on the distinction between positive and normative conceptions of morality. That the idea of human rights has not been accepted in various eras or climes does not prove that the idea is invalid or that it has limited relevance. For human rights are a normative, not a positive or empirically descriptive conception; they provide a rationally grounded moral model for how persons and groups ought to be regarded and treated even if existing systems of interpersonal and political relations depart from it. Even if "ought" implies "can," the obligations do not entirely lapse when existing social circumstances render them difficult or impossible. Such impossibility is not ingrained in the nature of things if it derives not from material conditions of life but from social practices, institutions, and traditions that can be changed by enlightened forms of individual and social action.

Much depends on which kinds of human rights are in question. The rights fall into a hierarchy according to the degree of their needfulness for action and successful action, so that when the rights conflict, those must take precedence that are more needed for action. Thus primacy belongs for the most part to the basic rights whose objects are such segments of basic well-being as life, physical integrity, and mental equilibrium, so that they require for their fulfillment not only food, clothing, and shelter but also freedom from torture and similar disabling practices. As this consideration already shows, while the distinction between political and civil rights, on the one hand, and social and economic rights, on the other, may be plausible in some contexts, the basic human rights include components from both sides of the distinction. A political system that excludes some persons from available food or subjects them to slavery cannot be excused on the ground that its traditions render impossible any other ways of treating the submerged groups.

Closely connected with such basic rights is the institution of the minimal state, which is characterized by the impartial application of the criminal law. Such law is morally justified insofar as it serves to protect all persons equally against harms to their basic and other kinds of well-being.

There are several steps between such basic human rights and the kinds of political and civil human rights enshrined in constitutional democracy. Such a democracy is morally justified, in the first instance, because its civil liberties are an important application of the human right to freedom. As such, they are vital components of the dignity of persons as rational agents who should be free to express and communicate their thoughts. In addition, a constitutional democratic government derives its legitimacy from the method of consent, which is an institutional application of the right to freedom. This method may, of course, operate in many different ways. But effective civil liberties are not merely a secondary kind of right, to be installed only after basic well-being has been assured. On the contrary, such liberties also function as important protections for the equal basic rights of all the persons in a society, since without them the rulers may favor the basic well-being of some groups at the expense of others. The contemporary drives for greater democratization in the republics of the former Soviet Union, China, and elsewhere show that although the ethnocentric objection has considerable empirical justification in terms of positive conceptions of morality, it also has important counterexamples that suggest an opposite, normative dynamic in the direction of human rights as here conceptualized.

These considerations are also relevant to the particularistic objection that some moral relations require a preferential rather than an impartial status for their members. I have dealt with this question in some detail elsewhere,[8] so here I shall be very brief. We must distinguish two different possible relations between universalist and particularist moralities. One relation is negative, such that particularist moralities may contradict the requirements of universalist morality. To take an extreme example, Nazi morality upheld the killing of persons who did not belong to what the Nazis considered as their own superior community. Such a negative relation is morally wrong, and its wrongness can be readily proved through the rationally justified principle of human rights.

A second relation between universalist and particularist moralities is affirmative, such that the particularist moralities fall within, because they are justified by, the universalist morality. In this relation the particularist moralities apply and supplement the requirements of the universalist morality rather than contradict them. In this way, for example, the particularist morality whereby family members give preferential consideration to one another's needs and interests is justified by the universalist principle of human rights, because this principle, especially through its freedom component, justifies the formation of voluntary associations, including families with their particularist preferential purposes. Thus justified particularist moralities provide no counterexample to the universalist principle of human rights.

To be emphasized especially in this and other contexts is the strong connection between human rights and human dignity. However much the status of persons as free rational agents may be attacked or submerged by one or another sociopolitical system, it is their dignity as such persons that the human rights express and protect. Since these rights have as their objects the freedom and well-being that are the necessary conditions of agency and of generally successful action, and since to have these rights is to be in a position to make justified claims to have their objects, as persons become progressively aware of their dignity as such agents they tend to reject the conditions that the ethnocentric objection adduces as empirical or ideological constraints on the rights.

THE EGOISTIC OBJECTION AND THE COMMUNITY OF RIGHTS

Let us now turn to a second kind of objection against the thesis that human rights provide the basis of common morality. This objection, which I call the *egoistic*, focuses on the "morality" aspect; it goes back at least to Bentham and Marx.[9] According to this objection, the self as conceived in human rights doctrines is purely self-interested, self-centered, and amoral. In opposition to this view, I hold that the idea of human rights involves what I call *the community of rights*. By this I mean that human rights, correctly understood, entail a certain communitarian conception of human relationships, one that is focused on mutuality of consideration and social solidarity.

In some views, including the egoistic objection just mentioned, the phrase "community of rights" is an oxymoron: "rights" and "community" are held to be mutually opposed. According to this objection, rights presuppose competition and conflict since rights are intended as guarantees that self-seeking individuals will not be trampled in their adversarial relations with one another. Community, on the other hand, involves the absence of such conflicts: it signifies common interests, mutual sympathy, and fellow-feeling. According to this contrast, because a right involves a claim that a person makes for the support of his or her interests, it evinces an adversarial preoccupation with fulfillment of one's own desires or needs regardless of broader social goals. Hence it operates to submerge the values of community and to obscure or annul the moral responsibilities that one ought to have to other persons and to society at large. But it is held that when persons maintain the relations of community that make for social harmony, there is no need for rights. The claiming of rights, then, is held to be egoistic and antithetical to morality.[10]

To address this objection, it is important first to avoid a utopian idealization of the idea of community. In particular, it is a serious error to extend to a whole society the preferential warmth of close familial and friendship ties, as in the vast series of utopias from Plato's *Republic* to Marx's "classless society." That human rights, as the normative property of distinct individuals, can serve as the indispensable basis of social solidarity realistically conceived can be shown by an analysis of the logical structure of such rights. According to that structure, every human has equal rights to freedom and well-being against all other humans. Hence every human is the respondent or duty-bearer as well as the subject or holder of human rights; precisely because each has rights against all the rest, every other person also has these rights against him, so that he has correlative duties toward them. The concept of human rights thus entails a reciprocal universality: each person must respect the rights of all others while having his or her rights respected by all others, so that there must be a mutual sharing of the benefits of rights and the burdens of duties. Human rights require mutuality of consideration and thus a kind of altruism rather than egoism. By such a reciprocally universal conception of human rights, each individual's personal claim to and protected property in the necessary goods of action are combined with a responsibility for interests shared in common with all other persons.

In the first instance, the duties required by the universality of human rights are negative: each person must refrain from removing or interfering with the freedom and well-being of all other persons. This well-being ranges from life and physical integrity to such goods as self-esteem and education. But the duties are also affirmative, requiring active assistance in circumstances where one person can help another to avoid drowning, starvation, or other threats to his basic well-being without comparable cost to himself. In broader social contexts where basic well-being and equality of opportunity (which involves additive rights) can be fostered only by collective action, the affirmative duties require appropriate governmental provisions so far as practicable, but they also require individuals' advocacy of other persons' rights to these goods and taking the necessary steps toward their support, including taxation.

In these ways, then, human rights have important implications for social policy. The negative rights require the minimum state referred to above, which serves to protect equally the freedom and basic well-being of all persons. The affirmative rights require the supportive or welfare state, which gives assistance to persons who cannot maintain their well-being by their own efforts. Such assistance, however, is not open-ended.

In this regard the principle of human rights diverges sharply from John Rawls's "difference principle,"[11] which requires that all economic goods be equalized for all persons unless, and to the extent that, the economic levels of the least advantaged can be raised by some persons' having greater wealth and income. This principle could operate to maintain the lesser advantaged persons in a permanent condition of recipience and dependency.

In contrast, the affirmative rights of the Principle of Generic Consistency or the principle of human rights are intended to secure and maintain the abilities of *agency* on the part of all persons who cannot develop and use these abilities by their own efforts. Whatever assistance they are given must be intended to enable such persons to acquire the personal and other resources whereby they can be productive agents on their own behalf. This point marks one of the major results of basing human rights in the needs of agency.

That these affirmative social policies require taxation of the more affluent does not entail that their right to freedom is violated, that is, unjustifiably infringed. Basic rights, such as the rights of starving persons to food, as well as additive rights to such goods as education, take precedence over the rights of other persons to make full use of all their wealth, since the objects of the former rights are more needed for agency than are the objects of the latter rights.

Although only some persons may need to be rescued from deprivation while other persons are taxed in order to provide such rescue, this duality does not prevent the affirmative rights in question from being a part of common morality in both the substantive and the judgmental senses. These rights, as derivative from the principle of human rights, involve that each person always has, as a matter of principle, both the right to be treated in the appropriate helping way when he or she has the need and the duty to act helpfully when circumstances arise that require such action and when he or she then has the ability to do so; this ability includes the consideration of cost to oneself. In this way the universality of the affirmative human rights is dispositional even if not always occurrent; or, to put it in a related way, even if the rights are not always universally exercised, they are always universally had. Hence they remain an important substantive part of common morality. Because the principle of human rights entails this requirement of mutual aid where needed and practicable, it is a principle of social solidarity, as against exclusive preoccupation with private interest.

This point also bears on the adversarial phase of the egoistic objection. When important rights are threatened or violated, forceful insistence on their fulfillment is quite in order. But when mutual rights are effectively recognized, and especially when this recognition is stabilized in effective institutions, the adversarial stance can and often does give way to an atmosphere of mutual respect and civility. An example of this contrast is provided by the relations between whites and blacks in the American South before and after the passage and enforcement of civil rights legislation. The desiderated removal of adversarial relationships may well depend on the implementation rather than the rejection of rights.

The community of rights thus embodies a more sober and realistic but also a safer conception of human community than is expressed in the various organicist utopias. It indicates that whatever the merits that are claimed for more close-knit conceptions of human community, a community of persons, especially one that is to be feasible in large-scale societies, must protect the mutual and equal rights of all persons. The community must respect all persons' dignity as rational agents who are aware of the needs of their agency and of their equal rights to the fulfillment of these needs, as entitlements of which they cannot be justifiably deprived simply because their communities demand it of them. Such a community of rights thus embodies the conception of human agents as reasonable persons who take due account of one another's agency needs, each respecting others' rights as well as one's own and maintaining a certain equitableness or mutuality of consideration between oneself and others, as required by the reciprocal universality of human rights. Thus the reasonable self, within the community of rights, recognizes that it has obligations toward others as well as rights against others.

SUBSTANTIVE AND JUDGMENTAL CHALLENGES

If the principle of human rights, or the Principle of Generic Consistency, is to function as the normative and substantive principle of a common morality, it must meet two further kinds of challenges. One is substantive: it must be shown that the principle can serve to clarify, and perhaps also to resolve, the manifold conflicts of perceived interests and positive moral conceptions that give rise to moral problems. This is a gigantic task that, for many reasons including those of space, I cannot attempt here.

Relevant clues can, however, be given. Since freedom and well-being in its three levels, as the generic features of action, are the central objects of the human rights, they underlie the more specific objects of moral disputes. And because these objects fall into a hierarchy of degrees of needfulness for action, the principle of human rights indicates how conflicts involving these objects can be resolved. This is why, for example, the rights not to be lied to or stolen from are overridden by the rights not to be murdered or to avoid starvation when these rights are in conflict. In various related ways the principle of human rights can also give guidance on a vast array of other moral problems, both as to their contents and as to the justifiable methods for resolving them.[12] It must also be recognized, however, that a host of complex factual considerations are relevant to many of these problems.

A second kind of challenge that the principle of human rights must meet is judgmental or metaethical: it must be shown that the principle, as the valid or normative conception of morality, can also be accepted as a positive conception. As explained above, the principle of human rights serves as a basis of a common morality in the normative-judgmental sense in that, because it has a rational justification, it ought to be accepted by all persons as valid for their thought and action. This justification can indeed be grasped by every agent who is minimally rational—with the logical and conative capacities that characterize all normal persons—for, in sum, it consists in pointing out that each actual or prospective agent must uphold for himself or herself certain generic rights of agency, and that he or she must also acknowledge these rights for all other actual or prospective agents, since they have the same qualities on which one's own necessary attribution of the rights are based.

To explicate such acceptance of the principle of human rights, it is not necessary that humans be portrayed as exclusively rational, let alone reasonable. On the contrary, apart from the obvious unrealism of such portrayal, the very basis of human rights is in the self-interested, conative drives of agents who seek to achieve their purposes. The principle of human rights represents the rational structuring that analysis and argument provide for this conative foundation. And insofar as persons are both conative and rational, they will accept the principle as valid for their actions and institutions.

Such positive acceptance is greatly facilitated by the presence of appropriate moral institutions and traditions. A constitutional democracy like that of the United States can progressively embody and effectuate in its institutions central phases of the principle of human rights, and this helps to support an effective unification of the normative and positive conceptions of a common morality. More generally, as hitherto suppressed groups become aware of their rights—frequently by noting the contrast between their condition and the condition of others who more fully enjoy the rights—they become concomitantly aware of those aspects of their worth and dignity as rational agents that underlie and justify their valid claims to the freedom and well-being that are the necessary conditions of their action and generally successful action.

It is to such a unification of positive and normative considerations that the United Nations Universal Declaration of Human Rights refers in its preamble when it points out that "disregard and contempt for human rights have resulted in barbarous acts which have outraged the conscience of mankind," and when it asserts that "the advent of a world" in which human rights are respected "has been proclaimed as the highest aspiration of the common people."[13] The concerns indicated here are far more than a rhetorical "manifesto"; they indicate that, amid the continuing conflicts of interests, of positive moralities, and of violations of human rights, a normatively common morality based on human rights, and thus on the community of rights, can be regarded as judgmentally common to all persons as conative and rational beings.

In this context the bearing of religion on morality becomes especially pertinent. On this complex topic I must here confine myself to certain essentials that are directly related to the considerations presented above. To begin with, morality in its normative conception is logically independent of religion: what is morally right and wrong, and the principle underlying this distinction, can be ascertained by purely rational means. But in the effectuation of moral norms—making positive in beliefs and especially in actions and institutions the contents of the normative conception of morality—religion can be of help. It can provide rhetorical and dialectical motivations that lead many persons to act morally and to support institutions and policies that promote human rights. In all of this, however, morality is normatively the independent variable, even if, in positive terms, it may to some extent be causally dependent on religion for the positive effectuation of its norms.

When it is said that without religion the "public square" is morally "naked" and a moral "vacuum,"[14] this is properly to be construed as an empirical claim about the indispensability of religion for the positive effectuation of normative morality. As such, the claim is historically contingent, and it suffers from the double fault that it confuses normative and positive morality and that it does not spell out adequately the principle and contents of normative morality. Viewed as a generalization about American public life, the contention is seriously misleading and in fact false. Religion has been and is neither a necessary nor a sufficient condition of the presence and influence in American society of normative morality, the morality of human rights with its humane concerns for the equal protection of freedom and well-being. First, religion is not a necessary condition. With regard to many institutional developments in American society and politics that have incorporated valid moral norms, including, in the twentieth century, the various New Deal reforms and the Great Society programs of civil rights, not only was their normative moral rightness independent of religion but their positive espousal and acceptance can also be accounted for independently of religion. More generally, it is simply false that in American public life there is no influential source of normative morality other than religion. This ignores not only basic aspects of the whole American constitutional structure but also the leavening and moderating influence of American pluralism and the deep concern for justice among many nonreligious persons and groups. Second, religion is far from a sufficient condition of the positive effectuation of normative morality. Many religious currents in American society have not been on the side of moral rightness; consider, for example, the anti-Semitic pronouncements of Father Coughlin, the Reverend Gerald L. K. Smith, and other religious figures during the 1930s. The influence of religion, then, can be morally ambiguous and indeed vicious.

If it is contended that illiberal, morally sinister religious figures like Coughlin and Smith were not examples of "true religion," the question arises of how true religion can be distinguished from false in a non-question-begging way. After all, the devil can cite Scripture for his own purposes. This point also indicates that there is probably as much diversity among American religious protagonists as in other areas of public life, so religion cannot be looked to as the unifying basis for which its adherents appeal. The case remains, then, that if the powerful force of religion is not guided and controlled by the normative morality of human rights, it can eventuate in a Torquemada or Ayatollah Khomeini as well as in a John Courtney Murray or Martin Luther King.

Because morality is the independent variable with regard to moral rightness, the frequently great power of religion in public life must be evaluated, with regard to its own rightness or wrongness, by reference to moral norms ascertained independently of religion. Insofar as religion can help to secure the effectuation of human rights, its help is to be welcomed. But its normatively subordinate role and consequent normative limitations should be clearly understood.

For the fuller comprehension of this issue, it is important to avoid the fallacy of disparateness.[15] This fallacy is committed when, in comparing two objects X and Y, one depicts them at different levels or in different respects, especially when one depicts X at an ideal or normative level and Y at an actual or positive level. Thus, in comparing religion and rational morality, I have in part depicted religion at the level of its actual positive manifestations, while I have depicted rational morality at the level of its rational normative justification. If, however, one looks at the actual positive level of ethical rationalist philosophers, such as the opinions about Jews expressed by such thinkers as Voltaire and Kant, what emerges is much more disquieting.[16]

To avoid the fallacy of disparateness, it is vitally important to keep in mind that what is directly relevant to the moral evaluation of religion that I have emphasized is the normative conception of morality. The positive departures of some rationalist moral philosophers from the precepts of this normative conception do not invalidate the distinction between the normative and the positive conceptions, nor do they remove the rational and moral validity of the normative conception presented above. This latter conception provides the standard by which all positive conceptions, including those of religionists and of philosophers, must be evaluated.

CONCLUSION

I have tried to show in this essay that the question of a common morality requires for its adequate treatment a recognition both of the judgmental distinction between positive and normative conceptions of morality and of the substantive distinction between particularist and universalist moralities. I have argued that, amid the manifold conflicts of positive moralities and perceived interests, the principle of human rights provides the normative basis of a valid universalist morality. Among the rational grounds of its universal validity is the fact that the principle is rationally derived from the necessary conditions of action and generally successful action, so that it must logically be accepted by every rational agent.

I have further tried to show that the ethnocentric and egoistic objections to the principle of human rights can be given adequate answers, which culminate in the normative moral conception of the community of rights. The principle of human rights can also surmount the challenges posed both by the vast array of substantive moral problems and by the need to bring to positive judgmental and institutional effectuation the valid moral norms established by rational analysis and argument. This involves making what is normatively a common morality also positively common as a matter of judgmental and institutional acceptance. I have also briefly discussed the bearing and limitations of religion regarding such positive effectuation.

From these considerations it is clear that two further kinds of effort are needed in the whole sphere of common morality. First, continued rational scrutiny must be given to the analysis and argument that are required for the fuller understanding of the normative basis of morality and of its manifold applications to human actions and institutions. Second, both great vigilance and continuing efforts are needed to bring the normative principle of human rights closer to positive effectuation.

NOTES

1. See Alan Gewirth, *Reason and Morality* (Chicago: University of Chicago Press, 1978), chaps. 1–3. For briefer versions of the argument, see my *Human Rights: Essays on Justification and Applications* (Chicago: University of Chicago Press, 1982), pp. 3–9, 41–67; "The Rationality of Reasonableness," *Synthese* 57

(1983): 225–47; and "The Epistemology of Human Rights," *Social Philosophy and Policy* 1, no. 2 (Spring 1984): 1–24.

2. Ibid.

3. For some of my main replies to objections, see *Reason and Morality*, pp. 82–102, 112–28; *Human Rights*, pp. 67–78; "Replies to My Critics," in E. Regis, Jr., ed., *Gewirth's Ethical Rationalism* (Chicago: University of Chicago Press, 1984), pp. 205–15; "Why Agents Must Claim Rights: A Reply," *Journal of Philosophy* 79 (1982): 403–10; "On Rational Agency As the Basis of Moral Equality," *Canadian Journal of Philosophy* 12 (1982): 667–72; "Rights and Virtues," *Review of Metaphysics* 38 (1985): 745–51; "Why There Are Human Rights," *Social Theory and Practice* 11 (1985): 235–48; "From the Prudential to the Moral: Reply to Singer," *Ethics* 95 (1985): 302–4; "The Justification of Morality," *Philosophical Studies*, 53 (1988): 245–62. See now Deryck Beyleveld, *The Dialectical Necessity of Morality: An Analysis and Defense of Alan Gewirth's Argument to the Principle of Generic Consistency* (Chicago: University of Chicago Press, 1991).

4. For this objection see Alasdair MacIntyre, *After Virtue* (Notre Dame, Ind.: University of Notre Dame Press, 1981), pp. 204ff.; Michael J. Sandel, *Liberalism and the Limits of Justice* (Cambridge: Cambridge University Press, 1982), pp. 158ff., 179ff.; Sandel, ed., *Liberalism and Its Critics* (New York: New York University Press, 1984), pp. 5–6; A.J.M. Milne, *Human Rights and Human Diversity* (Albany: State University of New York Press, 1986), pp. 2–4; Adamantia Pollis and Peter Schwab, *Human Rights: Cultural and Ideological Perspectives* (New York: Praeger, 1979), chap. 1.

5. See H.L.A. Hart, "Are There Any Natural Rights?" *Philosophical Review* 64 (1955): 176–77, 182; Isaiah Berlin, *Four Essays on Liberty* (London: Oxford University Press, 1969), p. 129; MacIntyre, *After Virtue*, pp. 65ff. For the denial of the concept of rights in Roman law, see Henry Sumner Maine, *Dissertations on Early Law and Custom* (London: John Murray, 1891), pp. 365–66, 390; Michel Villey, *Leçons d'histoire de la philosophie du droit* (Paris: Librairie Dalloz, 1957), chaps. 11, 14; W. W. Buckland, *A Textbook of Roman Law from Augustus to Justinian* (Cambridge: Cambridge University Press, 1963), p. 58.

6. See my *Reason and Morality*, pp. 98–102. See also A.W.H. Adkins, *Moral Values and Political Behavior in Ancient Greece* (London: Chatto and Windus, 1972); Brian Tierney, "Tuck on Rights: Some Medieval Problems," *History of Political Thought* 4 (1983): 429–41.

7. Aristotle, *Nicomachean Ethics* 3.1–5; Thomas Aquinas, *Summa Theologica* 1.2.6–17. See also Alan Donagan, "Thomas Aquinas on Human Action," in Norman Kretzmann et al., eds., *The Cambridge History of Later Medieval Philosophy* (Cambridge: Cambridge University Press, 1982), pp. 642–54.

8. See Alan Gewirth, "Ethical Universalism and Particularism," *Journal of Philosophy* 85 (June 1988): 283–302.

9. See Jeremy Bentham, *A Critical Examination of the Declaration of Rights*, in B. Parekh, ed., *Bentham's Political Thought* (New York: Barnes and Noble, 1973), pp. 261, 268ff.; Karl Marx, *On the Jewish Question*, in R. C. Tucker, ed., *The Marx-Engels Reader*, 2d ed. (New York: W. W. Norton, 1978), p. 43; Tom

Campbell, *The Left and Rights* (London: Routledge and Kegan Paul, 1983), pp. 14–15, 22.

10. See Richard E. Flathman, *The Practice of Rights* (Cambridge: Cambridge University Press, 1976), pp. 183ff.; Joseph Raz, "Right-Based Moralities," in Jeremy Waldron, ed., *Theories of Rights* (Oxford: Oxford University Press, 1984), pp. 196–97.

11. John Rawls, *A Theory of Justice* (Cambridge: Harvard University Press, 1971), pp. 75ff.

12. I here refer to some of my own efforts to develop "applications" of the principle of human rights. See *Reason and Morality*, chap. 4 ("Direct Applications of the Principle") and chap. 5 ("Indirect Applications of the Principle"). The latter chapter also includes sections on "The Completeness of the Principle" (pp. 327–38) and "Conflicts of Duties" (pp. 338–54). See also *Human Rights*, part 2, entitled "Essays on Applications," comprising eight essays on such topics as the prevention of cancer, the relief of starvation, civil disobedience, and the effectuation of civil liberties. See also more recent essays such as "Human Rights in the Workplace," *American Journal of Industrial Medicine* 9 (1986): 31–40; "Economic Rights," *Philosophical Topics* 14 (1986): 169–93; "Professional Ethics: The Separatist Thesis," *Ethics* 92 (1986): 282–300; "Reason and Nuclear Deterrence," *Canadian Journal of Philosophy*, supp. 12 (1986): 129–59; "Moral Foundations of Civil Rights Law," *Journal of Law and Religion* 5 (1987): 125–47; "Private Philanthropy and Positive Rights," *Social Philosophy and Policy* 4, no. 2 (Spring 1987): 55–78; "Human Rights and Academic Freedom," in Steven M. Cahn, ed., *Morality, Responsibility, and the University: Studies in Academic Ethics* (Philadelphia: Temple University Press, 1990), pp. 8–31.

13. The Universal Declaration of Human Rights is reprinted in many places. See Ian Brownlie, ed., *Basic Documents on Human Rights*, 2d ed. (Oxford: Clarendon Press, 1981), pp. 21ff.

14. See Richard J. Neuhaus, *The Naked Public Square: Religion and Democracy in America* (Grand Rapids, Mich.: William B. Eerdmans, 1984). Some important aspects of this issue are discussed, from different points of view, by Stanley Hauerwas and David G. Smith in *Nomos XXX: Religion, Morality, and the Law*, ed. J. Roland Pennock and John W. Chapman (New York: New York University Press, 1988), pp. 110–42.

15. On this fallacy, see Alan Gewirth, "Normative 'Science' and Positive 'Ethics'," *Philosophical Review* 69 (July 1960): 311–30.

16. See, for example, Arthur Hertzberg, *The French Enlightenment and the Jews: The Origins of Modern Anti-Semitism* (New York: Schocken Books, 1970), especially chap. 9; Paul Lawrence Rose, *Revolutionary Antisemitism in Germany from Kant to Wagner* (Princeton, N.J.: Princeton University Press, 1990), especially chap. 7.

Chapter 2

COMMON MORALITY AND KANT'S ENLIGHTENMENT PROJECT

Alan Donagan

I S THERE any prospect that all societies and cultures in the world will
one day accept the same morality? No. Is there any prospect that their
mores or ways of living will become much more alike? Yes, provided
that the socialist and "third world" societies adopt market systems of
economics, as it now appears that they will.

How can societies have much the same mores and yet not the same
morality? The thinkers of the eighteenth-century Enlightenment, who
laid the foundations of twentieth-century social and political science,
were in a position also to lay the foundations for an adequate twentieth-
century moral philosophy because they saw that the answer to this question must throw light not only on what morality is, but also on how its
content is determined. Whether they did what they could have done, however, is disputed. Adam Smith's admirers do not contend that his *Theory
of the Moral Sentiments* has the authority of his *Wealth of Nations*. And
although not a few philosophers maintain that the greatest of the Enlightenment philosophers, Immanuel Kant, not only correctly identified the
foundation of morality in his pioneering *Grundlegung zur Metaphysik
der Sitten* but also demonstrated in his late and uneven *Metaphysik der
Sitten* the structure of the specific moral systems that can be built on that
foundation, others deny it.[1]

I maintain that Kant succeeded in what he set out to do, and, incidentally, that the view of morality he worked out can hope for widespread
acceptance in a peaceable and free multicultural world. He succeeded
because of a connection he divined between religion and the new social
sciences. He recognized, as many Christians do not, not only that the
principles of his own country's Christian morality, which he revered, are
presupposed by the Christian faith in all its branches, and so are not its
product, but also that the Christian faith can be preached to all nations
only because those principles depend on what is common to all human
beings, no matter what their race or society. In addition, he perceived
that the new Enlightenment social sciences depended on a related presup-

position: that social and political differences are to be explained historically, as humanly intelligible responses to different physical and social conditions.

Morality, as Kant presents it, is traditional Christian morality demystified and universalized. It does not presuppose the truth of the Christian faith, but is presupposed by it. It does, however, presuppose an Enlightenment view of human society, and it entails liberal views of both economics and politics. Kant maintained, rightly in my opinion, that the human race has little prospect of a decent, peaceable, and prosperous future unless substantial bodies of opinion everywhere come to accept this morality. In what follows I outline its structure and explain the reasons Kant gives for its various features, interrupting exposition to examine objections to it that have been found plausible. I do not, however, follow the order of Kant's exposition in any of his writings, and I disregard the blind alleys into which he was sometimes diverted.

WHAT MORALITY IS AND WHY IT MATTERS: SOCIOLOGICAL PRELIMINARIES

What is morality? Kant's tacit point of departure is a sociological fact: while all societies, and many groups within them, impose a set of customary dos and don'ts on their members' conduct, many but not all societies recognize a smaller set of dos and don'ts, usually more vaguely defined, that measure the conduct of human beings everywhere. The concept of morality is the concept of such a smaller set of dos and don'ts. One mark of a civilized society is that its members share this concept, for only because they have it do civilized people acknowledge that human conduct everywhere is properly judged by standards accessible to members of societies other than their own, whose opinions they are not entitled to ignore. The concept of morality is therefore inseparable from the concept of a potential community of all human beings, de jure membership of which gives rise to duties that are more fundamental than those arising from de facto membership of particular societies, although they are compatible with them.

While all civilized persons agree that there are requirements on human conduct as such, they do not agree about what those requirements are. In part that is because they do not agree about what human beings are. Some opinions about what human beings are, such as that members of certain races are not fully human, can be disregarded as demonstrably false. Others that cannot be so disregarded—for example the Hindu doctrine that all living beings are transmigrating souls in a world governed by a morally non-neutral law of Karma, who are in some lives rational and in others not—morally divide those who hold them from those who hold contrary doctrines. Since in this paper it is impossible to discuss these differences, I can only give notice that here a doctrine contrary to the Hindu one will be assumed: namely, that each animal, human or not, is a living being distinct from every other, and that what happens to human animals depends solely on their interaction with a morally neutral natural environment, with their fellow-humans, and with whatever supernatural beings (gods or demons) there may be. This doctrine is common both to the major monotheistic religions (Judaism, Christianity, and Islam) and to nontheistic naturalism. I believe it to be true, but I shall not try to show that it is.

Although those who assent to these assumptions about human beings and the natural world they inhabit can and do disagree about morality, their disagreements are not as a rule expressed in differences of conduct. The extent of their disagreements is therefore often concealed. Thus a Chinese Maoist and a Chinese Christian may both refuse to practice or countenance abortion except when the mother has been subjected to constraint or her health is endangered. Yet the sameness of their conduct in this respect is not agreement in morality: the Maoist believes that the Chinese Communist state will not flourish unless Chinese parents have all the children they can, and that its claims are superior to all others; the Christian, while believing that China's population is excessive and should be limited by all legitimate means, also believes that killing freely conceived unborn children who are not endangering their mothers is murder. With respect to abortion, the mores of a Maoist China and of a Christian China would be much the same, but not their morality.

It is fortunate for us as human beings, even though it may confuse us as philosophers, that nonmoral reasons abound for disapproving of most kinds of action of which anybody disapproves for moral reasons. As Henry Sidgwick pointed out over a century ago,[2] generalizing an observation already made by Kant,[3] the mores of a society of moral egoists, who believe it to be everybody's sole duty to do whatever will maximize his or her own happiness, would be much the same as those of a society of utilitarians, who believe it to be everybody's sole duty to maximize the general happiness, or even as those of a society of "intuitional" moralists, who believe themselves to intuit the soundness of the roughly Christian moral tradition of Victorian England. Although moral pluralism—the doctrine that those who accept one view of morality can nevertheless recognize a contradictory view of it as equally acceptable—is absurd, every sane person, theist or atheist, egoist or Kantian or utilitarian, can agree that living in a peaceable and law-abiding society is a good which it is a moral duty to promote, and that violence to persons, fraud, breach of contract, and invasions of freely chosen family relations and of justly acquired property are evils contrary to that good. In other words, as Kant and Sidgwick saw, those who thus agree may hold different views of morality. Most of us prefer not to think about this, and only think about it when it is thrust upon us by exceptional cases. We can agree to disagree about morality only because our moral disagreements do not as a rule give rise to different mores.

Up to a point even actions of kinds believed to be morally wrong can be tolerated. Liberals who believe it to be morally wrong to advocate totalitarianism of any form also believe themselves morally obliged to safeguard the legal right of totalitarians to commit the moral wrong of urging their vicious opinions on others. Yet the range of moral tolerance is limited. In many cases, those who condemn actions of a certain kind as morally wrong also believe themselves morally obliged both to prevent others from doing such actions and to refuse to do them even though the law of the land requires it. Nearly all of us believe ourselves to have both obligations with respect to murder. Hence, if we believe it to be murder to procure an abortion or to kill in an unjust war, we cannot in good conscience either stand idly by while others procure abortions or accept lawful induction for military service in what we believe to be an unjust war. Thus the internal peace of any society is imperiled in those exceptional cases in which a strong body of opinion within it denounces actions of a certain kind as morally intolerable, and another strong body affirms that any human being has the right or even the duty to do actions of that kind.

Because popular moral outrage is commonly ugly, cruel, and misdirected, the Enlightenment philosophers considered it a moral duty to combat socially divisive moral errors. And because many of the most cruel and misdirected actions for the suppression of moral wrong have been done in the name of one religion or another, they believed that establishing moral truth would tend to eliminate religious superstition. Enlightenment moralists like Kant, who were not hostile to religion as such, hoped to purify established religion of superstition. Others, however, held that religion is necessarily superstitious. Of those others, most hoped to establish a morality for human beings as such, independent of all religion; but some became moral nihilists, and attacked morality itself as, along with religion, an imposture. By a *coincidentia oppositorum* of which religion affords other examples, the superstitious deny any place within their religion for a universal human morality on the same ground as moral nihilists dismiss the Enlightenment project: that there are no requirements on human beings simply as human. Both deny that anything universally human underlies the mores of any religious or social-political community. The superstitious maintain that one particular religious community is sanctioned by divine power, and morally nihilistic free spirits deny it, but except in that one special case, both agree that all systems of mores are to be studied with disenchanted objectivity as expressions of nondivine social power.

Since requirements on conduct vary in kind, moralists may simply be disregarded unless they make plain what kind of requirement they take a moral one—one governing human conduct as such—to be. The proposition that human beings in the United States are legally required not to commit murder could be disregarded if those who put it forward could not explain what kind of requirement a legal one is, and how it requires whatever it does. As Wittgenstein once remarked, the first question raised by uttered sentences of the form "Thou shalt . . ." is "And what if I do not?" Legal requirements derive from social institutions exercising coercive force, but not all requirements are coercively enforced. In logic we are taught the law of noncontradiction, which can be expressed as a requirement: "Thou shalt not affirm both a sentence and its contradictory." If you ask, "And what if I do?" a sufficient answer is that if you make such a double affirmation you will both assent to a sentence and dissent from it. Of course you can persist and ask, "And what if I do that?" If you ask it, it would be idle to answer you; a peaceable response would be to flee your approach. If you do not in practice recognize requirements on what you, as human, may affirm in your thinking, your fellows cannot communicate with you. But other than thinking, are there any such requirements on what human beings, as human, may do?

THE TRUTH-CONDITIONS OF MORAL PROPOSITIONS: KANT'S INNOVATIONS

Asking what a requirement on human conduct as such might be is another way of asking "Under what conditions is it true to say that human beings as such are required to conduct themselves in a certain way in a certain situation?" When we know those conditions, we shall also know what we are disregarding if we disregard them.

Among Christians the answer most commonly given assimilates moral requirements to legal ones. All human beings are regarded as subjects of a divine sovereign, whose laws they are required to obey on pain of divine judgment and punishment. The divine law has been promulgated in the canonical Scriptures—in particular, the Mosaic decalogue as set out in Exodus 20: 1–17. The defect of such an answer was made clear once for all by Plato in *Euthyphro* 10a–11a. If human beings are required not to commit murder, say, only because God has forbidden it in divinely revealed law, and if God has not so forbidden it because they are independently required as human beings not to commit it, then they are not required as human beings not to commit it. They have an overwhelmingly strong reason not to, for it would be insane to break the law of an all-knowing and all-powerful sovereign; but that is not a moral reason—a reason binding upon them as human, as distinct from subjects of a divine sovereign.

Although they all accepted Plato's objection to identifying morality with divine positive law, the Enlightenment philosophers diverged in their views of what it is. Those in the empiricist tradition concluded that the only requirements on the conduct of human beings must arise from certain of their feelings, which were sometimes obscurely attributed to a moral "sense." The most persuasive theory of this kind I have encountered is John Stuart Mill's in the brilliant third chapter of *Utilitarianism*, "Of the Ultimate Sanction of the Principle of Utility."[4] The objection to all such theories is that having some particular capacity for feeling, or some particular sense, even if having it is normal in human beings, is not essential to them as rational animals. If Mill were right, then abnormal human beings who do not *feel* approval, in the strict psychological sense, for promoting the happiness of sentient creatures generally, lack the internal ground for conducting themselves morally (that is, according to the principle of utility), which Mill himself considers ultimate. They may do so in response to external sanctions—for example, they may desire not to forfeit the approval of others—but they have no internal sanction, no reason as human beings, for it.

Because of this, Kant, along with most Enlightenment nonempiricists, concluded that the requirements of morality must arise not from feeling but from reason, to which human beings necessarily have access as rational animals.[5] St. Thomas Aquinas and other medieval scholastics anticipated them, along with many Protestants.[6] According to Aquinas, God's commands proceed from God's reason: the eternal reason by which he has created all things and governs them. Morality (or natural law, as Aquinas called it) is therefore only derivatively a set of divine commands; primarily, it is a set of requirements that reason itself imposes on human conduct, that reason being found infinitely and perfectly in God and derivatively and finitely in human beings. It may therefore be defined as *"quaedam participatio legis aeternae in rationali creatura."*[7] God's eternal law provides for each creature according to its nature; and since human beings are by nature rational animals, it provides that they are to conduct themselves according to requirements of reason. Hence, in thinking out how, as rational beings, they are required to conduct themselves, they are participating in God's legislation for them. They are capable, if they seriously set about it, of understanding why the divine law for them as human, as revealed to Moses, is as it is.

What, then, is it for rational animals to be required as rational to conduct themselves, except in their thinking, in this way rather than that?

Perhaps because it is as unpretentious as it is deep, Kant's answer has been widely misunderstood.[8] It depends on distinguishing two functions of reason and noticing an implication of that distinction. Reason has both the theoretical function of investigating what is true and what is false and the practical function of investigating what, in this situation or that, is to be done or not to be done. The results of successful investigations of the former kind are propositions whose contradictories are false; those of the latter kind are intentions to act the alternatives to which are irrational. Kant observed that propositions about the irrationality of proposed alternative intentions are true or false, even though those intentions themselves are not. Although evident when pointed out, many philosophers have failed to see it. And since there are theoretical propositions about the rationality of acts of practical reason, Kant saw that the problem of what the propositions of moral theory are saying—what their truth-conditions are—is solved: they are propositions about whether it is rational or not, in a certain kind of situation, to act in a certain kind of way.

Kant's distinction between theoretical and practical reason presupposes that there are requirements of reason on human conduct, just as there are on theoretical thinking. If so, they will presumably resemble the requirements of logic on theoretical thinking. But are there any? Hume denied it: only passion can move us to act, he maintained; reason cannot. Against him, Kant's first observation about practical reason is that there are requirements to which it undeniably gives rise: namely, those of technology or skill. Human beings wish to bring about a multitude of ends, and they therefore investigate how this or that end can be brought about most efficiently, that is, most cheaply, or with least sacrifice of other ends. A completed investigation into means and costs yields both a theoretical and a practical conclusion: the theoretical one that a certain means is the most efficient and least costly way of bringing about a wished for end; and the practical one that, unless the intention to bring about that end is abandoned, it is irrational not to adopt that means. Such a practical conclusion, as Kant points out, is conditional or "hypothetical": if the means is not adopted, abandon the end, and if the end is intended, adopt the means. One or the other must be chosen, on pain of irrationality.[9]

The procedure by which Kant reaches this theoretical proposition about practical reason deserves study. As he himself noticed, it closely resembles that by which the rules of classical logic are established: a process of showing that they can be rejected only by assenting to and dissenting from the same proposition.[10] Rejecting the cheapest and most efficient means to an end resembles dissenting from the consequent of a hypothetical proposition while assenting both to it and to its antecedent. However, as Kant also noticed, moral requirements are not conditional upon whether an end is in fact adhered to; they require everyone in certain situations to act for the sake of certain ends. Hence rejecting a moral requirement, if there is such a thing, does not resemble assenting to a conditional proposition and its antecedent and dissenting from its consequent; it is not analogous to self-contradiction.

Unfortunately, Kant's own treatment of conditional requirements has led some philosophers to refuse to recognize any proposition in moral theory unless denying it can be shown to involve something resembling logical falsehood.[11] Skepticism of that sort is absurd even in philosophy of mathematics, and there is no reason to countenance it in moral theory. Rebutting it, however, does call for accuracy and candor in setting out the lines on which Kant shows that acting for certain ends is required of human beings as rational.

Doing so takes us to his second observation about practical reason: that, unless there are ends it unconditionally requires its possessors to make their own, it can require no conduct of them as its possessors.[12] Are there such ends?

From the Greeks to the present, it has been widely held that human beings as such naturally seek happiness. Kant acknowledges not only that they do but that it is rational for them to do what they reasonably judge will promote their natural end. On the face of it, a presumptive morality of rational egoism would follow: that, other things being equal, it is irrational for any human being not to do whatever actions he or she rationally judges will contribute more to his or her happiness than any available alternatives might. That is Sidgwick's first "method of ethics." Appearances, however, deceive. The conditions of any human being's happiness are, according to Kant, opaque to reason. No one can hope for anything more reliable than "counsels of prudence." Hence, since the principle of rational egoism cannot be rationally applied, it cannot require any actions of human beings as such.[13]

Is any end of action both sanctioned by reason and such that it can be rationally applied; if so, what is it? The ground of Kant's answer to this question is his third and perhaps most important contribution to the theory of practical reason. It is a distinction between two kinds of end. In drawing it, he was anticipated by scholastics,[14] although his contemporaries and successors ignored or misunderstood what he had done. His point of departure was that both the Greek and the modern conception of an end as something to be brought about by action—as something "producible" (*bewirkender*)—is incomplete. In general, an end (*telos, Zweck*) is something for the sake of which something is done. It is true that some ends are producible; "happiness" may serve as a name for one's success, in a complete life, in getting produced whatever producible ends he or she wishes for. Producible ends, however, presuppose existing beings for whose sake they are produced; that is, every producible end presupposes a "self-existent" (*selbständiger*) end. Overlooking this, most philosophers have been blind to the self-existent ends that lie behind the producible ends people have. If they had not been blind to them, Kant implies, they might have perceived that each human being necessarily regards himself or herself as "a self-existent end, and can recognize that all others necessarily so regard themselves, on the same rational ground."[15] Unfortunately, he does not expressly say what he took that rational ground to be. Can we reconstruct it?

Kant suggests that he believed that ground to be that human beings necessarily conceive of themselves as social creatures of a sort that is unique among terrestrial animals.[16] Termites, ants, and bees are social creatures, but their social behavior is programmed, not adopted as the result of rational discussion and agreement. Nonrational animals can have no part in institutions such as law and compensation or punishment for actions contrary to rationally accepted norms; not even those who contend that gorillas, chimpanzees, or whales are rational contend that those species participate in such institutions or could do so. Human beings—the only terrestrial animals known to be rational—cannot live full human lives except in communities in which their conduct is regulated by commonly accepted laws and by a variety of other institutions and private arrangements. For them, treating one another as full members of the same community is the same as treating one another as self-existent ends: as existing beings for whose sake those laws, institutions, and arrangements exist. It is true that throughout human history there have been many human political societies, that most human beings are members of only one such society, and that in most such societies most members have not been full members. But normal adult rational beings cannot rationally think of themselves, or of one another, as unfit for full membership in some political community, for they cannot rationally think of themselves as unfit by nature for taking a full part in the life of such a community. Hence, to the extent that any of them are excluded from such membership, they cannot rationally think of their exclusion except as a misfortune to be explained by private interest or prejudice, not by reason.

Requirements on the conduct of human beings as such, Kant observes, "[do] not rest at all on feelings, impulses and inclinations; [they] rest merely on the relation of rational beings to one another, in which the will of a rational being must always be regarded as legislative, for otherwise it could not be thought of as an end in itself."[17] In short, no normal human adult can seriously deny any of the following four propositions:

1. My own conduct is determined by my will, in the light of my own thinking about what to do;

2. The conduct of every other mature rational being is determined in the same way;

3. Among terrestrial beings, human beings are unique in that their significant behavior is conduct that is so determined;

4. Among all beings whatever, rational beings are unique in that only they can discuss how to coordinate their conduct according to agreed rules, in which each would be regarded as a self-existing end, and how to enforce those rules.

It follows from these propositions that among terrestrial beings, only humans can form the concept of an end in itself, can govern their conduct according to their conclusions about what beings, if any, fall under that concept, and can form communities the members of which recognize that they are required so to govern their conduct. From this, Kant proceeded to a fourth proposition about practical reason: that anyone who asks the question whether beings of any sort are marked off from those not of that sort as ends in themselves may rationally answer that among terrestrial beings only human ones are so marked off. "Morality," Kant concludes, "consists in the relation of every action to that legislation through which alone a realm of ends (*ein Reich der Zwecke*) is possible. This legislation, however, must be found in every rational being."[18]

Objections to Kant's Doctrine That Practical Reason Requires Its Possessors to Think of Themselves as Ends in Themselves

Objections of two sorts are directly made to Kant's doctrine that practical reason requires its possessors to think of themselves as ends in themselves. Some are skeptical; others deny that rationality, an abstract concept, can ground requirements on the concrete actions of flesh and blood human beings.

The simplest skeptical objection to Kant's doctrine is that it is logically possible to assent to all four of the propositions that are its grounds and still deny it. Yet skeptical cavils of this sort are dismissed in other fields. Even in mathematics axioms are accepted because of considerations that are dialectical (that is, in which alternatives are explored) and holistic (that is, in which account is taken of all the evidence—the apparently adverse as well as the apparently favorable). Such a process always leaves open the possibility that an accepted axiom will be replaced by another, although for the present it would be methodologically silly not to work with it. It is perverse to demand that moral philosophers dispose of skeptical doubts that no one takes seriously elsewhere.

Kant has drawn attention to a set of facts that not only distinguishes rational beings from all others but also requires them to distinguish how they treat one another from how they treat everything else, at least in the respect that it is only one another's conduct they can attempt to change by rational argument. The same set of facts also implies that, if any nonrational being were in fact an end in itself, neither it nor any other such being could act upon that consideration. It would be cruel and thus wrong for any rational being to kill an antelope for food by setting hungry wild dogs onto it so that he or she could shoot it; but no ecologist would allow that wild dogs act cruelly or wrongly in killing prey in the painful way they do. Outside the realm of rational beings, nothing treats anything, even itself, as an end in itself. No nonrational animal killed by a predator thinks of itself as wronged because no nonrational animal thinks at all. It seems to me to follow that there is no good reason why rational beings should recognize anything but one another as an end in itself. If so, the only serious question that remains is whether there is any reason why they should recognize one another as such ends. Was not Kant right in thinking that it matters that a communal life according to mutually accepted reasons is possible for them, but only if they so recognize one another? In this practical case, is not reasoning from *posse* to *esse* sound?

Such reasoning is dialectical (it takes account of skeptical objections), practical (it considers whether or not to accept a certain reason for acting or not), and holistic (it purports to set forth all the facts about acting for ends relevant to what rational beings might recognize as an end, together with the implications for communal life both of recognizing one another as ends and of not doing so). It implicitly acknowledges that the practical conclusion to recognize each rational being as an end in itself is not such that the reasoning for it cannot be rejected without assuming some logically impossible proposition. On the other hand, Kant maintains that no one in his right mind can reject the reasoning for it. He confidently leaves each reader to reach his or her own verdict.

Alasdair MacIntyre has developed a disguised variant of the skeptical objection from the undeniable fact that Enlightenment moralists, even those who describe themselves as Kantian, have not in fact accepted one another's conclusions.

> If those who claim to be able to formulate principles on which rational moral agents ought to agree cannot secure agreement on the formulation of those principles from the colleagues who share their basic philosophical purpose and method, there is once again *prima facie* evidence that their purpose has failed, even before we examine their particular contentions and conclusions.[19]

To me the differences between Enlightenment moralists seem to be what might have been expected from philosophers who are in substantial agreement about morality but who differ in intellectual formation and temperament. Why should Kantian moralists agree completely about Kantian moral philosophy any more, say, than Thomist natural theologians about Thomistic natural theology? And why should not the stricter Kantians take comfort from fellow-travelers like John Rawls, just as the stricter Thomist natural theologians, confronted with Ockhamists and fideists, take comfort from fellow-travelers like Francisco Suarez?

"Yet are you not troubled by the fact that most moral philosophers who have read Kant are not Kantian in any sense: for example, they do not agree with Kant that practical reason requires its possessors to regard one another as ends in all their actions?" I agree only to the extent that I am persuaded that they have understood Kant's thought as, I believe, most Kantians today do: for example, his distinction between producible and self-existent ends. The Kant whom most Kantians defend is not the Kant whose doctrines are described in anti-Kantian polemics from Hegel to MacIntyre. Does not the utilitarian slogan "Each for one, and none for more than one,"[20] suggest that utilitarians who grasp Kant's distinction between self-existent and producible ends will have difficulty in rejecting it—and whatever follows from it?

Of those who understand Kant's conception of rational beings as self-existent ends, which in fact reject it, and on what grounds? I leave Nietzsche's abusive and antihuman rhetoric to those with a taste for it; it seems to me to disqualify itself as reasoning.[21] However, there is a tradition traceable to Hegel according to which grounding morality on human rationality "homogenizes" human beings and so exalts a tendency in modern mass society to "undermine the communities or characteristics by which people formerly identified themselves and put nothing in their place."[22] The mistake of all such objections derives from an error that pervades much Hegelian criticism of non-Hegelian philosophy: the error of believing that abstracting a property of something, and examining what follows from having that property, implies that that thing has no other properties.

It is perfectly true that Kant rejects the "communities or characteristics by which people formerly identified themselves"—and distinguished themselves from other people—as grounds for morality, but he did so not to deny that human beings are community-forming creatures or that they have characteristics in common with some but not all others that affect which communities they choose to join, but to determine the rational limits on the kinds of community they may aspire to form or join and the kinds of distinguishing characteristics they may cultivate. Far from homogenizing human beings, Kantian doctrine assumes that they cannot be homogenized. At the same time, it rejects as contrary to practical reason any political community that claims to determine the producible *tele* or ends their members must devote their lives to bringing about, as Hegel and his followers admire the ancient Greek *polis* for doing. Kant differs from Hegel and his post-Hegelian critics in his freedom from the illusion that human beings will ever be completely at home in any society there ever has been or ever will be on earth, and hence from the illusion that decent members of a society in which ethical truth is fully recognized cannot be alienated from it or from their fellows. Hegel's idealization of the Greek *polis* is as indefensible as his delusion that, while the elected bourgeois legislatures of France and Britain neither did nor could concretely embody universal reason, the pre-1848 Prussian monarchy did not but could have done so. Given the inescapable propensity to corruption of everything human, whether individuals or institutions, alienation that is remediable can be remedied only by intensifying alienation that is not. A moral theory may be true and yet alienation persist after it becomes generally accepted. As Kant more and more came to recognize, his moral theory implies that every human being is a *viator* whose destination is not to be at home in any actual earthly community.[23]

How Kant Determines the Content of Morality

If Kant was right in concluding that the existence of morality presupposes that practical reason imposes unconditional requirements on the conduct of its possessors, and that it could not do so unless it recognized certain existing beings as ends, in the sense of beings for whose sake its possessors rationally act, then certain conclusions about the structure of morality follow.

The fundamental requirement that practical reason imposes on its possessors is that they treat one another equally, as beings for whose sake they must act. From this fundamental requirement certain "side-constraints" (the expression of Nozick's) follow on what they may rationally do.[24] The principle of these side-constraints is that no rational being may be used simply as a means to doing something for the sake of anybody else. Hence no possessor of practical reason may interfere in activities of others in which the status of everyone else as an end—their dignity—is respected. Violence and fraud may not be used against those who are not violating the dignity of others even if, on balance, good will come of their use.

However, more than side-constraints follow from the fundamental requirement. One does not treat other rational beings as ends equally with oneself unless one supports their innocent projects as far as one can without disproportionate loss to one's own. That may require one actively to help them as well to protect them from wrongful interference by others. Thus it does not follow that no one may be a means to benefiting another. No rational being may be *simply* a means to benefiting another, but every rational being is required, so far as it is in his or her power, to be a means for the good of others. Yet the benefits anyone confers on anyone else must be in a system of social relations in which those who confer them are ends equally with those on whom they are conferred. Contractual exchanges of benefits between equals are among Kant's models of social interaction in which no party is treated as a mere means. Models of its negation are enforced exchanges of benefits between slaves and masters and bargains driven with the unfortunate to which equals would not have agreed.

Despite the familiar charge that Kantian morality is individualist and nonsocial, Kant insisted in the first volume of *Metaphysik der Sitten*, the *Rechtslehre*, that much of what makes civilized life is possible only in a political society.[25] A good will exercised outside a civil society is as good as a good will exercised in one, but it realizes many fewer moral possibilities. Since practical reason requires us to benefit one another, without any of us being reduced to mere means to others' ends, it also requires us to join with our fellows in setting up a political society if we do not live in one, and, if we do, in supporting the one in which we live. Outside political societies neither peace nor prosperity are possible: there is no way of resolving honest differences of opinion about what is due to each from each and no way of compelling compliance with the enforceable parts of morality by those tempted to flout them.

Since all human beings are equally one anothers' ends, each of us has duties to himself or herself as well as to others. And since, subject to the requirements of practical reason, rational beings each pursue their own happiness as they conceive it, it is rational for normal human adults to be self-supporting, either as individuals or as members of freely formed families, and for nonadult children to be supported primarily by their parents. Yet even in communities of farming families it would be irrational if there were no communal arrangements for looking after the unfortunate: young orphans, widows with young children, the disabled, and the aged. In more complex industrial societies it would be irrational if, besides such arrangements, there were not also others to ensure that those seeking work could find it on terms that respected their dignity as self-existent ends.

Given that each normal adult rational being is primarily required to support himself or herself, one would be irrational both in pursuing one's own well-being as one conceives it and in supporting others in pursuing theirs, if one did plan to do both effectively. One is not required to take every opportunity either to improve oneself or to help others; everyone has so many opportunities of both kinds that one must choose among them. What is required is that one give short measure neither to oneself nor to others. For most people, the stronger temptation is to give short measure to others, but Dickens's Mrs. Jellyby reminds us that for some the opposite is the stronger temptation. Both in improving oneself and in supporting others' pursuit of happiness, reason requires not that one act in any specific way in any specific situation, but that one make and act upon rational plans.

In making such plans, one must plan to observe the side-constraints imposed on one's actions by the requirement that in all one's intentions every rational being must be regarded as a self-existent end. One may not violate a side-constraint either to improve oneself or to help others because the ground of plans to do both is that every rational being, oneself included, must be treated as a self-existent end in all of one's actions. This is the ground of St. Paul's dictum—which has so puzzled utilitarians and other consequentialists—that even for the glory of God it would be wrong to do evil that good may come.[26]

OBJECTIONS TO HOW KANT DETERMINES THE CONTENT OF MORALITY

The major social problems of Kant's time were the persistence of unfree political, social, and economic institutions and warfare between sovereign states for political ends to which their citizens were assumed to be mere means. Although he wrote under a galling censorship that made the candid publication of his political views impossible, in his treatment of public law in the first volume of *Metaphysik der Sitten* he disguised a powerful argument for a liberal republican society as an analysis, heavily indebted to Rousseau, of the nature of all political societies, including the Prussia of his day.[27] A year before publishing this penetrably disguised manifesto of political liberalism, denouncing aggressive war as a means to any morally legitimate political end,[28] he had already ensured that in the illiberal and nationalist Europe that emerged from the Napoleonic wars he would be ridiculed as a mere theorist, ignorant of how society works, and too arrogant to confess it. He would also be despised as an ideologist of capitalist individualism by left-wing intellectuals who blamed warfare and political repression not on illiberalism but on market liberalism. Objections of both sorts continue to be made.

The most persistent objection to Kant's determination of the content of morality is to its deductive structure. Does not a system in which propositions about specific requirements of practical reason are deduced, with the aid of specificatory minor premises, from first principles, presuppose that those principles are self-evident, independent of the precepts derived from them? Is not Kant's system, in short, "foundationalist"?[29] Would it not be viciously circular unless its principles were "established on grounds that do not presuppose the acceptability of some or all of the system derived from [them]?"[30]

No, it would not be. This objection rests on a misunderstanding of the purpose, in any field, of putting a body of thought into deductive form, or even into axiomatic form, in which all undemonstrated propositions must be expressly stated in advance. In mathematical logic a theory is put into axiomatic form primarily to make it possible to test it by ensuring that what is claimed to follow from it, true or false, does so rigorously. The result of Frege's attempted axiomatization of arithmetic was to show that one of his axioms was false. Yet a deductive system like Kant's system of morality is not axiomatic. In it specific requirements are deduced from a single moral principle (that it is irrational of possessors of practical reason not to treat themselves and each other as self-existent ends), but this occurs by way of an indefinite number of nonmoral specifications of kinds of failure to treat others as self-existent ends—a number that is constantly being augmented, and of which any may be revised or even repudiated. Yet a deductive system of this sort can be tested much more rigorously than the clouds of unsystematic "intuitions" that are all most moralists will commit themselves to, although less so than an axiomatic system.

If a deductive system makes intelligible a considerable body of hitherto unsystematic beliefs, without implying anything to which serious objection can be offered, then it is rational to accept provisionally deductions from its principles about which no one hitherto has had any opinion at all; and it is a secondary purpose of deductive systems to provide such reason for accepting its derivative propositions. In morality as in law, deductive systems are refined as new consequences are drawn from them and found wanting, but it is intelligible that a stage will be reached at which it is reasonable to suppose that all future refinements will be in its nonmoral specificatory premises, not in its principles. Jewish and Christian moralists hold that this stage was reached millennia ago, when the moral parts of the Mosaic Torah were promulgated. Kant agreed with them, although he believed that the biblical formulations of the principles of morality could be improved upon.

Those who object that this is foundationalist fail to distinguish what is systemically fundamental from what is epistemically fundamental. The principles of any deductive system, moral or other, are systemically fundamental: its derived propositions are explained by reference to them, and they are not explained by reference to anything higher. They are not, however, epistemically fundamental; no part of any intellectual system is. Epistemically, a deductive system stands if it has no consequences that must be rejected as false for any reason, if no more comprehensive alternative is equally unobjectionable, and if no equally comprehensive one better explains what it explains. Its principles are accepted on holistic grounds and can always be called in question as new evidence comes to hand, but, as long as there is no reason to question them, the system's derivative propositions are accepted because they follow from its principles.

The propositions by which Kant arrives at his fundamental moral principle—that reason is practical, that practical reason is not confined to means-end or cost-benefit calculations, that there can be no unconditional requirements of practical reason unless there are self-existent rational ends as well as producible ones, and that rational beings are such ends—are offered not as self-evident but as inseparable from a variety of beliefs most of us share or can be brought to share. The very structure of the two morally substantive sections of *Grundlegung*, which is reflected in their titles, "Passage from Common Moral (*sittliche*) Rational Cognition (*Vernunfterkenntnis*) to Philosophical" and "Passage from Popular Moral *Weltweisheit* to Metaphysics of Morals," shows that at every stage his theory grows out of a steadily deepening reflection on common moral thinking.

The second continuing line of objection to Kant's moral theory is to its universality and abstraction. Sometimes it is complained that it is "unhistorical." The charge is vague, but the reply to it need not be. Kant saw the danger to Enlightenment civilization both from nationalist and imperialist wars and from the attitudes that go with them, in which members of one nation-state disregard the dignity of members of others as self-existent ends; he also saw that the only possible remedy was to expose those attitudes as irrational. To reject his exposure, as Hegel did, and to deny content to a morality of humanity, as distinct from the *Sittlichkeit* of this particular *Volk* or that, even if it is not intended to serve the interests of any particular nationalism, is as blind in theory as it is pernicious in practice. Without varieties of community human life is impoverished, but what makes a community different from others, precious though it may be, cannot provide its members with standards by which to judge when its life has gone rotten. Decent human variety presupposes recognition of common human dignity.

What holds for communities holds, even more emphatically, for religions. Every religion has something to learn about human decency from the practice of some other religions. But Kant's Enlightenment morality implies that what any acceptable religion offers is not a distinctive morality but a remedy for the state of those who already have a more or less adequate conception of the morality common to all such religions, but who flout it in practice. Most religions are radically false, and many are morally evil. But if any religion is true, as I believe Christianity is, it will satisfy the test proposed by Jesus: by its fruits you shall know it. Human beings can, if they work at it, tell whether the fruits of a religion are sound or rotten because, as Kant saw, they can find by reflection on their own situation the self-existent ends of all rational action. Christianity, along with some other religions, teaches that, besides the finite self-existent ends we encounter in each other, there is an infinite self-existent end to know whom is perfect happiness. But that cannot invalidate ordinary human moral knowledge; as St. John explained, we cannot love God, whom we have not seen, unless we love one another, whom we have.

NOTES

1. Immanuel Kant, *Grundlegung zur Metaphysik der Sitten*, 2d ed. (Riga: J. F. Hartnoch, 1786), and *Metaphysik der Sitten*, 2d ed. (Koenigsberg: F. Nicolovius, 1798). Two page numbers are given for all passages quoted or cited from Kant; the first refers to the original edition, and the second refers to the appropriate volume of the Berlin Academy's edition of Kant's collected works (vols. 4 and 6 respectively for the works cited in this note). For the former, I chiefly follow L. W. Beck's translation in *Immanuel Kant: The Critique of Practical Reason and Other Writings in Moral Philosophy* (Chicago: University of Chicago Press, 1949); for vol. 1 of the latter, J. Ladd, trans., *Kant: The Metaphysical Elements of Justice* (Indianapolis, Ind.: Bobbs Merrill, 1965); and for vol. 2 of the latter, James Ellington, trans., *Kant: The Metaphysical Elements of Virtue* (Indianapolis, Ind.: Bobbs Merrill, 1964).

2. In *The Methods of Ethics*, 7th ed. (London: Macmillan, 1907), pp. 162–75, 496–503.

3. *Grundlegung*, pp. 8–9 / 397–98.

4. "If there were not . . . a natural basis of sentiment for the utilitarian morality, it might well happen that [it] also, even after it had been implanted by education, might be analysed away. But there *is* this basis of powerful natural sentiment . . . [namely] that of the social feelings of mankind—the desire to be in unity with our fellow-creatures, which is already a powerful principle in human nature, and happily one of those which tend to become stronger, even without express inculcation, from the influences of advancing civilization" (J. S. Mill, *Utilitarianism* [Indianapolis, Ind.: Bobbs Merrill, 1957] pp. 39–40).

5. Although many utilitarians are empiricists and follow Mill, many are rationalists who on this point follow Kant—Sidgwick, for example (see *Methods of Ethics*, pp. 98–104).

6. See, e.g., John Calvin, *Institutio Christianae Religionis* (1559), 2.8.1.

7. "A certain participation by rational creatures in the eternal law," St. Thomas Aquinas, *Summa Theologiae* 1–2.91.2; cf. 1–2.100.1.

8. For a radical misunderstanding that distorted the development of ethics in analytical philosophy, see G. E. Moore, *Principia Ethica*, 2d ed. (Cambridge: Cambridge University Press, 1922), pp. 126–33.

9. *Grundlegung*, pp. 40–41 / 414–15. I owe this analysis of Kant's treatment of technological imperatives to Thomas E. Hill, Jr., "The Hypothetical Imperative," *Philosophical Review* 82 (1973): 429–50.

10. *Grundlegung*, pp. 44–45 / 417.

11. They do so with some encouragement from Kant himself, in his attempt to derive the whole content of morality from a principle of universalization. He

argues that it is irrational to act on any intention for which it would either be self-contradictory or contrary to your will to intend that everyone in similar situations should act as you intend to (*Grundlegung*, pp. 51–59 / 420–25, 80–81 /436–37). In his practice in *Die Metaphysik der Sitten* Kant abandons his doctrine in *Grundlegung* that the whole content of morality could and should be derived from his universalization principle by not attempting so to derive it. See my "The Structure of Kant's Metaphysics of Morals," *Topoi* 4 (1985): 61–72, especially 61–62; and my *Theory of Morality* (Chicago: University of Chicago Press, 1977), pp. 13, 57–59.

12. *Grundlegung*, pp. 64 / 428, 80–83 / 436–37.

13. *Grundlegung*, pp. 42–43 / 415–16.

14. Both Aquinas and Duns Scotus anticipate Kant here. See my *Human Ends and Human Actions: An Exploration of St. Thomas's Treatment* (Milwaukee, Wis.: Marquette University Press, 1985), especially pp. 3–17.

15. *Grundlegung*, pp. 64–66 / 428–29.

16. Especially in ibid., pp. 73–79 / 432–36.

17. Ibid., p. 76 / 434.

18. Ibid., p. 75 / 434.

19. Alasdair MacIntyre, *After Virtue*, 2d ed. (Notre Dame, Ind.: University of Notre Dame Press, 1984), p. 21.

20. "The greatest happiness principle . . . is a mere form of words without rational signification unless one person's happiness, supposed equal in degree (with the proper allowance made for kind), is counted for exactly as much as another's" (Mill, *Utilitarianism*, p. 76).

21. Curiously, these include Alasdair MacIntyre, who, referring to *Die fröliche Wissenschaft*, sect. 335, writes that "in five swift, witty and cogent paragraphs [Nietzsche] disposes . . . of what I have called the Enlightenment project to discover rational foundations for an objective morality" (*After Virtue*, p. 113). Of these five paragraphs, this is the one most directly about Kant:

> What? You admire the categorical imperative within you? This "firmness" of your so-called moral judgement? This "unconditional" feeling that "here everyone must judge as I do"? Rather admire your *selfishness* at this point. And the blindness, pettiness and frugality of your selfishness. For it is selfish to experience one's own judgement as a universal law, and this selfishness is blind, petty and frugal because it betrays that you have not yet discovered yourself nor created for yourself an ideal of your own, your very own—for that could never be somebody else's and much less that of all, all! (Friedrich Nietzsche, *The Gay Science*, trans. Walter Kaufmann [New York: Vintage Books, 1974], p. 265).

Kant, I imagine, would have been content to observe that Nietzsche's conception of unselfishness is illustrated to perfection by the argument of this passage.

22. Charles Taylor, *Hegel* (Cambridge: Cambridge University Press, 1975), pp. 412–14. The passages quoted appear in the selection reprinted in Michael J. Sandel, ed., *Liberalism and its Critics* (New York: New York University Press, 1984), pp. 177–97; Sandel's comment (p. 10) suggests that he is more impressed by Taylor's account of Hegel's criticism of Kant than by Taylor's own reservations about it (pp. 179, 191–97).

23. Taylor admirably exposes the unacceptability of Hegel's ethical theory, but he fails to bring out how paradoxical, on his own showing, it is. He argues convincingly that he held that "the last time that the world saw an effortless and undivided *Sittlichkeit* was among the Greeks" (*Hegel*, p. 378), and, just as convincingly, that one of Hegel's historical heroes is Socrates, who "undermined or broke with the *Sittlichkeit* of [his] people" (p. 377). As I think Kant would have said, "The case rests." For those who (like Hegel) continue to idealize the Greek *polis* after reading Plato, I recommend Simon Hornblower, *The Greek World*, 479–323 B.C. (New York, Methuen, 1983).

24. Robert Nozick, *Anarchy, State and Utopia* (New York: Basic Books, 1974), pp. 28–33.

25. Kant, *Metaphysik der Sitten*, 1:154–58 / 305–8.

26. See Samuel Scheffler, *The Rejection of Consequentialism* (Oxford: Clarendon Press, 1982), for a recent puzzled attempt to explain why nearly everyone agrees that consequentialism is wrong. Scheffler tacitly assumed that no satisfactory answer was available when he wrote. Kant's name is absent from its index.

27. See especially *Metaphysik der Sitten*, 1:203–12 / 318–23, 238–44 / 338–42.

28. Immanuel Kant, *Zum ewigen Frieden* (Koenigsberg: F. Nicolovius, 1796). This is translated into English as *To Perpetual Peace*.

29. For an example of this criticism, directed against my *Theory of Morality* rather than against Kant, see Jeffrey Stout, *Ethics after Babel* (Boston: Beacon Press, 1988), pp. 129–35. However, Stout's belief that Kant is a foundationalist appears in an aside on p. 169, to which attention is drawn in his index, p. 334.

30. Stout, *Ethics after Babel*, p. 130.

Chapter 3

THE NATURE AND BASIS OF HUMAN RIGHTS

David Little

W E ARE CURRENTLY confronted with two conflicting sets of claims and beliefs about our contemporary spiritual and intellectual condition. On the one hand, we are told we live in a "postmodern" world in which universal standards of truth and morality, standards that are believed to be applicable and justifiable independent of particular cultural or religious traditions, are simply unavailable. For example, Alasdair MacIntyre informs us bluntly that "human rights are fictions." That is so, he says, because there are no universally convincing reasons for believing in human rights, just as there are no such reasons for believing in witches or unicorns.[1]

MacIntyre goes on to argue, according to what has become a fairly fashionable line of thinking, that currently "the language of morality is in [a] state of disorder."[2] That is because the social and cultural contexts in which a common moral vocabulary once may have made sense, at least for Westerners, have virtually disappeared. We "possess . . . simulacra of morality, we continue to use many of the key expressions. But we have—very largely, if not entirely—lost our comprehension, both theoretical and practical, of morality."[3] Lacking common grounds, moral disputes are consequently interminable because they are irresolvable. What is true in the West in our encounters with one another is only amplified in the international community, as MacIntyre's comment about human rights makes clear.

From a somewhat different, though supplementary, perspective Richard Rorty contends that torturers, in inflicting pain on innocent people, are not betraying some essential principle of humanity, for there are no such principles. Rorty is sure that "there is nothing deep down inside us except what we have put there ourselves, no criterion that we have not created in the course of creating a practice, no standard of rationality . . . that is not obedience to our own conventions."[4] If we should come to affirm a prohibition against torture, it will be because we find it to be "pragmatically" justified—at least for our purposes, whatever they may happen to be.

Moreover, this general approach has its religious proponents. The redoubtable Stanley Hauerwas, for example, vigorously attacks the idea that there exists any usable "universal ethic grounded in human nature per se."[5] In some ways following MacIntyre, Hauerwas believes that any effort to make something important of assertions about universal human rights "fails to appreciate that there is no universal morality, but that in fact we live in a fragmented world of many moralities." Christian ethics, he says, is not to be commended to anyone "with the claim that we can know the content of that ethic by looking at the human."[6]

On the other hand, some advocates and defenders of human rights seem to suggest that there are certain moral beliefs and concomitant claims about the world that are universally true and universally justified. In the words of Patricia Derian, assistant secretary of state for Human Rights and Humanitarian Affairs during the Carter administration: "Electrodes applied to the gums shatter teeth in the same way in Manila as in Moscow. Cruelty knows no [distinctions] . . . ; the pain is universal, the demeaning and degrading of individuals is as hateful to those in the People's Republic of China, as it is in South Korea."[7]

Or as the Polish philosopher Leszek Kolakowski writes: "When we extend our generous acceptance of cultural diversity . . . and aver, e.g., that the human rights idea is a European concept, unfit for, and [not] understandable in, societies which share other traditions, is what we mean that Americans rather dislike being tortured and packed into concentration camps but Vietnamese, Iranians and Albanians do not mind or enjoy it?"[8]

In the same spirit the legal philosopher Ronald Dworkin, in a moving review of *Nunca Mas,* the report on the practice of torture by the Argentine military from 1976–1979, recommends a universal "taboo against torture." "The world needs . . . a settled, undoubted conviction that torture is criminal in any circumstance, that there is never justification or excuse for it, that everyone who takes part in it is a criminal against humanity. . . . Torture cannot be surgically limited only to what is necessary for some discrete goal, because once the taboo is violated the basis of all the other constraints of civilization, which is sympathy for suffering, is destroyed."[9]

I stand unflinchingly with the second group of philosophers, with those who suggest that there are universal, and even "objective," moral standards (and concomitant beliefs) that are in part associated with existing human rights norms. In what follows I try to provide the beginnings of a rationale for taking up such a position.

There are two parts to this rationale. First, I make some purely descriptive or, broadly speaking, sociological comments about the current place and function of human rights norms in the international community. Here I try to show that the "fragmentariness" of moral discourse, which certainly does exist in our world, is a more structured affair than Mac-

Intyre and Hauerwas seem to understand. Second, I address what is, for philosophical purposes, the heart of the matter—namely, questions of the definition and justification of human rights.[10] Here I try, no doubt at great risk, to rehabilitate a version of intuitionism. However unpopular that view is these days, I suggest that at least part of what intuitionists were trying to get at better conforms to our considered reactions to certain human rights statements than other more fashionable views do.

HUMAN RIGHTS AND MORAL DISCOURSE IN THE CONTEMPORARY INTERNATIONAL COMMUNITY

On a purely sociological or descriptive level, certain truisms about the role of human rights in international affairs are hard to square with claims about the radical fragmentation of moral language in our current experience. As one international relations observer remarks: "The idea that human beings have rights as humans is a staple of contemporary world politics."[11] Or, as another writes: "The international polity is changing, and global political processes now exist that can no longer be accounted for strictly in terms of interstate politics. . . . The internationalization of human rights concerns is part of this broader process. . . . To date the notion of a world society constitutes not a framework within which moral claims can be met, *but a vocabulary within which [those claims] may be articulated.*"[12]

Four things need stressing. First, there should be no controversy over whether human rights language is moral language. In the face of article One of the Universal Declaration—that "all human beings are born free and equal in dignity and conscience and should act toward one another in a spirit of brotherhood," or of the preamble to the Convention against Torture—that "the equal and inalienable rights of all members of the human family" "derive from the inherent dignity of the human person," there can be no reasonable doubt that these statements meet the standard criteria of morality. They are warrants for prescribing authoritative action, or action that takes priority and is regarded as legitimate, in part for considering the welfare of others.[13]

For example, there can be no doubt that human rights, as expressed in the international instruments, are understood as distinct from and prior to law. As the preamble to the Universal Declaration puts it, "human rights should be protected by the rule of law." That is, human rights are here understood to constitute an independent standard for formulating, interpreting, and criticizing law, and thus they are assumed to exist as a basis for moral appeal, whether or not they are in fact legally enforced in given circumstances.

Second, while it is true that under present international conditions by no means all human rights claims are satisfactorily accommodated, nor are all articles of the declarations and conventions uniformly interpreted and applied, it is hard to ignore the growing prevalence and significance of a common vocabulary in which claims from very different cultures are similarly articulated. People who deny these realities have not been paying attention to their newspapers. The fact these days that so much international attention is given to the petitions of human rights advocates all over the world—in the press, in diplomatic discussions, and in the reports of monitoring groups like Amnesty International, Human Rights Watch, and Helsinki Watch—attests to the remarkable momentum with which human rights are being internationalized.

What else are we to make of the expression of aspirations and demands, all couched in the shared vocabulary of human rights, that is occurring in so many diverse national settings? It would be impossible to understand the revolution now transpiring in Eastern Europe and the republics of the former Soviet Union apart from the language and categories of international human rights. Protesters passionately adopt the same language and categories to articulate their grievances in Tibet, Iran, Kuwait, Israel and the occupied territories, the People's Republic of China, South Africa, Honduras, and the Republic of Korea, to name a few places recently in the news.

Third, it must of course be admitted that an important degree of "fragmentation" and "disorder" in the moral discussion of human rights does exist. There are important disputes and differences of opinion in this area both within nations as well as among different cultural traditions, as the controversy over the Salman Rushdie affair exhibits.[14] However, it is no longer accurate, if indeed it ever was, to portray this fragmentation as disproving the existence of a deeply embedded common vocabulary. To a significant degree, the human rights vocabulary itself defines and structures the terms of the debate and the issues that are in dispute throughout the world.

The prominent and familiar controversies over "individual rights," ascribed without regard to race, creed, or color, versus "collective or communal rights," ascribed on the basis of race, creed, or color, have become a common problem *within* the national and cultural experience of nations across the globe largely because of a rather ironic set of circumstances. That is, many of the nations where these controversies now rage sought the right to pursue their own indigenous communal traditions on the basis of urgent appeals to universal human rights, rights that are premised on the principle of nondiscrimination.[15]

The right to political self-determination, for example, was characteristically demanded in response to colonial domination, a system perceived to have produced massive human rights violations, including extensive political and economic discrimination on grounds of race, ethnicity, and religion. Against that background, the new nations typically adopted modern constitutions formally promising that violations perpetrated under colonialism would not be continued, and usually instituting judicial and political systems designed accordingly.

On the other hand, the new nations understood it to be part of the right of self-determination to create societies in keeping with particular cultural and communal traditions. In advancing the "communal rights" of particular groups, these traditions were not altogether consonant with universal human rights standards, especially as regards the role of race, ethnicity, and religion as determinants of political and economic power.

Thus a wide variety of nations face a common dilemma that is created in large part by the human rights environment that produced them: How are nations who are in part, at least, committed to universal, nondiscriminatory standards to reconcile or harmonize those standards with countervailing indigenous standards? Regardless of whatever compromises are respectively worked out, it is unlikely that these nations will be able to escape the grip of the human rights vocabulary that is, for very important historical reasons, now embedded in their collective consciousness.

A fourth crucial reason, in addition to the circumstances of anticolonialism, helps to account for the current pervasiveness of a common human rights vocabulary. It is what we might refer to as the lesson of World War II, for it was as a consequence of that event that the human rights movement was initiated worldwide.

The war produced a new and profound anxiety over *the modern potential for political pathology* in people in every corner of the globe affected by the war. Specifically, the practices of fascism were taken to reveal what a system of arbitrary force amounts to, a system administered precisely according to the disciminatory criteria of race, creed, and color. It occurred to large numbers of people that the afflictions of the fascist countries were in some respects characteristic of the modern nationalist state. Given the appropriate conditions, the same kind of arbitrary force might easily be employed elsewhere, with similarly devastating results. Clearly, the specter of perpetuating the kind of political pathology perceived in World War II gave major impetus to the campaign to design an international system of human rights known as "Hitler's epitaph." The widespread apprehension in great part explains the remarkable international consensus achieved in 1948 in adopting the Universal Declaration and, later, the two major conventions on civil and political rights and on economic, social, and cultural rights.

On the one hand, the dramatic growth in the number of modern constitutional regimes in the postwar period helps to explain why the language of constitutional protections and human rights has resonated so widely and so persistently. On the other hand, it is the dramatic imbalance between the technology of force and the institutions of restraint that in large measure explains the urgency of the current appeal in favor of strengthening constitutional protections and human rights in so many diverse countries.

It ought to be added that the radically changing social, economic, and political conditions throughout the world resulting from economic development, industrialization, urbanization, and the like have severely modified the support and protection traditionally provided by the small, close-knit community.

> These intrusions have created a largely isolated individual who is forced to go it alone against social, economic and political forces that far too often appear to be aggressive and oppressive. . . . In such circumstances, human rights appear as the natural response . . . , a logical and necessary evolution of the means for realizing human dignity [in a changing social environment].[16]

DEFINING AND JUSTIFYING HUMAN RIGHTS

The position I try to defend is compellingly put forward in an article by William Gass called "The Case of the Obliging Stranger." The article begins in the following way:

> Imagine I approach a stranger on the street and say to him, "if you please, sir, I desire to perform an experiment with your aid." The stranger is obliging, and I lead him away. In a dark place conveniently by, I strike his head with the broad of an axe and cart him home. I place him, buttered and trussed, in an ample electric oven. The thermosat reads 450 F. Thereupon I go off to play poker with friends and forget all about the obliging stranger in the oven. When I return, I realize I have overbaked my specimen, and the experiment, alas, is ruined.
>
> Something has been done wrong. Or something wrong has been done.
>
> Any ethic that does not roundly condemn my action is vicious. . . . It is also interesting that no more convincing refutation of any ethic could be given than by showing that it approved of my baking the obliging stranger.[17]

Gass continues:

> If someone asks me, now I am repentant, why I regard my act . . . as wrong, *what can I do but point again to the circumstances comprising the act?* "Well, I put this fellow in an oven, you see. The oven was on, don't you know." And

if my questioner persists, saying, "Of course, I know all about *that*; but what I want to know is, why that is wrong?" I should recognize there is no use in replying that it is wrong because of the kind of act it is, a wrong one, for my questioner is clearly suffering from a sort of [*folly of moral doubt*] which forbids him to accept any final answer this early in the game, *although he will have to accept precisely the same kind of answer at some time or other.*

. . . It cannot be my baking the stranger is wrong for no reason at all. It would then be inexplicable. I do not think this is so, however. [The act] is not inexplicable; *it is transparent.* . . . [*Thus, the*] explanatory factor is always more inscrutable than the event it explains.

[For] how ludicrous are the moralist's "reasons" for condemning my baking the obliging stranger. They sound queerly unfamiliar and out of place. This is partly because they intrude where one expects to find denunciation only and because it is true they are seldom if ever *used*. But the strangeness is largely due to the humor in them.
Consider:
My act produced more pain than pleasure.
Baking this fellow did not serve the greatest happiness to the greatest number.
I acted wrongly because I could not consistently will that the maxim of my action become a universal law.
God forbade me, but I paid no heed.
Anyone can apprehend the property of wrongness sticking plainly to the whole affair.
Decent men remark it and are moved to tears.[18]

We may add a few examples of our own:

I would not like it if it were done to me.
If widely practiced, acts of this kind would diminish the chances for the survival of the species.
If people have any rights at all, they have a right not to be treated in that way (Hart, Shue).[19]
Such acts do not "work for us" (Rorty); they are not part of our "story" or tradition (MacIntyre, Hauerwas), nor are they consonant with "our own culture's best view of what moral truth or justified moral belief consists in" (Stout).[20]

Gass's general argument is obviously in the tradition of moral intuitionism. One of his two central points was anticipated, for example, in H. A. Prichard's famous essay first published in 1912, "Does Moral Philosophy Rest on a Mistake?" Prichard's affirmative answer to that question follows from the same conclusion Gass comes to, namely, that moral theories sound "queerly unfamiliar and out of place" as efforts to justify our reactions to acts like baking the stranger. Indeed, as Gass suggests, the attempt to supply justifying reasons of the sort mentioned would appear to be material better suited for Monty Python than for philosophical discourse.

Even though Gass's second point is not mentioned by Prichard, it conforms well to the spirit of intuitionism. It implies that far from providing justification for moral reactions of this kind, moral theories are themselves judged by how they handle acts like baking the stranger. As Gass puts it, "Any ethic that does not roundly condemn my action is vicious . . . [and] no more convincing refutation of any ethic could be given than by showing that it approved of [it]."

The first step in my strategy is simply to substitute certain human rights statements for Gass's example of baking the stranger. Consider again the comments by Patricia Derian and Ronald Dworkin condemning torture as universally wrong. We must readily admit that uncertainty will remain as to whether in some extreme circumstances torture might not be excusable—say, to extract from a terrorist information concerning the whereabouts of explosive devices, information that would help to prevent the death of large numbers of people. Moreover, there are likely some margins of unavoidable dispute among cultures as to whether a given form of treatment constitutes torture or not.

Nevertheless, can there be any reasonable doubt that some forms of torture—for example, inflicting severe pain on children for amusement or to terrorize and intimidate are *naturally* wrong and ought, as Dworkin urges, to be declared taboo for all the world? When the authors of *Nunca Mas* write, "Each time that a child suffered torture directly or witnessed the torture of his parents, he entered into a realm of horror [in some cases leading to suicide],"[21] can there be any reasonable doubt that acts of this sort are simply and transparently wrong in themselves, whoever may perform them and in whatever culture? Can there be any reasonable doubt that people who have systematically engaged in such acts have acted viciously in that they have violated something "deep down inside," something contrary to what it means to be a human being, and that they are therefore appropriately referred to, in Dworkin's words, as "criminals against humanity"?

As in other similar examples of moral revulsion—for instance, in response to extrajudicial execution for purposes of terrorizing and intimidating—our reactions to the torture of children and the like conform precisely to Gass's account. First, moral theories, insofar as they pretend to "explain" and "justify" why these acts are wrong, are little more than pompous distractions. In such instances the relevant questions concern only the verification of circumstances: Was a child in fact involved? Was torture willingly and deliberately performed for purposes of intimidating the parents, or was the torturer perhaps acting under duress? and so on.

If, after the evidence has been substantiated, someone still ventures to inquire why such an act was wrong, all that can be done is to repeat, perhaps more graphically, "the circumstances comprising the act": the child was three years old; while intermittently drinking coffee and smoking a cigar, the torturer administered severe electric shocks to the genitals of the child in the presence of its parents until they promised to retract their public criticism of government policies. Beyond that, requests for "reasons" why torturing children in that way is wrong becomes an occasion for doubting the mental and spiritual health of the inquirer.

Second, rather than requiring "further justification," circumstances like these establish a prior standard for evaluating theories of practical reason, including moral theories. That means, as Gass points out, that any theory that somehow finds a way to render acts with these precise characteristics to be permissible or even excusable is categorically invalidated. For example, when the Argentinian generals invoked a "national security ideology," based in part on an argument from necessity, as a way of excusing the torture of children during the "dirty war," such a conclusion (among others) itself became the basis for refuting the ideology. Any theory that systematically condones torturing children thereby demonstrates that it is a corrupt theory. Although Gass does not make the point, it follows that a theory also refutes itself to the degree that it dilutes or enfeebles the character of the primary intuition. Here Dworkin's use of the word "taboo" in regard to torture is instructive.

A taboo is a "sacred prohibition."[22] It is understood to go to the depths of human life; it verges upon a "sacred" realm, a realm beyond daily experience that is at once powerfully mysterious and fascinating. As such, a taboo attests to something beyond the control of human beings, something that is conceived to establish the conditions of human action in an "objective" way—in a way that must not be tampered with. Dworkin's suggestion that the taboo against torture protects the basis of "all the other constraints of civilization," namely "sympathy for suffering," is profoundly interesting in this regard. In any case, to talk of taboos is to talk, without embarrassment, of the inalterable and universal foundations of human life.[23] If it is appropriate to characterize the sort of intuitions that are associated with the torture of children as taboos, then, by extending Gass's account, any theory that weakens or in some way "denatures" that understanding is thereby self-refuting, just as theories that condone such acts would be self-refuting.

In my opinion, it does not take much effort to perceive that a number of the fashionable theories of practical reason—pragmatism, neotraditionalism (or whatever we are to call the emphasis on inherited cultural particularism as the context of practical reasoning), and related views—have precisely the effect of deconstructing or decomposing a belief in taboos in the sense we have identified them. If I understand them properly, it is, among other things, the point of several of these views to show how mistaken are the assumptions about the "inalterable and universal foundations" of human life, particularly the assumptions associated with "natural-rights liberalism" and its offspring, human rights philosophy. Accordingly, a conviction that there is, for example, a right against the recreational or intimidational torture of defenseless people that is universally justified, or "written on the hearts" of all people, as St. Paul says, is fallacious. From my point of view, such skepticism serves only to dilute or enfeeble the primary intuition we have been talking about.

Although I have no room here to supply documentation, from what I have read Rorty and Hauerwas appear to hold unconditionally that a belief in any kind of universal rights (or close substitutes) is fallacious. MacIntyre and Stout may be groping toward certain universal moral prohibitions on other than a rights basis, though the precise implications for action remain unclear, and the support for such views appears to fall far short of the requisite commitment to "inalterable and universal foundations" of human action.[24]

Some of the other aforementioned "reasons" in support of our primary intuitions appear to me not so much to undermine as to trivialize the intuitions and in that way to dilute them. It is fairly obvious that the "I-would-not-like-it-if-it-were-done-to-me" appeal does not cover the kind of intuition I am talking about. If we consider our reactions to torturing children, it is hardly a question of personal likes and dislikes. The matter is considerably weightier than that.

Similarly, to describe intuitions about prohibitions against torture as justified because they are instrumental toward some goal like preserving the species or maximizing pleasure or achieving some other idea of the good puts the cart before the horse. Assuming that Dworkin's account of a "torture taboo" is accurate, then the prohibition against torture may not be judged and justified with reference to some end or other. On the contrary, ends, ideas of the good, and the like are themselves evaluated as to whether or not they condone violations of such a prohibition and whether or not they weaken commitment to it.[25]

We are now in a position to address more directly questions of the definition and justification of human rights. Since a human right is a complex idea with moral, legal, and other aspects, we must make some preliminary clarifications. Given that a "right" *simpliciter* is an entitlement to demand a certain performance or forbearance on pain of sanction for noncompliance; that a moral right is a right regarded as authoritative in that it takes precedence over other action and is legitimate in part for considering the welfare of others; and that a legal right is warranted and enforced within a legal system, a human right, then, is understood as having the following five characteristics, according to the prevailing "human rights vocabulary." 1) It is a moral right advanced as a legal right. It should, as pointed out earlier, "be protected by the rule of law," thus constituting a standard for the conduct of government and the administration of force. 2) It is regarded as protecting something of indispensable human importance. 3) It is ascribed "naturally," which is to say it is not earned or achieved, nor is it disallowed by virtue of race, creed, ethnic origin, or gender. 4) Some human rights can be forfeited or suspended under prescribed conditions (under public emergency, for example), but several primary or basic human rights are considered indefeasible under any circumstances. 5) It is universally claimable by (or on behalf of) all people against all (appropriately situated) others, or by (or on behalf of) certain generic categories of people, such as "women" or "children." Those who are appropriately subject to such claims are said to have "correlative human duties."

The right against torture, which is enshrined in various major international instruments, is an example of a human right that satisfies all five characteristics. The prohibition of torture is assumed to be a moral right that is advanced as a legal right—it sets a universal political-legal standard. It is also assumed to protect something of indispensable human importance and to be ascribed "naturally" to all human beings, simply as human beings. It is one of the primary human rights that, legally understood, may not be suspended under any "exceptional circumstances" whatsoever. Finally, it is universally claimable by or on behalf of all human beings against all (appropriately situated) others. Thus, all people have a complex "correlative human duty": they must not perform torture, they must help protect against the practice, and they must aid those subjected to torture.[26]

As I hope is clear from the foregoing comments, I propose that the moral authority of the prohibition against torture rests finally and exclusively on an intuition or recognition of the transparent wrongness of at least certain forms of torture—such as, in this discussion, of the recreational or intimidational torture of children and other defenseless innocents.[27] The general features that constitute the wrongness of such acts are, it seems clear to me, *the arbitrary (or purposeless) infliction of severe suffering, that is, the infliction of severe suffering for no good reason.* Deliberately to inflict severe suffering upon defenseless individuals like children for some self-regarding purpose such as amusement or protection from political criticism is an important part of what the concept "moral wrongness" *has* to mean. Consequently, cases of that sort of practice, such as occurred in Argentina in the late 1970s, simply display these features, and in that sense they are "transparently wrong."[28]

It should be briefly explained why *all forms of torture,* and not just recreational or intimidational torture, have been outlawed in the international instruments. There are two related reasons. The first is the manifest irrationality of depending on the infliction of pain as a means of extracting reliable confessions. Cesare Beccaria called attention to the difficulties in 1764:

> The requirement . . . that pain become the crucible of truth, as if truth's criteria lay in some wretch's muscles and sinews, only confuses all relations. It is a sure means to acquit the sturdy villain and condemn the weakly innocent. . . . The result of torture, then, is a matter of temperament and of calculation, and varies in every person in proportion to strength and to sensitivity; so that it would be more the mathematician than the judge that could solve the following problem: given the muscular strength and nervous sensitivity of an innocent, find what degree of pain will make him confess to a given crime.[29]

Second, whatever utility there may be in employing torture in the extreme case, it appears impossible to prevent it, once introduced, from becoming the cause of widespread arbitrary suffering. In the words of the Amnesty International report *Torture in the Eighties*, "Once justified and allowed for the narrower purpose of combatting political violence, torture will almost inevitably be used for a wider range of purposes against an increasing proportion of the population."[30] Thus, torture of combatants or even of criminal suspects for interrogational purposes predictably degenerates into the unrestrained and thus arbitrary infliction of severe suffering, an outcome that, of course, violates our definition of at least part of the idea of moral wrongness.

The primary and indefeasible character of the right against torture begins to suggest how it might be related to other human rights.[31] Secondary rights, such as the rights of legal due process, political participation, freedom of expression, movement, and association, are rights suspendable under specified conditions enumerated in the international instruments. They would be understood as reliable means for preventing the arbitrary infliction of severe suffering like torture. Accordingly, secondary rights implement primary rights, and they are justifiable for that reason.[32]

These comments help, I hope, to illumine why the view I am trying out is an example of rational, rather than sensational intuitionism (of the Hutcheson and Shaftesbury sort). Wrongness is, accordingly, "cognizable" in that the notion has certain irreducible cognitive features, as already specified. Human beings may be expected to know enough to be able to recognize these basic features as deeply wrong, or taboo, and to begin to organize their lives accordingly, unless impeding or debilitating circumstances intervene to derail the prescribed recognition.

This last point has, of course, been the standard line of defense adopted by intuitionists when it is pointed out that not all human beings in fact have the same intuitions. If, for example, reference is made to societies like the Iks of Uganda, who allegedly act with systematic disregard for taboos against gratuitous suffering, it might be answered that they have been "morally handicapped" for having been banished from their traditional lands and way of life. Such a line of defense has always seemed perfectly reasonable, so long as one were convinced that taboos of the sort we have been proposing do exist.

It should be obvious that I see no reasonable grounds to doubt the taboo against arbitrary suffering as manifested in the practice of torture. Therefore, I would see no particular problem in describing as "handicapped" or "pathological" someone, or some group of people, who genuinely and systematically denied the universal and absolute wrongness of such a practice, particularly if such denials were acted upon. A judgment of that kind, of course, underlies the common international practice of condemning as "gross human rights violations" actions that typically include violations of the taboos we have been discussing.

I admit that intuitionists have usually gone too far both in the number and range of basic moral intuitions they claim, as well as in the degree of confidence they place in the ability of intuition to serve as a procedure for resolving moral dilemmas. My strategy is much more modest. At this point I am inclined to suspect that the list of primary intuitions or taboos is actually quite small, and that the notion of intuition, or whatever synonym we may identify, is relevant only in respect to them.

Beyond that is the fairly traditional idea that once the primary intuitions are in place, they will have to be applied, and conflicts among them resolved—as far as possible—by means of reason. This is a second sense in which my proposal is an example of rational intuitionism, and its role is suggested by Gass's comment that "no more convincing refutation of any ethic could be given than by showing that it approved of my baking the obliging stranger."

The procedure here is to determine, by means of both empirical and logical analysis, the extent to which any practical theory could be shown to approve of, to lead to, or to trivialize taboos against arbitrary suffering. It is at this point that the aforementioned examples of fascism and colonialism, as background for the post–World War II human rights campaign, become pertinent. The overall moral effects of these movements were, it seems to me, to "clarify the dimensions of our intuitions."

The record of atrocities committed in the name of fascism and colonialism served to shock people all over the globe into a new awareness of what we called the "modern potential for political pathology." It was not that in beholding fascist practices people came for the first time to believe that genocide or "geno-torture"—taking life or inflicting severe suffering on the basis of religious, ethnic, or racial criteria—was wrong and ought to be condemned and resisted. Rather, people came to see dramatized before their eyes the full pathological implications of certain discriminatory beliefs. Once the connections were demonstrated, all further arguments in support of those beliefs were silenced. To rephrase and adapt Gass's observation, after World War II no more convincing refutation of any set of beliefs could be given than by observing that it approved of (or led to, or trivialized) arbitrary suffering of the sort practiced during that period.

That form of refutation is now deeply embedded in the emerging world culture that is in part conveyed by the human rights vocabulary. All sets of practical beliefs in all parts of the world are now standardly subjected to what one could call "the antifascist test," and its variant, "the anticolonialist test." If it can be convincingly demonstrated that certain beliefs approve of, lead to, or trivialize arbitrary suffering of the sort associated with fascism and colonialism, very little else needs to be said.

In contemporary ideological disputes, all sides charge opponents with imposing one form or another of severe arbitrary suffering. Marxists and communists claim that capitalism enslaves workers in a system of "untold horrors, savagery, . . . and infamies," as Lenin put it.[33] Conversely, communism represents for capitalists a totally oppressive way of life. Islamic revolutionaries cite the record of what they regard as Western domination and exploitation in the Middle East in justification of their cause. For their part, Westerners view the extension of Islamic fundamentalism as a new form of tyranny.

Communitarians attack liberals for imposing their own biases and special interests under the guise of universal standards, while liberals charge communitarians with favoring ethnocentric and preferential political patterns. Regardless of whoever may be right or wrong in demonstrating the practical implications of certain assumptions and beliefs, there can be little dispute that the terms of moral argument are now deeply fixed and widely pervasive, illustrating the common reference point supplied by the events of World War II and the anticolonial aftermath.

There remain, of course, many unanswered questions. There are strictly philosophical problems, such as what sort of epistemology and ontology go with this view, as well as whether this position represents some kind of foundationalism, which is at present in such disrepute. It is also fair to ask whether this is at bottom a "rights-based" theory, and, if so, how such a theory might withstand some of the powerful objections currently in the literature. There are also questions oriented more directly to thinking about human rights. What is the relation of primary rights to the whole host of other rights contained in the international documents? How are conflicts among them resolved? These are but a few of the problems that need attention.

Even so, waiting until all the theoretical problems are solved before giving assent would, after all, contradict the kind of appeal that is made here. The whole idea is that the rapidly growing international consensus on human rights rests upon a few incontrovertible intuitions concerning some fundamental taboos, such as the taboo against torture. Given certain prevalent sociological conditions, it is "common sense" to honor those taboos by advocating and enforcing human rights. This position does not disparage theoretical reflection. But it does understand such reflection to be after the fact, rather than before it.

NOTES

The views expressed in this essay are the author's alone and are not to be taken as necessarily representing the outlook of the United States Institute of Peace. I would also like to thank my assistant, Darrin McMahon, for editorial assistance.

1. Alasdair MacIntyre, *After Virtue: A Study in Moral Theory* (Notre Dame, Ind.: Notre Dame Press, 1981), p. 67.

2. Ibid., p. 2.

3. Ibid.

4. Richard Rorty, *Consequences of Pragmatism* (Minneapolis: University of Minnesota Press, 1982), pp. xlii–xliii.

5. Stanley Hauerwas, *The Peaceable Kingdom* (Notre Dame, Ind.: University of Notre Dame Press, 1983), pp. 60–61.

6. Ibid., p. 63.

7. Patricia Derian, prepared statement, December 15, 1982, *Reconciling Human Rights and U.S. Security Interests in Asia*, Hearings before the subcommittees on Asian and Pacific Affairs and on Human Rights and International Organizations of the Committee on Foreign Affairs, House of Representatives, 1982, p. 483. The thrust of Ms. Derian's comments is 1) that the infliction of pain under the conditions mentioned is universally regarded as wrong ("demeaning and degrading"), and 2) that these universal reactions are valid. In other words, the statement has both descriptive and normative significance.

8. "Idolatry of Politics," unpublished paper delivered as the Fifth Jefferson Lecture of the National Endowment for the Humanities, 1986, p. 8.

9. Ronald Dworkin, "Report from Hell," *New York Review of Books*, July 17, 1986, p. 16. It is worth pointing out that although Dworkin's recommendation is clearly intended as universally normative, there is, as it stands, ambiguity over its justification. "The world needs . . . a settled, undoubted conviction" could mean that we ought now to invent and decide to adopt such a conviction, a conclusion that no doubt is compatible with antiobjectivist positions. Or it could mean that we need it because it is a prior and independent ("objective") moral condition of human life, *there to be discovered, not invented.* My impression is that Dworkin would incline toward the second position. In any event, in what follows I try to make the case for the second position.

10. In the light of some recent work on human rights, it is important to stress the need to attend specifically to questions of justification. It is popular these days to try to avoid the problem of the normative grounds of human rights beliefs by appealing to consensus. In *International Human Rights: Universalism vs. Relativism* (London: Sage Publications, 1990), p. 78, Alison Dundes Renteln writes:

"it is important to realize that there may be cross-cultural universals which empirical research might uncover. By seeking out specific moral principles held in common by all societies, one might be able to validate universal moral standards." No argument is provided to show if or how it might be possible to deduce normative conclusions from purely descriptive premises. Similarly, Jack Donnelly argues in *Universal Human Rights in Theory and Practice* (Ithaca, N.Y.: Cornell University Press, 1989), pp. 21–23, that we may be satisfied with a purely "analytic or descriptive" theory of human rights, rather than a "normative or prescriptive" one, because, for one reason, "there is a remarkable international normative consensus on the list of rights." It is enough, according to Donnelly, to show descriptively "the implications for social relations of taking human rights seriously." As my comments in the first section of this paper demonstrate, description of the role and implications of human rights in contemporary international politics is important. But for a full theory of human rights that is surely insufficient. Whatever consensus may now exist, it was hard won, to put it mildly, against the most severe challenges to the justifiability of human rights from fascists and others in recent history. There is no reason to think such challenges will not reappear. Indeed, as I mentioned at the beginning of the paper, serious philosophical challenges to human rights are in fact rather fashionable these days. It is hard to see how appeals to consensus answer these challenges, since critics may consistently assert that the consensus is mistaken and ought to change. Moreover, it seems clear that human rights language, like moral and other evaluative language generally, is self-committing in a way that descriptive language is not. Human rights, as formulated in the international instruments, call for commitment: "Whereas the peoples of the United Nations have in the Charter *reaffirmed their faith in fundamental human rights*, in the dignity and worth of the human person and in the equal rights of men and women" (preamble, Universal Declaration; emphasis added). This is very different from a statement that "the peoples of the UN have in the charter taken note of the fact that human rights are widely accepted." A full theory of human rights must address the self-committing character of human rights, or what philosophers call the 'supervenient' character of normative language. I contend that the supervenience or special normative or 'self-committing' character of human rights language is accounted for only by explicitly identifying a prior *moral* premise (the primary normative intuitions) in which the "rightness" of rights can logically be grounded. See Paul Taylor, "Social Science and Ethical Relativism," *Journal of Philosophy* 55 (1958): 32–44, for a thoughtful discussion of this issue.

11. R. J. Vincent, *Human Rights and International Relations* (Cambridge: Cambridge University Press, 1986), p. 7. See also Louis Henkin, *The Age of Rights* (New York: Columbia University Press, 1990), pp. 28–29:

> In response to pressures and influences both domestic and external, all kinds of political systems, all kinds of governments have accepted the idea of rights, have written rights into constitutions, and have undertaken obligations to respect them. No doubt the commitment of many countries to human rights is less than authentic and whole-hearted. Yet the fact of the commitment, that it is enshrined in a constitution, and that it is confirmed in an international instrument are not to be dismissed lightly. Even hypocrisy may sometimes deserve

one cheer for it confirms the value of the idea, and limits the scope and blatancy of violations. . . .

12. J. G. Ruggie, "The Future International Community," *Daedalus* 112 (Fall 1983): 105–6; emphasis added. See Antonio Cassese, *Human Rights in a Changing World* (Philadelphia: Temple University Press, 1990), pp. 63–64:

> It is a fact that the Universal Declaration and the various covenants, treaties and declarations that followed ended up involving and, as it were, "ensnaring" states which were opposed or indifferent to certain aspects of human rights, either due to their historical and cultural traditions or due to different ideologies. Thus, . . . the Socialist countries, having first shown perplexity over, and indeed hostility towards, the Universal Declaration, ended up collaborating in drafting it. Admittedly, they began by thinking of using it as a weapon in the Cold War. But they gradually came to believe in the Declaration as a great ethical and political decalogue that should inspire their actions. More or less the same thing happened to many Third World countries, which ended up energetically participating in producing, if not the Declaration (many of them were not yet independent in 1946–8), the 1966 Covenants [on Civil, Political, and on Economic, Social, and Cultural Rights]. . . . Admittedly, this process of unification remains at the moment mainly at a "rhetorical" level, that is, a normative and to some extent ideological one. But in a world as divided, and fragmented, as the international community today, the existence of *a set of general standards*, however diversely understood and applied, in itself constitutes an important factor for unification. (original emphasis)

13. An elaboration and defense of this view of the notion of morality is provided in David Little and Sumner Twiss, *Comparative Religious Ethics* (New York: Harper & Row, 1978), chap. 2.

14. In regard to the controversy over the publication of Salman Rushdie's *Satanic Verses* in September 1988, however, it would be a mistake to conclude that the fragmentation in moral assumptions is a simple cross-cultural conflict between Muslim and Western ideas. The situation is more complicated than that. Commitment to the norms of free expression and nondiscrimination are not all on the "Western" side. On April 9, 1990, the British High Court of Justice refused to extend the protection of an existing blasphemy law to Muslims living in Britain, while as much as admitting that the decision was unfair: "The mere fact that the law is anomalous or even unjust does not, in our view, justify the Court in changing it, if it is clear" (Regina v. Bow St. Magistrates Court—Ex Parte Choudhury). Conversely, there is evidence of commitment to the norms of tolerance and free expression from within the Muslim community; see Lisa Appignanesi and Sara Maitland, eds., *The Rushdie File* (Syracuse, N.Y.: Syracuse University Press, 1990). For a fuller treatment of the matter, see David Little, "Toward a European Peace Order: The Role of Religion and Human Rights," in *Europe in Transition: Political, Economic, and Security Prospects for the 1990s*, J. J. Lee and Walter Korter, eds. (Austin: Lyndon B. Johnson School of Public Affairs, University of Texas, 1991), pp. 257–70.

15. The African nationalist leader the Reverend Ndabaningi Sithole put it this way in 1959: "During the war the Allied Powers taught the subject peoples (and

millions of them!) that it was not right for Germany to dominate other nations. They taught the subjugated peoples to fight and die for freedom rather than live and be subjugated by Hitler. Here then is the paradox of history, that the Allied Powers, by effectively liquidating the threat of Nazi domination, set in motion those powerful forces which are now liquidating, with equal effectiveness, European domination in Africa" (cited in Paul Gordon Lauren, *Power and Prejudice: The Politics and Diplomacy of Racial Discrimination* [Boulder, Colo.: Westview Press, 1988], pp. 161–62).

16. Jack Donnelly, "Human Rights and Human Dignity," *American Political Science Review* 76 (1982): 312; cf. "Poorest Continent [Africa] Becoming Most Rapidly Urbanized," *Washington Post*, April 9, 1989, p. A1.

17. William H. Gass, "The Case of the Obliging Stranger," *Philosophical Review* 66, no. 2 (April 1957): 193. My emphasis.

18. Ibid., p. 198; all emphases are mine.

19. See H.L.A. Hart, "Are There Any Natural Rights? in A. I. Melden, ed., *Human Rights* (Belmont, Calif.: Wadsworth Publishing Co., 1970), pp. 61–75; Henry Shue, *Basic Rights: Subsistence, Affluence, and U.S. Foreign Policy* (Princeton, N.J.: Princeton University Press, 1980); see especially pp. 21–22, and n. 15, p. 182, for reference to Shue's reliance on Hart's famous hypothetical defense of natural rights. As Shue puts it, "if there are any rights (basic or not basic) at all, there are basic rights to physical security" (p. 21). Hart's argument is that if people ascribe "special rights" to others by undertaking such things as making promises, granting proxies, and entering into contracts, then they must assume that, absent such agreements, everyone is understood to have a "general right" (a natural right) not to be interfered with. The argument is hypothetical because the general right obtains only if people first agree to enter into "right-creating" institutions like promise-keeping.

20. Jeffrey Stout, *Ethics after Babel: The Languages of Morals and Their Discontents* (Boston: Beacon Press, 1988), p. 23.

21. *Nunca Mas* (New York: Farrar, Straus and Giroux, 1986), p. 307.

22. *Webster's New World Dictionary*.

23. It will no doubt be objected that taboos vary and change over time and from culture to culture. How can one be sure that beliefs in taboos as representing "the inalterable and universal 'foundations' of human life" are not simply projections conditioned by temporary and local circumstances? I do not deny that taboos change and vary. Much of moral experience undoubtedly involves the process of evaluating and accepting or rejecting beliefs put forward as taboos. My only point here is that, on reflection, whatever other taboos may be deemed irrational, superstitious, and so forth, a taboo against torture (of the sort specified) cannot seriously or imaginably be so regarded by a self-respecting human being. Thus a considered reaction to instances of torture of children such as occurred in the Third Reich or in Argentina in the late seventies can be adequately characterized only by means of a concept like taboo—as something whose violation must be regarded as an offense against the "foundations of human life."

24. For what is to my mind a thoroughly convincing account of the nihilistic implications of Stout's latest arguments, see the review of *Ethics after Babel* by Edmund Santurri, *Journal of Religion* 71 (January 1991): 67–78.

25. For criticism of the hypothetical defense of human rights offered by Shue, see note 31 below.

26. See Shue, *Basis Rights*, chap. 2 for a compelling discussion of the "correlative duties" implied in a commitment to human rights.

27. I am using "intuition" in the way G. E. Moore does in the preface to *Principia Ethica* (Cambridge: Cambridge University Press, 1965), p. x: "When I call . . . propositions 'Intuitions,' I mean *merely* to assert that they are incapable of proof; I imply nothing whatever as to the manner or origin of our cognition of them. Still less do I imply (as most Intuitionists have done) that any proposition whatever is true, because we cognise it in a particular way or by exercise of any particular faculty" (original emphasis).

28. I have sympathy for many of the suggestions about the foundations of human rights in Louis Henkin's important book, *The Age of Rights*, though I have one reservation. I agree when Henkin writes: "The idea of rights here distilled from contemporary international instruments responds, I believe, to common moral intuitions. . . . Those intuitions have not been authoritatively articulated. Developed during the decades following the Second World War, international human rights are not the work of philosophers, but of politicians and citizens. . . . The international expressions of rights themselves claim no philosophical foundation . . ." (p. 6). All this attests to the pretheoretical character of the moral reactions that appear to me to underlie current international human rights understanding. Indeed, I have tried to reinforce Henkin's suggestion in the second part of this essay. But I am less convinced when Henkin writes that the international expressions of rights "articulate no particular moral principles." The moral principle I mention and exemplify in this paragraph seems to me properly to characterize the "moral intuitions" involved.

29. Cesare Beccaria, *Essays on Crimes and Punishments*, cited by Cassese, *Human Rights in a Changing World*, pp. 89–90.

30. *Torture in the Eighties*, Amnesty International (London, 1984), p. 7.

31. See, for example, article 4 of the International Covenant on Civil and Political Rights, which identifies certain rights as "nonderogable" or unsuspendable even under legitimate emergency conditions. It is important to note that while there is as yet no fully authoritative and systematic legal theory of the hierarchy of human rights, nor, for that matter, complete agreement about how many primary rights exist, legal experts agree that there is a "small number (irreducible core) of rights"—at least the right to life and the prohibition of slavery, torture, and retroactive penal measures—that is *jus cogens*, or among the preemptory or overriding norms of international law. See Theodor Meron, "On a Hierarchy of International Human Rights," *American Journal of International Law* 80, no. 1 (January 1986): 11.

Meron draws an interesting conclusion: "Removal of the underbrush that clutters the landscape of concepts and nomenclature may make it possible to build a sounder, less amorphous structure of human rights, *which should be based on an enlarged core of non-derogable rights*" (p. 22; emphasis added). Two things are worth pointing out in this connection: first, by definition a preemptory norm (*jus cogens*) acts as a fixed and prior constraint upon all law. It does not depend for its validity upon state concurrence, nor are states free to modify it as they see fit.

Second, each of the "irreducible core" rights—those against torture, extrajudicial killing, slavery, and retroactive laws—amounts to a fundamental protection against the arbitrary infliction of severe suffering.

32. This is, at present, only a suggestion. It does seem clear that one valid traditional reason for supporting civil and political rights is the protection they are believed to ensure against tyranny, or what is the same thing, the arbitrary infliction of injury and death. Still, it may be that some of the derogable rights like freedom of speech have, in addition, more than just instrumental value. That needs to be thought through.

I do find this way of understanding the relation between primary and secondary rights superior to the proposal made by Shue, and in part supported by Nickel (see Shue, *Basic Rights*, 5–87; and James W. Nickel, *Making Sense of Human Rights* [Berkeley and Los Angeles: University of California Press, 1987], pp. 133–36). Shue argues that since a person who has been killed, enslaved, or tortured is incapable of enjoying any secondary rights, rights against such things must be regarded as primary or "basic," and thus they are, by implication, nonderogable. This proposal yields a peculiar result: torture and arbitrary life-taking would be prohibited *so that* persons could enjoy the rights of due process. There are two problems: first, it is more reasonable to think of the rights of due process as the desirable means of preventing arbitrary injury and suffering; second, there appears to be something transparently wrong about arbitrary life-taking and torturing. They are surely not wrong just because they make the enjoyment of other rights impossible.

33. V. I. Lenin, *The State and Revolution*, excerpt in Walter Laqueur and Barry Rubin, eds., *The Human Rights Reader* (New York: New American Library, 1979), p. 181.

Chapter 4

RELIGIOUS ETHICS IN A PLURALISTIC SOCIETY

Robert Merrihew Adams

ONE OF THE OBJECTIONS often raised against religious theories in ethics is that in a religiously pluralistic society they will be divisive, undermining the common, or shared, morality on which a society depends for its health. We would be better served, objectors suggest, by a purely secular ethical theory on which all could agree. The short answer to this objection is that there is a sense in which every society must, and therefore will, have a shared morality, but that a shared ethical theory is not required for such a common morality. And it is good that it is not required, for no comprehensive or foundational ethical theory, not even a secular one, is likely to meet with general agreement in any modern society that permits free inquiry. The development and advocacy of a religious ethical theory, therefore, does not destroy a realistic possibility of agreement that would otherwise exist. I believe this answer to be correct, and I try to develop it more fully in this essay.

COMMON MORALITY

Where in the moral life should we look for general agreement? Perhaps first at the beginning of it, in the moral education of children. A university course in moral philosophy may begin with problems of moral skepticism, but if the moral education of children began that way, morality would not exist as a social reality. Children begin early in life (in American culture, at any rate) to acquire the skills of moral *dis*agreement, but they will not have the materials for disagreement unless they first learn some moral facts. They learn that kindness, generosity, and gratitude are good, and that selfishness is bad. They learn that in general it is right for them to obey their parents, wrong to take or break what belongs to someone else, and so forth. Even in learning that certain things do "belong to" certain people, they are learning a partly moral fact that is important to the structure of a society. They do not quite have the concept of morality until they have learned to distinguish what is morally wrong from what is prohibited merely on account of tastes or preferences of their parents.

It is unlikely that this moral learning will "stick" unless the children find (as they normally do) that a central core of the moral "facts" they learned from their parents are also viewed as facts in the wider community. This common core, I argue, is not an ethical theory; borrowing a phrase from Rawls, we could call it rather an "overlapping consensus."[1] I do not mean to suggest that it exists in the minds of individuals in any sort of isolation from other, less widely shared beliefs. Beliefs belonging to common morality are taught to children in the closest association with more distinctive views and values of their parents, often in the context of a religious institution.

Beginning, as it does, with moral "facts" accepted on authority, moral learning requires little reasoning at first. Moral reasoning is an essential part of the practice of morality, however. Children do in time learn principles that tell us not so much which actions to perform as how to judge which actions we ought to perform. Among these are principles of universalizability ("Do unto others as you would have them do unto you"); fairness (rules should be applied consistently, and on the basis of the facts); and beneficence (it is good to do what is good for people, and bad to do what is bad for people). These principles enjoy general, even cross-cultural, acceptance. It seems likely that we have a natural affinity for them.

That we agree, broadly and roughly, on principles of this sort is important for one of the functions of morality, which is to provide a framework for trying to resolve by discussion practical issues in our common life. We give each other reasons to whose relevance and importance we have a shared commitment. In this way, for example, members of a philosophy department (who perhaps hold quite diverse views in ethical theory) may be able to reach agreement about the appropriate treatment of a particular student's academic situation, based on accepted principles of fairness and consistency in the application of rules, as well as a measure of agreement on the aims and standards of the academic program.

One of the most obvious expressions of a common morality is the criminal law. Defining a type of action as criminal normally expresses moral disapproval of it. And more than disapproval is involved; crimes are acts that society refuses to tolerate. To be effective, except in an oppressive police state, this intolerance requires a broad base of public support. In many jurisdictions of our own society, to be sure, the criminal law forbids some types of action (such as sodomy between consenting adults, or personal use of marijuana) that a substantial segment of the population does not regard as wrong. If enforced, however, such prohibitions are inevitably a source of conflict. A society in which most actions forbidden under the criminal law were not generally agreed to be morally wrong would be in deep trouble.

The law creates reasons for action, and in some cases the wrongness of a contrary action will be seen to arise from its legal prohibition. This is true of many violations of tax and traffic laws. The core of the criminal law, however, is the prohibition of certain types of action that are regarded as immoral independently of the law, and prior to it. On the wrongness of these actions we expect general agreement, not only within a given society but also among members of different societies. Travelers going from country to country can reasonably assume, without consulting lawbooks, that most forms of theft and physical assault will be forbidden wherever they go.

Judgments of honesty and dishonesty constitute an interesting area of shared morality, similar in some ways to the criminal law. It is widely agreed that lying and breaking promises are generally wrong. While these offenses are legally penalized only in special cases, we are apt to be quite intolerant of them in other ways. They are among the types of action we feel we should not have to put up with. This is no accident. Without shared disapproval of dishonesty and deception, human practices of communication and cooperative planning would be all but impossible.

ETHICAL THEORY AND THE LIMITS OF COMMON MORALITY

This area of general moral agreement has its limits, although they can hardly be defined with precision. Indeed, most particular points of moral agreement shade into controversy. The killing of human beings, and violent assault on them, are generally condemned—but there is deep disagreement about the morality of warfare, capital punishment, and euthanasia. We can agree about the general wrongness of stealing more readily than about the limits of individual property rights in relation to the state. Other things being equal, it is surely wrong to tell a lie—but are there exceptions, and if so, what are they? Opinions differ about these questions. Selfishness is bad; and often it is plainly recognizable. But what seems selfish to some may be regarded by others as the innocent pursuit of happiness, or even the laudable pursuit of personal excellence. While we agree on a number of principles of fairness, there is certainly much disagreement about what is fair in concrete situations. Moreover, we think it is important to hold open the possibility that we are wrong about some of the moral points on which we do agree. We must be prepared to give a hearing to the reformer who claims that all or most of us have wrongly condoned slavery or the slaughter of animals for food.

These limits of common morality are very important for the development of ethical theory. The moral life in its earliest stages is a response to the actual demands of those with whom the child is linked in society, and I believe that those demands still constitute a major part of moral motivation for virtually all adults. It might seem natural, therefore, to identify moral obligation with the demands of society. The main obstacle to this identification is the fact that society speaks with a divided voice on many issues, and that we believe society has sometimes spoken with an erring voice on important matters.

What counts as common morality, indeed, is not only imprecise but variable and relative to one's historical and cultural context. Common morality covers a larger area relative to North American society in the 1980s than it does in relation the whole contemporary human world. It covers an even larger area in relation to the set of subcultures within which a typical individual (even a fairly cosmopolitan individual) lives most of his or her life. We will rarely have to deal with people with whom we do not have significant fragments of morality in common, but finding the shared basis for moral discussion can be a difficult practical problem. The imprecision and relativity of the concept of a common morality would also pose a serious theoretical problem if I meant to define what is objective in morality as what is common. But that is not my intention.

Much ethical theory can be seen as trying to find the nature of moral obligation and the morally good in something that transcends the divided and fallible voice of society. Candidates for this role have included the Form of the Good, (human) nature, pure practical reason, and modern variants on these ideas. The commands of the gods were probably the first candidates, and I have argued elsewhere that an account of the nature of ethical right and wrong in terms of the commands of a loving God affords the best possibility of finding a transcendent ground of moral obligation that is consonant with the social nature of obligation.[2] Prescriptivist and existentialist metaethical views have also insisted on the possible transcendence of society's demands by individual moral decision, but at the expense of the objectivity of morals.

More relevant to our present purpose is another relation of ethical theory to the limits of pretheoretical agreement in morals. One of the main motives for ethical theorizing is to try to resolve rationally some or all of the moral issues that common sense seems to leave unresolved or doubtfully resolved. If disagreement or uncertainty prevails on a point of ethics about which we are concerned, we should surely want to think as clearly and carefully about it as we can. And we may well suppose that a general understanding of the nature and grounds of moral rightness and goodness would provide us with criteria that would be helpful in settling moral issues. In this way we might hope to reach firm and shared conclusions about previously debated questions in ethics.

These hopes have in large measure been disappointed. There are many points of ethics on which there is wide agreement, as noted earlier. But no comprehensive ethical theory commands anything approaching general agreement. I have mentioned several of the varieties of objectivism and subjectivism that flourish in metaethics. And in normative ethics utilitarianism is vigorously defended and vigorously opposed. Even among opponents of utilitarianism who agree in giving a fundamental place to rights and liberties, there are disagreements in both theoretical foundations and political conclusions as deep as those between Rawls and Nozick. Nothing in the history of modern secular ethical theory gives reason to expect that general agreement on a single comprehensive ethical theory will ever be achieved—or that, if achieved, it would long endure in a climate of free inquiry.

Even agreement on the encompassing framework of an ethical theory, moreover, will not necessarily lead to agreement on particular ethical questions. The difficulty of assigning values to the expected utility of alternative courses of action leads utilitarians to differ widely about concrete issues. This problem is not peculiar to utilitarianism, since any plausible ethical theory will count the goodness or badness of expected consequences as at least an important source of moral reasons. If we were to agree on a natural law framework for ethics, there would remain notorious possibilities for disagreement about whether a particular action (for instance, any particular sexual practice) is contrary to nature.

I certainly do not mean to suggest that ethical theory is useless, or that one cannot reasonably believe and advocate any ethical theory. I have my own opinions in ethical theory (I oppose utilitarianism, for example, and favor a form of divine command metaethics). And thinking hard about ethical theory can be of great benefit to the moral life. It helps one to form one's own ethical conclusions in a more reasoned and consistent way. It can deepen one's understanding of ethical issues and increase one's sensitivity to the whole range of principles and reasons on which people might want to rely in deciding them. This can hardly fail to be helpful in trying to find common ground with others in ethical discussion; and it is my experience that ethical theorists are fairly often able to propose for an ethical problem a reasoned resolution that will command wide acceptance. The point that I want to emphasize in the present context is that while ethical theory is very useful for our common moral discourse, it is not itself an area in which general agreement is to be expected.

Ethical theory is also not an area in which general agreement is needed for such common morality as we possess. The main features of that morality are learned rather early in life, as I have pointed out, whereas most people reach adulthood with little awareness of systematic ethical theory, as teachers of ethics know. It follows that our common morality is possible without a generally accepted ethical theory, since it is possible with virtually no ethical theory at all. It does not immediately follow, of course, that common morality remains possible when ethical theory is developed and turns out to be a subject fraught with deep and apparently permanent disagreements that are known to many of the leaders of society. In fact, however, that is the situation in ethical theory, and the common morality I have described still exists.

The impact of ethical theory on common morality is limited because virtually everyone has more confidence in the central dictates of shared morality than in any ethical theory as such. An ethical theory of whose correctness I am persuaded may reasonably lead me to depart from the teachings of "common sense" in a few cases. But if an ethical theory were to imply that lying, stealing, and killing people are not generally wrong—so much the worse for the theory. Ethical theorists are generally at pains to establish that their theories do not have such consequences, and if possible they try to show that they can explain the "data" of common morality. Utilitarians, for example, try to show that lying generally has bad consequences (and hence less expected utility than truthfulness). The relation of ethical theory to common morality bears some resemblance to the relation of physical theory to ordinary beliefs about physical objects. The belief that a pint of mercury is heavier than a pint of water was prevalent long before quantum mechanics came on the scene, and it will still prevail a hundred years from now, even if quantum mechanics has by then been long superseded. Similarly, most of the precepts of common morality can be expected to survive the vagaries of ethical theory.

RELIGIOUS ETHICS AND COMMON MORALITY

In view of the controversial character of religious theses, does their introduction into ethical theory undermine common morality or diminish the chances for ethical agreement? No, we may reply on the basis of the foregoing argument, for there is no realistic chance of general agreement on even a secular ethical theory, and common morality does not depend on agreement in ethical theory. I believe this answer is substantially correct; but it needs some qualifications, or the observance of some distinctions.

First we must be clear that we cannot plausibly assert the moral innocence of *all* religious theses, nor should we want to. Some religious theses have had horribly immoral consequences. For examples we have only to think of the religious or quasi-religious teachings that have led people to think it right to commit what we should call murder, on a larger or a smaller scale. Some religious beliefs, on the other hand, such as those that inspired many of the leaders in British and American movements to abolish slavery in the eighteenth and nineteenth centuries, have surely been better than the common morality of their time and place, and have provided a prophetic basis for correcting it.[3] My claim then is not that religious theses cannot be opposed to common morality, but that the fact that a thesis is religious does not imply that its inclusion in an ethical theory is subversive of common morality.

While we may reasonably hope that a religious ethics will in general support the demands of common morality, we must also expect that it will include additional demands that are not part of common morality. This fact is perfectly compatible with common morality, provided that common morality is conceived as the large area of overlap of the diverse moralities of different people and groups of people. If common morality were conceived as the complete morality of every participant, then it would seem to be in competition with the various religions and their ethics, and from their point of view it would appear as something like a false religion. But I think it is more accurate to regard common morality as a set of agreements among people who typically also hold other, less widely shared ethical beliefs.

With regard to religious and other theories in the field generally, if not happily, called "metaethics," it is also important to distinguish between what we may call the semantics of morals, the metaphysics of morals, and the epistemology of morals. I take my examples from divine command theories, though they are certainly not the only theological theories in this area. A simple divine command theory in the *semantics* of morals might claim that in the discourse of theistic believers, 'wrong' simply *means* 'forbidden by God'. This theory would seem to imply that a common morality, or even common moral discourse, between theists and atheists is impossible, since the atheists can hardly mean the same thing by 'wrong'. Such a view might therefore tend to undermine common morality. But it seems more likely that the theory will be seen as refuted by the manifest actuality of common moral discourse between theists and atheists.

One might still try to maintain a theological theory in the semantics of morals, modifying it to try to explain how ethical comunication between believers and nonbelievers is possible. I once pursued this line, arguing that the meaning of 'wrong' is partly the same and partly different for theists and atheists.[4] Now, however, I am inclined to embrace a religiously neutral semantics of morals. I think that the meaning of 'wrong' is the same for theists and atheists, but that one can understand that meaning, and be a competent user of the word 'wrong', without knowing the nature of wrongness. All that the meaning of 'wrong' tells us about the nature of wrongness is that wrongness is the property (if there is one) that best fills a certain role.[5] Whether there is such a property and, if so, what it is, are questions not for the semantics but for the metaphysics of morals.

It is in the *metaphysics* of morals, then, that I would now maintain a divine command theory of the nature of wrongness. It says that the property of being contrary to the commands of a loving God is the property that best fills the role indicated by the meaning of 'wrong', and therefore it is the property of wrongness. This theory in the metaphysics of morals is not likely to conflict with any of the dictates of common morality. It purports instead to explain the nature of the obligation that is involved in those dictates. Our agreement on the general wrongness of lying, stealing, and killing need not be disturbed by disagreements in the metaphysics of morals about what wrongness consists in, any more than our agreement that two plus two equals four need be disturbed by disagreements in the metaphysics of mathematics about the nature of numbers.

It is important at this point that I am thinking of common morality only as a loosely recognizable set of overlapping agreements. If you think of it as a well-defined structure of thought, and particularly if you think of it as an autonomous system to be sharply distinguished from other systems of ethical thought, you may be more disturbed by the suggestion that a rationale for some of the concepts used in it can be given best in theological terms, or in other relatively controversial terms. That might seem to compromise the autonomy of the common morality.[6] I do not believe, however, in a common morality that is sufficiently theoretical to have an autonomy that might be compromised in this way.

It is in the *epistemology* of morals that the most serious questions arise about the compatibility of religious theories with common morality. Divine command metaethics, as I have conceived it thus far, is not a theory in the epistemology of morals, although it implies a need for such a theory. It is a conceptual truth that a command does not exist unless it has been in some way issued, promulgated, or communicated to those who are subject to it. Divine commands must therefore have been revealed if they are to ground moral obligations; so divine command metaethics requires, in effect, a theory of revelation, in the sense of divine self-disclosure. But many different theories of revelation would be compatible with divine command metaethics in the general form in which I have developed it.

For present purposes we may adopt a rough division of revelation into "general" and "special" forms. General revelation takes place through facts about life and the world that are generally accessible to human beings, and through tendencies of belief and feeling that are natural to human beings or at least widely and commonly present in people of different places, times, and cultures. The cross-cultural tendency of people to regard lying as generally wrong, for example, can be regarded as a general revelation of a divine prohibition. Special revelation, on the other hand, takes place through more particular phenomena that have a more or less precise location in history. It may be addressed only to one person or one community; if it is to be more widely disseminated, it will be known to most people only through a link of tradition or culture that connects them with the original source. Divine commands made known through sacred texts, authoritative traditions, or unique personal inspirations would be examples of special revelation. It is possible to believe, as the Deists did, in general revelation alone, or in special revelations that only republish general revelation. There have also been those who have believed that God's commands are promulgated exclusively through special revelation. On the whole, however, I think it has been more typical of the Jewish and Christian traditions to believe both in general revelation and in special revelation that adds something to the general revelation— whether or not the terminology of "revelation" is employed in this way.

A theory of *general revelation*, as such, creates no problems for common morality. The principles that have wide enough acceptance to be genuinely a part of common morality can plausibly be regarded (by divine command theorists) as commands of God generally revealed. If the consensus favoring some of these principles is relatively recent, the disagreement of earlier generations or cultures can be accommodated by the idea of "progressive revelation" that is a feature of some theories of general as well as special revelation. And the bases of ethical belief that are given theological significance by a theory of general revelation are for the most part those that are generally acknowledged in our common moral reasoning. This is not to say that no socially controversial ethical precept could be regarded as generally revealed. Unlimited exploitation of other living things for human benefit, for example, although regarded by many as morally appropriate in principle, might be viewed by others as contrary to the will of God revealed in nature; the latter might view the former as insensitive to a revelation available to all in the structure of nature and our capacity to respond to it.[7] There is no reason to expect a theory of general revelation to be more disruptive of shared moral discourse than any other theory in the epistemology of morals.

Theories of *special revelation*, particularly those that recognize no other way of knowing God's commands, may seem more disruptive. If one thinks that right and wrong are constituted by God's commands, and that those commands are promulgated exclusively in special revelation, how can one take seriously the reasons offered in ethical discussion by those who do not believe in that special revelation? Even some quite extreme theories of special revelation, however, leave more room than might at first appear for sharing moral discourse with nonbelievers. Consider a view according to which God's will is made known *only* in the Bible. Unless their exegesis is quite bizarre, those who hold this view will agree, for example, that killing, stealing, and lying are generally wrong, and that it is good to relieve human need. They will in fact accept most of the normative principles that serve as reasons in the shared discourse of common morality regarding concrete ethical issues. And, in applying these principles to particular cases not described in the Bible, they will face many of the same difficulties, and rely on most of the same patterns of reasoning, as anyone else. They will of course think that many of their fellow citizens do not accept the only ultimately valid ground of belief in the moral principles they share; but this disagreement about metaethical foundations need not be a barrier to the giving and accepting of reasons based on the principles. In some cases, to be sure, their views may keep them from carrying an ethical discussion very far. If their hermeneutics is rigidly authoritarian, there may be some socially controversial issues, perhaps in sexual morality, on which they will hold firmly to principles for which they are not prepared to give any reason except an appeal to religious authority, and against which they will not seriously entertain any argument at all.

Could a theological epistemology of morals come into more serious and systematic conflict with the requirements of common moral discourse? Consider what we may call an "exclusively charismatic" epistemology of morals, according to which ethical truths are made known only in personal inspiration, on a case-by-case basis. Since no general ethical principles are revealed according to this theory, those who hold it (if anyone does) will not accept general principles as reasons for any ethical conclusion, and they will thus be unable to participate in the exchange of reasons that constitutes common moral discourse. But is this a theory of anything that is still recognizable as a morality? Can we conceive of a moral education that does not involve the teaching of certain normative principles as generally binding? It is very doubtful whether we should count as a morality any form of life or thought that does not embrace at least a large proportion of the general principles that belong to common morality. And since acceptance of a large proportion of these principles— and of ordinary forms of reasoning—is all that is required for entry into common moral discourse, it is hard to see how anything that is truly an epistemology *of morals*, theological or nontheological, could conflict radically with the requirements of common moral discourse.

CONFLICT AND DEMOCRACY

Many political theorists, both liberal and communitarian (Rawls and MacIntyre, for example), seem to think that more agreement in ethical theory than I believe possible is required for a really good social order. While in various ways they wish not only to recognize but to preserve possibilities of disagreement, they think that we ought to hold in common a conception of justice that is sufficiently developed theoretically to give us at least some hope of arriving at reasoned agreement about moral issues in politics, so that we will not have to resolve them through conflict of brute political forces.[8] It is controversial whether religious ethical theories are likely to be incompatible with such a common theory of justice, but some certainly suspect that they are.[9]

In my opinion the best response to this suspicion is to argue that agreement on a theory of justice is not required for a society as good as we can reasonably hope to achieve. What is required, in addition to the rather untheoretical jumble of agreements I have already described as common morality, is agreement on some principles of *constitutional law*, which can also be described as agreement on the forms and limits of acceptable conflict. Obviously agreement shades into disagreement in constitutional law as well as in morals; we simply need widespread agreement on a sufficiently large and central area of the subject. My argument amounts to a rationale for constitutional democracy, a rationale broadly inspired by the thought of Reinhold Niebuhr, though I make no attempt to follow him in detail.

One of Niebuhr's greatest contributions is the extensive and many-sided development of his perception of the inevitability of conflict in even the best of social orders. He admired Marxism's realistic view of conflict in pre-Marxist societies, but he saw that this realism evaporated into utopianism when the Marxist gaze was turned to what would happen after the triumph of the proletariat—and that the utopian belief in the end of conflict served to justify institutionalization of a particularly repressive and coercive form of conflict. Authoritarianism has often been sentimental or naively optimistic about conflict, thinking that the solution to the problem of conflict within a society is the establishment of a good and wise authority—the philosopher-king or the dictatorship of the proletariat, for example. Because the good and wise authority would deserve the trust of everyone, there would be no need for anyone (or, at any rate, for any good person) to oppose the authority. Ideally, therefore, conflict should disappear. But no authority is really good and wise enough to deserve such trust; and the authority's sins and errors will be perceived more clearly, as Niebuhr argues, by those whose power is less.

In practice, therefore, authoritarianism leads only to worse forms of conflict. People are intimidated from disagreeing with the authority, or if they do become conscious of differing with the opinions or interests of the authority, they are forcibly prevented from giving effect to their views. Alternatively, they present a threat of change that is much more violent than it would be in a less authoritarian political order, and they provoke a more violent reaction.

A democratic political order, by contrast, is an open, reasonably fair and honest, minimally coercive system for the nonviolent working through of social conflicts. There is more than one way of trying to resolve a conflict without violence. One way is to try to reach agreement on the right solution through reasoning. That is the method that rationalistic assumptions in political theory should lead us to expect in a really good social order. Much of the recent literature on moral problems of a pluralistic society seems to proceed on the assumption that agreement achieved through rational persuasion is the main alternative to violence. This assumption may well be a main source of fears that the influence of religion on ethical beliefs bearing on our common life will be damaging, for even those most interested in reasoning about religious issues do not usually have great hopes for the achievement of agreement thereby.

There are other alternatives to violence, however. One that is important in democracy and most other political systems is compromise. It requires no extraordinary experience to recognize that it is commonly less important for the peace of a community that people believe that the result achieved was right in principle than that they feel that everyone got something and no party to the controversy was crushed. Compromise shares with majority vote the advantage that it does not require anyone to admit an error. Agreeing, as a result of rational persuasion, that the other party was right may often be the most virtuous way of ending a dispute, but it is rarely the easiest. We would be wise not to expect too much of it if we are devising ways for ordinary sinners to live together.

The method of nonviolent conflict resolution that is most characteristic of democracy is majority vote,[10] and it is not a form of rational persuasion. Plato was surely right in contending that a majority vote is not a plausible way of determining the most rational conclusion to a debate. If we want a concrete way of registering an agreement reached by reasoning, consensus (or perhaps a 90 percent vote) would seem to be the indicated procedure. Of course consensus is not a workable method of government, because too often it is impossible to obtain a consensus. That is in large part because reasoning about moral issues in politics too often fails to lead to agreement. It seems particularly unlikely to produce consensus on the most theoretical issues. We had better not need an agreed theory of justice, because we are not likely to get one.

In Niebuhrian perspective this too is a manifestation of our sin. One of the reasons (though not the only one, in my opinion) why we often cannot reach agreement about moral issues is that our excessive interest in our own welfare, and even more in our own power and our own reputation for rightness, distorts our judgment in profound but largely hidden ways. Rationality, as Niebuhr insisted, is an essential resource for combating this blindness, but the distortion is too subtle and too deeply rooted to be eradicated by reasoning; excessive confidence in the objectivity of our reasoning will only make us easier prey to self-deception.

Majority rule is a symbol whose reality is elusive. What it unquestionably does provide is the most obviously fair procedure for determining the result of a vote or election. And I believe that votes and elections are best seen as a form of ritual combat that provides not only for the decision of political issues but above all for a nonviolent transfer of power. Without some such institution, power will be transferred not at all or with violence. The knowledge of this fact will tempt those without power to violence and those with it to repression and preventive violence. That is in fact what happened in earlier, more authoritarian stages of our own political culture, in which opposition was often hardly distinguished from treason. The violent results can be seen in the history of England—a relatively stable society—during the centuries in which monarchs ruled as well as reigned. From the Norman conquest to the time when the transition to parliamentary government made possible the concept of "His (or Her) Majesty's *loyal* opposition," almost half the reigns came to a violent end, belying the power of the hereditary principle to avert conflict.

The concept of a loyal opposition is indeed an even more fundamental feature of our political tradition than majority rule. Such approach as we have made to an ideal of majority rule has come only through very strenuous efforts over more than a century to free the right to vote from restrictions and impediments related to economic status, gender, and race. But these efforts have taken place in the context of constitutions that already provided ways in which opposition to current policies and leadership could be expressed without disloyalty, and could possibly prevail. The existence of such a constitution does require widespread agreement in the society, not on a theory of justice, but on the constitution itself. More than agreement, it requires clear commitment to certain principles of constitutional law on the part of all or almost all of the groups and individuals possessing significant power in the society. They must trust each other to pursue their conflicts within the limits established by the constitution. Most important, they must trust each other to refrain from the most blatant forms of violence, fraud, and deception, and to yield power when they lose certain votes.

It has proved possible for adherents of very diverse religions and ethical theories—not to mention very diverse social and economic interests and ideals—to maintain a common commitment to a constitution of this sort, and to maintain it through gradual change and development of the constitution itself. How is this possible? Why are we willing to yield power nonviolently to political movements we vigorously oppose? No doubt the answers to these questions are very complex, and the emotional grip of political tradition on a nation plays an important part. But it is surely an important factor that the violence and other evils attendant on both anarchy and authoritarianism make it easy for adherents of quite different ethical theories to conclude that it is better for them, and for others, to take turns losing and gaining power in a constitutional regime than to try to cling to power by brute force, even though considerable goods may be lost when power is lost.

It is thus the desirability of a relatively nonviolent and uncoercive political order that provides, in my opinion, the strongest reason, with the widest appeal, for agreement on a more or less democratic constitution. This motive is fully as compelling from a communitarian as from an individualistic point of view. And it will generally support developments that would make the constitution more liberal and more democratic; the protection of civil liberties obviously makes the society less coercive, and the aim of providing nonviolent ways for social conflict to be carried on is served by the extension of political participation to all groups in the society.

This view involves a frank acceptance of conflict, which is to be kept within agreed limits but not eradicated. The fear of even relatively nonviolent conflict is one of the subtlest and most dangerous enemies of liberty and of justice, especially when the fear masquerades as a dream of untroubled social harmony. Conflict is inevitable—and, I would add, not altogether undesirable. The meeting of will with will, which almost always involves conflict at some level, is the very substance of personal relationships, which would not be fully personal without it. It is through conflict, or something like it, that we know the otherness of self and other. The oppositions that arise between our wills and our parents' wills are necessary for our differentiating ourselves from them. The fact that the world is in some ways contrary, and in some ways unresponsive, to our wills is what keeps us from regarding it all as an extension of ourselves. This fact takes on metaphysical dimensions in the philosophy of Berkeley, who defines the "reality" of sensible things partly in terms of the involuntariness of our sensations of them. Interpersonally, the independence of will from will, as manifested from time to time in conflict, is essential to the reality of relationship. We have learned to be suspicious of marriages in which the spouses claim they have no fights. In politics, likewise, conflict could hardly be eradicated without excluding from the political process the selfhood of most of the individuals, and the identity of many of the groups, in the society.

This is not to say that a democratic constitution should be viewed merely as rules for a contest of naked self-interest. It is important for the health of a democratic society that the participants, and especially the leaders, should often try sincerely to do what is fair and what is best for people in general. This of itself does not eliminate conflict, since our views of what is fair and best can conflict as much as our self-interest. But a democratic political order could hardly function if there were not a large measure of agreement in the society about what is right. One feature of democracy for which this is essential is the mutual respect and trust between opposing political leaders without which the self-restraint that limits the forms and methods of conflict would hardly be possible.

The moral agreement democracy needs, however, is not to be found in a common ethical theory or even in a common theory of justice, but in the unsystematic plurality of agreements that constitute common morality. These agreements make it possible to approximate consensus on some moral issues in politics. They do not enable us to settle all issues about justice by reasoning together; they leave some such issues to be settled by contests of will and political strength within the limits set by the constitution. But that is a large part of what democratic institutions are for.

Democratic institutions, of course, are no guarantee against injustice, and in fact they have often permitted it, as have all other forms of human government. All strong human interests (and that definitely includes religious interests) can tempt persons or groups to acts of injustice. But the argument that therefore it would be better for political society if religion, as a source of passionate interests, could be avoided altogether will rightly seem to religious persons no more persuasive than the observation, doubtless true in some sense, that we would cause a lot less trouble if we were all dead. Most of the meaning and value of human life depends on strong interests, and those who have serious religious interests will see them as particularly important for the meaning and value of life.

Can Religion Flourish in a Pluralistic Society?

Thus far I have argued that believers' use of religious theses in their ethical theories is not a threat to the sort of common morality that is possible in a pluralistic society and necessary for the health of the society. I want to conclude with a look in the opposite direction, at the question whether pluralism is a threat to the health of religious ethics, or indeed of religion itself. The American political and religious communities have tended to answer this question in the negative, pointing with some satisfaction to the fact that the percentage of participation in organized religion is much higher in America than in most of those industrialized countries in which a single religious tradition has been historically established. Disturbing questions are also raised, however, as to whether this complacency is warranted. Are religions in our pluralistic society like the seedlings Jesus described that spring up quickly in rocky soil but have no deep root (Mark 4:5–6)? Does the untidy array of moral principles and political institutions on which our society does agree constitute its real religion, the "civil religion" of America, as it is often called? Are the plurality of faiths that most of us officially profess left thereby with the form, but without the power, of religion (2 Timothy 3:5)? Are those faiths so marginalized by their exclusion from the realm of what is commonly accepted in society that it is difficult or impossible for most of their adherents to realize their relevance to the political, cultural, and professional aspects of their lives, or to make them the sort of organizing principle of an integrated life that religion is supposed to be?

There is undoubtedly much to be said for an affirmative answer to these questions; and they are reinforced by developments in the study of religion that call our attention to the intimate relations between religion and culture. We know that in preliterate societies religion is so inextricably interwoven with other aspects of the culture that even to speak of religion as a separate category is to import an alien conception from our life into the understanding of theirs. We are charmed, and sometimes inspired, by the way in which religion has permeated everyday life through total cultural acceptance in many times and places, even in more complex and developed traditions such as those of Christianity. We see that this permeation was made possible by the religious unanimity of a complete society, and that it is not possible, at least not in the same way, in a pluralistic society. As we think about these things we may be tempted to ask whether we can really, in the fullest sense, have a religion unless we all have the same religion.

Similar concerns arise as we think about what it is for an individual to acquire a religious faith. Attention to the role of story and ritual in religion, and to the integration of verbal and nonverbal behavior in a religious "form of life," support the view that becoming an adherent of a religion cannot be adequately described in terms of forming beliefs alone, that it is in many ways like learning a language or a complex social skill.[11] Such skills are in general best learned by total immersion in the language or practice, and better learned the earlier in life one begins. These thoughts could easily lead to the view that the ideal situation for religion is one in which people are steeped from earliest childhood in a single religious tradition that organizes their whole social experience—and that no other arrangment can be more than a second best for religion.

These views do not seem to me entirely wrong. I am personally addicted to a pluralistic society with rather fluid boundaries between the diverse traditions in it. I think such a society has great advantages in what it makes possible, both in the rich awareness of human potentialities and achievements and in the development of individual and ecclesiastical autonomy and identity. Even if we wanted to, most of us will not be able to avoid living in a society that is more or less of this type. Nonetheless I agree that something religiously (and culturally) valuable may be lost in these circumstances. We cannot reasonably hope to enjoy in a pluralistic society *all* the advantages of a religiously homogeneous society. "The best things in life" do not necessarily cost money, but they are rarely "free."

Some social arrangements seem to have few advantages, but all have disadvantages.

I will argue here simply that from the particular viewpoint of Christianity there is something questionable about excessive nostalgia for a religiously homogenous society. Christianity as we know it took shape in the religiously, culturally, and ethnically pluralistic society of the Roman Empire. The Christian religion would never have existed if its formation and transmission required a totally Christian social context. And today the Christian church is growing most rapidly in regions whose historic traditions are quite alien to those that have been most closely associated with Christianity.

Characteristic of the Christian tradition is a distinction, if not always a separation, between church and nation, and between church and state.[12] By contrast Judaism, as the dominant faith of an ethnic group and deeply connected with their sense of nationhood, does not make the former distinction so clearly; and Islam, as a faith that began in a militant campaign to reshape a whole society, is less inclined to distinguish between religious and political institutions. These distinctions in Christianity are undoubtedly connected with the fact that it began as the faith of a minority within both its original Jewish ethnic group and the larger society. The New Testament, however, is already deeply marked with both distinctions. The distinction between church and nation aroused divisive controversy at first, but the New Testament is unanimous in characterizing Christianity as a movement that does not aspire in any ordinary historical way to political power, and in tracing this stance to Jesus himself. Because these distinctions shape its self-conception from the outset, Christianity is intrinsically adapted to existence in a pluralistic environment.

Christian theology in the twentieth century has rightly emphasized the early church's resistance to religious syncretism. But it is clear from such a document as the Epistle to Diognetus that Christians of the first centuries also were conscious of sharing with most of their pagan neighbors enough ethical convictions to constitute what I would call a common morality—and that both their disagreements and their agreements with the rest of their society were important to the identity of typical Christians as such.

It is not hard to locate historically the point at which the creation of an all-embracingly (if not ideally!) Christian society and culture became a real possibility. This happened with the conversion of Constantine—a development that is widely deplored in the church today. I do not deplore it. It is hardly thinkable that the church that had survived the rigors of the persecution of Diocletian would have declined Constantine's offer of imperial favor. The Christianization of the empire, and of the European civilizations that succeeded it, had both advantages and disadvantages, from both Christian and more generally human perspectives, as does the pluralism of our own society. The Christian tradition has certainly been enriched by the realization of some of the possibilities of a comprehensively Christian society and culture. Some aspects of specifically religious and distinctively Christian life and thought were developed after Constantine in a way that may not have been possible, and at any rate did not happen, in the embattled minority church of the martyrs. My main thesis, however, about the Constantinian turning point in the history of Christianity is that one does not have to regard it as a fall from grace to see that the religiously homogeneous society to which it led cannot plausibly be regarded as the only setting in which Christianity can flourish.

Indeed the church had barely begun to be politically and culturally successful before there arose, in the monastic movement, the first of many attempts to recreate, within a church that had become too all-embracing, a functional equivalent of the distinction between the church and the world. The need felt by many Christians for such a distinction is connected with the importance of *conversion* in the Christian tradition—an importance that seems hard to reconcile with the idea that the best attainable sort of Christian life would have to begin with childhood education in a totally Christian social context. I have no wish to propound an extremely conversionist theology of the Christian life and no objection in principle to infant baptism, in part because I think that birth or adoption into a Christian family does often mark the single most decisive point in a person's initiation into Christianity. But with such examples as Paul and Augustine, how can we suppose that childhood immersion in a Christian culture is a uniquely privileged mode of entry into Christianity?

The case of Augustine seems specially worthy of attention. By virtue of his *Confessions* his is perhaps the paradigmatic spiritual journey for Western Christendom. It is clear that despite early exposure to Christianity, his way led through a sampling of the variety of religious alternatives offered by the still pluralistic Roman world, including a period of commitment to Manichaeism. And if we are inclined to think that the things he was most ashamed of in his personal relationships were not always those he ought to have been most ashamed of, we may also be less ready than he to deplore his spiritual wanderings. It was clear indeed to Augustine himself that much that he had gleaned from pagan culture, particularly from the Platonic tradition, remained a part of his eventual Christian awareness of God.[13] Conversion, as we find it in Augustine, is not merely a matter of turning out of one way into another. It is also, and perhaps much more, a matter of reintegrating one's life, and one's sense of the world, around a new center—or, as in Augustine's case, around a center that may not be entirely new.

Viewed in this way, conversion is a necessary feature of Christian existence even for people who have been Christians all their lives. All Christians have a recurrent need not only for repentance but also for reintegration of self and world around Christ. The idea that a Christian community can present its children with a preintegrated life is in my opinion inconsistent with the transcendent and eschatological dimensions of Christianity. Christianity is more than a practice or social skill that can be taught. It is also a framework for grappling with realities that no church can control—realities including not only (and most notably) God, but also sin, suffering, interpersonal and political conflict, and all the marvelous diversity of the human and natural world and of our own psychology. In these confrontations one's life and one's awareness are inevitably changed profoundly enough, from time to time, to require a new reintegration—religiously, a new step of conversion. And because the church is not the perfected Kingdom of God, the breaking, dissolution, or reshaping of some of our most religiously sanctioned patterns may be part of what is required to bring us nearer to the Kingdom. For such a pilgrimage, I think, a pluralistic society is not a less favorable environment than a religiously homogeneous society.

NOTES

For their help to me in revising this paper I am grateful to groups of students and faculty at Yale University, at California State University, Sacramento, and at UCLA, and particularly to Richard Fern and Gene Outka, and to Karen Orren for her written comments. Suggestions from the editors, and from a reader for the press, were also helpful.

1. John Rawls, *A Theory of Justice* (Cambridge, Mass.: Harvard University Press, 1971), p. 388.

2. Robert M. Adams, "Divine Commands and the Social Nature of Obligation," *Faith and Philosophy* 4 (1987): 262–75.

3. It is not my intention here to debate the question whether the influence of religion on human history has been more good than bad. I doubt whether that question has a clear answer, and it would certainly be beyond my competence to give it an answer.

4. Robert M. Adams, "A Modified Divine Command Theory of Ethical Wrongness," in Gene Outka and John P. Reeder, Jr., eds., *Religion and Morality* (Garden City, N.Y.: Doubleday Anchor, 1973), pp. 318–47; reprinted as chap. 7 of Robert M. Adams, *The Virtue of Faith and Other Essays in Philosophical Theology* (New York: Oxford University Press, 1987).

5. I have expounded this view much more fully in "Divine Command Metaethics Modified Again," *The Journal of Religious Ethics* 7 (1979): 66–79; reprinted as chap. 9 of my *Virtue of Faith*.

6. I wonder whether some concern such as this moves Jeffrey Stout in his criticism of Basil Mitchell's proposal of a theological "rationale" for "the traditional

conscience" (Mitchell, *Morality: Religious and Secular* [Oxford: Clarendon Press, 1980], p. 120). Stout seems to fear that Mitchell's approach might undermine common morality. He writes: "until theism proves able to gather a reasonably broad rational consensus around a specific conception of the good, an eventuality that now seems remote, we probably should not follow advice like Mitchell's. The risks of reviving religious conflict like that of early modern Europe are too great" (Jeffrey Stout, *Ethics after Babel* [Boston: Beacon Press, 1988], p. 222f.). This fear seems implausible. It may be debated whether our society still contains the seeds of really disastrous religious conflict. But in any event it is most unlikely that such a conflict would be either ignited or averted by theories about the foundations of ethics. Stout's fear is the more surprising because he seems largely to agree with me about the limits of the moral agreement to be expected in our society. He does suggest, however, as in the reference to "*rational* consensus" (my emphasis) in the above passage, common morality requires for its viability a certain rational coherence. Perhaps he thinks this rational coherence would be threatened if the common morality employs concepts that depend for their best rationale on beliefs not generally shared; I am tempted to read pp. 221–25 of *Ethics after Babel* as such a suggestion. I think the only kind of common morality for which we can realistically hope is too untheoretical either to need or to sustain the sort of rational coherence that would figure in such a worry.

7. This would be the view of James M. Gustafson in *Ethics from a Theocentric Perspective*, vol. 1 (Chicago: University of Chicago Press, 1981), except that he would substitute 'purpose' for 'will'. See also the interesting treatment of environmental issues as an area of ethics in which religious reasons are likely to make a difference in Kent Greenawalt, *Religious Convictions and Political Choice* (New York: Oxford University Press, 1988).

8. John Rawls's position on these topics is subtle, and perhaps still in development, or even change. I am not certain how far I am disagreeing with him. Clearly he does not accept, and wants very much to avoid, the conclusion that religious theories about the foundations of ethics as such are a threat to justice or democracy. In "Justice as Fairness: Political not Metaphysical," *Philosophy and Public Affairs* 14 (1985): 223–51, he has minimized his theoretical commitments in a way that he did not in *A Theory of Justice*. Already in *A Theory of Justice* he grants that "in a nearly just society . . . [t]here can, in fact, be considerable differences in citizens' conceptions of justice provided that these conceptions lead to similar political judgments" (p. 387; cf. p. 517). But the proviso incorporated in this statement is significant. It still seems to me that Rawls underemphasizes the combative aspects of a democratic polity and tends to overestimate the level of theoretical agreement in political ethics needed for an attainably just society.

9. See Richard Fern, "Religious Belief in a Rawlsian Society," *Journal of Religious Ethics* 15 (1987): 40–46.

10. I do not mean to imply that majority vote is the only method of nonviolent conflict resolution to be found in democracies. Democracies also require law courts, for example. I believe also that some constitutional restraints on majority rule, such as those provided by the Bill of Rights in the United States, are highly desirable in a democracy. And I think it is not a defect in a democratic constitution

if its actual workings give those who care most about a particular issue more influence in deciding it than is proportional to their numbers.

11. See George A. Lindbeck, *The Nature of Doctrine* (Philadelphia: Westminster Press, 1984). I do not mean to ascribe to Lindbeck any objection to a pluralistic society.

12. Here a distinction between nation and state is presupposed but not elucidated in a systematic way. An example may help to make clear what I have in mind. The Austro-Hungarian Empire was a multinational state whose jurisdiction for some years included part, but never all, of the Polish nation.

13. Aurelius Augustinus, *Confessions*, bk. 7, chaps. 9, 20.

Chapter 5

AUGUSTINIANISM AND COMMON MORALITY

Gene Outka

> Christians, whose reformers perished in the dungeon or at the
> stake as heretics, as apostates, as blasphemers—Christians,
> whose religion breathes charity, liberty and mercy in
> every line . . . that they, having gained the power of
> which they were the victims, should employ it
> in the self same way . . . in vindictive
> persecution . . . is most monstrous.
> *John Stuart Mill*

TWO APPEALS lie embedded in Mill's honorable judgment. One is
to sheer consistency. Those who protest persecution when they
are victims contradict themselves if they persecute others when
they acquire power. The other is to explicit convictions. Those who define
themselves by a religion enjoining charity, liberty, and mercy violate these
injunctions when they use their power to persecute others.

These appeals doubtless go well together in giving Mill's judgment the
force it has. Still, each appeal presented by itself asks us to weigh distinct
considerations. The first extols noncontradiction in our de facto judgments and practices. If we reach one verdict when we are on the receiving
end, we should not reach its opposite when we are on the giving end. The
appeal by no means requires that its hearers hold Christian beliefs. The
second appeal takes these beliefs as a point of departure and forbids a
certain practice in light of them. This appeal shows why Christians should
denounce vindictive persecution, whether they are on the receiving or the
giving end.

We can readily associate each appeal with one of two main senses of
"common morality" often distinguished and hardly less often opposed.
Each sense involves a quite different answer to the question, who are
"we" who share some identifiable morality?

The first answer is, "all of us who bear the human countenance." To
take the appeal to consistency as shared in this inclusive sense assumes
something common to human beings as such. It assumes we are so constituted that to demand "similar treatment for similar cases" can and should

get its hold on all of us. The demand never goes out of fashion or ceases to be relevant. It is generally negotiable. Its normative force need not require that we hold only certain substantive beliefs or belong only to certain traditions. We can appeal to non-Christians as well as to Christians. We can appeal to all human beings. We say this, even though we recognize of course that in fundamental respects distinctive substantive beliefs and cultural traditions define what we care about. But the demand in question applies to, and merits acknowledgment by, all human beings.

The second answer is, "all of us who share a determinate manner of life, one that is shaped and governed by particular narratives." What is common includes a set of judgments about what *we* do and do not do. The "we" refers to an identifiable tradition or particular community: we Jews, Christians, Muslims, Marxists, Navahos, Japanese, and so on. The "what we do and do not do" refers to judgments about right and wrong that we in the tradition or community accept. The judgments lie either within or beyond the moral pale for us. We in the community adhere to this manner of life; it is not peculiar to an individual. And we are prepared to commend values that promote the well-being of the community as a whole. Our morality has a thickness: in the array of beliefs that give it intelligibility, in the total commitment for which it calls, in the distinctive requirements we urge on one another and criticize one another for failing to meet.

Modern moral philosophers nuance and defend one or the other of these answers (goaded respectively by Kant and Hegel), and attempt on occasion to reconcile them. Though I do not isolate what I examine here from such discussion, I try to add to the stock of issues debated nowadays. The aims of my inquiry are three.

First, I want to engage a definite tradition and standpoint. I begin with a certain determinate content that the second account of common morality forces us to confront. And I work from a vantage point within the religious tradition Mill mentions. The vantage point is Augustinianism. It is only one in a tradition of enormous complexity. I choose it because its historical influence is vast and because it yields distinctive and I believe valuable insights for modern discussion. Augustine himself casts a massive shadow over the West. To reckon with him is no intramural exercise. He has correctly been called the father both of Roman Catholicism and of the Reformation. His approach to questions about common morality anticipates later answers on both sides. Moreover, Augustinianism serves to reopen a subject that modern debates largely ignore. This subject takes its bearing from Augustine's well-known moral pessimism, his vivid awareness of sin and evil. To insist, as he does, that our moral performance is frequently dismal is one way to introduce distinctive questions about the prospects for common morality.

Second, although I work from a particular vantage point within a determinate tradition, I select one that promotes more than a hermetically sealed morality, that is, one that does not consign in advance every generally negotiable moral appeal to the flames. Within its own web of belief, Augustinianism displays openness, for example, to an appeal to the Golden Rule that can and should get its hold on all of us. And it mixes appeals we tend to assign to one or the other of the accounts of common morality I introduced above. Some of the most interesting results come, I think, from studying instances of such interplay. The instances I examine include Augustine's treatment of the Golden Rule, lying, and motives that purport to sway human beings in all times and places.

Third, I want a vantage point that enlarges horizons and yet permits comparison with modern views. To scrutinize a tradition that antedates the Enlightenment and maintains even now some critical distance from key features of its legacy serves to enlarge horizons. At the same time, many detect traces of Augustinianism in more pessimistic strands of Western political thought, from Hobbes to Madison. I illustrate the critical distance and the comparative possibilities by attending briefly to one adherent to Augustinianism in the twentieth century, Reinhold Niebuhr. I also refer to certain views in more recent moral philosophy that the tradition I examine here confronts. The relevance of the early treatment of Augustine for contemporary debates emerges clearly, I hope, in the last section.

Augustine: Immutable Justice, Ineradicable Sin

Let us go at once to Augustine's texts. Those who defend a common morality shaped and governed by particular narratives ask inevitably which interactions with surrounding communities such morality demands, permits, and forbids. Augustine himself writes that the community of believers "while it sojourns on earth, calls citizens out of all nations, and gathers together a society of pilgrims of all languages, not scrupling about diversities in the manners, laws, and institutions whereby earthly peace is secured and maintained, but recognising that, however various these are, they all tend to one and the same end of earthly peace. It therefore is so far from rescinding and abolishing these diversities, that it even preserves and adapts them, so long only as no hindrance to the worship of the one supreme and true God is thus introduced."[1]

Augustine gives the society of pilgrims then wide leeway in accommodating the "diversity of peoples." Much properly depends on when and where they live. Usually they are wise to abide by the laws and customs of the particular city or nation in which they reside. Not only do conventional agreements vary among societies at a given time, but customs change within each society over time. Further still, our finitude restricts our ability to discern the rationale for the agreements and customs of societies that came before us. We do well to admit that people "whose days upon the earth are few, cannot by their own perception harmonize the causes of former ages and other nations, of which they have no experience, and compare them with those of which they do have experience."[2]

In their common life however, those within the church must not permit a readiness to accommodate to end in sheer permissiveness and relativism. Philosophers who become Christians, for example, may have to renounce certain beliefs, such as Manichaean ones. And if their clothing styles or manner of living prove "indecent or self-indulgent," they should abandon them. Moreover, though pilgrims may choose freely among the contemplative, active, and composite modes of life, they all must accept certain boundaries. "No man has a right to lead such a life of contemplation as to forget in his own ease the service due to his neighbor; nor has any man a right to be so immersed in active life as to neglect the contemplation of God."[3]

Finally, beyond the modes of life that those within the community enjoin on one another, there is the demand of justice that binds all those who seek to secure and maintain an earthly peace. Here too Augustine draws back from permissiveness and relativism. Although justice accommodates diversity (in the relevant sense), it does not, qua standard of normative appeals, undergo variation. "Some . . . thought that there was no such thing as absolute justice but that every people regarded its own way of life as just. For if justice, which ought to remain immutable, varies so much among different peoples, it is evident that justice does not exist. They have not understood, to cite only one instance, that 'what you do not wish to have done to yourself, do not do to another' cannot be varied on account of any diversity of peoples."[4]

Let us focus on Augustine's "one instance," the Golden Rule as part of that justice whose normative force he thinks does not vary. It is here that he comes closest to Mill's first appeal.

Justice and the Golden Rule

Augustine normally treats the Golden Rule as an appeal to interpersonal consistency and as a willingness to test one's actions toward others by reversing roles. Often he commends it in its negative form. "That which to thyself thou wouldest not have done, do not thou to another." He also cites a variant that suits Mill's judgment totally: "What thou art unwilling to suffer, be unwilling to do."[5]

The appeal gets its hold on us because it identifies two practical questions each of us can answer.

The first question is this: What, honestly, am *I* unwilling to suffer or have done to me? "For who hath taught thee that thou wouldest have no other man draw near thy wife? Who hath taught thee, that thou wouldest not have a theft committed upon thee? Who hath taught thee, that thou wouldest not suffer wrong, and whatever other thing either universally or particularly might be spoken of? For many things there are, of which severally if questioned men with loud voice would answer, that they would not suffer."[6]

Augustine thinks the question extends to promoting good as well as to avoiding harm. "Again, of doing kindnesses, not only of not hurting, but also of conferring and distributing, any hungry soul is questioned thus; 'thou sufferest hunger, another man hath bread, and there is abundance with him beyond sufficiency, he knoweth thee to want, he giveth not: it displeaseth thee when hungering, let it displease thee when full also, when of another's hungering thou shalt have known.'"[7] He cites too the case of a stranger who comes to one's country and wants shelter. When refused, the stranger protests that the country is "inhuman." Augustine comments: "He feeleth the injustice because he suffereth; thou perchance feelest not, but it is meet that thou imagine thyself also a stranger."[8]

We can ask a second question, a question to which his appeal to imagine oneself a stranger points. Should I not admit that the things I am unwilling to suffer I should not do to other persons because they are requisitely similar to me? "Come, if thou art not willing to suffer these things, art thou by any means the only man? Dost thou not live in the fellowship of mankind? He that together with thee hath been made, is thy fellow; and all men have been made after the image of God, unless with earthly coveting they efface that which He hath formed. That which therefore to thyself thou wilt not have to be done, do not thou to another."[9]

That each of us can answer both questions means for Augustine that the Golden Rule is commonly knowable, prior to or apart from the moral law the Decalogue specifies. "Of this truth [the Golden Rule], even before the Law was given, no one was suffered to be ignorant, in order that there might be some rule whereby might be judged even those to whom the Law had not been given."[10] The written law addresses those who seek to evade such judgment when they complain that they lack essential knowledge of what they should do and forbear. They refuse to recognize what is within them to know, and the written law sends them back, as it were, to themselves. "Because men, desiring those things which are without, even from themselves have become exiles, there hath been given also a written law; not because in hearts it had not been written, but because thou wast a deserter from thy heart, by Him that is every where thou art seized, and to thyself within art called back."[11]

These texts indicate how seriously Augustine takes Golden Rule appeals, and how widely relevant he finds them. Such appeals, as one instance of justice that transcends social and cultural diversity, can and should get their hold on all of us. It makes sense to refer to them when we consider the limits to impose on the pursuit of our own interests, limits we then impose on anyone in situations like ours. It makes sense as well to refer to them when we consider more demanding claims positively to further the interests of others as we would our own. To protest "double standards"—arbitrary exception making, inconsistent application of judgments when persons and situations are relevantly similar—wherever we encounter them, to attempt to put oneself in another's shoes, to try to identify imaginatively with his or her narrative: when we perform these and similar exercises, we follow the Golden Rule. Perhaps he would find it unsurprising that variants of the Golden Rule appear in all of the world's major religions.[12] Perhaps he would also welcome the labors of philosophers down to the present to trace more precisely the rule's affinities to a cluster of moral notions that include, alongside justice, universalizability, interpersonal consistency, reversibility, reciprocal acceptability, impartiality, equality, and the challenges, "How would you like it if someone did that to you?" and "What if everyone did that?"[13] In any event, the wide-ranging relevance he ascribes to the rule points, at a minimum, in the direction of the first account of common morality.

Lying

I turn now to Augustine's prohibition against lying, where beliefs falling under the second account of common morality exert more explicit control. Augustine devotes two treatises to this subject.[14] Once again his concern is not with fitting accommodations to social and cultural diversity. Rather he seeks normative judgments that bind invariantly as justice itself does. The subject of lying, he observes, arises unavoidably in everyday interactions, for both believers and nonbelievers. What then is a lie? Augustine sets aside jokes and false things we say that we believe to be true. We lie when we have one thing in our minds and express something else in words, or by other signs. Lying inheres in the desire to deceive, whether or not we succeed. "Whence also the heart of him who lies is said to be double; that is, there is a double thought: the one, of that thing which he either knows or thinks to be true and does not produce; the other, of that thing which he produces instead . . . , knowing or thinking it to be false."[15] "Now clearly, language, in its proper function, was developed not as a means whereby men could deceive one another, but as a medium through which a man could communicate his thought to others. Wherefore to use language in order to deceive, and not as it was designed to be used, is a sin."[16]

To describe and evaluate lying in this way does not settle a well-worn question: May or even should we tell lies for well-intentioned, charitable reasons? Augustine locates this question in the midst of eight cases of lying he assesses.

(1) The lies we utter on behalf of "the doctrine of religion," when we teach and learn it, are for him the worst lies of all. He finds them absolutely intolerable. Throughout his second treatise he attacks, for example, certain Catholics who pretend to be members of a heretical group (the Priscillianists) in order to discover the group's hiding places. (2) Within the exceptionless prohibition against unjust harm he includes telling a lie that hurts any other person. (3) Within the same prohibition he also rules out telling a lie that hurts another person but that helps someone else, "even if the hurt be slighter than would the hurt to him unless the lie were told."[17] (4) He next contends that lies which neither hurt nor help anyone else still hurt those who tell them. People who gratuitously lie he calls liars; they delight in lying, and they corrupt their own integrity. (5) He likewise thinks that lies which hurt no one else but are told to be pleasant in conversation hurt the tellers, because such folk care more about pleasing their listeners than about the truth. (6) The point where he admits that estimable disputes occur concerns those lies told by people who incontestably mean well, lies that hurt no one else and benefit someone else. He considers this hard instance. A man hides his money to prevent its loss by theft or violence, and another knows its location. Should the one who knows lie if a third party (perhaps with suspicious designs) asks where the money is? Augustine recalls his contention that lying hurts the teller. He also argues that the Decalogue's prohibition against bearing false witness retains normative force on its own, as the other prohibitions against stealing, killing, and adultery, severally do. Lying remains culpable in itself; it is never a neutral or indifferent matter. (7) Lies that hurt no one else and benefit someone else, told to a judge who interrogates, are also to be avoided. Suppose a just and innocent person, or perhaps a culprit, takes refuge with a Christian. The Christian is asked about the place of hiding, and knows that the person sought will be put to death. This instance Augustine treats as a conflict between lying and betrayal (for even with a culprit, "it belongs to Christian discipline neither to despair of any man's amendment, nor to bar the way of repentance against any"[18]). He thinks the Christian should say nothing at all, and take the consequences. (8) Lies that hurt no one else and do good, to the agent or someone else, in preserving a person from "corporal defilement," are finally to be avoided. Integrity of mind is greater than bodily hurt, and among evil things those we do are greater than those we suffer.[19]

Augustine does not offer these judgments complacently or smugly. In the first treatise he acknowleges how much arguments for less absolutist verdicts move him. And even though such arguments fail to persuade him in the end, he allows that of the eight cases of lying, "a man sins less when he tells a lie, in proportion as he emerges to the eighth: more, in proportion as he diverges to the first."[20] Lies do differ in seriousness; we can compare what is better with what is worse and chart progress of a kind. But what we pardon or tolerate we must not honor. We can sin less, yet not, not at all.

The Interplay Nuanced

Augustine combines confidence in the legitimacy of untechnical appeals to a kind of generalized self-interest with more specific verdicts that show the ongoing influence of particular beliefs. He declines to choose between consulting one's own preferences, suitably expanded, and other judgments about actions held to be wrong in themselves. Yet this combination makes room for different sorts of reciprocal influence, and it allows attention to distinctive considerations on each side. I want now to take note of additional nuances at work.

1. At points, particular beliefs influence Augustine's understanding of the Golden Rule itself. In one case he endeavors to forestall a standard objection to the rule, namely, that it authorizes the transfer of unworthy desires. He endorses the efforts of some interpreters to add "good things" to the actual wording of the rule in order to "prevent any one from wishing other men to provide him with unseemly, not to say shameful, gratifications—luxurious banquets for example—on the supposition that if he returned the like to them he would be fulfilling this precept."[21] These efforts he regards as unnecessary only when we exegete the Golden Rule in New Testament Greek to include "good" in its meaning. To respond to the standard objection in this way shows his readiness, at times at least, to link his understanding of the rule to substantive beliefs about what are goods and evils.

In another case he offers a specific verdict about lying that addresses a further standard objection to the Golden Rule. We noticed how he maintains that appeals to the Golden Rule not only serve to set limits on the pursuit of our own interests but involve positively promoting the interests of others as we would our own. According to this objection, the rule supplies incomplete guidance at best, or proves unacceptably indeterminate at worst, because the relation between the setting of limits and positive promotion remains uncertain. Issues about this relation extend all the way to modern debates in ethical theory and politics: Does the prohibition against doing harm always trump the injunction to promote good? Do we commend a limited morality of rights or a more demanding utilitarian beneficence? If we attempt to retain a place for each, do we opt nonetheless for a lexical ordering? Though Augustine's discussion of lying displays no notable commitment to the language of rights, it comes down on the side of setting limits.

So far, the combination takes this form. On the one hand, the Golden Rule generates broad normative appeals, ranging across a spectrum of actions. It offers a criterion for judging which actions are right and wrong. The appeals certainly support a case against lying in general. Augustine contends, for example, "that even a deceiver is unwilling to be deceived by somebody else."[22] On the other hand, the indeterminateness of the Golden Rule to which I alluded is overcome, in part, where particular judgments serve to order and give specificity to wider normative appeals. When Augustine claims that there can be no "just lie,"[23] his judgments about lying inform his account of justice as well as the reverse.

2. At other points the prohibition against lying encompasses considerations the Golden Rule does not address. Why the prohibition matters, how far those who violate it go wrong, cannot be ascertained solely by appeals to the rule. Augustine on lying develops a pattern of reasoning about religious and moral absolutes whose influence proves enormous. Two features distinguish this attempt to defend normative judgments that bind invariantly from the one conducted on behalf of justice and the Golden Rule, and they enter substantially into our own inquiry.

a. The religious and moral significance Augustine ascribes to lying includes but is not exhausted by his concern for what tends to the end of earthly peace. He believes that lying threatens not only earthly peace but also one's relation to God and personal integrity. And the goods so threatened are incommensurable with such peace.

That lying has generally pernicious effects on the life of communities he does not deny. Indeed, he contends that works evil in themselves— lying, thefts, adulteries, blasphemies—"subvert human affairs and all manners and laws."[24] His own concerns center on the havoc that lies wreak within the community of believers. Those who lie to ingratiate themselves, or to win some temporal advantage, or to gain converts, can never be entirely trusted to speak the truth. To accept or approve of lying at any time undermines "all discipline of faith."[25] Once we "break or but slightly diminish the authority of truth, . . . all things will remain doubtful: which unless they be believed true, cannot be held as certain."[26]

Identifying such effects is integral to his case against lying. But we must beware of reductive accounts of such effects. Lying corrupts the integrity of the teller, as we have seen, and this holds good even as it also undermines communal discipline or jeopardizes pursuit of earthly peace. We flatten out his cumulative case unless we include in our sense of "effects" the injury lying does to the self's own reflexive condition. And he connects the notion of personal integrity to other beliefs about how human beings are constituted and what witness the Bible gives. He distinguishes integrity of body from integrity of mind, as we have also seen. The latter we must prefer if a choice ensues, for its life is permanent. Above all, a congruency obtains between integrity of mind and a right relation to God. Lying never aids or abets *this* relation. "Each man departs from eternity just in so far as he departs from truth."[27] The prohibition against lying resides in God's will. Violations are eventually punished. Augustine examines the biblical passages that appear to condone certain lies. He argues that, on closer inspection, either the passages do not do so, or they honestly report transgressions that readers should not imitate. He refers often to a passage from the Psalms: "you make an end of liars" (5:6). Invoking God's will supplies the final religious rationale for saying that we should not do this evil that good may come.

b. Augustine's focus on the self, and his account of self-love, involve appeals that differ from those routinely made on behalf of the Golden Rule. In the case of the latter, we have noticed how he shares the assumption that the rule's sting is directed against injustice as arbitrary exception making. We ask what we are willing to have done to us, and we generalize our verdicts accordingly. In the case of lying, however, other assumptions come into play, assumptions that surface elsewhere in his work and contribute to his theory of action. I shall mention three.

First, to love oneself rightly requires taking account of the power one has in one's own case, a power that proves irreducibly distinctive for every agent. Augustine's well-known stress on a developed notion of the will supports this view of proper self-love. And the view is positively correlated with love for God. Such love includes cleaving to God, and cleaving includes personal activity, a power of assent that is essentially one's own, a total commitment of the will.[28]

Second, attending to this power also disposes Augustine to stress the self's decisive role in its own corruption. He ties the notion of "final" corruption to uncoerced consent. What this implies for ascriptions of culpability is caught when he writes: "whose the deed, his the sin."[29] Actions do not become one's own when they are committed upon one, without approval or consent. He can even write: "though murder is a greater sin than stealing, yet [for the agent] it is worse to steal than to suffer murder."[30]

Third, Augustine opposes the view that "no deed is so evil, but that in avoidance of a worse it ought to be done."[31] One should advise, admonish, condemn, and otherwise attempt to dissuade someone who intends to do wrong, but if all attempts fail, one is not then bound to prevent the wrong by a sin of one's own. Moreover, one should not be intimidated by those who say: "Thou has done it as well as he; for he had not done this, hadst thou done that."[32] He takes the case of a man who confesses that he intends to commit parricide. It is absurd to suppose that the one who hears the confession commits parricide also unless he slays the man (lacking all other means of prevention) before the deed can be carried out. In short, to give priority to what remains in one's own power leads to some strict drawing of lines. One should "prefer to avoid that which would be his own sin, rather than that which would be another's. Nor would the latter become his act . . . because he might avoid it if he would commit a sin of his own."[33]

3. That lying possesses such independent religious and moral significance leads many to confine Augustine's treatment of it altogether to those who belong to the community of believers. One is not surprised that modern writers such as Sissela Bok conclude that Augustine's "complete prohibition against lying, even in circumstances of threats to innocent lives, must, in order for it to be reasonable, rely on some belief that the lie is associated with a fate 'worse than death.'"[34] Yet what of those who lack this necessary belief? Is Augustine's case against lying irrelevant to them? Is it irrelevant in its entirety, or only at those points where theological beliefs hold explicit sway? And most important here, does Augustine himself confine his case to the community of believers? Is he content to speak esoterically?

I read him as follows. He addresses judgments about lying first to the particular community. The case as we have examined it falls largely under Mill's second appeal. Among Christians at least, Augustine thinks the judgments never go out of fashion or cease to be relevant. Yet he proceeds to move outward, in two stages.

First, he interprets inclusively the "neighbor" in the second love commandment: "Because a man, therefore a neighbor," and "Every man is a neighbor to every man."[35] Love of neighbor is finally universal in scope. Believers share distinctive loyalties and communal bonds, but no human being is to be excluded from the range of their active concern. So far, he justifies expansion outward for reasons internal to the Christian tradition—the injunction to love one's enemies. Yet such particularist justification still requires normative universal love to do material work. Believers are to transfer some of their commitments to wider communities. They are, for example, to apply the prohibition against lying not only to neighbors inside their own community but also to those outside of it. One of the most egregious tenets the Priscillianists put forward is that "with them who are not our neighbors in society of the truth, nor, so to say, our co-members, it is lawful and right to speak a lie."[36] Augustine cannot be content to speak esoterically if it authorizes practices of this kind.

Second, he sometimes moves even further outward, so that the case against lying includes occasional unsystematic overtures in the direction of the first account of common morality. It is hard always to distinguish judgments that apply to all human beings, for reasons internal to the tradition, and those that merit acknowledgment by all, by those outside as well as inside the particular community. I have mentioned examples of the latter: lying is a subject all of us care about in our ordinary interactions. It confounds the basic purposes that Augustine takes human language to have. Its destructive effects on earthly peace hardly exhaust the insidious harm it does, but they remain integral nonetheless to the case he offers.

Thus we look in vain for some exact line of demarcation between the two accounts of common morality. It is not as if the Golden Rule is sufficient unto itself for the comprehensive case against lying that Augustine puts before believers. But it is also not as if the harm lying does is reinterpreted so thoroughly that all its aspects are intelligible only to believers. Its destructive effects overall on social life are palpable. And to find typically among deceivers an unwillingness to be deceived is subject, again, to a general protest against injustice as arbitrary exception making. Each person can ask the two practical questions the rule enjoins, and thereby take counsel with the wants of his or her own "heart." Perhaps the rule serves to start a conversation to which believers and unbelievers enjoy access. It furnishes an other-regarding trigger of sorts. To be sure, Augustine incorporates the rule into the larger scheme whose center of gravity is God. The rule does not in itself supply knowledge of this scheme, but it is not at variance with the scheme.

The status of the case against lying seems then, in a final analysis, not wholly discontinuous from the one he accords to justice and the Golden Rule. First, *deception is characteristically unwelcome.* Although customs vary and circumstances alter, no change in epistemic contexts might one day result in a community whose members honor lying in the way communities known to him honor truth telling. The confidence that no such epistemic context will emerge stops short of an insistence that all must agree to the full range of his own strict verdicts. Augustine's awareness of legitimate controversy appears too strong for this. His sense of how the grain of religious and moral appeals goes warrants at least, however, a presumption against lying in every time and place. Second, *deception is rife de facto.* If this were not so, he would devote less effort to the casuistry of lying. We face a human world in which the presumption against lying collides interminably with violations. This state of affairs echoes one that the normative force of the Golden Rule makes evident more generally. Put simply, he finds the Golden Rule massively violated in fact. People flagrantly, often cruelly, reverse it. They treat others precisely as they do *not* want others to treat them. His excruciating awareness of this reversal fans his moral pessimism. Indeed, such awareness tends to shift the characteristic focus for moral reflection. He gives comparatively less time to conceptual elucidation of the rule and more time to instances where the attitudes and actions he thinks the rule obviously mandates are transgressed. In a word, failures in actual performance worry him conspicuously. The shift points to the ineradicable presence of sin and evil in human life.

Augustine's claim that deceivers do not want to be deceived, but that transparent reversals of the Golden Rule occur with depressing frequency, anticipates the far-reaching generalizations about human beings to which I finally turn.

Two Generalizations about Human Beings

The generalizations central to Augustinianism on which I concentrate are intimated in a single sentence: "For there is nothing so social by nature, so unsocial by its corruption, as this race."[37]

1. Each generalization epitomizes a set of religious, moral, and anthropological claims. That we are social by nature is interpreted in terms of the God-relation above all. Augustine (John Burnaby correctly remarks) would conclude Kant's famous statement as follows: "'Nothing can possibly be conceived, in the world, or even out of it, which can be called good without qualification, except'—union with God, *adhaerere Deo*."[38] Fellowship with God is the greatest of all goods, the only source of inexhaustible happiness, the herald of our final destiny. Augustine takes pains to emphasize that we are also social by nature in our relations with one another. As we have seen, the appeals to justice and the Golden Rule and the strictures against lying derive part of their intelligibility from the fact that they promote positive bonds between people. And Augustine offers other observations: for instance, human sociability, ratified and reinforced by the commandment to love our neighbors as ourselves, should extend to the whole human race; the family is the primary "natural bond of human society"; friendship is an important natural good.[39] To see social life as "natural" is to accept these several claims as constitutive of human flourishing.

That we are unsocial by corruption is likewise a religious claim. But moral and anthropological claims also play a role. "Corruption" is associated at Augustine's hands with sin, an irreducibly religious and theological notion. Some terrible flaw, mysterious, deeper than any social and political arrangement, seemingly intractable, curves us in on ourselves. We turn away from fellowship with God and thereby deny, in a primal act of self-destructiveness, the greatest of all goods, the source of our own complete happiness. This turning away is a matter of our own willing. Again, Augustine's worries center less on epistemology than on performance. "In Augustine's Christian outlook . . . , the perversity in the will can never be sufficiently explained by our lack of insight into the good; on the contrary, it makes us act below and against our insight, and prevents this from becoming fuller and purer."[40] This unwillingness to follow our insight has pernicious effects on our relations with others, leading often to failure and betrayal. The course of nations and empires, moreover, no less than personal relations, is infected by strife, lust for power, and greed.

2. Both generalizations are justified in a way that corresponds to their meaning. Data internal to the Christian tradition serve as Augustine's decisive sources. Such data include the Bible quintessentially (the longer he lived the more the Bible supplanted Plato and Plotinus in his thought and/or transformed the Christian Platonism), and the church fathers who preceded him. "Decisive" means that without them we lack awareness of our total situation. His depiction of fellowship with God is the central case in point. Yet even in *The City of God*, the work of his old age, we encounter references to matters "evident, not only from divine authority, but also from such reasons as can be adduced to unbelievers."[41] True, he often issues critical verdicts in light of theocentric convictions. For example, unbelievers refuse to countenance evidence against fanciful descriptions of how fully happy we can be through our own exertions because pride induces wishful thinking. He seeks to show that just as God is not "organic to the world," so the supreme good cannot be found in this life, and we cannot be happy by our own resources. But more than aggressive criticism is sometimes at work. Consider the first generalization. Augustine allows that philosophers are right to insist that the life of the wise must be social. He praises Cicero for advocating the cause of justice against injustice. And he thinks everyone, unbelievers and believers, desires peace, not only in our domestic circle but even when we wage war. He offers this sweeping assessment: "Whoever gives even moderate attention to human affairs and to our common nature, will recognise that if there is no man who does not wish to be joyful, neither is there anyone who does not wish to have peace."[42]

This justificatory pattern continues when we turn to the second generalization. A calamity bedevils all of the human history we know. The calamity's origins lie for Augustine in the biblical account of Adam's original sin, where pride injects disorder into our social world, so that fellowship with God and among human beings is perpetually jeopardized. The calamity's consequences show themselves on every level of human striving. Augustine relies on the Bible for his characterization of original sin and the universal significance he attributes to it. He appropriates the Pauline confession that he does not do the good he wants to do, but the evil he does not want is what he does. In a word, it is from the Bible and tradition, and the grace of God to which they attest, that he also knows about this calamity, and that it is of our own making.

Yet he finds this second generalization reinforced, unthematically but powerfully, in the personal lives and institutional arrangements he observes. After insisting that the life of the wise must be social, he turns at once to enumerate grievances of which human life is full. They extend to friendships and family relations. "On all hands we experience these slights, suspicions, quarrels, war, all of which are undoubted evils." Our foes can come from our own household. "If, then, home, the natural refuge from the ills of life, is itself not safe, what shall we say of the city, which, as it is larger, is so much the more filled with lawsuits civil and criminal, and is never free from the fear, if sometimes from the actual outbreak, of disturbing and bloody insurrections and civil wars?"[43]

3. We should avoid mistakes that, he thinks, overestimate and underestimate the influence of the second generalization on the first. We overestimate the devastating effects of sin and evil unless we adhere to two convictions. First, sin and evil remain parasitic on a good creation. The fall, to which Adam's transgression consigns us, never replaces creation. This means, as we consider the prospects for a common morality, that we retain "traces," "vestiges," "semblances," or "images" of our sense of justice. The appeal the Golden Rule encapsulates continues its normative hold on us. We can employ these traces to judge particular economic, legal, and political institutions.[44] Notions of "civilized society" are not all chimerical. They have genuine if fallible application. The traces prove crucial to us, although they are shadowy now. It follows that we can assess, and so praise and condemn, relative degrees of virtue and vice among persons and groups. Rulers differ in the wisdom they display and justice they enforce, and fortunate are the people whose ruler is wise and just. Augustine contrasts the early Roman rulers, for example, with those who came later. The former preferred honor and glory to avarice and luxury, and so achieved a laudable measure of "civic" virtue. He qualifies his praise, however, in a characteristic way. The early Romans sought applause for their valor rather than the approval of their own conscience, and so they lacked true virtue. He finds their achievements impressive but flawed.[45] Second, recall his insistence that no one is allowed to be ignorant of the truth of the Golden Rule, so that all may be judged. We cannot evade responsibility by claiming ignorance of specific moral laws. This condition too persists. At least we should not attempt to deny our status as morally capable creatures, as accountable persons.

We underestimate the devastating effects of sin and evil unless we see that the traces of justice and awareness of accountability we retain stand under permanent siege. We can document with melancholy ease palpable reversals of the Golden Rule, in every community. Thus it is unsurprising that the earthly peace we standardly affirm remains precarious in the best of times. Though we may praise and condemn relative degrees of virtue and vice among persons and groups, no achievement is wholly secure. Our personal triumphs encounter new temptations. Our ability actually to achieve equity and order in our social and political arrangements is uncertain and unstable, continually subject to further outbreaks of factionalism, opportunism, and oppression.

4. The generalizations provide a framework Augustine interprets determinately and regards as encompassing in scope. That is, the array of beliefs he employs to elucidate each generalization discloses his allegiance to a definite tradition. Yet he appears also to think that we cannot produce a community of human beings to whom these generalizations fail to apply: the "we cannot" possesses general force and ongoing relevance.

His reasons for the latter thought remain chiefly within the web of particular, expressly articulated convictions. He believes, for example, that Christianity has a message with objective significance; that the two great love commandments identify an order that is *there* and that we can plot the forms our idolatry takes; that the travails of Adam and Eve begin a narrative about the character of postfallen existence that obtains for all of us prior to the eschaton. And he draws on these beliefs to assess and criticize teachings and performances both inside and outside the tradition. Further complexities surface, however, when Augustine includes reasons that *he* insists can be adduced to nonbelievers. We have noted an uncertain amalgam of such reasons. That we are social creatures receives support from a variety of sources. He consults workaday experience; Cicero's praise of justice is welcome; all desire peace; some grievances are, in the eyes of all, undoubted evils. To be sure, the reasons adduced to all prove to confirm, reinforce, and elaborate what he finds in the data that distinguish the tradition. Still, he is prepared to introduce certain appeals that not only apply to all but merit acknowledgment by all. To acknowledge their force does not require conversion to Christianity. And Christians, though rightly more concerned about conversion, are also concerned with making these appeals succeed, even among those who never convert. Here is a point where Augustine has cumulative reasons to be generous rather than critical. He shows no fear that concern for the success of these appeals must threaten obedience to God or otherwise undermine particularist convictions.

ONE TWENTIETH-CENTURY AUGUSTINIAN: OUR CAPACITY FOR JUSTICE AND OUR INCLINATION TO INJUSTICE

Reinhold Niebuhr self-consciously perpetuates in this century certain features of the Augustinian legacy. Describing Augustine as "a more reliable guide than any known thinker,"[46] Niebuhr extends Augustine's two generalizations: "Man's capacity for justice makes democracy possible; but man's inclination to injustice makes democracy necessary."[47]

To an important extent, Niebuhr construes our capacity for justice along lines he finds in Augustine. Appeals to justice must accommodate, without becoming hostage to, the "diversity of peoples." Niebuhr thinks Augustine allows "for the endlessly unique social configurations which human beings, in their freedom over natural necessity, construct."[48] Yet Niebuhr reaffirms what he takes to be the traditional teaching Augustine upholds, namely, that appeals to justice bind not simply by virtue of special revelation or the authority of any particular society. The biblical text Niebuhr cites (which Augustine echoes when he refers to the written law that sends us back to ourselves) is Romans 2:14–15: "When Gentiles who do not possess the law carry out its precepts by the light of nature, then . . . they show that what the law requires is inscribed on their hearts, and to this their conscience gives supporting witness." Still, Niebuhr does not reiterate here all of what we found in Augustine. Though he insists that appeals to justice can and should get their hold on all of us, he gives little attention to the Golden Rule as such. And he often attaches primary importance to calculations of consequences. When he argues that certain actions, including lying, are generally prohibited, he relies more than Augustine on estimates of social effects. He offers no absolute priority rule on the relation between setting limits and positive promotion. Despite these differences, he continues to defend the overall relation between Augustine's two generalizations. He links our capacity for justice to a good creation on which sin and evil remain parasitic. This limits his moral pessimism. It is not so deep that he posits a single egoistic spring of motivation. Since we never efface completely our status as morally capable creatures, or do without the "organic and loving relations" that mark our interdependence,[49] Niebuhr rejects with Augustine the picture of human beings as essentially antisocial, aggressive, and competitive. Our status survives the recognition that violations of justice occur everywhere. But it cannot survive the attempt to redescribe and reevaluate the violations so that they themselves are made to look good.

Niebuhr's most valuable insights come when, under the second generalization, he considers our inclination to injustice. I shall concentrate on his version of the claim that we cannot produce a community of human beings to whom the second generalization as well as the first fails to apply, and that this "we cannot" possesses general force and ongoing relevance. I can thereby further indicate how Augustinianism's vivid awareness of sin and evil introduces distinctive questions about the prospects for a common morality.

Niebuhr continues to interpret our inclination to injustice within the larger framework of sin. And sin involves "a craving for undue exaltation" that extends in two directions. "The Bible defines sin in both religious and moral terms. The religious dimension of sin is man's rebellion against God, his effort to usurp the place of God. The moral and social dimension of sin is injustice. The ego which falsely makes itself the centre of existence in its pride and will-to-power inevitably subordinates other life to its will and thus does injustice to other life."[50] Not desire or creativity as such, but inordinancy, the overweening movement of pride, *superbia*, hubris, connects the two dimensions.

He contends that for all of its logical and moral difficulties, the doctrine of original sin takes the measure of such inordinancy more adequately than ancient and modern alternatives. He thinks Pascal is right: "Certainly nothing offends us more rudely than this doctrine, and yet without this mystery, the most incomprehensible of all, we are incomprehensible to ourselves."[51] As Niebuhr restates and defends the doctrine, he once again displays striking affinities with Augustine. To be sure, he subjects Augustine's account to immanent critique. Augustine errs in tracing the *origins* of the calamity that bedevils us. Niebuhr rejects with countless others "the myth of the fall of man as a historical fact. With that rejection we can dispose of all nonsense about a biologically inherited corruption of sin."[52] In this respect, he believes Kierkegaard's *The Concept of Anxiety* represents an important advance over the Augustinian legacy.[53] Sin is existentially inevitable but not ontologically necessary. The insecurity of life itself and anxiety about our finitude supply a context of intelligibility for sin, yet we never fully explain it by any antecedent. Like freedom, it presupposes itself.

To accept the advance, we need not, however, jettison an Augustinian awareness that the *consequences* of sin show themselves everywhere and on every level. Indeed, Niebuhr also contends that in the case of political rulers, Augustine fails to carry his own insights far enough. Augustine weighs the dangers of tyranny less realistically than the dangers of anarchy. The later Calvinists do better in attaining this crucial realism.[54]

How and how far Niebuhr promotes such Augustinian awareness, and what more specifically the promotion implies for common morality, I sketch under the following two headings.

Human Malleability and Its Limits

Through the doctrine of original sin, Niebuhr writes, "one may understand that no matter how wide the perspectives which the human mind may reach, how broad the loyalties which the human imagination may conceive, how universal the community which human statecraft may organize, or how pure the aspirations of the saintliest idealists may be, there is no level of human moral or social achievement in which there is not some corruption of inordinate self-love."[55] The "universality of an ego-centric corruption" exempts no area of our lives and no one of us. Niebuhr dwells on the sins of pride: pride of power, knowledge, virtue, and religion. The latter is a final battleground, never simply an un-ambiguous quest for God.

Again, the first generalization about human beings is not thereby dis-placed. We remain accountable creatures. No essentially egoistic picture of human beings will do. Morever, Niebuhr discriminates between rela-tive degrees of justice that various people and communities manage to realize; he insists that these degrees demonstrably matter; and he extols (and practiced) political activism. Yet he also sees our craving for undue exaltation as too constitutional to be removed altogether by any social and political realignment. Thus he claims that the universality of an ego-centric corruption both allows important moral discriminations and sets upper limits to our malleability. Each side repays examination.

He takes as indispensable the Pauline assertion that all have sinned and come short of the glory of God (Romans 3:22–3). However, it can imperil moral discriminations. He proceeds to distinguish between sin and guilt. Those "who are equally sinners in the sight of God need not be equally guilty of a specific act of wrong-doing in which they are involved."[56] He insists that "Biblical religion" stresses inequality of guilt as much as equality of sin. "Specially severe judgments fall upon the rich and the powerful, the mighty and the noble, the wise and the righteous. . . . The strictures of the prophets against the mighty . . . are consistently par-tial."[57] And "in the teachings of Jesus this prophetic note of moral dis-crimination is maintained without reservation."[58]

This note prompts Niebuhr to go beyond Augustine in emphasizing the moral relevance of socioeconomic conditions. "Biblical religion . . . is too realistic to obscure the fact that socio-economic conditions actually deter-mine to a large degree that some . . . are tempted to pride and injustice, while others are encouraged to humility."[59] No natural depravity distin-guishes capitalists from poor laborers, for example. The former commit more injustices against the latter than the latter commit against them by virtue of the greater power they possess. Power disposes egos to expand vertically and horizontally.[60]

Socioeconomic conditions can account for only so much, however. Our craving for undue exaltation is a tendency no specific social and po-litical arrangement either establishes or eradicates completely. Niebuhr builds on Augustine's insistence that "the seat of evil" lies finally in the self.[61] When we deny this, we pay a heavy price in sentimentality and miscalculation. Niebuhr locates versions of the denial in the optimism a liberal culture displays toward social engineering, psychiatric help, educational reform, and economic reorganization. "The conception of human nature which underlies" this culture, "is that of an essentially harmless individual."[62] Certainly we should endorse such efforts insofar as they harness and beguile the tendency, and achieve higher degrees of relative justice. But we go wrong to assume that our problems of justice reflect wholly unique local circumstances, or that we solve them once and for all by addressing immediate and specific causes.

To see the tendency in question as too constitutional to be removed altogether by any social and political realignment, he amplifies in two directions. First, we should resist utopian and perfectibilist schemes. The tendency sets upper limits to our malleability, and he contends that the historical outcome of utopian ventures backs up his claim. Second, we should resist ethical and political versions of Manichaeism. These versions attribute to specific differences among us the power to explain, exhaustively, the corruption that bedevils us, and they dichotomize people accordingly. Niebuhr criticizes especially the inflexible "class basis of virtue and vice" he associates with communist movements. But a sense of the universality of an egocentric corruption relativizes many other economic, political, cultural, sexual, and racial differences. It evokes controversial assessments. "Must we not say to the rich and secure classes of society that their vaunted devotion to the laws and structures of society which guarantee their privileges is tainted with self-interest; and must we not say to the poor that their dream of a propertyless society of perfect justice turns into a nightmare of new injustice because it is based only upon the recognition of the sin which the other commits and knows nothing of the sin which the poor man commits when he is no longer poor but has become a commissar?"[63] Niebuhr continues to insist that the seat of evil lies in an internal dialectic within the substantive self. To ignore this is to risk breathing new life into Manichaean divisions of humankind. We are tempted again to promote our cohesiveness and consolidate our virtue through ostracism and terror. To take the insistence seriously is to expect new outbreaks of injustice after we succeed in achieving redistributions of power that accord more nearly with our sense of justice. But to repeat, we should never deny that such successes count; we should seek tirelessly to realize them; we should reckon with the influence of particular socioeconomic conditions; we should start with an antiaristocratic bias. Still, the new holders of power will not prove immune to the tendency and so to the possible censure that Mill's first appeal authorizes. Niebuhr thinks there is something finally humane in the insistence. It leans against the self-righteousness that accompanies Manichaeanism of every stripe, and it thereby encourages humility and mutual forbearance that bind us together.

Democracy and Accountable Power

That new outbreaks of injustice will occur until the eschaton is a prediction for which communities do well to make general provision in their institutional arrangements. Whatever common morality we envisage should reckon with the pressures our constitutional tendency exerts. Niebuhr argues that such reckoning leads at the level of social and political morality to claims like these: "no one is good enough or wise enough to be completely entrusted with the destiny of his fellowmen"; "irresponsible and uncontrolled power is the greatest source of injustice."[64] We enhance prospects as we deliberately shape our institutions to take these claims into account. "Christianity knows that a healthy society must seek to achieve the greatest possible equilibrium of power, the greatest possible number of centers of power, the greatest possible social check upon the administration of power, and the greatest possible inner moral check on human ambition, as well as the most effective use of forms of power in which consent and coercion are compounded."[65]

Tyranny and anarchy are the perils we must continuously avoid, and democratic arrangements are the most perspicuous devices for doing so. Niebuhr writes extensively about democracy, not only about its strategies to promote the equilibrium and dispersal of power, but also about the refusal to spare any center of prestige from critical review, the role of universal suffrage as a form of control over the leaders of society, specific insights "biblical faith" furnishes for defying the authorities of this world and for extolling human dignity, the greater adequacy of Madison's Calvinistic approach to the problems of government than Jefferson's simple libertarianism, democracy as a false religion, and so on. He believes his defense of democracy elaborates key Augustinian themes.

That we retain our capacity for justice means that our practical reason serves as an organ of judgment upon egoistic self-interest. Not all moral appeals should be reduced to ideology. Democratic strategies assume our reason can, with sufficient regularity, thus acquit itself. This assumption supports in turn assigning a positive role to government. Niebuhr accepts that government has an ameliorative role associated with the Augustinian legacy, "the power to subdue recalcitrance"; but he also ascribes to government, if not a fully pedagogical role in the inculcation of virtue, at least the capacity to "guide, direct, deflect and rechannel conflicting and competing forces in a community in the interest of a higher order."[66]

That we are inclined to injustice means that our practical reason also serves egoistic self-interest. Niebuhr returns to various cases of special pleading in our social and political thought, such as the arguments members of dominant groups employ to secure their gains and defend their privileges. Democratic strategies therefore assume in addition the continuous presence of an "ideological taint," as when, with appalling resourcefulness, we misuse our reasoning powers to justify and otherwise promote ourselves and the groups of which we are a part. We do so inordinately, often unquestioningly, sometimes ruthlessly. Democratic strategies aspire nonviolently to circumscribe this predictable misuse.

THE TWO GENERALIZATIONS REEXAMINED

I distinguished initially two broad accounts of common morality and proceeded to concentrate on a version of the second. When we asked what the two generalizations within the tradition mean and how they are justified, we found them to be decisively elucidated and supported from data internal to it. Yet we also found them confirmed and reinforced by an amalgam of wider appeals.

Augustinianism falls between the extremes we tend to associate with the Enlightenment and sectarianism. On the one side, the beliefs internal to the tradition are not seen as incidental and finally dispensable aids to a tradition-independent morality. They influence variously but substantially the account of morality those in the tradition offer. We saw that Augustine justifies his strictures on lying in relation to various particular beliefs, such as the belief that it threatens one's relation to God and personal integrity as well as earthly peace. Those in the tradition resist radical insulation, where we suppose the appeals give us all that we need morally, and where we consign the convictions altogether to a realm of private, optional, individual ideals. To be acceptable, appeals that point in the direction of the first account of common morality must never make redundant the convictions that distinguish the tradition. On the other side, beliefs internal to the tradition authorize appeals to justice, for example, as similar treatment for similar cases. Again, it will not do to see these appeals as alternatives to the religious and moral life the tradition enjoins. Rather, they are themselves integral to such life. The first and not only the second part of Mill's judgment is continuously employed. Moreover, those in the tradition take these appeals to impinge on an audience whose membership is, some of the way, open-ended. The relevance of the appeals does not require us always to resort, explicitly and in every detail, to convictions that distinguish the tradition.

We need to mark more exactly the particular space Augustinianism occupies between these extremes. To do so, I focus once again on the two generalizations, this time as they confront a host of modern and postmodern developments. I close by examining aspects of this confrontation.

Justice and an Overall View

That we are social by nature is, by itself, the least contestable of claims. Believers and nonbelievers can assent to it. But of course it never arrives self-interpreted. We saw that within Augustinianism it means fellowship with God, above all. And we can hardly examine here the questions about this supremely important conviction. What we can viably consider is Augustine's defense of the Golden Rule as an instance of appeals to justice that derive part of their intelligibility from the positive bonds they help us to establish and foster, and the violations of these bonds that they help us to identify, criticize, and seek to reduce.

I referred earlier to the attention modern philosophers pay to the Golden Rule as part of a family of notions that includes interpersonal consistency or universalizability, the role-reversal test, and the generalization argument. To attribute to Augustine a position within recent debates about the Golden Rule carries undeniable hazards. Certainly his defense omits many instructive contemporary refinements. But we also learn when we examine Augustine's defense on its own terms and decline to invoke recent debates as the sole or definitive point of reference. Our findings here suggest the following.

1. The rule articulates something essential. It authorizes appeals that persons from various cultures can recognize as pertaining to themselves. Henry Sidgwick allows that the rule's effect is "to throw a definite *onus probandi* on the man who applies to another a treatment of which he would complain if applied to himself," and that the "practical importance" of this work is beyond dispute.[67] To avoid singling ourselves out arbitrarily, to press role-reversal questions: we saw how Augustine employs the rule to make these appeals in ordinary social relations. And the comparative simplicity of his case displays the normative work the rule characteristically does. For him the appeals appear too basic to warrant concluding that we are simply creatures of custom, if this means that the future is so up for grabs that members of a later community might very well dismiss them. More than anything else, I would argue, it is these appeals that not only apply to but merit acknowledgment by all.

We see a certain continuity between the way Augustine employs the rule and the efforts to eliminate arbitrary discrepancies that many take to be a hallmark of post-Enlightenment liberal morality. Here are two examples of these efforts. "The thought that a universality test can provide a criterion of moral acceptability may be expressed quite simply as the thought that if we are to act as morally worthy beings we should not single ourselves out for special consideration or treatment." "The person who adopts an egocentric policy . . . must also recognize in the 'other', a being who is like himself in the relevant respects and who, therefore, . . .

must be addressing to him an implicit question as to the justification for this non-equivalent mode of treatment just *as he himself would do if the positions were reversed.*"[68]

As it happens, the first statement by Onora O'Neill occurs as she discusses the ethics of Kant, and the second by Frederick Olafson comes as he discusses the ethics of Mill. The affinities to Augustine's case are manifest. How much should we make of this? I find three replies most cogent. First, various parties, some of whom plainly antedate liberal morality, subscribe to "the requirement that everyone shall be judged by the same standard . . . in the sense that everyone shall judge everyone else by the standard by which he judges himself."[69] The continuity shows that the requirement is not liberal morality's unique possession. Second, any such continuity never permits us, however, to reduce Augustine's case to an idiom totally commensurable with liberal morality, or to view it as merely anticipating Kant or Mill, or to measure its adequacy in terms of their distinctive theories. Third, we should nonetheless distinguish between an insistence that his case is not the same as theirs and a demand that the cases must always differ utterly. We have seen that Augustine wants these appeals to succeed. He is prepared to converse and to welcome support, without fearing that his particular beliefs must inevitably be eviscerated.

2. Yet the rule does not furnish complete guidance. It lacks the status of a modern supreme principle of morality as such, which allows for a strictly deductive order of epistemic dependence. We found in the texts we examined that Augustine combines confidence in the legitimacy of untechnical appeals to a kind of generalized self-interest with specific verdicts that show the ongoing relevance of particular beliefs. The combination means that neither the appeals nor the verdicts simply collapse into the other, and that we encounter various sorts of reciprocal influence.

On the one side, Augustine's confidence assumes that the content of what agents normally want for themselves is not completely variable and arbitrary. It proves implausible and evasive to suppose otherwise. Our initial review of Augustine's defense of the rule showed him to appeal to basic wants about which he thinks there is demonstrably widespread consensus. "We"—here the vast majority, inside and outside the Christian tradition—do not want someone to try to entice our spouse to commit adultery; we do not want our possessions stolen; we do not want to be deceived; we want bread when we are hungry; we want shelter and welcome in a strange location. (Compare the primary goods John Rawls defines as "things which it is supposed a rational man wants whatever else he wants."[70]) As Alan Gewirth observes, the traditional Golden Rule "is most plausible when it focuses on certain standard desires which all persons are normally thought to have for themselves, such as protection against physical violence and other harms."[71] This focus Augustine sustains.

On the other side, Augustine invokes particular beliefs about substantive goods and evils. He believes that certain actions, in themselves, are sins. We have seen him introduce such beliefs when he responds to a standard objection to the rule, that it authorizes the transfer of unworthy desires. Modern discussions usefully locate two difficulties the objection signals. (1) The rule fails to reckon sufficiently with the possibility that what an agent wants qua recipient may not accord with what the actual recipient wants. The rule proves too hospitable to agents who are quarrelers, seducers, fanatics, hard hearted, and so forth.[72] (2) The rule fails to reckon sufficiently with the possibility that the wants on which a particular agent and recipient agree turn out to be immoral or mutually destructive. The rule proves again too flexible, so that it permits sadomasochistic practices between consenting adults, "co-dependent" patterns involving substance addiction, and so on. The substantive beliefs help to guard against excessive hospitality, where the recipient is oppressed by the agent's contingent wants, and where the agent is oppressed by the recipient's contingent wants. The beliefs help likewise to guard against excessive flexibility by specifying certain moral and immoral actions and disallowing mutually destructive practices and patterns.

The move to combine assumptions about certain rational wants with more particular beliefs dissatisfies many modern defenders of a supreme moral principle. Gewirth, for one, thinks that once we invoke particular beliefs about what are goods and evils, we leave the rule no even semi-independent work to do. He takes Augustine expressly to task. For "in order to apply the Rule one would already have to know, independently of the Rule, what are the moral goods and evils"; and so "the Rule would no longer be a first moral principle determining what are moral goods and evils."[73] He thinks Augustine's account renders the rule superfluous.

Gewirth's criticism ignores the focus on certain standard desires that he himself points out makes the traditional Golden Rule most plausible, and which we saw that Augustine sustains. Moreover, Gewirth's own defense of the rule leads him to incorporate it into and finally equate it with a supreme principle in his own ethical theory, the principle of generic consistency. He takes a common morality that confines itself entirely to the first account as I sketched it to be rationally demonstrated by this very principle.[74] He distinguishes as he goes between a normatively moral sense and a morally neutral sense of "rational."[75] An assessment of Gewirth's distinction falls outside our concerns, but the texts we have examined draw us back from imposing it on Augustine. More generally, our findings show no comparably ambitious claim in Augustine. Though the rule articulates something essential, it lacks for him the status of a supreme moral principle. Again, we have seen that Augustine's appeals to the rule support a case against lying in general; but we have also seen that his particular judgments about lying reduce the indeterminacy of the appeals by ordering them and giving them specificity. And his judgments bring in other underived assumptions about lying and its importance.

We must draw a similar contrast with efforts to assimilate the rule to utilitarianism as the supreme moral principle. Peter Singer, for example, proceeds from the rule's acknowledged ubiquity. He judges it significant that the rule arises independently at different times and in different ethical and cultural traditions (found, for instance, in Rabbi Hillel, in Jesus, in the Mahabharata). "In each case," he writes, the rule is "seized on as something fundamental to ethical living, a foundation from which all else can be derived."[76] Augustine treats it as fundamental, but not as this all-sufficient foundation.

3. The meaning the rule has, and the weight it is accorded in any fuller account of justice and love, stand more subtly and pervasively in relation to other beliefs held. We see this in Augustine's case especially at two points. (a) His own appeals to a kind of "generalized self-interest" show a certain construal of that phrase. The exercises he believes the rule induces us to perform are comparatively expansive and generous. We are to impose limits, to be sure, on the pursuit of our own interests, limits we then impose on anyone in situations like ours. But we are also positively to promote the interests of others. We are not only to protest double standards wherever we find them, but we are also to show active sympathy and imaginative identification by trying to put ourselves in the other person's shoes. Alternatives to this understanding are familiar. He does not concentrate, for example, on self-interested bargains. He does not commend a calculated policy of tit for tat, equivalent repayments, or a demand for retribution. He stands generally in the line of interpretation that brings the rule into close proximity with the love command, a line to which Aquinas, Luther, and Jonathan Edwards subsequently belong.[77] (b) The element of arbitrariness on which Augustine finds it most plausible and honest to focus is the misfit between what agents want for themselves and the ways they treat and react to the treatment of others. It is profoundly disquieting that victimizers are so often incensed when victimized; adulterers rage against the infidelity of spouses; deceivers feel betrayed when deceived; unsparing critics are touchy about being criticized. His sensitivity to the misfit is linked finally to convictions about post-fallen existence, our endemic craving for undue exaltation. It is in this context that Augustine finds the rule indispensable in the performative exercises it enjoins us to undertake, and as it reminds us of unwelcome truths about ourselves.

In short, his account of the rule displays a pattern to which Alasdair MacIntyre is right to call attention: "Conceptions of justice and practical rationality generally and characteristically confront us as closely related aspects of some larger, more or less well-articulated, overall view of human life and its place in nature."[78]

Pessimism and Prospects

That we are unsocial by corruption is a more contestable claim. Certainly "corruption" is a term we should not toss around. I sought to indicate how Augustinians understand it within a framework of sin. Yet this understanding should itself be scrutinized with extreme care.

Such scrutiny is often specifically theological. We meet Karl Barth's insistence, for example, that the essence of sin is not the denial of sin but the denial of reconciliation.[79] And we encounter feminist criticism that Niebuhr attends too much to the sins of pride and neglects the sins of sloth.[80] My concern, however, has centered not on how to enrich or modify a substantive account of sin, but on how to view the framework itself. We have seen that Augustinians refuse any simple either/or. They decline to abstract their account of sin from data internal to the tradition and community. And they decline to speak only esoterically. They see biblical narratives as depicting a world that obtains not only for believers, and they see the depiction confirmed, reinforced, and elaborated in the personal lives and institutional arrangements they observe. This order of knowledge should never be reversed. Yet its circularity proves virtuous.

I want now to trace further implications of contending that the second generalization as well as the first discloses allegiance to a definite tradition and still possesses general force and ongoing relevance.

1. To refuse an either/or is not primarily an apologetic procedure. That is, what matters chiefly is fidelity to what the tradition confesses and not defense to a non-Christian audience. Neither Augustine nor Niebuhr as we have read them seeks to transcend their tradition and adopt the assumptions and commitments of those outside.[81] Their center of gravity remains the community where sin is recognized and interpreted.

Moreover, awareness of sin, in comparison with awareness of justice and the Golden Rule, may rely more explicitly on data internal to the tradition. One obvious reason is that sin is unpalatable to contemplate and painful to experience; we resist awareness in complex ways. Another reason is that sin is defined not only in moral and social terms, but in religious terms as well, and this points to irreducibly distinctive theological claims. Niebuhr affirms, for example, that only a "religion of revelation" permits us to recognize that "collective pride is the final form of sin." We possess in ourselves no vantage point for such recognition; it is "possible only within terms of a religion of revelation in the faith of which a voice of God is heard from beyond all human majesties and a divine power is revealed in comparison with which the 'nations are as a drop of a bucket' (Isaiah 40:15)."[82]

2. The recognition of sin is thought nevertheless to be a true recognition. To avoid systematic apologetics is not to forsake the distinctive compound of theological interpretation and a refusal to speak only esoterically. For Augustinians sin matters generally, however unpleasant it is, however mysterious it remains. We then have to do with more than a picture of human beings that happened to capture much of the Western world for centuries, yet lacks all claims to permanence.

We saw for example that Augustine finds the depiction of sin confirmed, unthematically but powerfully, in the history of nations and empires. And to claim as Niebuhr does that the universality of an egocentric corruption will persist until the eschaton and that it sets upper limits to our malleability means that historical developments, while they alter our possibilities and prospects at numberless points, will not allow us for long to drop the claim as an item we no longer find interesting. For the corruption continues to intrude too tenaciously to make credible attempts merely to change the subject.

Compare two sets of remarks that take the French Revolution as their point of departure. Richard Rorty praises "what political utopians since the French Revolution have sensed," namely, "that changing languages and other social practices may produce human beings of a sort that had never existed before." He wishes to extol a line of thought that "sets aside questions about both the will of God and the nature of man and dreams of creating a hitherto unknown form of society," "where we treat *everything*—our language, our conscience, our community—as a product of time and chance."[83] Niebuhr observes that "a French revolutionist of the eighteenth century can be as cruel in his religious fervour as the 'God-ordained' feudal system which he seeks to destroy."[84] He wishes to show that eliminating the hegemony of organized religion does not eliminate intolerance, which can be comparably self-righteous and vindictive, and that events in the twentieth century add their own tragic documentation. In this respect at least, changing social practices have not produced human beings of a sort that never existed before. When Rorty cites George Orwell's list of practices resumed in the twentieth century, he ironically provides what Niebuhr could view as confirmation of the claim in question: "imprisonment without trial, the use of war prisoners as slaves, public executions, torture to extract confessions, the use of hostages, and the deportation of whole populations."[85] It appears to Niebuhr that despite the undeniable variety and variability of human beings and their social worlds, and the relative degrees of justice whose instantiations we can in some measure reliably locate, the second as well as the first generalization possesses ongoing relevance.

3. To confront such relevance is important, but not all-important. We must remember the mistakes Augustine thinks we make when we overestimate the influence of the second generalization on the first. Sin remains parasitic on a good creation; unsocial behavior corrupts natural sociality. Pointing out how the second generalization is confirmed mandates a certain degree of moral pessimism although, as we have seen, it too is limited. And we must distinguish such pessimism from, in broad terms, moral cynicism and moral skepticism.

The differences from cynicism are shown in Niebuhr's case for the relevance of sin in vindicating democratic strategies. We saw how it is a datum with him that unchecked and unaccountable concentrations of power lead to injustice. Prospects for common morality go best when we strive to shape our institutional arrangements to forestall such concentrations. The claim about sin disposes us to regard the datum as sufficiently fixed to serve as a criterion by which we estimate which particular arrangements are fitting, and predict what occurs when arrangements are unfitting. To take the measure of the datum is not an end in itself. Rather, it is thought to serve the humane end of promoting just arrangements by keeping in view permanent threats we face. And the efforts expended in such promotion make sense only as we refuse to posit a single egoistic spring of motivation.

The differences from skepticism are less straightforward. Martha Nussbaum argues that belief in "original sin impedes the reasoning of each reasoner, as well as making it difficult for a reasoned view to win acceptance."[86] She is not alone in presuming that such belief encourages deference to authority and lessens the demand for good reasons. In this case, our findings warrant two replies.

First, we must indeed face soberly our resourcefulness in misusing our reasoning powers for self-promotion. Niebuhr's references to an "ideological taint" suggest that sin can not only disorder the will but disorient the mind. At times it seems that reason's operations are so infected, even moral arguments so corruptible, that sin has epistemic consequences, generating its own hermeneutics of suspicion. Yet the basic relation between the two generalizations sets a limit. Chronic suspiciousness must not subvert all confidence in our capacity for justice, all efforts to challenge arbitrary discrepancies and to press role reversal questions. Augustinians will thus show severely qualified sympathy with Bernard Williams when he commends Nietzsche as "the voice of a genuinely disturbing skepticism." Nietzsche "makes it hard to take at their face value many of the sorts of moral assurances which almost all the work, whether in ethical theory or otherwise, still takes for granted." Williams's special target is utilitarianism, which rejects "some of our conventional beliefs, but on the basis of an unquestioned belief in impartial benevolence which is itself traditional, and also a miracle of moral and theoretical over-confidence."[87] Augustinian pessimism alters this assessment. Utilitarianism errs not because it believes in benevolence (though Augustinians may interpret the content and status of benevolence differently), but because it underestimates the forces arrayed against benevolence.

Second, to ask what these forces are leads us back to Augustine's worries about performance. Sin is linked, we recall, to a perversity in the will that makes us act below and against our insight into the good. Challenged then are intellectualist assumptions that once we get our epistemology right, we will get our praxis right. We suffer from moral as well as intellectual weakness. And nothing is performatively secure. We enjoy no guarantees that whatever progress we achieve will be maintained. The worries about performance should not, I think, lead us to deny that moral and intellectual weakness often flow together. Consider for example the importance of *perceptions* in determining how to take the inclusiveness Augustine commends (recall too, "because a man, therefore a neighbor"). Which features we *recognize* as requisitely similar, which faces as fully human, prove historically to be far from self-evident. These perceptions may vary across epochs and cultures, and they may depend in part on particular traditions and narratives. Deliberately and emphatically to include various races and both genders alters and expands our actual perceptions. All failures to see may not reduce simply to bad faith.[88] Within Augustinianism, the accent falls nonetheless on the self-serving and self-justificatory aspects of such failures.

This tightly forged link to the will distinguishes then the account of what is wrong with us, and so too the kind of humility on which to focus. Though we cannot neatly divide performative from epistemic humility, we should attend especially to the former. One indication comes from Niebuhr's insistence that the Bible is distinctive "in its subordination of the problem of finiteness to the problem of sin."[89] Assuredly both problems remain ineradicable, inside and outside religious communities. Niebuhr claims that a suitably complex humility was absent too frequently from the Protestant and Roman Catholic communities in the religious wars that preceded the seventeenth and eighteenth centuries. The Enlightenment, though it too often lacked humility in both senses, can be seen as a judgment on the inability of the Christian communities of that period to conclude these wars on theological rather than secular grounds. Still, the hardest look, here as elsewhere, centers on failures in actual performance. Less attention is paid to perspectival finitism and the epistemic humility it yields. And doubts about our de facto virtue are not tantamount to humility about our knowledge of basic harms that the

Golden Rule helps us to recognize. To this extent, what receives emphasis are not the impediments sin may bring to the reasoning of each reasoner. The tradition we have examined thereby agrees with but furnishes a distinctive perspective on the sentiment Williams well expresses: "We need a politics that makes ethical sense of individual lives, and we need it to be psychologically and socially realistic."[90]

NOTES

For invaluable assessments of earlier drafts I am indebted to Susan Owen and John Reeder. For instructive discussions and suggestions I am grateful to Matthew Berke, Margaret Farley, Richard Fern, Rowan Greer, Alfred Grindon, George Hunsinger, Cathleen Kaveny, David Little, Ping-cheung Lo, Robert McKim, Gordon Marino, Cyril O'Regan, Russell Reno, Nancy Sherman, Kathryn Tanner, and Sondra Wheeler.

1. Augustine, *The City of God*, book 19, trans. Marcus Dods (New York: Modern Library, 1950), p. 696.

2. Augustine, *Confessions*, book 3, trans. Albert C. Outler (Philadelphia: Westminster Press, 1955), p. 70.

3. *City of God*, book 19, p. 698.

4. Augustine, *On Christian Doctrine*, trans. D. W. Robertson, Jr. (New York: Liberal Arts Press, 1958), p. 92.

5. Herbert A. Deane canvasses the various formulations of the Golden Rule Augustine employs in *The Political and Social Ideas of St. Augustine* (New York: Columbia University Press, 1963), pp. 85–86.

6. Augustine, *Expositions on the Book of Psalms*, psalm 57, ed. A. Cleveland Coxe (Grand Rapids, Mich.: Eerdmans, 1956), p. 230. My references will be to this volume, no. 8 in the first series of *The Nicene and Post-Nicene Fathers*, ed. Philip Schaff. Most of the texts I cite on the Golden Rule appear also in Augustine, *The Political Writings*, ed. Henry Palucci (Chicago: Gateway Editions, 1987), pp. 153–58.

7. *Expositions on the Book of Psalms*, p. 230.

8. Ibid.

9. Ibid.

10. Ibid., p. 229.

11. Ibid., p. 230.

12. See, for example, W. A. Spooner, "The Golden Rule," *Encyclopædia of Religion and Ethics*, ed. James Hastings (New York: Charles Scribner's Sons, 1914), 6:310–12.

13. See Henry Sidgwick, *The Methods of Ethics* (London: Macmillan, 1963), pp. 379–80; Marcus G. Singer, *Generalization in Ethics* (New York: Knopf, 1961), pp. 15–17; Singer, "The Golden Rule," *Philosophy* 38 (October, 1963): 293–314; Singer, "Golden Rule," in *The Encyclopedia of Philosophy*, ed. Paul Edwards (New York: Macmillan, 1967), 3:365–67; R. M. Hare, *Freedom and Reason* (New York: Oxford University Press, 1965), pp. 85–125, 155–85; Hare,

"Abortion and the Golden Rule," *Philosophy and Public Affairs* 4 (1975): 201–22; Hare, *Essays in Ethical Theory* (Oxford: Clarendon Press, 1989), pp. 144, 191–211, 248; J. L. Mackie, *Ethics: Inventing Right and Wrong* (Harmondsworth, Eng.: Penguin, 1977), pp. 83–102; Alan Gewirth, *Reason and Morality* (Chicago: University of Chicago Press, 1978), pp. 169–71; Gewirth, "The Golden Rule Rationalized," in *Human Rights: Essays on Justification and Applications* (Chicago: University of Chicago Press, 1982), pp. 128–42; Alan Donagan, *The Theory of Morality* (Chicago: University of Chicago Press, 1977), pp. 58–59; Alasdair MacIntyre, *Against the Self-Images of the Age* (Notre Dame, Ind.: University of Notre Dame Press, 1978), pp. 96–108; Nelson T. Potter and Mark Timmons, eds., *Morality and Universality: Essays on Ethical Universalizability* (Dordrecht: Reidel, 1985).

14. Augustine, *On Lying* and *To Consentius: Against Lying*, trans. H. Browne (Edinburgh: T & T Clark, 1988), vol. 3 in the first series of *Nicene and Post-Nicene Fathers*, ed. Philip Schaff, pp. 455–500.

15. *On Lying*, p. 458.

16. Augustine, *Enchiridion*, trans. Albert C. Outler (Philadelphia: Westminster Press, 1955), p. 353.

17. *On Lying*, p. 466.

18. Ibid., p. 469.

19. Ibid., p. 476.

20. Ibid., pp. 476–77.

21. *City of God*, book 14, p. 450.

22. *Enchiridion*, p. 348.

23. *To Consentius: Against Lying*, p. 495.

24. Ibid., p. 488.

25. *On Lying*, p. 463.

26. Ibid., p. 466.

27. Ibid., p. 463.

28. Charles Taylor, *Sources of the Self: The Making of the Modern Identity* (Cambridge: Cambridge University Press, 1989), p. 137.

29. *On Lying*, p. 465.

30. Ibid.

31. Ibid., p. 464.

32. Ibid., p. 465.

33. Ibid.

34. Sissela Bok, *Lying: Moral Choice in Public and Private Life* (New York: Vintage Books, 1979), p. 47.

35. Oliver O'Donovan, *The Problem of Self-Love in St. Augustine* (New Haven, Conn.: Yale University Press, 1980), p. 122.

36. *To Consentius: Against Lying*, p. 482.

37. *City of God*, book 12, p. 410. R. A. Markus translates *discordiosum* as "anti-social" in his *Saeculum: History and Society in the Theology of St. Augustine* (Cambridge: Cambridge University Press, 1989), p. 95.

38. John Burnaby, *Amor Dei: A Study of the Religion of St. Augustine* (London: Hodder & Stoughton, 1947), p. 183.

39. Deane, *Political and Social Ideas of St. Augustine*, pp. 78–79.

40. Taylor, *Sources of the Self*, p. 138. Peter Brown observes: "it was most unusual to insist, as Augustine does, that no man could ever sufficiently search his own heart, that the 'spreading, limitless room' was so complex, so mysterious, that no one could ever know his whole personality; and so, that no one could be certain that all of him would rally to standards, which the conscious mind alone had accepted." *Augustine of Hippo* (Berkeley and Los Angeles: University of California Press, 1975), p. 179.

41. *City of God*, book 19, p. 669.

42. Ibid., p. 687.

43. Ibid., p. 681.

44. Deane, *Political and Social Ideas of St. Augustine*, p. 97.

45. Ibid., p. 51.

46. Reinhold Niebuhr, *Christian Realism and Political Problems* (New York: Charles Scribner's Sons, 1953), p. 146. For a recent study that notes Niebuhr's debts to Augustine, and that attempts more generally to show how fruitful Augustine's political ethics prove to be for debates about liberalism and constitutional theory, see Graham Walker, *Moral Foundations of Constitutional Thought: Current Problems, Augustinian Prospects* (Princeton, N.J.: Princeton University Press, 1990). For another recent collection of essays on various aspects of Augustine's ethical thought, see William S. Babcock, ed., *The Ethics of St. Augustine*, JRE Studies in Religious Ethics 3 (Atlanta, Ga.: Scholars Press, 1991).

47. Reinhold Niebuhr, *The Children of Light and the Children of Darkness* (New York: Charles Scribner's Sons, 1972), p. xiii.

48. Niebuhr, *Christian Realism and Political Problems*, p. 132.

49. Reinhold Niebuhr, *The Nature and Destiny of Man* (New York: Charles Scribner's Sons, 1949), 1:275.

50. Ibid., 1:179.

51. Ibid., 1:243. Pascal continues: "there are two truths of faith of equal importance: one, that man in his native state, or state of grace, is raised above the whole of nature and made like God, participating in his divinity; the other, that in his state of corruption and sin he has fallen from this estate and become like the animals. These two propositions are both equally sound and certain." *Pascal's Pensées*, 247, trans. Martin Turnell (New York: Harper, 1962), pp. 170–71.

52. Niebuhr, *Christian Realism and Political Problems*, p. 199.

53. Søren Kierkegaard, *The Concept of Anxiety*, trans. Reidar Thomte (Princeton, N.J.: Princeton University Press, 1980). For an argument that Kierkegaard joins Kant and Schleiermacher in criticizing an Augustinian account of original sin, but that he advances the discussion by solving problems they fail to solve, see Philip L. Quinn, "Does Anxiety Explain Original Sin?" *Noûs* 24 (April 1990): 227–44.

54. Niebuhr, *Nature and Destiny of Man*, 1:221.

55. Niebuhr, *Children of Light and the Children of Darkness*, pp. 16–17.

56. Niebuhr, *Nature and Destiny of Man*, 1:222. Later Niebuhr expresses dissatisfaction with this distinction and confesses: "I remain baffled in my search for an adequate description of the situation which will allow for discriminate

judgments between good and evil on the one hand, and which will, on the other, preserve the Biblical affirmation that all . . . fall short before God's judgment." "Reply to Interpretation and Criticism," in *Reinhold Niebuhr: His Religious, Social, and Political Thought,* ed. Charles W. Kegley and Robert W. Bretall (New York: Macmillan, 1961), p. 437.

57. Niebuhr, *Nature and Destiny of Man,* 1:223.

58. Ibid., 1:224.

59. Ibid., 1:225.

60. Ibid., 1:226. Cornel West critically considers whether Niebuhr extends these claims about power adequately to relations between the United States and the third world in the post–World War II period. See *Prophetic Fragments* (Grand Rapids, Mich.: Eerdmans; Trenton, N.J.: Africa World Press, 1988), pp. 144–52.

61. Niebuhr, *Christian Realism and Political Problems,* p. 121.

62. Niebuhr, *Children of Light and the Children of Darkness,* p. 18.

63. Niebuhr, *Christian Realism and Political Problems,* pp. 113, 11.

64. Niebuhr, *Children of Light and the Children of Darkness,* p. xiv.

65. *Reinhold Niebuhr on Politics,* ed. Harry R. Davis and Robert C. Good (New York: Charles Scribner's Sons, 1960), p. 182.

66. Niebuhr, *Children of Light and the Children of Darkness,* p. 44.

67. Sidgwick, *Methods of Ethics,* p. 380.

68. Onora O'Neill, "Consistency in Action," in *Morality and Universality: Essays on Ethical Universalizability,* p. 172; Frederick A. Olafson, "A Passage in Mill's *Utilitarianism,*" *Morality and Universality,* p. 111.

69. MacIntyre, *Against the Self-Images of the Age,* p. 104.

70. John Rawls, *A Theory of Justice* (Cambridge, Mass.: Harvard University Press, 1971), p. 92.

71. Gewirth, "The Golden Rule Rationalized," p. 132.

72. Ibid., pp. 128–29.

73. Ibid., p. 134.

74. See also Jan Narveson, "The How and Why of Universalizability," *Morality and Universality,* p. 3.

75. Gewirth, "The Golden Rule Rationalized," p. 133.

76. Peter Singer, *The Expanding Circle: Ethics and Sociobiology* (New York: Farrar, Straus & Giroux, 1981), pp. 136–37.

77. Thomas Aquinas, *Summa Theologica,* 1–2. 99., a.1, ad 3; from *Summa Theologica of St. Thomas Aquinas,* trans. Fathers of the English Dominican Province (New York: Benziger, 1947), 1:1032; Martin Luther, "Secular Authority: To What Extent It Should Be Obeyed," in *Martin Luther: Selections from His Writings,* ed. John Dillenberger (Garden City, N.Y.: Doubleday Anchor, 1961), pp. 400–401. See also Ping-cheung Lo, *Love and Imitation in the New Testament and Recent Christian Ethics* (Ph.D. diss., Yale University, 1990), especially pp. 34–38, 119–22. The case of Edwards is doubly instructive. He brings his interpretation of the Golden Rule into proximity with the second love commandment in *Charity and Its Fruits,* e.g., sermon 7, "Charity Contrary to a Selfish Spirit." See *The Works of Jonathan Edwards: Ethical Writings,* ed. Paul Ramsey (New Haven, Conn.: Yale University Press, 1989), especially 8:264–66. Ramsey, in his introduction, maintains that the "swapping places" which the rule enjoins extends

even to enemies because Edwards employs finally a Christological understanding of what substituting ourselves in the stead of others involves (pp. 23–27). This understanding elevates the standards of bottom-line appeals. Yet in *The Nature of True Virtue*, Edwards takes Golden Rule arguments as fundamental to his depiction of conscience. And this depiction forms part of what I call here the first account of common morality. Conscience for Edwards is not an intuition but a relation, a relation of the self's consciousness to itself. "To do that to another which we should be angry with him for doing to us, and to hate a person for doing that to us which we should incline to and insist on doing to him, if we were exactly in the same case, is to disagree with ourselves, and contradict ourselves" (pp. 589–90). Edwards thinks that "unless men's consciences are greatly stupefied," Golden Rule appeals are "naturally and necessarily suggested," and "habitually, spontaneously, instantaneously, and as it were insensibly arise in the mind" (p. 591). Common morality is for Edwards a "splendid thing," though never tantamount to true virtue. The two converge and still diverge, because true virtue requires the first love commandment, "absolute benevolence to God." See Ramsey, pp. 53–59. A full-blown comparison of Augustine and Edwards on these matters would yield illuminating results.

78. Alasdair MacIntyre, *Whose Justice? Which Rationality?* (Notre Dame, Ind.: University of Notre Dame Press, 1988), p. 389.

79. Gene Outka, *Agape: An Ethical Analysis* (New Haven, Conn.: Yale University Press, 1972), p. 251.

80. See Susan Nelson Dunfee, "The Sin of Hiding: A Feminist Critique of Reinhold Niebuhr's Account of the Sin of Pride," *Soundings* 65, no. 3 (Fall 1982): 318–24. For general remarks on the relation between pride and sloth, see my "Universal Love and Impartiality," in *The Love Commandments: Essays in Christian Ethics and Moral Philosophy*, ed. Edmund Santurri and William Werpehowski (Washington, D.C.: Georgetown University Press, forthcoming).

81. For elaboration, see William C. Placher, *Unapologetic Theology: A Christian Voice in a Pluralistic Conversation* (Louisville, Ky.: Westminster/John Knox Press, 1989); William Werpehowski, "*Ad hoc* Apologetics," *Journal of Religion* 66 (1986): 282–301.

82. Niebuhr, *Nature and Destiny of Man*, 1:215.

83. Richard Rorty, *Contingency, Irony, and Solidarity* (Cambridge: Cambridge University Press, 1989), pp. 7, 3, 22.

84. Niebuhr, *Nature and Destiny of Man*, 1:203.

85. Rorty, *Contingency, Irony, and Solidarity*, p. 169.

86. Martha Nussbaum, "Recoiling from Reason," *New York Review of Books*, December 7, 1989, p. 41.

87. Bernard Williams, "The Need to be Skeptical," [London] *Times Literary Supplement*, February 16–22, 1990, p. 164.

88. Conversation with Sondra Wheeler led me to make this point about perception, though she is not responsible for the formulation I offer.

89. Niebuhr, *Nature and Destiny of Man*, 1:178.

90. Williams, "The Need to be Skeptical," p. 164.

Chapter 6

CLAIMS, RIGHTS, RESPONSIBILITIES

Annette C. Baier

> God having design'd Man as a sociable Creature, made him
> not only with an inclination, and under a necessity to have
> fellowship with those of his own kind; but furnished
> him also with Language, which was to be the great
> Instrument and common Tie of society.
> *John Locke*

Disputes about Rights

OUR SOCIABILITY is a matter not just of our tastes but of our capacities. Language does more than help us cater to our sociable tastes; it is itself a social capacity, one that we enjoy exercising. We may learn it largely by spontaneous imitation, but others teach us its finer points, and we both need and welcome initiation into the various roles that speech involves—teacher and learner, speaker and hearer, asker and answerer, proposer and seconder, challenger and defender, proclaimer and dissident. Speech, once we are fully initiated into it, introduces us to the plurality of social roles that are briefly taken on by speakers, and to the social expectations of who is to play which role when. We learn when it is our turn to speak, and what sort of speech we may make. In learning this we learn our rights as language users. Since our language is shared with those from whom we learn it, and since we all learn the full range of speech acts, there is a built-in tendency for us to see our rights as speakers not as special rights but as shared rights, and to see our due "turn" at speaking to be to an equal share of the speaking time. Our nature as speakers is such that we can be counted on to use speech to claim universal rights to speech and to contest some of these claims. Our nature, more generally, is such that we can be counted on both to voice claims to a variety of universal human rights and to contest such claims. We are a right-claiming and right-recognizing species, and these claims have a built-in potential for contested universalization.

Every group of human beings with any sort of social organization—that is to say, every group of human beings—recognizes something very like rights, as well as responsibilities, attaching to roles other than speech roles within that organization. The rights or protorights of parents with respect to their children, of chiefs over their warriors, and other such role-related rights, will be recognized. Because we are social animals, one of whose socially learned activities is talking, we have words naming these fairly long-lasting roles that some play and forms of words in which role players can claim their rights, and in which others can at times contest them—contest their content and their scope. We are a challenging and defensive species; there is always someone around to ask, "Why should the chief not merely get first pick of captives after a battle, but be able to take as many as he wishes as his slaves?" And there will usually be someone around to answer such a challenge, to tell us in detail about precedent, time-honored custom, stability, constitutional prerogatives. The very nature of speech virtually ensures this. Since we are talking animals, and since we do divide the social labor into a variety of roles with a variety of powers and responsibilities, roles that we do not all take turns in assuming, there will regularly be challenges to role-related rights, and defenses of them, and there will be claims to the extension of some rights and disputes about the legitimacy of such claims.

Other animal species with any analogue of status in human communities, such as apes, who recognize some degrees of dominance in a troop, often have habits that mitigate the inequality that dominance introduces. The social device of dominance itself avoids mutually disadvantageous infighting, but its cost is high for the dominated. The various rituals of deference, and of begging and response to begging, reduce this cost. We are a species who recognize status (and so avoid the war of all against all) and who have a strictly limited willingness both to beg and to give to those who beg. The conditions of the form of human justice that recognizes universal human rights include not only moderate scarcity, vulnerability to the resentment of one's fellows, and limited generosity, all of which Hume recognized, but also a limited willingness to beg, a considerable unwillingness to ask, even when—if we did ask the powerful for a handout—it would perhaps be given to us. What we regard as ours by right is what we are unwilling to beg for and willing only within limits to say "thank you" for. We are becoming less and less willing either to beg or to give to beggars. The increasing tendency to talk of universal rights and to extend their content correlates with this decreasing ability to beg or to respond generously to beggars.

Before this century, the famous proclamations of rights were not of universal human rights. Charters and bills of rights have typically been assertions or reassertions of the rights of some limited group. The Magna Carta asserted the traditional feudal rights of barons against the king, and, in Hume's words, "introduced no new distribution of the powers of the commonwealth, and no innovation in the political or public law of the kingdom." Although it introduced "some mixture of Democracy" into the constitution, it also "exalted still higher, the Aristocracy," who then became "disorderly and licentious tyrants," what Hume calls "a kind of Polish Aristocracy."[1] The American Bill of Rights spoke of, and meant, the rights of men, not of women, and it did not even refer to all men, since slaves were excluded. This is typical of proclamations of rights. They voice the grievances, or the remembered grievances, of some group against some present or past oppressor. They may demand an extension of what hitherto was a right of a more circumscribed group, but there will always be some who are affected by the right-holders' exercise of their rights who are implicitly or explicitly excluded from those on behalf of whom the rights are claimed. Slaves, nonlandowners, the poor, women, criminals, children, and nonhuman animals have all been out-groups in relation to those in-groups who have claimed their rights in famous proclamations and manifestos. There is a perceptible drive to generalization, a questioning of monopoly rights, but even famous clarion cries like "the poorest he that is in England has a life to live as has the richest he" spoke of he's, not she's, seeing the woman's life as merely an adjunct to the man's. A century passed after this famous protest by one of Cromwell's soldiers before women like Mary Wollstonecraft and Ann Lee doubled the pool of rights-claimants by including women in it, Ann Lee having the insight to see one root sustainer of their exclusion, a patriarchal religion.[2] She was a true radical; the four-personed God she worshipped was two-fourths female, so that equality of the sexes as well as of the races was assured in her Shaker version of Christianity.

Human nature displays its contradiction-engendering variety both in Ann Lee's bold universalizing moves and in her refusal to allow her faithful what had been a near-universal implicit right, the right to reproduce one's kind. She perhaps saw that the other root-sustainer of the oppression of women was marriage itself, that the inherent dynamics of sexual reproduction, along with the different asymmetric natural powers men and women possess in reproduction (men to force sexual intercourse, women to obscure or conceal the paternity of their children, which men want kept clear and revealed) regularly produce some variant of a trade in women, and their consequent oppression. Her radical remedy was a renunciation of the assumed general right to sexual intercourse and to parenthood, or perhaps more accurately, a granting of a monopoly of that right to those outside the Shaker community. The damned were to provide the blessed with continuers of their faith. This new mix of universal and special rights—a universal gender-blind, race-blind right to participate in the running of the community, as well as in all forms of skilled work (tradition has it that the circular saw was invented by a

Shaker woman), along with the denial of a general right to parenthood—lasted amazingly long. The mutual parasitism between the damned and the saved worked fairly well for a century and a half.

Fascinating and multiply instructive as this bit of cultural history is, I cite it only as an example of a dramatically great universalizing impetus, an extension of some rights accompanied by an equally dramatic reduction of other rights. We are a species who claim and contest rights, and the contest is especially great when claims are made about universal rights, but we are also a species who trade rights, who relinquish old ones for new ones, who circumscribe some in order to extend others. Rights by their very nature tend to clash. Ann Lee's husband's time-honored marital rights clashed with the radical rights that she claimed in founding a new ascetic woman-led religion, and he did not last long as one of its adherents. Rights must be constantly balanced and adjusted—that is part of their nature, and it expresses the nature of us their creators. We are not merely claimants and contestants, we are plea bargainers, compromisers, fixers, and adjusters. To construct any list of rights that we can take seriously and live without infringing, we must deny or severely limit other worthy candidate-rights, ones others will likely proclaim. Different groups make different trade-offs among the candidates for universal rights. We at present give more weight to the universal right to free expression than to what might well seem the equally vital universal right to an unmolested childhood. So we in effect allow child pornography, and we even tolerate, in the name of freedom, the market of so-called snuff movies, which the purchasers believe, sometimes correctly, to have involved the actual abuse, torture, and death of the involuntary child (and other) "actors." Our current trade-off of universal rights is as bizarre as was the Shakers', and it seems almost to vindicate their belief that sex is the devil.

Lists of universal rights, if they are both to cohere and to receive anything like general assent, must be so vague as to be virtually empty. Usually they combine vagueness with an implicit limitation of the class of rightholders and a consequent limitation of those whose assent is deemed of any consequence. Life, liberty, and the pursuit of happiness did not mean the life of Indians and slaves or the liberty of women, nor was it later interpreted to include the Mormons' original version of the pursuit of happiness. This declaration was a protest by white, male, largely land-owning (or at least land-possessing) colonists against a colonial power, just as the Magna Carta was a protest by Norman barons who in the previous century had, along with their royal leader, seized and conquered English soil. The barons protested against that leader's successor, who, they thought, was encroaching on what they had expected to be their own powers over the conquered land and people. In both cases a set of expropriating conquerors quarreled among themselves over the division of the fairly recent spoils. The rights asserted were those of an upper class against a previously acknowledged sovereign, with only token concern for the dispossessed, indigenous population and with no intention whatever to extend the claimed rights to those who traditionally had been relegated to an inferior status, namely slaves and women.

There was nothing radical in the demands of the American "revolutionaries." The extent of the British royal power to tax had been disputed ever since its inception as a substitute for feudal military service. The American "revolution" was cheered on by many European conservatives, who rightly saw that no radical social experiment was afoot, merely a redrawing of national boundaries so that a new sovereign state emerged. Unlike the French Revolution, which struck terror into the hearts of privileged classes everywhere, the American "revolution," for all its prohibition of titles, reaffirmed most of the traditional European class prejudices and its traditional sexist and racist attitudes. De Tocqueville noted (and shared) the racism, and he was impressed at the freedom of young unmarried white American women, compared with that of their French counterparts, and at the willing bondage of the married women. He saw only one class, a merchant class of those intent on gaining wealth. (That is to say, he saw only one class *among the white males.*) While he noted and discussed slavery and variations in wealth, he apparently did not see the differences between free men and slaves, landowners and the landless, capitalists and wage earners, and employers and employed, as class differences. Viewed from his aristocratic vantage point, the absence of the top two European classes, royalty and nobility, amounted to a total abolition of classes. But that was surely a distorted view. Like many claims about rights, the Americans' claims were mainly protective and conservative, not innovative or radical. The radical proclamations came later, from the reformers, abolitionists, feminists.

Claims to rights, even ones cast in universal or pseudo-universal form beginning with the phrase "all men . . . " or even "all persons . . . ,"[3] can be used to shore up and protect traditional privileges (by which I mean merely rights or powers that not all have, although most would like to have them), as well as to attempt to claim powers or liberties not yet possessed. Bills of rights can serve either a conservative or a radical reforming purpose. What they do depends on the relation of their content, and understood scope, to the political and social system within which the claims are made. In our social context, to affirm the universal adult right to a vote by secret ballot is simply to reaffirm our present system. To claim the right of every able-bodied citizen to meaningful work for a living wage would be revolutionary. But in Singapore or (until recently)

Russia it would be merely to reassert the going system. Different societies have made different trade-offs between the perennial candidates for universal rights. We have traded in so-called welfare rights for individual liberties. Although the preamble to the Declaration of Independence speaks of rights to life and to the pursuit of happiness, we interpret these in the most minimal and negative way. For instance, we do not see adult gun owners to have violated a child's right to life when the child is shot by another child who has taken his or her parents' legally possessed and loaded gun to enhance their game of cops and robbers. We see no such violation when a person dies of lung cancer after years of sitting in committees with pipe-smoking colleagues or years of living in a city where the profits of the local rich come from air-polluting steel mills. Nor do we see the right to the pursuit of happiness to have been infringed when Vietnam veterans have to "pursue their happiness" in hospitals and mental hospitals, or when the unemployed and homeless must pursue it in ventilator shafts in our cities in the winter. We have put the emphasis on the free pursuit, not on the chances, of achievement. It does not seem to worry most of us that, within our system of free enterprise and formal equality of opportunity, we have one of the worst male-female differentials in earnings among the so-called developed nations,[4] that starting salaries in the academic profession are on average two thousand dollars lower for women than for men, and that the difference increases in the higher ranks.

We seem effectively to fear bureaucratic intervention and its abuses far more than we fear inequity and unfair inequality. This may be the lasting heritage of that rebellion against a central authority which gave this nation birth. But, as I have emphasized, that was a rebellion of the haves, not of the have nots, and one traditional role of central authorities has been to act as defender of "the people," in the old sense of that term, that is to say the underprivileged, against the greed and domination of the barons, landowners, and capitalists. "We the people" need to organize ourselves and to have agents and spokesmen if we are effectively to assert our claims against those claiming to be superior to the people, be they kings, barons, oil barons, state governments, officials, exploiting profiteers, or profiteering arms dealers and warmongers.

The *Oxford English Dictionary* gives as very early senses of the English word "people" (a transliteration of the Latin *populus*) the terms "persons in relation to a superior," as in "peers and people" (*populus senatusque*); "the commonality, the mass of the community as distinguished from the nobility and ruling class"; and, interestingly, "those to whom one belongs, the members of one's tribe, family, association, church, etc." Other senses of the word include laypersons, as distinct from clergy, and a very old sense in which all animals are people, many of them, however, "feeble people." The family resemblance in all these senses is the exclusion of governors, superior authorities, and overlords, so that "government by the people" becomes a splendid paradox.

The language of rights can be used to defend and to challenge entrenched powers and privileges. It can be used by both sides in any contested issue, by kings and subjects, employers and employees, capitalists and the unemployed, monopolists and free marketeers. There is no agreement on what anyone's rights are. Even as far as positive legally recognized rights go, it takes lawyers' wrangling and court procedures to decide what a given person's rights are. And when we go beyond legal rights to moral rights and human rights, the wrangling spreads from lawyers to all of us. Is the language of rights then morally empty or neutral? Does it give no guidance to our lives as moral beings?

Rights as Rights of Disputants

It is often claimed that, although the concept of a right had a secure if limited place in Roman law, the conduct of our moral and social debate primarily by assertions of rights is a modern phenomenon. Since Grotius and Hobbes, the main question—outside the Kantian tradition, which keeps the Thomistic primacy of law-imposed obligations—has become not what responsibilities or duties we have but what rights we have. In the rights tradition duties are seen to be founded on others' rights to their performance. In the Thomistic and Kantian tradition, a recognized right is seen merely as a specific obligation that binds another to act in a specific way. Laws come to be seen to protect and recognize prior rights, not to found them. If there really is this difference between, say, Grotius and Aquinas, and between moral debate conducted in the language of basic rights and that conducted in the earlier language of basic laws and obligations (a language Kant preserves), it would be somewhat surprising if it made no substantive difference, if it were a merely verbal change. It will be more likely that some of the reasons for the supposed change would be changed perceptions of what needed emphasis, of where the burden of proof lay, of what procedures of discourse would best express the range of moral convictions that were competing to be heard, and that the language of rights did assist such shifting of agendas and of emphases. Changes in other social structures, such as the courts and legislatures, changes in the relation of church power to secular power, contests of jurisdiction between canon law and civil law, and disputes between Catholics and Protestants might be cited as explanatory causes for why the language of rights became the lingua franca of moral discussion. I am not a historian, nor an anthropologist, nor a lawyer, so I shall merely wave a deferential hand in the directions of such explanations. Instead I claim the philosopher's traditional arrogant prerogative of transcending the nitty gritty of historical change and of attempting to give a "transcendental deduction" of the very possibility of the development in question, or, to put it less pretentiously, to suggest that a special feature of the concept of a right encouraged such development.

My thesis, not a new one,[5] is that the language of rights is the language of language users who are becoming conscious of themselves as individuals. As a first step in that process they—we—are prone to fetishism. Especially when we have not only language but also the institution of private property, we like to make, out of our own powers, spiritual fetishes in the form of rights, things we have and can trade. The powers thus externalized and objectivized are our individual powers to participate in and benefit from cooperative practices, most fundamentally in speech. If there is any basic right, it is the right to be heard, to participate in normative discussion. One's first claim is the claim to a voice, to one's turn to speak and be listened to. It is to speech itself, and the cooperation needed to learn and use a language, to which we can turn to see where rights or protorights can always be found, and to see why disagreement about rights is normal, once we can not only exercise or attempt to exercise our speakers' rights but also speak about rights, to turn our discussion on to them. For disagreement is one of the distinctive cultural products that speech makes possible. Without speech, there can be (and usually is) conflict, but not disagreement. My grandmother used to say to her quarreling grandchildren: "Little birds in their nest agree." She was a wise woman, but there is reason to disagree doubly with this bit of folk wisdom. Some little birds peck weaker little birds to death in the nest, and even those that peaceably coexist cannot, properly speaking, be said to agree. For what is there for them to agree about? Lacking language, and so lacking any way of making proposals, they cannot second or agree with any, nor dispute and disagree. Language gives us the "moral equivalent" both of conflict and of harmony, of fighting and of accord and mutual aid. And, just as important, it diversifies the forms both of accord and of discord.

Locke, whose views I invoked at the outset, was well aware of the vital importance of speech not just as an expression of but as a foundation for our moral natures. In his splendid writings on education, he discusses first the needs of the prespeech child: needs for fresh air, loose clothing and freedom of movement, regular cold foot baths, a plain diet replete with fresh fruit, as much sleep as is wanted, a variety of homemade and eventually self-made playthings, patient, confident, but unrelenting toilet training, and gradual training in hardiness, self-denial, and respect for parental authority (the latter training is to be accomplished without reliance on either the rod, except as a "last resort," or counter-productive bribing by "sugar plums."[6] The punishment of clear disapproval and its consequent shame and the reward of esteem and its consequent pride are to suffice). He then considers the child's initiation into the arts of speech as well as into other civilizing arts like dancing (which he says gives both "graceful motion" and "becoming confidence" to children).[7] In his long discussion of the arts of language, Locke downplays the importance of teaching rules of language. As in ethics, in language one learns by "practice more than rules."[8] Most of this long discussion is devoted to what we would call the pragmatics, not the semantics or syntax, of language, to initiation into speech act competence rather than vocabulary, grammar, or composition, which he thinks children will soon pick up for themselves. His concern is that children learn to play an appropriate role in the conversation going on around them, that they learn not to interrupt, continually to contradict what others are saying, or to engage in "loud wrangling," but also that they learn to take some active part in the conversation.[9] Locke thinks the last lesson is easy to teach, unless the child's spirit is already broken by misuse of the rod. He discusses at length the need for young people to learn to avoid such rudeness of speech as disrespectful interruption, "self conceited" contradiction, and "positive asserting and the Magisterial Air."[10] He finds these faults not only in beginners in the arts of conversation but also among "grown People, even of Rank amongst us." "The Indians," he continues, "whom we call Barbarous, observe much more Decency and Civility in their Discourses and Conversation, giving one another a fair silent hearing, till they have quite done, and then answering them calmly, without Noise or Passion."[11] I think therefore that I can claim the support of John Locke for the thesis that the right to a fair hearing, to one's turn to speak, is a fundamental right.

I turn also to Hobbes, one of the other thinkers usually credited with bringing the language of rights from the moral background into the moral foreground, for an account of what the power of speech introduces into human life. Speech, Hobbes says, is "the most noble and profitable invention of any other . . . without which there would have been neither Commonwealth, nor Society, nor Contract, nor Peace, no more than among Lyons, Bears and Wolves."[12] The uses of speech, according to Hobbes, are, first, to use words as "Markes or Notes" to register noticed important facts or to register long trains of thought, as a possibly private aide-mémoire. The second use, more interesting for my purposes, is as "Signes," to "signify one to another what they conceive or think of each matter, and also what they desire, feare, or have any other passion for." Language enables us not only to "register" our findings concerning causes and effects, but to "counsell and teach one another" and to "make known our wills and purposes, that we may have the mutuall help of one another."[13] He proceeds to show how a vitally important product of speech is the capacity to count and number things, and to reckon or reason. Here reasoning is essentially reckoning in interpersonally settled "signs," and the reckoning process is more than that desire-regulated train of thoughts or imaginings which can spy out the likely future for us or reconstruct some past train of events—a capacity Hobbes thinks is "common to Man and Beast."[14] Reason, and "right reason," require a common currency of words, and a shared standard of correct reckoning. "For no one man's Reason, nor the Reason of any one number of them, makes the certaintie . . . the parties must by their own accord set up for right Reason the Reason of some Arbitrator or Judge, to whose sentence they will both stand."[15] Hobbesian reason is a human cultural invention cotemporal with the invention of authority, and several of the uses of speech that he had earlier analyzed must go into the creation of reason and the setting up of a court, or arbitration panel, of right reason. He had already claimed that "True and False are attributes of Speech, not of Things. And where Speech is not, there is neither Truth nor Falsehood."[16] Reason is a way of reckoning that preserves truth, and right reason settles disputes about truth, and about reckoning. The disputes themselves are made possible by speech, by "affirmation" and the use of "negative names" in refusal and denial. Hobbes carefully lists the moods into which speech users will need to go from time to time, "interrogative, optative, infinitive," as well as the soon for him to be crucial imperative mood. But along with "Commandement" he lists "Narration, Syllogisme, Sermon, Oration" among the sorts of speeches we will produce, forms of speech to praise or magnify, and that form of speech which "is by the Greeks called Μακαρισμός, for which we have no name in our tongue."[17]

Hobbes does not support my claim that speech gives us the moral equivalent both of accord and mutual help and of conflict and mutual attack. He joins Locke in deploring the use of speech in raillery and ridicule, and he says it is an "abuse" of speech to use words "to grieve one another: for seeing nature has armed living creatures, some with teeth and horns, and some with hands, to grieve an enemy, it is but an abuse of Speech to grieve him with the tongue."[18] Hobbes takes these "abuses" of speech in insults and dishonorings (including such withdrawals from the conversation as falling asleep while another is speaking) to be among the important causes of that "war of all against all" for which he invokes the verbal antidote of right reason, and of contract. Insofar as such verbal "abuses" flourish in "the natural condition of mankind," they are taken by Hobbes to be just as "natural" to speech users as the more constructive "uses" of speech that get us out of that condition. My claim that where there is speech there will be disagreement, wrangling, and dispute—that where there is diction there will be contradiction—can then be made

Hobbesian, as long as it is true that where there is use, there will also be abuse. In any case, verbal disagreement and contradiction need not degenerate into dispute, let alone into grievous insult. Both disagreement and the need to find ways of settling those that degenerate into dispute and impassioned conflict can be taken to be consequences of the "most noble and profitable invention of speech."

This noble invention makes everyone who becomes a language user a claimant—one who advances verbal claims, listens to how they are received, defends them, and sometimes corrects, amends, or retracts them. As participants in conversation we acquire the protorights to have our say, to affirm or deny what others say, to be heard. Sometimes those rights are anything but equal. Children in bygone epochs were restricted to a minimal conversational role in the presence of their elders, and Plato gives Socrates' coconversationalists the role only of providing Socrates with material for correction and of yea-saying his moves. Most human conversations, especially about the norms to govern human communities, have been elitist instead of democratic conversations, in that the majority of the people play the role merely of reciting "amen" to whatever their "betters" had concluded. Still, the fact of speech itself empowers each speaker. The minimal and basic power to say "no," to protest, is there from the start, as is the power to interrupt, to clamor for a say, when others monopolize the conversation. These powers, sometimes very costly to exercise, are, I suggest, the foundations of human rights.

They do not themselves dictate the specific content of any right that may reasonably be claimed, but they do direct attention to individual participants. Rights belong to individual persons, and they are rights to what individuals can have and do. They may belong to individuals as occupants of thrones or White Houses, and they may come to be recognized as belonging also to artificial persons, to corporations and states. Any right is someone's right, in a sense in which it need not be true that any law is someone's law, or even that any responsibility is someone's. Our generation may collectively have a responsibility to clean up rivers, lakes, and the atmosphere, but until we appoint officers with special powers and responsibilities to see to this, the responsibility is not yet any single person's; it belongs to us collectively, not yet distributively. By contrast, if we of our generation have a right to, for instance, social security benefits because of what we have paid in, we have that distributively. Each of us has it. The language of rights is the language of speakers becoming conscious of themselves as individual participants in the cooperative practice of speech and in other cooperative practices. Rights claimants are cooperators conscious of themselves as individuals, claiming what they see as their due share of the fruits of cooperation.

The Peculiarity and the Parasitism of Rights

I do not think it is very controversial to claim that the use of the language of rights is one that draws attention to the presence and claims of individuals. Most of those who have recently written on the origins of our concept of right and on the distinctive features of rights-based moral theories are agreed on this (Richard Tuck, Ronald Dworkin, J. L. Mackie, Joseph Raz, Joel Feinberg),[19] and most critics of rights-based theories object precisely to this "individualism," to what is seen as an over-attention to individual demands and claims at the expense of attention to needs of the collectivity, needs that no single person may be voicing. If this "possessive individualism" is to be distinctive of the language of rights, and not a universal unvarying feature of all moral discourse, then one would expect that rights attach to single individual persons more basically than do obligations (which in their original sense are ties between two or more parties) or responsibilities and duties. The latter may be jointly possessed and jointly performed. Laws typically are laws of groups, not of individuals, and respect for law is something that a community can show collectively as well as individually. The language of rights directs attention to individual persons, not as duty-bearers or contributors to the human task but as beneficiaries or claimants to a share of what is produced by the performance of that task. Nor is this all. The language of rights pushes us, more insistently than does the language of duties, responsibilities, obligations, legislation, and respect for law, to see the participants in the moral practice as single clamorous living human beings, not as families, clans, tribes, groups, classes, churches, congregations, nations, or peoples.

Given the complicated and repeated inversions that Richard Tuck has traced in the medieval history of the concepts of *ius* and *dominium* in relation to *lex*, it takes a rash philosopher to suggest that there is any one thread linking the changing uses, that gives us a basis for a contrast with the concept of obligation (*obligatio*) and of responsibility. I shall make a rash suggestion covering the earliest use of *ius* in Roman law, where it was what a successful contestant in a dispute won;[20] through the later *iura praediorum*, which entitled home builders to conduct their drains through neighboring homeowners' property and to block their daylight to some degree; on through the medieval interpretation of Justinian (after the rediscovery of the *Digest* in the twelfth century), for whom justice is the continuing determination to give everyone his or her *ius* (and for whom *dominium* is a kind of *ius*); through the Renaissance lawyers such as Francois de Connan, to Grotius and beyond. De Connan says that the *ius* of a settler on vacant land, for example, differs from the consequent and correlative obligation of others not to dispossess him, and from his having legal case to enforce discharge of that obligation in its "reason, role and scope," not in its "cause, matter and end."[21] The "scope" of the right is a single settler, who is to have *dominium* over the settled land. The scope of the obligation is other individuals and collectives such as municipalities or religious orders. My suggestion concerns just this difference in scope, role, and order of reasons that de Connan perspicuously presents. Rights, I suggest, differ from obligations in that they primarily attach to individual persons, whereas parties to a tie of obligation and responsibility holders can as easily be collectives as individual persons. Rights differ also in their individuation, since what rights we recognize is affected by this key fact; we see them as essentially the possessions of single persons, whereas our obligations can include such things as no single individual could possibly do, things such as repaying a national debt, or cleaning up our rivers. Obligations and responsibilities are what we have collectively or individually, and they involve things that can be done either cooperatively or singly. Rights primarily have individual living persons in their scope, and they pertain to actions that single individuals can perform or to goods that individuals can possess.

This is not, of course, to deny that de Connan's point that the rights of a settler give rise to obligations of later-comers could be applied as readily to a group of Benedictine monks, obedient to some religious superior, or to a family, as to a single settler. The right may belong to some group, who can therefore claim, "*We* have right to this land." But when they— the monks, for example—say that, the claim is different from their recognition of their obligations when they say, "We have an obligation to organize soup kitchens for the local paupers and to offer up masses for the souls of our departed brethren." Their obligations include things that only a collective can do, whereas none of their rights requires a collective either to claim or to exercise. When rights are possessed, as of course they can be, by an "us" rather than a "me," that is accidentally not necessarily the case. But some obligations and responsibilities, including very important ones such as obligations to future generations, must be ours not mine, and any that are mine must, like individual monks' duties to officiate in certain ways at certain places and times, grow out of the arrangements made to discharge the collectively owned obligation—that is, the division of that moral task into individually dischargeable derivative duties.

I suggest, then, that throughout the twists and turns of the history of the concepts of *ius*, *dominium*, *droit*, *recht*, and right, they remain concepts more closely tied to single persons and the sort of goods they can have (liberty, control of material goods, power to command others), than is the wider-ranging and, in my view, more fundamental concept of responsibility.

If we look at Grotius's use of the term *ius*, which is often taken to inaugurate our modern tradition of rights-based moral and social theories, we find him appropriately starting by considering what sort of good a single living person can possess and which of these goods are transferable to others. Inalienable goods are life, honor, and freedom, and so rights to them are to be inalienable. Other goods possessible by single human beings, such as land and labor power, are alienable or *wandelbaer*. (In his discussion Tuck makes the interesting claim that the recognition of a right to liberty, treated as *dominium* or total control, and so including the right to renounce, was convenient to slave traders, who could persuade themselves that the Africans whom they traded had already renounced liberty for life. Molina's and Suarez's recognition of a right or *dominium* to individual liberty was, ironically enough, part of the justification of slavery, while Grotius's limitation on that right—his doctrine that liberty was an inalienable good—was a step in the direction of delegitimizing slavery and the slave trade.[22]) Thus Grotius can give his famous definition of a right as "a moral quality annexed to the person enabling him to have or do something justly."[23] Rights are the sort of thing most naturally annexed to individual persons, since they pertain to goods or powers that can be enjoyed or exercised by a single person, occasion by occasion. This is not to deny that for the very existence of the goods that rights secure (life, or free speech) there must have been some earlier cooperative activity (between parents, between parent and child, between language transmitters and those to whom it is transmitted). Rather, I make the simple claim that "I live and I speak, and so I exercise my rights to life and speech" makes very easy sense to us, whereas "I made a law" or "I made reparations to the American Indians for their past mistreatment" makes little sense. Laws must be collectively made, many obligations must be collectively discharged, but rights attach essentially to individual persons, and only derivatively to collectives.

Obligations and responsibilities can refer to the sorts of action that must be done collectively, so that for the discharge of the obligation a group must organize itself and divide the moral labor. If we, as a generation, are to fulfill our obligation to future generations, we must appoint officials with specific duties. Moral labor, the moral task, in this case as in many others, must be divided up by social agreement. It does not come naturally predivided, as does labor in childbirth. I have in the past challenged the view that because we have a responsibility or an obligation to clean up our messes for the sake of the future generations who could be poisoned by those messes, future generations therefore must be said to have rights against us, rights to unpoisoned air and water.[24] But if we did want to support that view, such rights would not be collectively possessed by each successive generation; the air at that time, would not be rationed, each person to his or her fair quota. Air divides itself into the lungs breathing it, river water cools or quenches the thirst of those bathing in or drinking it, without need for any allocative agency. (When a resource is scarce, as it may be, allocation will be necessary, but then the case for cross-generational obligations and rights immediately becomes more questionable. How much coal should we leave our great-grandchildren's generation? This is an unanswerable question, unlike the easily answered, "Should we leave lakes and rivers polluted or unpolluted?"[25]) Even when a resource is not scarce, it may take organization to give each person a turn at access to it; the job of such organizers will not be to "divide" the collective entitlement but to facilitate receipt of a self-apportioning and self-renewing good. My thesis, then, is that while collective responsibilities and obligations are not, or not always, self-apportioning, collective rights are. If someone fails to get access to, for example, the collective inheritance of the Western European literary tradition, it will be because someone or some community denied that person an education or access to public libraries, or because he or she did not act upon the opportunity of access. It is not that the other library users greedily consumed that person's portion as well as their own. By contrast, our collective obligation to pass on this tradition to the next generation is not self-apportioning. We do need to organize ourselves and allocate special responsibilities to some in order to discharge this collective obligation.

This feature of rights—that, once recognized, they do not have to be allocated, but come as it were preallocated—may explain why many say that respect for basic rights requires us merely to refrain from interfering with each other's exercise of these basic rights. I can get my air, continue my life, enjoy my liberty and public libraries, and have my right of reply to charges against me, without having to wait to discover which air is my air, which life my life, which liberty mine, which books the ones I am allocated, which say is my say. To discharge my responsibilities, however, I must first find out what my responsibilities are, I must consult my fellows. I think that this popular doctrine, that rights define a sort of core morality that demands of mutual right respecters an essential minimum of cooperation and coordination, is half-right. Rights do define a sort of individualist tip of the iceberg of morality, which needs no extra organization to stay afloat because it is supported by the submerged floating mass of cooperatively discharged responsibilities and socially divided labor. Basic rights, I argue, are rights of access to self-allocating public goods.

The right to one's say illustrates well this parasitism of rights on other less individualist moral concepts. If the "say" in question is a reply to criticisms levied against one, then indeed it is easily seen who has it, and in a sense what it is that one has. But for how long can I speak in my own defense and expect my accusers to listen? The rules that fix the substance of what counts as my say must be socially agreed ones, agreements that it may take courts or other organizations to reach. The same is true of my right to life. In a sense it is correct that, in order for it to be respected, all that others must do is not kill me. But although that may seem clear enough when I am a reasonably tough adult, it was less clear when I was a helpless newborn, and will be less clear if I become a helpless old person. Cooperation is needed to specify the precise content of such a right, as well as to preserve the supply of the good that gives this right its name and its individuality. Cooperation between parents, or perhaps between a state that issues a license of parenthood and individual potential parents, is needed for the reproduction of human life in a form that can still be seen as a good. Similarly, cooperation is needed both to preserve the liberty to which we have a right and to specify its limits and scope. We need cooperation to keep our various wells self-supplying and unpoisoned, as well as to regulate access to such wells.

So, although basic rights are those that individuals can have, exercise, and enjoy, it is as individual participants in a cooperative practice that we have basic rights, individual as they intrinsically are. Rights can be claimed, and when any attempt is made to claim or to "vindicate" any of these individual rights, the claim and the vindication have to employ the socially coordinated practice of speech. The claimants and vindicators must exercise some social powers as participants in discourse. Such declarers, proclaimers, and vindicators may often shout to the empty air, be heard but laughed out of court, or be contradicted or heckled or shouted down, but the very attempt to claim rights exercises basic hard-to-suppress rights to speak up for oneself and one's people, rights that the public good of speech itself gives us. We the people, once adult, have some actual equality of the essential powers of speech, not only with one another but also with any contrasting overlords. We may not all be equally eloquent or get equally wide audiences, and some may speak in accents or dialects that reveal origins more "lowly" than others, but that need not impair communicative force, especially the force of protest. "People" is a collective noun for an aggregation of individuals who can follow each other's speech and gesture and so can make claims and counterclaims, both on one another and on any would-be overlords. But for this sort of community—constituted by a common language or a mutually comprehensible collection of languages—to exist, the individuals making up "the people" must be seen not as "autonomous," each making her or his own laws, but as members of a "republic of letters," obeying common conventions of speech and accepting shared responsibilities to protect the common wealth that speech brings. Ends in ourselves we may be, each of us a separate valuable source of voice, suggestion, and demand, but we hold this status only as members of a republic of such ends in themselves. Only as participants in a cooperative practice can we have any rights. The concept of responsibility, of being properly responsive to our fellow cooperators, is the more fundamental one, and its linguistic origins are obvious. Rights are the tip of the iceberg that collective and individual responsibilities support.

Such a foundation for the concept of a right—basing it on our human nature as individual speakers who transmit our powers and standards of speech to new arrivals—leaves open as a matter of unending debate the question of what universal rights, other than the equal right to have one's say, can plausibly be claimed. Still, it might seem to prejudice the question of the content of such rights toward the rights of freedom of speech and worship, toward procedural rights and away from so-called welfare rights. Consent will seem to become as basic as the framers of the United States Constitution made it, and the concerns of those who were unhappy until the Constitution was amended with explicit recognition of the rights to speak, to put speech to religious uses, to assemble to talk, and to petition, appear eminently appropriate. To what more appropriate end can the language of rights be used than to claim the rights intrinsic to language participants? Lest it be thought, however, that I am retracting my earlier claim that speech is the moral equivalent of discord as well as accord—that rights themselves are the moral human equivalent of talons, saber teeth, horns and antlers, and instruments of self-defense and attack as well as mutual aid—let me add a remark about the second amendment, the claimed right to keep and bear arms at all times. If rights are spiritual weapons, and the right to speak is the great equalizer, should they be used to secure what they can replace? If the first amendment seems a natural starter for a bill of rights, the second seems a most unnatural follow-up. The language of rights does not rule out any particular content, but it does make some proposed contents to universal rights look a little dangerous for the very survival of the formal structure of right-recognition itself. The right to rebel against tyrants is one of the oldest and most venerable claimed rights, and it is indeed a last-resort right, the right to resort to violent self-defense when its moral equivalent (debate, petition, protest, wrangling, and litigation) fails. Such appeals to God-or-Nature must remain an ultimate last resort, a dangerous safeguard, but they are a borderline case of what can count as the exercise of a right, if rights pertain essentially to one's role-related powers in a cooperative enterprise, and if their point is to offer a better way than fighting of settling perceived conflicts of interests. Such a limit case right must be recognized, I think, just as much as the quintessential right to speech, if we recognize any rights. But to recognize the right to rebel against tyrannical governments is one thing; to recognize a right to keep arms at all times is quite another. In fact, it seems almost to contradict the very idea of recognizing any rights—an invitation to revert to raw force and violence, away from their civilized and cooked variants of contradiction, protest, disputation. It is a bit like using one's powers of speech to take a vow of silence, as Trappists do. It is indeed possible with the forged cultural instrument of a social practice of rights-recognition and protection, but it is an anomalous and self-endangering thing to do. It is the right to cease to rely on appeal to one's rights. And since rights, like a monetary currency, depend for their very existence on trust in them, then the right to distrust them, and to promote that distrust, is a strange and right-undermining right.

RIGHTS, INTERESTS, RESPONSIBILITIES

The language of individual rights naturally leads to the concept of an individual human interest. Individual interests come to be seen as what rights protect, and the individuation of interests piggybacks upon that of the rights that protect them. Often we claim rights before we are very clear about the value of what we are claiming, so that consciousness of our vital interests demands more of us than awareness of our rights does. Indeed, I would say that the language of vital interests is the proper complement, perhaps even successor, to the language of rights. Perceived vital interests are rights that have transcended or transvalued themselves, and once we talk the language of interests, we are bound to recognize as vital public as well as private interests. Meanwhile, we have both concepts, rights and interests. The language of rights, once we have it and while we still use it, will and should be used to protect what we see to be vital and protectable individual human interests. I see no reason why we should not include the so-called welfare rights among the universal rights we recognize. If the role of rights is to mitigate the effects of dominance without requiring begging, then there should be rights to whatever vital goods we the people can otherwise only get by violence or by begging— that is, to food, shelter, and help when we are not yet capable or are incapacitated. But our perception of what we want to fight or beg for if we cannot otherwise claim them, of which interests are vital, and our collective ability to cooperate so as to protect these interests, vary greatly from culture to culture and from epoch to epoch. Even in one culture at one time there probably will be considerable disagreement.

If we do allow that there is a right to self-defense, even with violence, that right, like the right to a share of the earth's common stock of food or the right to one's turn at useful paid work in the community into which one is born, will be based on an interest different from any specifically speech-related interests. Rights to self-defense, to work, and to join the "banquet of life" are all as much "welfare rights" as they are "procedural rights." None of them has anything intrinsically to do with speech or with the roles we play as speech participants. But it would surely be absurdly narcissistic to use our powers of speech to talk only about talk, or to use our capacities to claim and to recognize claims, to propose and to second, to declare and to vindicate, only to protect that very capacity. The language of rights is worth protecting only if it finds something other than itself to talk about, and only if it is used to assert some rights in addition to the right to speak. It must indeed protect itself, if it is to protect any human interest. Unless it is protecting, as best the current conditions allow, some vital human interests in addition to our vital interest as participants in speech, however, it will become merely a branch of contemporary literature, of talk about talk, and the United States Constitution with its past and future amendments will be merely texts about texts. We do have a fundamental and vital interest in our cooperative practice of speech, and in the rights it gives birth to, but we surely have an equally vital interest in other cooperative practices (now thoroughly permeated by speech), such as the production of food and shelter and the care of the very young, the sick, and the very old. As Locke's account of a good education emphasizes, no one becomes a participant in that most noble and civilizing practice of speech unless first fed, sheltered, and treated as one of us, the people. It is only decent filial piety for participants in the language of rights, in speech becoming conscious of itself, to use that language to recognize rights to the greatest equal protection that we collectively can afford to those basics of human life that our exercise of our rightly treasured power of speech itself presupposes. The most primitive of these basic prerequisites is protection against torture, against the infliction of pain that substitutes screams and groans for voice. That is indeed so basic that it seems too weak to say that the victims of torture are victims of the violation of a right. They are victims of violation itself, of violence at its most evil. If we have any responsibilities, the responsibility to prevent torture, to respond to the cries or stifled cries of the tortured, is surely the most self-evident. Unless we recognize that, we renounce morality itself.

Speakers, conscious of themselves, recognize the rights that speech essentially entails. Right-recognizers, conscious of their dependence on and debts to those who sustain human life, protect as best they can the interests that must be protected if human lives are to be sustained. Rights to speak, to one's turn (in speech, and in all those civilizing procedures that define turns), sustain the very possibility of any rights and so of any alternative to begging as a way of softening the effects of dominance. The so-called welfare rights sustain rights-claimants. We have a vital interest in the goods protected by both sorts of rights. But rights are only the tip of the moral iceberg, supported by the responsibilities that we cooperatively discharge and by the individual responsibilities that we recognize, including responsibilities to cooperate, in order to maintain such common goods as civilized speech and civilized ways of settling disputes. For it takes more than rights to settle disputes about rights.

NOTES

This paper is a revised version of a talk given at the University of Pennsylvania in March 1987, during a Bicentennial conference on human nature organized by Charles Kahn. I have been helped by the discussion on that occasion, and by comments by my colleague Robert Brandom.

1. David Hume, *History of England* (Indianapolis, Ind.: Liberty Classics, 1985). The first quotation is from the second appendix, the others from the end of chap. 23.

2. For an account of Ann Lee and the Shaker faith she founded, see Edward D. Andrews, *The People Called Shakers: A Search for the Perfect Society* (New York: Oxford University Press, 1953) and Henri Desroche, *The American Shakers: From Neo-Christianity to Presocialism* (Paris: Editions de Minuit, 1955), trans. and ed. John K. Savacool (Amherst: University of Massachusetts Press, 1971).

3. "Person" is a status term, for Pufendorf and the dominant tradition, as much a will-imposed "moral entity" or artifice as "sovereign" or "slave."

4. "Week in Review," *New York Times*, 21 December 1986.

5. See Stanley Benn and Richard Peters, *The Principles of Political Thought* (New York: Free Press, 1965) (earlier published as *Social Principles and the Democratic State* [London, England: Allen and Unwin, 1959]). In chap. 2 of that work (on which I cut my social philosophical teeth), Benn and Peters link respect for persons with the attitude shown by Socrates when he reasoned with a slave. "For what has a man's social position to do with the truth or falsity of what he says? . . . If we are prepared seriously to attend to what another person has to say, whatever his personal or social attributes, we must have at least a minimal respect for him as the source of an argument." They attribute the germs of this idea to Karl Popper, who had developed it in seminars. It obviously has a strong family resemblance to the theses defended more recently by Jürgen Habermas.

6. John Locke, *Some Thoughts Concerning Education* (Menston, England: Scholar Press, 1970), sec. 83.

7. Ibid., sec. 196.

8. Ibid., sec. 185.

9. Ibid., sec. 145.

10. Ibid.

11. Ibid.

12. Thomas Hobbes, *Leviathan* (London: J. M. Dent & Sons; New York: E. P. Dutton, 1914), chap. 4.

13. Ibid., chap. 4.

14. Ibid., chap. 3.

15. Ibid., chap. 5.

16. Ibid., chap. 4.

17. Ibid., chap. 6.

18. Ibid., chap. 4. Hobbes here adds a significant qualification: "unlesse it be one whom we are obliged to govern; and then it is not to grieve, but to correct and amend."

19. Richard Tuck, *Natural Rights Theories: Their Origin and Development* (New York: Cambridge University Press, 1979); Ronald Dworkin, *Taking Rights Seriously* (Cambridge, Mass.: Harvard University Press, 1978); J. L. Mackie, "Can There Be a Rights-Based Theory?" in *Theories of Rights*, ed. J. Waldron (New York: Oxford University Press, 1984); Joseph Raz, "Rights-Based Moralities," in Waldron, *Theories of Rights*; Joel Feinberg, "The Nature and Value of Rights," *Journal of Value Inquiry* 4 (Winter 1970): 243–57.

20. See Tuck, *Natural Rights Theories*, p. 8.

21. Quoted in ibid., p. 40.

22. See ibid., p. 54ff.

23. Grotius, *De Jure Belli ac Pacis* 1.11.1.5.

24. I have discussed this in "Rights of Past and Future Persons," in *Responsibility to Future Generations*, ed. E. Partridge (Buffalo, N.Y.: Prometheus Books, 1981). Republished, in part, in *Morality in Practice*, ed. James P. Sterba (Belmont, Cal.: Wadsworth Publishing Co., 1985).

25. I have discussed this in "For the Sake of Future Generations," in *Earthbound*, ed. Tom Regan (New York: Random House, 1984).

Chapter 7

FEMINISM AND UNIVERSAL MORALITY

MARGARET A. FARLEY

FEMINISTS have understandable reasons both to reject and to promote belief in a common or universal morality. The social construction of moral norms is hardly anywhere more evident than in the history of interpretations of women's roles and duties in the family and in society. The suffering caused by what are now judged to be mistaken views of women's "nature" and its laws has moved many feminists to a deep skepticism regarding moral norms in general. Yet insofar as feminism is a movement aimed at the well-being of women, it has an important interest in understanding what truly is for women's good—and in arguing for the basic intelligibility of that good. And insofar as feminism has an ultimate aim of enhancing the well-being of all human persons—women, men, children—its interests extend to understanding human good, individual and social, and to pressing claims that require some agreement on what constitutes and serves that human good.[1] In other words, despite a sharp sense of the historical and social relativity of moral norms, the moral commitments and political agendas of many feminists lead them to articulate (or at least to imply) some version of a common morality. However, simply to attribute to feminists a general assumption about the possibility of a common human morality underestimates the seriousness of feminist critiques of traditional theories of universal morality. It also obscures the quite drastic differences among feminist theories that have emerged in the twentieth century.

On one reading, feminist theorists take as many positions on the possibility of a common morality as might be found in the main streams of late twentieth-century philosophy, theology, political theory, psychology, and literary criticism. Feminists speak out of and back into classical, analytical, phenomenological, neo-Kantian, Marxist, pragmatist, deconstructionist, hermeneutical, and other waxing and waning traditions and currents of thought. Therefore, they are as cautious, skeptical, ironical, revisionary, deconstructive, or reconstructive as their disciplines have become. Yet there is a difference. Because feminist theory retains a connection with feminism as a movement (a movement against the subordination of women to men and against any basic patterns of relationship that are characterized by the domination of some persons over others), feminist theory is never without a strong challenge not only to relate to particular women's experiences but also to mediate some universally sharable moral insights. This, however, may turn out to be an impossibly conflicted task.

This essay aims to explore the possibilities for a feminist theory that will include a coherent notion of universal or common morality. This is an important project for feminist theory and, I think, generally for both moral philosophy and theological ethics. On the one hand, if a theory of common morality is to be sustained, it needs to satisfy a specifically feminist critique (a critique that incorporates gender analysis). On the other hand, if feminist theory is to accommodate some of feminists' deepest concerns, it must at least ask about the universal relevance and intelligibility of its own moral claims.

I do not propose here to survey all of current feminist theory, looking for signs of a theory of common morality. Nor will I test the many historical and contemporary theories of universal morality against a feminist critique. I will try to locate in feminist theory some key criticisms of possible theories of common morality and some central reasons why a common morality must be sought. I will then attempt to frame some elements for a feminist theory of common morality.

The Feminist Case against a Common Morality

Feminists resist theories of common morality primarily because they have been harmful to women (and to some men). In the name of universality, of a total view of human nature and society, such theories have in fact been exclusive, oppressive, and repressive of women and of men who do not belong to a dominant group. Whether consciously or unconsciously, the formulators of such theories have inaccurately universalized a particular perspective; as a result, the needs and moral claims of some groups and individuals have been left out, their roles and duties distorted, and their full voices silenced. What is thought to be "common" morality, when examined with an eye for gender bias—or for class, race, religious, or other deep-seated biases—turns out not to have universal extension and to incorporate seriously mistaken moral requirements.

Theories of common morality, then, are not, in fact, universal; more than this, they distort what should be valid moral claims. They are not only inadequate, but false; not only false, but injurious. Such charges do not by themselves rule out the possibility of a valid universal morality. They only challenge the ones that have been developed thus far. For some feminists, this means that a moral theory can be corrected, expanded, improved upon; indeed, for these theorists the very possibility of a feminist critique implies a more adequate perspective for discerning universal moral norms. For other feminists, the problems with any theory of universal morality are more radical, even to the point where such a theory must be ruled out—if not in principle, at least in any foreseeable historical practice.

Feminist theories have diverged through the last three decades on some very fundamental questions. They have agreed that the subordination of women to men is unjustifiable and that it is sustained by false and inadequate interpretations of what women are—what they can do, what they desire, what kind of relationships they ought to be able to form. But feminist theorists have disagreed on the causes of gendered hierarchy, on its remedies, and on the nature of its interaction with other forms of dominance and subordination. Some of these disagreements stem from the varying philosophical alignments that have marked feminist analyses all along, and others have emerged in conjunction with changes in feminism as a movement. The bases of disagreements often go as deep and are as comprehensive as whole worldviews. In its own considerable pluralism, then, feminism provides formidable obstacles to a common morality; yet it may instance the potential of plural perspectives to allow and even support some common moral norms.

Alison Jaggar's categorization of contemporary feminist theories is useful for understanding the variety of feminist descriptive and normative proposals.[2] Jaggar's focus is on theories of society, but she argues that feminist theories of society have developed along with understandings of human nature, which in turn have involved commitments regarding the nature of human knowledge. She identifies four major categories (or what she sometimes calls paradigms) of feminist theories: liberal, traditional Marxist, radical, and socialist. Each general category encompasses numerous variations but has its own unitary focus. In the twentieth century these categories have tended to follow one another in importance within feminist thought; that is, they have emerged chronologically in terms of attention and number of adherents, though they all represent points of view still held within feminism today.

Liberal feminism, in Jaggar's sense, incorporates a view of human nature that emphasizes rationality, autonomy, and individual fulfillment.[3] Its central moral principle is traditional philosophical liberalism's respect for persons, based on the equal dignity of rational agents and on the requirements of rationality itself insofar as reason identifies unconditional moral obligations or provides the warrants for a social contract.[4] Like traditional liberalism, the feminist version has believed in the possibility of objectivity in scientific and moral knowledge; it has seen its own critical function as that of challenging liberalism to consistency and to true impartiality in its recognition of and respect for every human person. Feminists' particular task has been to demand acknowledgement of the full humanity of women and, with this, the extension of principles of liberty and equality to women as well as to men.

Liberal feminism, then, more than any other major form of feminist theory, has tended to support the possibility of a universal morality. Since the 1792 publication of Mary Wollstonecraft's *Vindication of the Rights of Women*, mainstream feminism has struggled to complete what it assumed to be a truly human moral point of view by (*a*) "adding" insights drawn from women's history and experience; (*b*) claiming for women a "sameness" with men as human persons and as full citizens; and (*c*) asserting the autonomy of individual women and the rights of self-determination for women as members of a group. Discouragement with liberalism has grown among feminists (as among others), however. Its perceived failure to emancipate women (after two centuries of theoretical critique and political action) has convinced many feminists that an "additive" approach to political theory is not sufficient. While few feminists want to lose civil liberties or a newfound sense of individual selfhood, they nonetheless have come to demand of liberal norms and ideals more than a simple extension to include women. The content of liberalism itself requires major change, and its claims as an impartial, objective, universal moral theory are in serious doubt.

To feminists, this form of liberalism fails to take account of the particular historical situations of women. It is content to divide areas of public life from private, so that even where liberal ideals appear to alleviate women's oppression, alienation remains in sexual relations, child rearing, and the support services of ordinary housework. Aristotle's *polis* depended on a sexual division of labor, and modern liberal societies seem to need it no less. Appeals to neutral reason are ineffective before the convictions of the powerful, and where they are heard, they leave out whole spheres of human life and dimensions of the human personality. Many feminist critics of liberalism target, then, its tendency to dichotomize and to rank mind and body, reason and emotion, public and private, autonomy and community. Its theoretical deficiencies mask its support of the subordination of some persons to others on the basis of gender, class, race, and other human particularities that liberalism claims to have transcended.

Not surprisingly, *Marxist feminism* has provided a significant alternative for some of the feminist critics of liberalism.[5] Traditional Marxism offers an explanation for the failures of abstract rationality.[6] It contends that moral norms and ideals are not universal and ahistorical, the achievement of a neutral and solitary observer; they are socially constructed. Even human nature is a historical construction, fashioned out of the interaction of biology, society, and the physical environment—limited by material needs in a concrete and particular situation, subject to the purposes of a ruling class. Relational but not completely relativist, Marxism allows for some objectivity in the physical sciences and a *telos* for moral understandings. For while moralities are conventional, they are part of the human struggle for liberation. The dominant class determines the moral and political norms of a society (and the structures that make norms convincing), but the voices and actions of the oppressed can bring about revolutionary change. The introduction of a feminist point of view will not, then, be irrelevant to the liberation of women and the achieved equality of all persons.

As attractive as Marxist analysis is for feminists, and as helpful as it has been in addressing the problems of liberal philosophy and political theory, it has nonetheless not satisfied many feminists as a theoretical basis for understanding the social construction of gender. In its concern for economic analysis, traditional Marxism leaves intact the separation of the public world and the private. In its preoccupation with production, it fails to take seriously the historical nature of reproduction. But above all, traditional Marxism has insufficient theoretical room for either gender or racial analysis. Within its framework, women as women cannot constitute a class, nor is race as such a determinant of class. The tools are missing, therefore, for some of the needs of a feminist theory.

Radical feminism challenges both liberal and Marxist feminism. If Marxism fails to take gender seriously enough, radical feminists make it the central problem. If liberal feminism appreciates the perspectives of women as starting points on the way to understanding women's full humanity, radical feminists begin and (to an important extent) end with the experience and the ways of knowing that are particular to women. These challenges go a long way toward specifying what is otherwise an unwieldy category.[7] For whatever else radical feminists are, they are convinced that the most basic form of all oppression is patriarchy, and that patriarchy is neither a mere anomaly in an otherwise liberal justice nor a form of domination that is solely derivative of economic power.

Gender provides the (often invisible) framework for every social relation. Hence, the radical feminist task is to understand how gender is socially constructed and to explore its influence, especially in the private sphere of family life, sexual relationships, and spirituality. For some earlier radical feminists the goal was to eliminate gender differences; for many later radical feminists the goal has been to reclaim the differences between women and men—to retrieve women's culture, to revalue woman-identified emotion in relation to reason, embodiment in relation to transcendent mind, and caring in relation to abstract principles of justice. No longer afraid that acknowledging gender differences will inevitably result in discrimination, many radical feminists are as concerned with the repression of women as with their oppression.

The radical feminist agenda, then, is both to free women's bodies from the power of men and to free women's minds and hearts from the cultural and psychological bonds of patriarchy. This turns out to be one task, for the human person is an organic whole. The task depends importantly, however, on the recognition and release of women's special powers of knowing. For some this takes the form of spiritual insight, made possible by participation in communal rituals.[8] For others it is the less mystical process of consciousness-raising, the sharing of women's experience in a way that leads to new self-understanding and insight into human (especially women's) possibility. Variously inspired by the analysis and literary innovations of Mary Daly, the psychological studies of Carol Gilligan, the bold and mysterious *écriture féminine* of French feminists, and the powerful theories and expressions of countless other feminists, radical feminism makes women themselves the focus of exploration and the organizers of their own liberation.[9]

Still, many feminists are not satisfied with what radical feminism has been able to provide thus far by way of theory. While it pays attention to gender and to women's experience and to the integration of body and mind, affectivity and knowledge, and the private sphere and the public, it is finally not sufficiently historical for some feminists, not sufficiently political for others. Some fear that the new emphasis on differences between women and men is neither warranted nor wise, for it slips too easily into traditional stereotypes and threatens to reinforce once again the subordination of women to men. Moreover, it ignores the diverse histories of individual women and groups of women. And finally, however special women's ways of knowing may be, there remain troubling questions of the social construction of knowledge, the dichotomization of (for example) justice and care, the particular or universal relevance of woman-identified values as the human ideal.

Feminist theory has continued to develop, however, and Jaggar's last category incorporates key elements from both traditional Marxist and radical feminist theory.[10] What Jaggar calls *socialist feminism* is like Marxism in its assertions that understandings of human nature and society are socially constructed and that prevailing worldviews reflect the interests of the dominant class. It also agrees with traditional Marxism that the perspective of the oppressed is epistemologically privileged because it is more likely to be impartial (though not disinterested) and comprehensive, since its interests are more likely to serve the wider social good. Like radical feminism, socialist feminism believes Marxism to be mistaken in not taking particular account of gender in its analysis of oppression. Radical and socialist feminists have stood together in considering patriarchy to be the major social problem in both private and public arenas. But socialist feminists want to address the interconnections of gender and class and race and age, and they require more systematic and critical studies of women's experience, particularly women's experience in the shared social practice of the struggle for liberation. Like radical feminists, socialist feminists want to raise the importance of emotion as a source of knowledge as well as affective power, but at least for Jaggar this involves a critical analysis of historically structured emotional responses.

With these four versions of feminist theory the possibilities for a theory of universal morality are clearly limited but not eliminated. Liberal feminism, sobered by the recognition of its capacity to conceal oppression as well as to reveal it, still looks to a basic set of rights and responsibilities for all human persons. Traditional Marxist feminism, appreciative of the role of power in sustaining historically situated worldviews, still aims at overcoming alienation in the attainment of a universally intelligible human social good. Radical feminism trusts the capacities of women to discover or to create who they are and what they need—sometimes even in an essential sense. Socialist feminism, historical and materialist, pragmatic and provisional, aims nonetheless at a more adequate systematic explanation of oppression for the sake of an ultimate transformation of society.

Developments in feminist theory, however, emerging out of each of the four types and out of the interaction among them, have generated sharper obstacles to formulations of universal morality.[11] Two developments in particular call into question the possibility of any overarching feminist theory of morality. The seeds of both are in the call by many feminist theorists for a critical revaluation of human embodiment, affectivity, and the ordinary housekeeping of life, and in the insistence by all feminist theorists on the inclusion of a woman's perspective.

The first development marks an intensification of the long-standing concern that feminists have had to pay attention to women's bodies. While it is true that early forms of feminism attempted to prescind from women's embodiment (opposing, for example, the strictures of "anatomy is destiny"), women soon began to "reclaim" their bodies. With such reclaiming has come the recognition that feminist analysis is irrevocably bound up with the historical, the particular, the situated, the contingent—all of which effectively resist universal interpretation. That which had been considered most "natural," abstracted as it was from women's experience and therefore easily universalized by its interpreters, now seems almost completely subject to social construction for its meaning. The last bastion for some versions of universal morality seems lost before sustained feminist critique.

The second development is not unrelated to the first. It involves the deconstruction of "women's experience" by women whose experience is marginal to that of the dominant class of women, and by postmodernist feminists who are suspicious of any grand narratives, even those that include the perspectives of women. The critique that feminist theorists have lodged against false universalization from men's experience to "human" experience has been turned on feminism itself, with the charge that the experience of some women—white, middle-class, Western, heterosexual—has been falsely universalized to represent all women. Women of color, lesbian women, working-class women, women from across the world have pressed the question of whether or not there is anything common in women's experience, or whether the delineation of a "women's perspective" must simply replicate the situation in which those with power always privilege their own voices while silencing others'.

The issue is again not simply one of adding many voices in order to make what is partial more representative of a whole. It is the issue of whether or not women as women do have anything in common, and, again, whether there can be "any account of 'human nature' that, in the guise of a universal account, doesn't end up conflating the situation of one group of humans with the situation of all?"[12] It is the issue, moreover, of why gender analysis without class, race, and cultural analyses can only be distortive, why the abstraction of gender from the full situatedness of persons conceals the patterns of their relationships. Feminists increasingly insist, for example, that patriarchy in Western culture cannot be understood without an analysis of why marriage determines a woman's class but not a man's; that a slave woman's situation is not understood simply by adding together what it means to be a woman and what it means to be a slave; that the race of white women as well as black women determines their experience of sexism; and that invisible but "compulsory" heterosexuality must be recognized if all the forms of sexism are to be seen.

Postmodernist trends in contemporary feminist theory coalesce (despite tension) with the challenges of women whose experiences have been heretofore undervalued or ignored.[13] Along with Lyotard, Derrida, Foucault, and others, some feminists have come to doubt whether any theory can transcend particular power relations and historical situatedness to critique large social and institutional structures. Perhaps no one can attempt to identify common elements in women's (or men's) experience without suppressing voices different from his or her own and without mistaking the contingent for the essential. The dangers of abstraction may finally outweigh any cognitive or political advantage it once seemed to have. To move in this direction, of course, threatens to leave feminism without the tools for a universal critique of structures of domination and subordination. For even categories like "gender," "race," and "class" must be deconstructed, possibly to the point where they are useless for social and ethical theory. At this extreme in feminist theory, all theory as theory is vulnerable.

THE FEMINIST CASE FOR A COMMON MORALITY

Nevertheless, feminists continue to theorize, and arguments for a common morality continue to be made. If theories of universal morality have been distortive and harmful, theories of unmitigated relativism are no less so. The problem of representing particulars as universals is bound up with the problems of coercion and violence. But the problem of recognizing no universals at all is also a problem of conflict and power, and it limits or eliminates the possibility of a common cry for justice. Thus Sandra Harding is not alone in believing that "relativism is not a problem originating in, or justifiable in terms of, women's experiences or feminist agendas."[14] Feminists tend to appreciate the observation of Mircea Eliade that historicism is promoted in nations where history has not been a "continuous terror."[15] So long as oppression, hierarchies of power, and relative visibility of lives are part of human society, it is not possible to conclude that everyone's analysis is equally plausible, that everyone's voice carries equally adequate "truth." Indeed, to adopt historical and cultural relativism as a solution to the inadequacies and falsehoods of universalism may be to abandon the field to the powerful or to struggle for position on a model of human relationship that offers nothing more ultimate than conflict—a model that feminists have consistently rejected.

A feminist case for common morality stands on more than the needs of a political agenda, however. It stands primarily on the convictions that human persons can and ought to experience moral claims in relation to one another and that some of these claims can and ought to cross (though not ignore) the boundaries of culture and history. These convictions presuppose some commonality in human experience—in the experience of what it means as a human person to rejoice and to be sorrowful, to be protected or violated, nurtured or stifled, understood or misjudged, respected or used. Whatever the differences in human lives, however minimal the actuality of world community, however unique the social arrangements of diverse peoples, it is nonetheless possible for human persons to weep over commonly felt tragedies, laugh over commonly perceived incongruities, yearn for common hopes. And across time and place, it is possible to condemn commonly recognized injustices and act for commonly desired goals. The range of universal moral norms may be narrower than traditional ethical theories supposed, but it does exist. The content of universal morality may be modest and in many ways provisional, but it is not empty. Beyond the critique of universal norms lies caution and care but not arbitrariness or indifference, and not completely isolated moral systems.

The dissonance between such convictions and the new awareness of differences among women is probably more apparent than real. Feminist theorists are wary of identifying commonalities in women's experience, but they do not dismiss them altogether. Thus Josephine Donovan and others insist that there are some "determinant structures of experience under which women, unlike men, have nearly universally existed."[16] These structures include the political subordination of women to men, the assignment of women to major tasks in the domestic sphere, women's participation in economic production for use but not exchange, and significant physical events of the female body such as menstruation, childbirth, and breast-feeding. The meaning of these structures is socially constructed, and hence variable, but women who reflect on them across cultures and classes usually find something in their language and in their consciousness (and therefore in their experience) that is shared.

Those who have done the most to challenge an assumed commonality in contemporary women's experience are women who belong to minority groups in the United States and women from areas of Africa, Central and Latin America, and the many parts of Asia. The goal of their challenge, however, has not been to isolate women from one another, as if differences were eternal barriers. Nor has it been to offer particular stories of particular histories that are simply parallel to every other history—entirely relative in their meaning to the contexts in which they have developed. Rather, they have spoken of themselves as "long-suffering custodians of truth," bringing from the Third World protests against cruelty, violence, and injustice.[17] They have presented what they believe to be serious feminist theories of universal significance.[18] They have argued that differences can make community possible, but only if the differences are confronted and respected.[19] These writers are as opposed to unmitigated moral relativism as to false and inadequate universalisms.

If feminist theory is to incorporate some form of common morality, however, it is of course not enough for it to interpret moral norms and ideals only for women. It must incorporate or transcend not only the differences among women but the differences between women and men. If it is a theory of common morality, it must somehow be accessible to men, somehow cross the boundaries of gendered experience and understanding as well as the boundaries of culture and race and class. Some feminist theories are therefore less suited to address issues of common morality than others. For example, proposals like Carol Gilligan's regarding the moral development of women come close (despite repeated caveats) to sanctioning one set of norms for women and another for men.[20] Still, most feminists who bring women's perspectives to bear on questions of morality rely on the general (and potentially universal) intelligibility and moral force of the arguments they make. They do not assume that these arguments are plausible only to women. In articulating moral claims and ideals, in advocating the transformation of society, they presume some analogy in the experiences of differently situated persons—some basis for perceiving moral challenges and possibilities, some inkling of similarity even in difference.[21]

What feminists think about universal morality is perhaps clearer when the issues are concerned less with method than with ethical behavior and social policy. Here the lessons of particularity are not forgotten, but neither are the compelling needs and rationales of universality. The demystification of moral rules in spheres historically important to women is profound. Evidence mounts for historical social construction of the meaning of sexuality, parenthood, marriage and family, technology, war, birth and death. What counts as courage, honesty, loyalty, integrity becomes open to exploration. The loosening of taboo moralities and the relaxation of moralism is welcome and freeing to women. Some behaviors are no longer interpreted primarily as moral matters—as in the evaluation of many sexual arrangements. Other behaviors are newly understood as morally required, even though their meaning is deeply culture-relative—as in the forms that honesty takes in culturally shaped interpersonal relations.[22] Moreover, disagreement among feminists on specific moral questions sometimes relativizes perspectives, and the political arena becomes the appropriate setting for the adjudication of conflict and the struggle with uncertainty, as with the issues of abortion, eugenics, pornography, prostitution, etc.[23]

But as relativism rises in importance for feminists, so in a way does a feminist commitment to universal morality. If there is demystification of taboos, for example, so is there demystification of double standards for women and for men. This is as true in decisions about medical treatment as it is in traditional patterns of sexual activity, and it prompts calls for unitary systems of morality.[24] In addition, feminist respect for particularity and diversity is not criterionless, and feminism works hard to sustain some critical distance from every context. Hence it is difficult to imagine a feminist perspective in which sexism could be approved, although to some extent what counts as sexism may be culture-relative. And while feminists have failed (and still can fail) to critique racism or classism, most feminist theorists today would call for self-criticism in that regard. Again, while there is something fundamentally contextual about the experience of embodiment, feminists have universalized bodily integrity as a reality and a value that ought not to be violated. While the meaning of sexuality is importantly socially constructed, and gender is understood differently in various historical contexts, feminists have not hesitated to critique—across cultures—actions such as footbinding, female genital circumcision, spouse abuse, sexual harassment, reproductive coercion, slavery, and rape.[25] The critical perspective needed for rejecting such practices is itself dependent upon social influences, but neither feminism as a movement nor feminism as a theory has accepted complete identification with a society or a culture. To acknowledge a point of view is not necessarily to relinquish some claim to universal validity.

The vantage point for a feminist critique of individual actions as well as social practices—women's as well as men's—is a commitment to the well-being of women, and within and beyond that to the well-being of all human persons (and, for many feminists, within and beyond that to the well-being of all the world). It is these commitments that motivate both respect for diversity and a desire for universality. Insofar as refinement of theory serves this commitment today, feminism is searching for a more adequate theory of differences and a more integrative theory of universal norms. The search is not a sectarian one, but one that has much to do with a common morality. As part of that search, I want to consider briefly two possible elements in a feminist theory of common morality. The first is a view of the human person, woman-person or man-person, that tries to take account of feminism's concern for both selfhood and relationship. As such it risks the charge of essentialism, the dangers of abstract universalism, and a form of naïveté in affirming still a "subject." Yet it seems worth considering. The second is an approach to moral action-guides that tries to move beyond current feminist theoretical tensions between justice and care. It will encounter the problems of "realism" and again the dangers of universalism. But it will aim to integrate context and principle.

ELEMENTS FOR A FEMINIST THEORY OF COMMON MORALITY

Autonomy and Relationality

The commitment of feminism to the well-being of women implies, as I have noted earlier, some understanding of what constitutes women's well-being. An early conviction of contemporary feminism was that at the heart of what is good for women is autonomy, in the sense of both self-legislation and self-determination. Women needed to take hold of their own lives, to refuse the subordinate position that rendered them passive in relation to an active male, to trust their own insights and articulate their own self-understanding. Because autonomy belonged to women as personal beings with the capacity to determine the ultimate meaning of their own lives, they could make claims for respect as persons, valuable in themselves and not merely as instruments in the service of the community—or of the human species, the family, or men. An important part of the claim to respect for autonomy was the right to bodily integrity, the right not to be touched or invaded or used as embodied beings without their own free choice or consent.

An affirmation of autonomy as the central feature of the human personality is not without its theoretical and practical limitations, however. As we have seen, feminists (along with others) have been critical of the connotations of exaggerated individualism, detached spectatorship, and Faustian desires for control that Western notions of autonomy have carried. Therefore, throughout the development of contemporary feminist theory there has been a strong tendency to consider another feature of persons (and another aspect of women's well-being) as important as autonomy—the feature that can be called "relationality."

The tendency of women to emphasize relationships in their approach to morality provides the focus for much of feminist moral theory today. The general response to Carol Gilligan's work testifies to the importance of this approach, as does the interest in earlier studies by Nancy Chodorow, Dorothy Dinnerstein, and others. At stake here, though less clearly articulated than descriptions of psychological patterns of relating, is a view of women, but also of men, in which the capacity for relationship is as significant a characteristic of human persons as the capacity for self-determination. Like autonomy, relationality underlies the value of persons in themselves. Because persons can know and be known, love and be loved, they are both self-transcendent—expansive beyond what they are in any given moment—and self-possessing—capable of knowing and loving themselves not in spite of knowing and loving others, but through it and in it.

But also like autonomy, relationality has its theoretical and practical limitations. Feminists tend to be aware, for example, of the destructiveness of an emphasis on relationship that fails to respect autonomy. They are more critical of situatedness in communities and traditions than are many recent communitarian philosophers.[26] Women's experiences of submersion in roles, the tyranny of traditions, and the potential oppressiveness of communities warn them of the need for moral limits to community.

Feminist moral theory, then, needs both autonomy and relationality. Against "modernist" rationalism, it can show that autonomy is ultimately for the sake of relationship; against conservative forms of communitarianism, it can argue that relationships without respect for individuality and autonomy are destructive of persons—and, historically, especially destructive of women; against postmodernist diffusion of the self as subject into a network of systems and the womb of language, it can maintain that enduring relationships make an autonomous self ultimately possible.

The meaning of both autonomy and relationality will be importantly influenced by history and by culture. Feminist theory offers neither a "view from nowhere" (unsituated and therefore universally entirely true) nor a "view from everywhere" (protean and uncommitted, dancing from one conversation to another).[27] Yet feminist notions of autonomy and relationality suggest necessary directions for a common human morality.

Beyond Care-versus-Justice

Closely aligned with considerations of relationality and autonomy is another set of questions generated by the present emphasis on "caring" in feminist moral theory. I have already signalled some difficulties with the current formulations of an ethic of care, but it bears further probing. The issues it raises are in a way critical for a feminist theory of universal morality.

On the basis of empirical studies, Carol Gilligan has argued that there are two very different moral systems, two independent approaches to moral questions, that cannot be combined.[28] They are gender-specific in that men largely prefer a "justice" ethic, while women most often prefer an ethic of "care." In contrast to an ethic of justice—which Gilligan characterizes as concerned for individual freedom, social contracts, a ranked order of values, fairness, and an emphasis on duty—an ethic of care in Gilligan's sense focuses on relationships between persons, cooperation, communication, and caring. Justice, in this view, is the value that reinforces individuation and separation of persons, and care is the value that represents connectedness.

On the face of it, Gilligan's ethic of care responds to many feminist concerns. It takes seriously the experience of women, and it gives credibility to considerations of affectivity. It balances individualistic tendencies in Western society with an equal appreciation of relationship. Despite its popularity among feminists, however, it has provoked some serious feminist disagreement. Critics have raised at least two questions about its descriptive and interpretive adequacy. They ask if, insofar as there are these different approaches to moral questions, they are gender-identified, and if "justice" and "care" accurately describe the kind of moral reasoning that most people engage in. Responses to the first concern have been more numerous, and many of them cast serious doubt on the validity of Gilligan's conclusions.[29] I am, however, more interested in the second problem, since it anticipates the first and addresses directly the question of the possibility of a universal morality.

To some extent the participants in Gilligan's and related studies do offer identifiably different sorts of answers to questions about moral situations. They give different reasons for sometimes different solutions to the problems presented. It is not so clear, however, that the reasons differ precisely because some are appeals to justice and others to care. Nor is it at all clear, as Gilligan implies, that some appeal to principles and others to relationships. It is possible, for example, to interpret references to what is "fair" as a way of being faithful to a relation, and to regard references to worries about preserving a relationship as worries about being accepted, judged fairly, and so on. It is certainly the case that nonviolence—the most mature consideration in moral choices according to Gilligan's ethic of care—is as much a *principle* as fairness is. There is, in other words, a lack of conceptual clarity in Gilligan's findings.

The major question to be pursued, however, is how do persons reflect on moral questions and make moral choices—and, beyond that, how they ought to. The more persuasive feminist response to this question would be one that did not insist on the *inevitability* of a dichotomy between reason and emotion, justice and care, principles and persons. My own conviction is that all human choices are choices of both reasons and emotions, and that we evaluate both our reasons and our emotions according to some norms.[30] Whenever we are confronted with alternative actions we consider the alternatives only if we have some desire to do them, whether out of care or a sense of duty, fear, or some other already-present emotion; the desires—the leaning toward pleasure or duty or fear or care or whatever—arise from some more fundamental affective response (call it fundamental care, or love, or affective affirmation), some fundamental relationship with ourselves or with someone or something else.

But affectivity, emotions of whatever kind, are not, when they are *chosen*, morally neutral. That is, not even caring is necessarily morally good. There are forms of care that have destroyed individuals and groups. There are forms of relationship, based on whatever reasons and emotions, that are harmful to persons. The problem for our moral lives and our moral theories is how to evaluate our care, our love, our relationships: according to what norms is care helpful and not harmful? The problem, one might say, is whether and how caring may be just.

This question, however, poses another hurdle in the formulation of a common morality. What can count as "justice"? Surely not only fairness, surely not only fidelity to a social contract. In its most general and classical sense, justice means giving to each her or his "due." Broadly speaking, this would seem to require that justice take account of the concrete reality of the one to whom it is due, whether what is relevant in this concrete reality is a contract or a basic human need or the history of a shared commitment or all of the above and more. But theories of common morality have dwindled precisely because we despair of knowing the concrete reality of anything.

There is a sense, however, in which feminist theory almost always incorporates some "realism" in its moral epistemology. The assumption is that real persons and real things not only exist apart from the perceptions of human ideas of them, they also require respect and set a kind of limit to the meaning that can be imposed on them. Feminist skepticism regarding knowledge of concrete reality is not total, nor does acknowledgement of the social construction of reality rule out efforts at discovery of aspects of reality that are in some sense "already there." This is not surprising in a theory generated by a movement whose goal is, at least in part, that women's concrete reality be attended to. Perhaps in spite of some philosophical commitments, feminists persist therefore in trying to understand better the society in which they live, the experience that is theirs, the people with and for whom they struggle. The kind of realisms they oppose are those that reify ideas or that presume total explanations, that require no mutual search and admit no particular relative perspectives. But otherwise feminism asks for attention to reality—for the unmasking of hidden powers, the making visible of what has been ignored, the acting on at least what is less false in human interpretation.[31] For most feminists "reality" is not infinitely malleable, not neutrally open to an infinite number of interpretations at any given point in time. Even deconstruction is used for the sake of better understanding, and it can serve a wiser care. Gender analysis itself is necessary if the concrete reality of persons is not to be falsified or unjustly distorted. Like the human body, the meaning of almost everything is socially constructed, but there are limits beyond which some constructions will end in destruction.

To attend to reality and to care for it justly may seem too general a requirement to satisfy our need for a common morality. Yet if this obligates us to respect autonomy and relationality, particularity and shared needs, embodiment and human hope, we shall have more morality in common than we have perhaps ever had. The very task of specifying our obligations, and the form of its process, will be part of our just care.

NOTES

1. The feminists to whom I am referring generally in this essay are primarily North American and Western European. Yet more and more feminist theory is being shaped by international and cross-cultural feminist voices. The importance of these voices for the kinds of questions this essay addresses is immense—something that will, I trust, be evident as my discussion unfolds.

2. Alison M. Jaggar, *Feminist Politics and Human Nature* (Totowa, N.J.: Rowman & Allanheld, 1983). There are numerous other typologies for feminist theory, but Jaggar's seems particularly relevant to the questions of a common morality. I am using her categories heuristically, however, so that the features of each as I identify them sometimes go beyond (and sometimes fall short of) the descriptions Jaggar offers. See alternative typologies in Josephine Donovan, *Feminist Theory: The Intellectual Traditions of American Feminism* (New York: Frederick Ungar, 1985); Elisabeth Schüssler Fiorenza, *In Memory of Her: A Fem-*

inist Reconstruction of Christian Origins (New York: Crossroad, 1983), pp. 7–36; Beverly Wildung Harrison, *Our Right to Choose: Toward a New Ethic of Abortion*, chap. 3 (Boston: Beacon Press, 1983); Carol S. Robb, "A Framework for Feminist Ethics," *Journal of Religious Ethics* 9 (1981): 48–68; Rosemary Radford Ruether, *Sexism and God-Talk* (Boston: Beacon Press, 1983), pp. 214–34; Linda Alcoff, "Cultural Feminism versus Post-Structuralism: The Identity Crisis in Feminist Theory," in *Feminist Theory in Practice and Process*, ed. Micheline R. Malson et al. (Chicago: University of Chicago Press, 1989), pp. 295–326.

3. Individual feminists cannot easily be assigned to these categories because feminist theories are continually developing and because the categories indicate elements of theories (methods, sources, particular concepts) that turn out to be separable from a theory as a whole—elements that then are able to appear in more than one category of theory. Jaggar herself (whether intentionally or not) sometimes assigns an individual feminist to more than one category, as, for example, when she instances Christine Delphy for traditional Marxism, radical feminism, and socialist feminism. This is why it is difficult to provide a list of feminist thinkers who would now willingly wear the label "liberal." An early and utterly clear representative of Enlightenment liberal feminism is, of course, Mary Wollstonecraft's *A Vindication of the Rights of Women* (rpt., Baltimore: Penguin, 1975). Others who are often remembered as launching historically significant liberal feminist appeals include Elizabeth Cady Stanton, Sarah Grimké, Susan B. Anthony, Sojourner Truth, and Harriet Taylor. Currently it may be more helpful to indicate some of the important feminist explorations of liberal theory (which have varying degrees of sympathy for a liberal feminist point of view, and some of which embody serious criticisms of traditional liberalism). These include: Jean Grimshaw, *Philosophy and Feminist Thinking* (Minneapolis: University of Minnesota Press, 1986); Zillah Eisenstein, *The Radical Future of Liberal Feminism* (New York: Longman, 1981); Lenore Coltheart, "Desire, Consent, and Liberal Theory," in *Feminist Challenges: Social and Political Theory*, ed. Carole Pateman and Elizabeth Gross (Boston: Northeastern University Press, 1986), pp. 112–22; Christine Di Stefano, "Liberalism and Its Feminist Critics," *American Philosophical Association Newsletter* 88 (June 1989): 35–38; Genevieve Lloyd, *The Man of Reason: "Male" and "Female" in Western Philosophy* (Minneapolis: University of Minnesota Press, 1984); Susan Moller Okin, *Women in Western Political Thought* (Princeton, N.J.: Princeton University Press, 1979); Iris Marion Young, "Impartiality and the Civic Public: Some Implications of Feminist Critiques of Moral and Political Theory," in *Feminism as Critique: On the Politics of Gender*, ed. Seyla Benhabib & Drucilla Cornell (Minneapolis: University of Minnesota Press, 1987); Jean Bethke Elshtain, *Public Man, Private Woman: Women in Social and Political Thought* (Princeton, N.J.: Princeton University Press, 1981).

4. Among the more obvious current representatives of this tradition are John Rawls, *A Theory of Justice* (Cambridge: Harvard University Press, 1971); Alan Donagan, *The Theory of Morality* (Chicago: University of Chicago Press, 1977); Ronald Dworkin, *Taking Rights Seriously* (Cambridge: Harvard University Press, 1977); Alan Gewirth, *Reason and Morality* (Chicago: University of Chicago Press, 1978).

5. Among feminists who have explored the possibilities and limits of a Marxist feminism are Michele Barrett, *Women's Oppression Today* (London: Verso, 1980); Jane Flax, "Do Feminists Need Marxism?" in *Building Feminist Theory*, ed. *The Quest* staff (New York: Longman, 1981); Lydia Sargent, ed., *Women and Revolution: A Discussion of the Unhappy Marriage of Marxism and Feminism* (Boston: South End Press, 1981); Angela Davis, *Women, Race, and Class* (New York: Random House, 1981); Linda Nicholson, "Feminism and Marx: Integrating Kinship with the Economic," in Benhabib and Cornell, *Feminism as Critique*, pp. 16–30.

6. In addition to Marx's own writings (especially his early writings), feminists have tended to take most seriously such Marxist interpreters as Georg Lukács, *History and Class Consciousness: Studies in Marxist Dialectics*, trans. Rodney Livingstone (Cambridge, Mass.: MIT Press, 1971); Karl Kautsky, *Ethics and the Materialist Conception of History*, trans. J. B. Asken (Chicago: University of Chicago Press, 1907).

7. Radical feminism is the broadest of Jaggar's four categories. There is, as she acknowledges, no single radical feminist analysis. Jaggar even wonders whether in a short time the category may have to be elided with socialist feminism. But whatever the evolution of theory in this regard, it is still helpful to talk about radical forms of feminism with some historical status. For my present purposes, this category stretches to include elements of the work of such diverse feminists as Shulamith Firestone, Ti-Grace Atkinson, Charlotte Bunch, Kate Millett, Adrienne Rich, Mary Daly, Susan Griffin, Catherine MacKinnon, Carol Gilligan, and Luce Irigaray. My characterization of the category should make it clear which elements I am identifying. As for the individual thinkers (as we shall see), there are other elements in their works—sometimes because their work has developed and changed—that make them representatives of socialist feminism as well. For a fuller perspective on radical feminism with important added assumptions and configurations, see Bell Hooks, *Feminist Theory: From Margin to Center* (Boston: South End Press, 1984), especially chaps. 1–4, 11–12.

8. A good deal of the growing movement in feminist spirituality illustrates this. See, for example, Starhawk, *The Spiral Dance: A Rebirth of the Religion of the Great Goddess* (San Francisco: Harper & Row, 1979), and *Dreaming the Dark* (Boston: Beacon Press, 1982); Margot Adler, *Drawing Down the Moon*, rev. ed. (Boston: Beacon Press, 1986).

9. See, for example, Mary Daly, *Gyn-Ecology: The Metaethics of Radical Feminism* (Boston: Beacon Press, 1978); Carol Gilligan, *In a Different Voice: Psychological Theory and Women's Development* (Cambridge: Harvard University Press, 1982); Carol Gilligan, Janie Victoria Ward, and Jill McLean Taylor, eds., *Mapping the Moral Domain: A Contribution of Women's Thinking to Psychological Theory and Education* (Cambridge, Mass.: Center for the Study of Gender, Education, and Human Development, 1988); Luce Irigaray, *Speculum of the Other Woman*, trans. Gillian C. Gill (Ithaca, N.Y.: Cornell University Press, 1985); Hélène Cixous and Catherine Clément, *The Newly Born Woman*, trans. Betsy Wing (Minneapolis: University of Minnesota Press, 1986); Sara Ruddick, *Maternal Thinking: Toward a Politics of Peace* (Boston: Beacon Press, 1989). Not everyone would consider all of these writings to be representatives of radical

feminism, but they are all concerned with what they identify as aspects of women's experience, nature, and ways of knowing that are particular to women (different, therefore, from those of men).

10. At the time of writing her book on *Feminist Politics and Human Nature*, Jaggar indicated that socialist feminism was perhaps the "most questionable" of her four paradigms, since it seemed a small modification of either Marxist feminism or radical feminism. She included in it feminist thinkers whose systematic work on gender or class contributed to the kind of analysis described here. Hence this category included Juliet Mitchell (who also qualifies as a traditional Marxist feminist), Nancy Chodorow (who can also be considered a radical feminist), Sandra Harding, Ann Ferguson, and Jaggar herself. Exploration of and from this perspective can be found in Iris Young, "Beyond the Unhappy Marriage: A Critique of the Dual Systems Theory," in *Women and Revolution*, ed. Lydia Sargent (Boston: South End Press, 1981); Zillah Eisenstein, "Some Notes on the Relations of Capitalist Patriarchy," in *Capitalist Patriarchy and the Case for Socialist Feminism*, ed. Zillah Eisenstein (New York: Monthly Review Press, 1979); Christine Delphy, *Close to Home: A Materialist Analysis of Women's Oppression*, trans. Diana Leonard (Amherst: University of Massachusetts Press, 1984); Hooks, *Feminist Theory*.

11. Jaggar does not follow these developments very far in *Feminist Politics and Human Nature*, though she does signal them from the beginning (see p. 12). In a later work it is clear that the developments have progressed very far indeed; see Alison M. Jaggar and Susan R. Bordo, eds., *Gender/Body/Knowledge: Feminist Reconstructions of Being and Knowing* (New Brunswick, N.J.: Rutgers University Press, 1989).

12. Elizabeth V. Spelman, *Inessential Woman: Problems of Exclusion in Feminist Thought* (Boston: Beacon Press, 1988), 79. For similar formulations of the problem of the interconnectedness of identity factors and the necessity of seeing their interconnections for understanding human oppression, see the groundbreaking study of Okin, *Women in Western Political Thought*; Hooks, *Feminist Theory*, chap. 1; Hester Eisenstein and Alice Jardine, eds., *The Future of Difference* (New Brunswick, N.J.: Rutgers University Press, 1985); Delphy, *Close to Home*, especially chap. 2; Elizabeth Meese and Alice Parker, eds., *The Difference Within: Feminism and Critical Theory* (Philadelphia: John Benjamins, 1989); Pateman and Gross, *Feminist Challenges*.

13. Helpful insights into postmodernist philosophy and its uses in feminist theory can be found in: Linda J. Nicholson, ed., *Feminism/Postmodernism* (New York and London: Routledge, 1990); Barbara Johnson, *A World of Difference* (Baltimore: The Johns Hopkins University Press, 1987); Benhabib and Cornell, *Feminism As Critique*; Ann Garry and Marilyn Pearsall, eds., *Women, Knowledge, and Reality: Explorations in Feminist Philosophy* (Boston: Unwin Hyman, 1989); Joan W. Scott, "Deconstructing Equality-versus-Difference: Or, the Uses of Poststructuralist Theory for Feminism," *Feminist Studies* 14 (Spring 1988): 33–50; Evelyn Keller, *Reflections on Gender and Science* (New Haven, Conn.: Yale University Press, 1985); Jane Flax, *Thinking Fragments: Psychoanalysis, Feminism, and Postmodernism in the Contemporary West* (Berkeley and Los Angeles: University of California Press, 1990).

14. Sandra Harding, "Introduction: Is There a Feminist Method?" in Sandra Harding, ed., *Feminism and Methodology: Social Science Issues* (Bloomington: Indiana University Press, 1987), p. 156.

15. Mircea Eliade, *Cosmos and History: The Myth of the Eternal Return* (Princeton, N.J.: Princeton University Press, 1954), pp. 151–52.

16. Donovan, *Feminist Theory*, pp. 172–73. See also Emily Martin, *The Woman in the Body: A Cultural Analysis of Reproduction* (Boston: Beacon Press, 1987), pp. 4, 201.

17. Katie G. Cannon, foreword to *With Passion and Compassion: Third World Women Doing Theology*, ed. Virginia Fabella and Mercy Amba Oduyoye (Maryknoll, N.Y.: Orbis Books, 1988), p. vii.

18. See the analysis of women's role in Salvadoran society presented in *A Dream Compels Us: Voices of Salvadoran Women*, ed. New Americas Press (Boston: South End Press, 1989).

19. See, for example, Hooks, *Feminist Theory*, chap. 4.

20. Gilligan, *In a Different Voice*. This is not to question the usefulness and importance of Gilligan's findings in respects other than universal relevance. It must also be noted that Gilligan qualifies her conclusions in this study and succeeding ones, emphasizing that the justice and care perspectives are precisely that—perspectives, and they can be part of women's or men's approach to morality. Nonetheless, her work has been interpreted by many others to show a fundamental (however socially constructed) divergence in women's and men's moral sensibilities. This emphasis is clear in, for example, Nel Noddings, *Caring* (Berkeley and Los Angeles: University of California Press, 1984). Sara Ruddick's theory of "maternal thinking" allows more explicit room for men's access to understanding and acting from this moral perspective; see Ruddick, *Maternal Thinking*, pp. 44–45.

21. For a treatment of analogy as model of relationship and basis of moral epistemology, see Caroline Whitbeck, "A Different Reality: Feminist Ontology," in *Beyond Domination: New Perspectives on Women and Philosophy*, ed. Carol Gould (Totowa, N.J.: Rowman & Allanheld, 1984), pp. 64–88. For examples of straightforward ethical analysis from a feminist perspective but obviously offered for general understanding, see Harrison, *Our Right to Choose*; Barrett, *Women's Oppression Today*; Sharon D. Welch, *A Feminist Ethic of Risk* (Minneapolis: Fortress Press, 1990).

22. See Adrienne Rich, "Women and Honor: Some Notes on Lying," in *On Lies, Secrets, and Silence: Selected Prose, 1966–78* (New York: Norton, 1979), pp. 185–94.

23. One of the most interesting issues in this regard is prostitution. Feminists have been outraged by the growth of sex industries, especially in, for example, southeast Asian countries. It seems impossible from a feminist point of view not to condemn the blatant exploitation of women whose economic dependency (and often the economic dependency of their countries) makes them vulnerable, and whose experience is of relentless terror. On the other hand, the voices of women prostitutes in very different circumstances are beginning to be heard, and the last word does not yet seem to be in. See, for example, Gail Pheterson, ed., *A Vindication of the Rights of Whores* (Seattle: The Seal Press, 1989). On other issues, see

Jean Bethke Elshtain, "The New Eugenics and Feminist Quandaries," *Lutheran Forum* 23 (1989): 20–29; Celeste Michelle Condit, *Decoding Abortion Rhetoric: Communicating Social Change* (Urbana: University of Illinois Press, 1990); Linda Gordon, "Feminism and Social Control: The Case of Child Abuse and Neglect," in *What Is Feminism: A Re-examination*, ed. Juliet Mitchell and Ann Oakley (New York: Pantheon, 1986), pp. 63–84. Other studies of interest to feminist analysis include: Charles Bernheimer, *Figures of Ill Repute: Representing Prostitution in Nineteenth-Century France* (Cambridge: Harvard University Press, 1989); Alain Corbin, *Women for Hire: Prostitution and Sexuality in France after 1850*, trans. Alan Sheridan (Cambridge: Harvard University Press, 1990); John Boswell, *The Kindness of Strangers: The Abandonment of Children in Western Europe from Late Antiquity to the Renaissance* (New York: Pantheon, 1988); Daphne Read, "(De)Constructing Pornography: Feminisms in Conflict," in *Passion & Power: Sexuality in History*, ed. Kathy Peiss and Christina Simmons (Philadelphia: Temple University Press, 1989), pp. 277–92.

24. A recent survey of court decisions in the United States has turned up a revealing pattern of gender differentiation in acceptance of patient wishes regarding refusal of medical treatment. See Steven H. Miles and Allison August, "Courts, Gender and 'The Right to Die,'" *Law, Medicine & Health Care* 18 (Spring–Summer 1990): 85–95.

25. The tension that some feminists experience, however, in seeming to judge a culture other than their own can be seen in the study of the practice of clitoridectomy among African women. See Hanny Lightfoot-Klein, *Prisoners of Ritual: An Odyssey into Female Genital Circumcision in Africa* (Binghamton, N.Y.: Haworth Press, 1989).

26. For an overview of feminist theory insofar as it converges and diverges with communitarian thought, see Benhabib and Cornell, *Feminism as Critique*, pp. 12–13.

27. For a succinct critique of deconstructionism and the "view from everywhere," see Susan Bordo, "The View from Nowhere and the Dream of Everywhere: Heterogeneity, Adequation and Feminist Theory," *American Philosophical Association Newsletter on Feminism and Philosophy* 88 (March 1989): 19–25.

28. Gilligan, *In a Different Voice*; see also Gilligan, "Moral Orientation and Moral Development," in *Women and Moral Theory*, ed. Eva Feder Kittay and Diana T. Meyers (Totowa, N.J.: Rowman & Littlefield, 1987), pp. 19–33; and Gilligan et al., *Mapping the Moral Domain*.

29. For a summary of empirical studies challenging Gilligan's conclusions, see Martha T. Mednick, "On the Politics of Psychological Constructs: Stop the Bandwagon, I Want to Get Off," *American Psychologist* 44 (August 1989): 1118–23.

30. I only suggest here what obviously needs careful elaboration and justification. A more substantive outline of the theory at the basis of these ideas can be found in my *Personal Commitments: Beginning, Keeping, Changing* (San Francisco: Harper & Row, 1986), especially chaps. 3 and 7.

31. The phrase is Sandra Harding's in "Feminism, Science, and the Anti-Enlightenment Critiques," in Nicholson, *Feminism/Postmodernism*, p. 83.

Chapter 8

FOUNDATIONS WITHOUT FOUNDATIONALISM

John P. Reeder, Jr.

IN THIS ESSAY I assume that there is indeed, as Richard J. Bernstein
has argued, a way beyond the false alternatives of objectivism and
relativism. But I argue that everything depends on what one takes
that to be.[1] I first discuss the historical context and Bernstein's typology,
and then I try to set out a version of that way I call neopragmatism. The
thrust of my view is that the rejection of an "ahistorical" starting point
for justification, understanding, and agreement does not settle the substantive issues at stake in debates about a common or universal morality.
I suggest that the enduring question (one not settled by neopragmatism
itself) is whether there are grounds for morality in notions of humanity as
such. I assume that moral traditions are not necessarily untranslatable
and argue that understanding is possible on the basis of "concrete universals." Finally, I suggest that neopragmatism does not rule out claims regarding a universal morality—a form of Esperanto. Richard Rorty has
argued that Rawlsian liberalism does not require an ahistorical foundation;[2] I conclude by suggesting that a universalistic version of the liberal
tradition can also survive the loss of an ahistorical ground.

THE HISTORICAL CONTEXT

Alasdair MacIntyre has argued that the emotivists (and their continental
philosophical counterparts) thought they were talking about the nature
of moral language and belief *sub specie aeternitatis* but that they were in
fact merely reflecting a social fact of their, and indeed our own, time.[3]
Since moral norms had come loose from their moorings in an Aristo-
telian-Christian worldview, and since the Enlightenment had provided no
effective substitutes—that is, no warrants that could resolve moral debates—people have been molding moral convictions simply on the basis
of arbitrary personal preferences, manifesting their will to power. Thus
the various forms of emotivism are reinterpreted; they should not be seen
as theories of moral discourse and belief but merely as a reflection of the
general absence of workable justifications in a particular historical epoch.

This account seems historically out of kilter. Roughly, here is what I think has happened. Emotivism in various guises is not so much a reflection of a general social fact, but rather perhaps a particular reaction to the failure to find an ahistorical ground. Many of course have not been swayed by the view that moral standpoints are ultimately arbitrary. But others have at least been worried.[4] Faced with the evidence of moral diversity, and concluding that there is no starting point outside of one's contingent historical context, they have leapt quite understandably to the conclusion that all moral standpoints are ultimately unjustified. Thus over and above anxieties about particular moral issues, there has been a malaise in segments of Western culture and among some intellectuals in particular in regard to the "foundations of morals." When pretenders such as Aquinas or Kant are unmasked, some have said, nothing is left but arbitrary will, either in individual or collective forms.[5]

BERNSTEIN'S TYPOLOGY

Some philosophers and theologians have suggested that an ahistorical starting point and arbitrariness are false alternatives and that there is a way forward that escapes them both. Richard Bernstein, for example, has argued that what he calls objectivism and relativism are mistaken epistemological theories, both in regard to scientific and moral knowledge. He argues that a number of philosophers, both Anglo-American and European, have tried to chart a better course, which has affinities with pragmatist traditions. I begin with Bernstein, but develop my own typology of current positions.

What is objectivism, or as others often call it, foundationalism? In Bernstein's words, it is "the basic conviction that there is or must be some permanent, ahistorical matrix or framework to which we can ultimately appeal in determining the nature of rationality, knowledge, truth, reality, goodness, or rightness."[6] In short, moral foundationalism is any view that holds that moral knowledge is rooted in an ahistorical framework that furnishes certain universal, immediately justified (that is, admitting and requiring no additional justification), and immutable beliefs. A modification of the basic paradigm of moral foundationalism would be the view that while moral beliefs themselves are not foundational, the beliefs on which they rest—for example, beliefs about God or human nature—are. Thus either a moral belief(s) is foundational, or some other supporting belief(s) is. By means of such ahistorical, immediately justified, and immutable beliefs, furthermore, people in various cultures can understand each other's specific moral views; one can grasp the structure of the alien culture because there are certain common general beliefs; specific judgments, however, can vary widely due to differences in factual or metaphysical beliefs. But since there are basic moral agreements, people in one culture can persuade those in another whose specific judgments are different, provided both can attain sufficient agreement on factual or metaphysical matters.

What is "relativism"? In Bernstein's words, it is the view that

> the concepts of rationality, truth, reality, right, the good, or norms . . . must be understood as relative to a specific conceptual scheme, theoretical framework, paradigm, form of life, society, or culture. . . . [T]here is no substantive overarching framework or a single metalanguage by which we can rationally adjudicate or univocally evaluate competing claims of alternative paradigms. . . . [T]here can be no rational comparison among the plurality of theories, paradigms, and language games—that we are prisoners locked in our own framework and cannot get out of it.[7]

The crucial theses of this general view applied to moral epistemology are frequently said to be these: since there are no "foundations," the general criteria, the basic values or norms, on which one's entire moral system is based are ultimately arbitrary, whether these be cast as a product of a culture as a whole or as a function of individual will; moral cultures are conceptual schemes whose categories in some basic respects at least cannot be mutually translated or understood; and since moral schemes do not share basic criteria, there is no hope for a "single metalanguage" in terms of which cultures can persuade one another; intractable moral disagreement is to be expected.

What then is the position I shall heuristically label neopragmatism? What follows is a paradigm of some current views (which I will shortly try to amend); it does not reflect any particular author's views but is a compound of several.

Neopragmatism agrees with relativism that there are no ahistorical foundations. Neopragmatism insists, however, that the building blocks of moral systems are not arbitrary. In fact, insists the neopragmatist, the basic error at the heart of relativism is the retention of the deductive model of moral reasoning, which assumes as its foundationalist counterpart did that we reason solely from general principles or criteria to more specific judgments.[8] General principles or criteria on the neopragmatist account do not require any justification independent of their relation to specific judgments. Justification in morality consists of a dialectic between judgments in specific cases and the application of generalizations to new cases in light of which the generalizations themselves are modified. Generalizations are inductions from specific judgments applied analogously to new cases and modified in light of these new experiences.

Such a neopragmatist account does not deny that specific judgments are implicitly generalizable, for to say that a particular act is just, for example, is to say that it satisfies a certain description that could apply to other acts. The point is that convictions about the general description of just acts arise and are justified only in the context of specific judgments. Thus justification consists in a process by which one continually is trying to bring one's general and specific beliefs into a state of harmony or equilibrium.[9] Since justification does not consist in a deductive movement from an ahistorical, immediately justified, and immutable starting point, the loss of faith in such foundations does not require one to believe that the foundations are in fact arbitrary. One must rid oneself, the pragmatists insist, of the very metaphor of foundations itself.[10]

The neopragmatist, moreover, denies that moral systems are conceptual schemes into which we are locked in such a way that attempts at translation and understanding necessarily fail. Given the possibility of the enrichment of our own moral language through the process of learning another scheme as a new language, it is always possible, although often difficult, to achieve understanding.[11] If Foucault, for example, held that "epistemes" are conceptual schemes each of which is at least in part not initially understandable by another, such as "subjugated knowledges" that cannot be understood in the categories of the dominant episteme, then he would have been correct; but he would have been wrong if he claimed that the untranslatability was ultimate.[12]

Thus the neopragmatist does not accept the view that the foundations of morality are ultimately arbitrary or that we live in locked-in conceptual schemes that are at least in part simply not mutually understandable. The neopragmatist is also less pessimistic than the relativist on the possibility of agreement. The relativist sees the inevitability of intractable moral disagreement from the top down due to divergences in basic criteria. But the neopragmatist has discarded the very idea of "basic" criteria on which a moral system "rests." Thus the neopragmatist argues that we can work to try to discover convergences or *overlaps* in our moral, valuational, and factual beliefs—on the basis of which we can perhaps come to moral agreement. The neopragmatist does not deny that mutual understanding is often extraordinarily difficult, for some cultures may represent issues in such a way that we could not be said to be disagreeing about the same topic; nor does the neopragmatist deny that overlaps may in fact not exist. But the neopragmatist insists that once the metaphor of foundational differences is given up, there are ways to understand, and that we may be able to find overlaps that could lead to agreement. The neopragmatist will claim nonetheless (along with the relativist) that we should not hope for a moral Esperanto, a moral vocabulary that will replace our diverse and particular moralities; we should hope for partial agreements but probably not for widely shared justifications.

The neopragmatist has tried therefore to steer a course between the two false alternatives. Rejecting the metaphor of foundations common to both, the neopragmatist sees the possibility of complex intersections between webs of belief.[13]

JUSTIFICATION AND THE DEDUCTIVE MODEL

I now take up each of the three parts of the neopragmatist position and modify it in light of my own views. In this section on justification I deal with the relation between general and specific moral beliefs; in the section on understanding I take up the distinction between abstract similarities and concrete cultural and social locations; and in the final section on agreement I discuss universal in contrast to local moralities. First, the attack against the deductive model of justification.

On the neopragmatist paradigm as I have sketched it, moral reasoning begins with specific judgments; general principles are generalizations that are then applied analogously to new cases and modified accordingly. I believe that in many if not all moralities one finds a process of justification that is "dialectical" in the sense that the meaning of general principles or virtues is developed and modified in light of specific judgments. What I want to challenge is the notion that general categories arise only as generalizations and hence are justified only through the process of dialectical extension and modification. In my view, general criteria or standards such as "respect persons" or "seek human good" have a justification in some moral systems that is independent of the dialectical relation of the principles and virtues that express them (such as Rawls's principles of justice or a particular conception of the general virtues comprising the human good), and specific judgments about conduct and character. This is not to say that the criteria or standards are necessarily said to have the foundationalist status of ahistorical, immediately justified, and immutable first principles; nor is it to say that other beliefs that might be said to constitute their justification are necessarily given foundationalist status. The point is simply that in some cultural systems an attempt is made to anchor or ground a fundamental moral perspective independent of its relation to more determinate convictions.

For example, in the ethics of James Gustafson the fundamental perspective is established by reasoning from a set of metaphysical, valuational, and moral beliefs. He asserts that there is an ultimate force that has such and such a nature, its purposes are good, and one owes it a debt of gratitude; these beliefs combine to justify a basic moral stance: adhere to God's purpose (the well-being of the cosmos as a whole).[14] He makes no attempt to deny that some values and moral insights are present prior to the construction of the fundamental perspective, for clearly the purposes of God are judged good in light of the believer's values, and gratitude as a moral category is simply assumed. But God's purposes play a fundamental or foundational role in the believer's moral reasoning; this perspective is established or justified independent of its subsequent relation to determinate norms and judgments, which, as I read Gustafson, and as I think is the case elsewhere, are developed through dialectical application in a moral tradition and community. Gustafson's notion of what is good for human persons, other animals, and nature as a whole is developed in light of a host of beliefs; one might compare this to Rawls's derivation of principles of justice that express the moral equality of the veil of ignorance but require other beliefs to achieve their determinate form. The "obligations" that protect and promote such goods are applied in specific judgments and extended analogously to new cases, similar to Rawls's attempt to achieve reflective equilibrium between the principles and "considered moral judgments." But the fundamental perspective is *controlling* in the sense that notions of goods and obligations must be in accord with it. One can never consider only *human* good. A notion of distributive justice, for instance, should not be limited to the allocation of benefits and burdens among humans alone. The floor or fundamental perspective works as a constraint that informs but does not entirely determine the content of general virtues and principles. The latter are constructed by means of other beliefs in a dialectical process of application and reapplication.

A critic might reply to my suggestion as follows: you admit that Gustafson justifies in part his so-called foundational perspective by appealing to a specific moral judgment about a debt of gratitude; doesn't this show that Gustafson justifies general moral beliefs by bringing them into harmony with specific moral convictions (and other nonmoral beliefs, such as God's existence and nature)? My reply is that Gustafson does not begin by working toward a state of adjustment between general moral notions such as justice and specific convictions; rather he first establishes the moral floor on the basis of which he in turn works out dialectically a reflective harmony between general notions of goods, virtues, and obligations, and specific applications thereof. Thus gratitude helps establish the *floor*. The floor is established holistically—in virtue of several supporting grounds—but not by means of a dialectical adjustment between general and specific convictions.[15]

I have not argued that such a picture of moral reasoning exists in every morality, only that nothing in the neopragmatist attack on foundationalism rules out such a procedure. And I am not claiming that to be justified a moral belief *must* be legitimated in terms of a foundational moral perspective that itself is justified independently of the dialectical relation between determinate principles and judgments. My point is only that in some systems a moral floor is independently established that informs but does not entirely determine the dialectical relations of more determinate norms and judgments.

The Gustafson example also argues that neopragmatism should not rule out efforts to ground or anchor a fundamental moral perspective by reference to "reality" or the "nature of things." Moral criteria, it could be granted, are fully shaped only as they are developed and applied in light of other beliefs, but a general criterion or standard, such as respect for persons, could arguably be justified independently and directly on the basis of well-entrenched beliefs about the nature of things.

Some neopragmatists may not oppose appeals to a transcendent reality or human nature in relation to such a reality as part of a "thick" view of the human condition; they oppose the notion of human nature as such, the idea of features of human nature that appear across, and can be recognized within, various cultures.[16] Richard Rorty, for example, links appeals to human nature as such with the foundationalist attempt to find a permanent, ahistorical ground: "Contemporary intellectuals have given up the Enlightenment assumption that religion, myth, and tradition can be opposed to something ahistorical, something common to all human beings qua human." The Enlightenment attempt to find a view of a common human nature as such, independent of religious convictions, amounts to an effort to locate "an ahistorical natural center, the locus of human dignity, surrounded by an adventitious and inessential periphery."[17] To appeal to a "transcultural" human nature is to look for an "ahistorical self." Rorty's objection, therefore, may identify any justificatory appeal to human nature or, more broadly, to the nature of persons as such with the attempt to locate an ahistorical self and framework of moral knowledge.

One could read Rorty, however, as following Rawls—that one can bracket notions of the self for the purpose of liberal democratic beliefs into equilibrium: one can appeal to common sense and social science, and even to a common capacity to suffer, but he rejects any justificatory appeal to the nature of persons that specifies, for example, "the universal features of human psychology relevant to motivation."[18] Still, if I understand him, Rorty seems also to mount the broader argument against appeals to humanity as such.

Yet, it may be that all Rorty wants to oppose is the idea of an *ahistorical* essence or framework, that is, one that exists independently of any cultural construction. If the ahistorical framework is his only target, then it is hard to see, however, as Thomas McCarthy argues, why he would object to finding common features of human nature so long as these are constructed and recognized within "contingent" webs of concepts and beliefs.[19] In any case, it is not necessary to claim one has discovered a "transcendental subject" merely to assert that what Joel Feinberg, for example, calls "descriptive" or "commonsense personhood" is a well-justified view of the *nature* of persons, and one that could have appeal across a variety of cultures.[20] Without necessarily supposing that this conception somehow directly requires moral duties or rights, it can function (as it does for Feinberg and others) as an indispensable premise in an argument to the effect that only a person (which is not the same as merely being a member of homo sapiens) has full moral status.

To take another example, one closer to the notion of a self whose nature directly grounds basic moral requirements, Alan Gewirth's view that all human agents share valuational assumptions and a canon of reasoning need not be interpreted as an attempt to find a standpoint that escapes historical context; it can be read as an effort to uncover basic beliefs that on reflection at least human beings in cultures generally can acknowledge from the perspective of their own webs of belief.[21] In other words, Gewirth would be making a very strong and controversial claim about the content of cultures, and, of course, he proposes a specific justificatory argument as well (that the valuational assumptions and consistency yield basic rights). But he would not have argued for an ahistorical framework; he would have argued only for some strong commonalities *within* human history.[22]

My thesis, then, is that neopragmatism qua epistemology does not rule out an appeal to the nature of persons that is or can be shared across cultures. The substantive issue is whether we believe there are general features of persons that persons generally can acknowledge and that are relevant to the justification of moral belief.

When David Wong, for example, argues against conceptions of a single true morality, he is arguing that human nature does not have general features such that our beliefs about it decisively shape our conceptions of the good or the right.[23] For example, he criticizes MacIntyre's attempt to argue from what we are to what is good for us. MacIntyre as a thinker in the Aristotelian tradition argues that our good lies fundamentally in a commonly valued *relation* that is not privately possessed.[24] As the alternative to Nietzsche, MacIntyre wants to retrieve from the Aristotelian tradition not its metaphysical biology but its assumption that one can argue from what we are to what our good is. We are sufficiently like other living things or artifacts that the functional sense of good or excellence is appropriate. Our good, at least our fundamental good, is intersubjective.[25]

Wong's basic argument against a move such as MacIntyre's is that human nature is not sufficiently determinate for the argument to work. The critic can grant that our sociality requires that we have some form of morality and even that recognizably similar rules and virtues arise in various traditions. The critic can even grant that human nature is not so elastic, shall we say, that judgments about the good and the right are not subject to any constraints at all. A critic such as Wong can freely admit that there are minimal parameters of physiological and psychological health that rest on the evolved constitution of human nature. The critic denies that human nature is sufficiently determinate to retrieve the ancient dream of arguing from what we are to a vision of the "good for man," a thick or full theory of the good: "insofar as there is such a thing as a fixed human nature, remaining invariant from social environment to social environment, it is not sufficiently determinate to justify the claim that there is a determinate good for man, a complex of activities arranged in an ideal balance, which any rational and informed person would find the most rewarding."[26]

Other questions about justification also take us deep into the territory of debates about basic parts of the human psyche, such as reason, desire, emotion. Many contemporary thinkers have offered a critique of the picture of reason as entirely distinct from desire or emotion. This picture, which dates at least to the dispute between Enlightenment thinkers as to whether morality is a matter of "reason" or of "sentiment," and which is linked to a patriarchal division of gender traits, posits a distinction between rational grounds for belief and the supposedly arbitrary vagaries of feeling and desire. The critique of a reason-emotion dichotomy has led some contemporary feminists and others to propose a view that puts sympathy and benevolence at the center of morality, buttressed with assumptions about the good and various requirements of reason.

While feminist thinkers, for example, would be the last to assert they have discovered an ahistorical essence, many do argue against one cultural construction of the self in favor of another; their moral protest is anchored in a revised view of our limitations and possibilities. Many seek to uncover moral possibilities open to both sexes: both have as much capacity for compassion as for the autonomous choice of life-plans or for various forms of reasoning. Out of perceived dissatisfaction with inherited moral traditions, many feminists explore other possible forms of human interaction and make normative proposals against the backdrop of these options. They purport neither to have formulated an entirely nonmoral conception of the person nor to have simply proposed an alternative moral ideal ("autonomy" supplanted, or at least balanced against, "relation"). They make substantive proposals against the background of a revised view of moral capacities and limitations: we *can* be certain sorts of persons if we want to be.[27]

I have argued, then, for a more expansive view of justification that allows general criteria or standards to have their own backing and that recognizes the legitimate role of theological or nontheological assumptions about human nature. Substantive questions about justification, I have suggested, have to do with which of these assumptions are true.

UNDERSTANDING

If neopragmatism should not in principle rule out justificatory appeals to general features of human nature or persons, how is it possible that such appeals could be made across cultures? Are the images of the person in various cultures not only diverse but, in some cases at least, untranslatable, incapable even of being understood in the categories of the Other?

As an antifoundationalist, of course, the neopragmatist embraces the thesis that justification is relative to cultural context. The neopragmatist thus rejects any notion of abstract moral concepts independent of concrete social locations and traditions. Moral concepts are always part of historical traditions; they cannot be abstracted or removed from ways of life. But one sense of relativism that neopragmatists seem most urgently to want to defeat is the notion that we are locked into conceptual schemes between which there is no possibility of translation or understanding. The neopragmatist spurns not only the epistemologically spurious model of an uninterpreted reality or framework to which we have unmediated access, but the notion that reality is available to us only in ultimately untranslatable conceptual schemes.[28]

Even MacIntyre, for example, agrees that understanding is possible, although extreme steps could be necessary to overcome gaps in communication. Moral "languages" or traditions can be untranslatable in the sense that they have conceptual resources not present in other cultures, but MacIntyre does not hold that translation is ultimately impossible. The claim that moral concepts and standards are tradition-specific does not entail that we can never bridge traditions. By learning a "second first language" and by doubling back to enrich one's own tradition, one can connect the two.[29] Even when learning the new vocabulary, however, some might argue one still uses one's own concepts to grasp the new. For example, even if I had no vocabulary for egalitarian justice, I would still have to use my notion of what is equal or identical to grasp the new terminology of social equality in the second first language.[30]

MacIntyre's model in any case seems to fit some cultural confrontations. In other instances of cultural interaction, I would also argue for the possibility of understanding based on what Carol Gould calls "concrete universality." For example, if sympathy and benevolence were widespread or potentially widespread human phenomena, they would not of course appear in some abstract or ahistorical form; they would appear clothed in the conceptual garments of particular cultures. In this sense they would appear as concrete universals. Thus understanding and translation would take place on the basis of culturally concrete construals of sympathy and benevolence. Understanding and translation would proceed on the basis of analogical comparison and contrast: my concept of "love" is like and unlike your concept of "*karuna.*"

I am suggesting, then, that if concrete universals are culturally available, we may well be able to extrapolate analogically over a range of moral experiences. The notion of concrete universals seems to catch the phenomenon of structurally similar experiences constructed in different cultural idioms. The experiences never appear abstractly, but are always shaped in concrete cultural forms. As Gould argues, the universal is the union of common and differentiating features. Differences are as essential as similarities: "the universal cannot be abstracted or conceived apart from these differences, but exists only in and through them."[31] Since such universals would be concrete, one can be open to learning from others; no one tradition *possesses* the universal.

Debaters arguing whether something is a concrete universal will ask, does a sufficient degree of likeness exist, or is the similarity merely formal? Are there general features of human nature as such that can be recognized cross-culturally, features such as actual or potential capacities for compassion and benevolence, for various forms of reasoning (instrumental calculations, reciprocal exchanges, judgments of consistency, and so on), and for forming views of the good and for having certain basic values?

But even if we are able to learn second first languages and to use concrete universals as bridges to understanding, are there still, practically speaking, almost insuperable gaps in perspective between those concretely affected by actual situations of oppression and their oppressors, or those simply removed by distance or social location? It has been argued that only the oppressed are able to reflect adequately about their situation. If theory is helpful, it emerges from the oppressed.

It does make sense to suggest that those who are oppressed may have insights that others lack. We should *first* let the oppressed speak for themselves, as Sharon Welch argues, and learn from what they have to teach us—as white males have had to learn from women and people of color. In this sense a commitment to the oppressed requires a commitment to the "perspective of the oppressed."[32]

But closeness also sometimes produces distortion. For example, suppose it was argued that the only way the oppressed could gain self-identity and self-respect was to engage in violence.[33] Would we accept this view, privilege it in the strong sense simply because the author is a member of an oppressed group? If we have reason to think that others see a moral situation differently than we do, what they *ought* to do (in Gilbert

Harman's "inner judgment" sense) is a function of *their* own beliefs.[34] We can say, however, what they ought to do *if* they held our moral beliefs, and we can say they should hold them if we think that some of their beliefs are mistaken. While we must attempt first to learn from the oppressed—in this sense to privilege their view—it seems inescapable that in the end we must judge for ourselves, whatever our social location.

Furthermore, the oppressed who shape a new moral vision may not always recognize what they share with the "dominant episteme." The radical settlers on the utopian planet Anarres in Ursula LeGuin's *The Dispossessed* did not realize that they shared normative ground with the world they rejected; they erected a "wall" between themselves and Urras. It is dangerous, therefore, not to acknowledge connections between a "dominant episteme" and a "subjugated knowledge." Failure to see the positive connection between the dominant and the subjugated episteme obscures the fact that radicals still stand on some parts of the ship while repairing others; not acknowledging this connection can also be a form of dispossession.[35]

Some liberation theologians, however, do not erect a wall.[36] Welch, for example, criticizes Western conceptions of freedom and equality that have masked oppression (excluded women and people of color), but she seems explicitly to refashion these traditions as part of her new vision.[37] Out of solidarity or compassionate identification with the oppressed—the victims of "political terror and economic exploitation"—one seeks "freedom" and "justice"; one acts out of "concern for other races and classes, for the lives of all of those adversely affected by our political and economic systems."[38] One recognizes the danger of false universals—moral conceptions that mask their partiality and claim the status of a priori "absolutes"—but one goes ahead with "provisional" notions of freedom and justice, recognizing their contingency; one revises the tradition and is open to further revision.[39]

In conclusion, we find that we live in concrete social locations: understanding is difficult, but traditions are perhaps linked through concrete universals; we begin in "theory-laden" forms of social practice; we are oppressed, oppressors, or both, as Welch notes;[40] we construe our world through various moral vocabularies and modes of discourse. While there is difference, distance, and even discontinuity, there is also connection, sometimes of a surprising sort.

AGREEMENT

Even if appeals to general features of human nature are legitimate, and even if by way of concrete universals we can understand the Other across gaps of diversity and oppression, what hope do we have for agreement?

Should we look only for partial agreements, or for a common vocabulary? I do not argue here for a universal moral vocabulary that would entirely supplant diverse moral traditions, what Jeffrey Stout calls an Esperanto.[41] Such a universalism is possible, and indeed it has been the dream of moral revolutionaries in a variety of traditions, but it does not seem to me likely, given the empirical diversity of views of the cosmos and human nature in which moral convictions are embedded. Nor is it necessarily desirable, since a pluralism of moral opinion is the matrix out of which challenges to moral agreements can arise. I do however argue for a regulative universal vocabulary that can be supported by appeals to various features of human nature (or, more broadly, persons) analogically understood as concrete universals: an Esperanto in this more limited sense. To preserve "difference" but allow for "connection" I want to suggest that the evolving substance of the liberal tradition—corrected in the light of oppression and enriched by contact with other traditions—could serve as such an Esperanto.

Let us look first at objections that are often directed at the moral vocabulary of the liberal tradition even when it is confined to certain contexts (a local, shall we say, rather than a universal moral language). If we live in epistemic communities and traditions, a critic might say, then liberalism, for example in its Rawlsian form, is off to a false start.[42] Rawls asks agents to divorce themselves from their own personal history, to prescind from the natural-social lottery; to adopt moral principles of justice from the standpoint of the autonomously legislating self; and to transcend their particular traditions in favor of a common framework. But since individuals cannot divorce themselves from their identities, cannot adopt moral principles in isolation from other people, and cannot transcend their particular traditions, we cannot do what liberalism asks. And since we cannot, the principles of justice that liberalism produces turn out to be "tainted" with particularity; liberalism masks its own social location.

How would a Rawlsian neopragmatist reply to the charges of impersonal abstraction, unsocial isolation, and ahistorical universalism?[43] First, the Rawlsian would say that the required point of view is a moral perspective on one's history, not an escape from it. Indeed, the imperative to think of oneself apart from one's place in the natural and social lottery is itself a moral tradition, which has become accepted by the individual and in that sense has become part of the individual's web of belief and hence part of the individual's history and moral identity. A critic could say, however, that since we are locked in to our conceptual schemes (whatever the "our" signifies) we cannot understand the Other in order to reason about what we all need simply as persons; hence the attempt to adopt the perspective of anyone is futile. But the Rawlsian will reply that there are ways to communicate with and understand the other; we can transcend our place in the natural and social lottery sufficiently well to form a workable—if not perfect—conception of what persons need as persons.[44] Second, the isolation is not epistemological; the tradition is shared with others. And indeed the moral stance that has one look on oneself as anyone is itself a bond with others, for one identifies oneself, one defines one's moral identity, as an equal citizen in the kingdom of ends. One identifies with one's neighbor by thinking of oneself morally as any agent or person and by asking what "respect" for persons requires. Third, the common, i.e., shared framework of Rawls's proposal builds on a particular tradition, a web of belief; it is not an attempt to escape history to a transcultural foundation. It does, however, ask that the framework regulate the remaining moral beliefs of its adherents.

Rawls then has reinterpreted Kant's subject as a type of moral identity. Historically, we have moved in this tradition from being equal subjects of God, to equal subjects of foundationalist moral reason, to equal moral citizens whose epistemology at least in Rawls's hands escapes the false alternatives of foundationalism or relativism. And the Rawlsian liberal will readily admit that liberalism has sometimes been a mask for particular interest groups, but still insists that its promise has not been fulfilled; self-interest and false beliefs have marred the versions that have shaped Western society. Yet precisely in, for example, the civil rights or women's movements one can see the tradition correcting itself. The tradition strives not to erase "difference" but to provide a common framework in which all can flourish.[45]

Note again that Rawls, unlike Gewirth, for example, does not propose warrants that are intended to convince any agent, warrants pertinent to persons as such. Moreover, Rawls himself would not claim that he is proposing a *supplanting* Esperanto but would insist that his principles of justice are to function only as a common framework in terms of which to govern or *adjudicate* conflicts between the prescriptions of particular moralities. The Rawlsian, then, wants to create a framework built out of a pattern of existing moral conceptions.[46] The Rawlsian seeks a common vocabulary in addition to particular moral "languages." Rawls does not expect agents to share a wide range of values, but he expects a good number of them at least to have reasons from within their own web of religious or philosophical beliefs to adopt an adjudicatory framework above and beyond their particular moralities. Others will apparently accept it for its own sake "as in itself sufficient to express values that, under the reasonably favorable conditions that make a more or less just constitutional democracy possible, normally outweigh whatever other values may oppose them."[47] Since people from diverse traditions often have prior reasons to accept the theory of justice, the latter does not even govern, much less supplant, *those* reasons; it governs the *rest* of the particular moral traditions of those who assent to it. Where the consensus is not founded on a "wider doctrine" but accepted for its own sake, it still overrides opposing values. Rawls wants a consensus in the sense that various traditions adopt the framework of justice, which then takes priority over particular conceptions of the good and the right.[48]

How could a theory of justice such as Rawls's come to be accepted as a universal vocabulary or Esperanto, not supplanting, but regulating (through international agreements of various sorts) the interactions of otherwise diverse communities? There are at least three models of how this could happen.

First, there is the sort of an "overlapping consensus" referred to earlier: various and otherwise diverse "comprehensive and general" schemes will have their own reasons for supporting a public consensus on the justice of institutions. (For Rawls conceptions are "general in that they apply to a wide range of subjects, and comprehensive in that they include conceptions of what is of value in human life, ideals of personal virtue and character that are to inform our thought and character as a whole"; they refer to the "meaning, value and purpose of human life."[49]) Rawls's examples are a religious faith that supports toleration and other liberties, or a doctrine such as Kant's or Mill's. Presumably one could envisage a universalization of this process from within nation-states to their relations.[50]

Second, there is another sense of "consensus" that Rawls notes, a public view of justice that is accepted as sufficiently appealing in itself, without any support from a comprehensive and general scheme.[51] This, if I understand him correctly, is Rorty's preferred version of Rawlsian liberalism. A conception of justice or, more broadly, a common moral framework (whose substance for Rorty accords with the liberal tradition) needs no support from "comprehensive and general" religious and philosophical doctrines; these play a role only in the search for private perfection. The general moral commitment to equality and the particular considered judgments about freedom and well-being that Rawls tries to integrate could simply become *diffused* as they become attractive in and between various communities.[52]

Third, I want to propose that appeals to general features of human nature can perhaps furnish grounds for agreement. Appeals to forms of reasoning, to sympathy, and to shared values already seem to play a significant role as justifications for a common framework of justice.[53] Theorists will debate how to integrate these appeals and how they shape more determinate norms, but the process is already at work in and between communities. Indeed, we see in the growth of the human rights movement—including not only security and political but economic rights—a potentially universal regulative Esperanto. While Rawls allows a consensus (beyond its internal coherence) to be supported by comprehensive and general doctrines, Rorty may want it to be accepted simply for its own sake. On either alternative, comprehensive and general beliefs are detached from the public realm. My suggestion in contrast to both is that perhaps by way of appeals to analogous conceptions between traditions we can find common comprehensive and general reasons for common moral convictions. Diversity is not eliminated, but we could overcome to a certain extent the dichotomy of private and public conviction.[54]

I have argued that while neopragmatism may give us a correct epistemological orientation—we give up foundationalism and avoid false senses of relativism—it does not help us determine which sorts of warrants for the good and the right are available in whatever our web of belief may be. Neopragmatism does not rule out a search for grounds for our most general moral beliefs. Nor does it help us decide whether there are general motivating features of human nature that can be recognized across cultures. To resolve this debate we must repair to more specific arguments, just as a neopragmatist would expect.

I also contend that neopragmatism can appreciate the degree to which we live in particular and diverse webs of meaning and still allow for concrete universals as a basis of understanding. While keeping a sense of historical and social context, we should nonetheless not erect "walls" that separate cultures or even oppressors from the oppressed.

And finally, neopragmatism does not rule out an Esperanto that would regulate diverse traditions either within specific communities or even universally. We may find substantive analogies that could provide the grounds for shared convictions. But this is only a promissory note; the patient work of cultural understanding and argument remains largely to be done.

NOTES

I would like to thank all those colleagues who have read versions of this essay, especially one reviewer for Princeton University Press who suggested a radical pruning. Mark Hadley, Paul Lauritzen, Robert McKim, Gene Outka, Sumner B. Twiss, and Lee Yearley read the final draft.

1. Richard J. Bernstein, *Beyond Objectivism and Relativism: Science, Hermeneutics, and Praxis* (Philadelphia: University of Pennsylvania Press, 1983). I assume here that foundationalism in a certain sense is unjustified, but the debate is far from concluded. For an examination of senses of foundationalism and coherentism and an evaluation of arguments related to both, see Ernest Sosa, "The Raft and the Pyramid: Coherence versus Foundation in the Theory of Knowledge," in *Knowledge in Perspective: Selected Essays in Epistemology* (Cambridge: Cambridge University Press, 1991), pp. 165–91.

2. Richard Rorty, "The Priority of Democracy to Philosophy," in *The Virginia Statute for Religious Freedom: Its Evolution and Consequences in American History*, ed. Merrill D. Peterson and Robert C. Vaughn (Cambridge: Cambridge University Press, 1988), pp. 257–82. Reprinted in this volume as chap. 11.

3. Alasdair MacIntyre, *After Virtue: A Study in Moral Theory*, 2d ed. (Notre Dame, Ind.: University of Notre Dame Press, 1984), pp. 18–19, 112–13, 117–18.

4. Compare MacIntyre's sense of epistemological crisis, the sort of occasion when old concepts are deemed inadequate and new structures have to be invented (ibid., pp. 361ff.).

5. See MacIntyre himself, *Whose Justice? Which Rationality?* (Notre Dame, Ind.: University of Notre Dame Press, 1988), pp. 352–53; 395–96. See Jeffrey Stout, *Ethics after Babel: The Languages of Morals and Their Discontents* (Boston: Beacon Press, 1988), pp. 261–65 on this way of understanding emotivism—existentialism. See also J. B. Schneewind, "Moral Crisis and the History of Ethics," *Midwest Studies in Philosophy* 8 (1983): 525–42.

6. Bernstein, *Beyond Objectivism and Relativism*, p. 8.

7. Ibid., p. 8 (cf. pp. 11–12); p. 92.

8. Neil Cooper, for example, retains this model when he argues that unsupported "criteriological judgements" are logically prior to more specific moral beliefs. See *The Diversity of Moral Thinking* (Oxford: Clarendon Press, 1981).

9. Norman Daniels ("Wide Reflective Equilibrium and Theory Acceptance in Ethics," *Journal of Philosophy* 76 [May 1979]:258) distinguishes with Rawls between "narrow" and "wide" reflective equilibrium. I am indebted to Daniels who argues that "background theories" (with moral content) justify principles, independent of their fit with considered judgments; I also discuss later how in some systems there is also a justification of the background theory or perspective independent of the dialectical adjustment of principles and judgments. My title is an adaptation of a phrase of Daniels', "foundationalism without foundations" (ibid., p. 265). See also Daniels, "Reflective Equilibrium and Archimedean Points," *Canadian Journal of Philosophy* 10 (March 1980): 83–103; and "Two Approaches to Theory Construction in Ethics," in David Copp and David Zimmerman, eds., *Morality, Reason, and Truth: New Essays on the Foundations of Ethics* (Totowa, N.J.: Rowman and Allanheld, 1984), pp. 120–40.

10. Compare J. B. Schneewind, "Moral Knowledge and Moral Principles," in *Revisions: Changing Perspectives in Moral Philosophy*, ed. Stanley Hauerwas and Alasdair MacIntyre (Notre Dame, Ind.: University of Notre Dame Press, 1983), pp. 113–26, especially pp. 119–22. The general thrust of Rorty's argument in "Priority" is that reflective equilibrium—I assume in the "wide" sense—is sufficient.

11. See Stout, *Ethics after Babel*, chap. 3 and MacIntyre, *Whose Justice?*, chap. 19.

12. See, for example, Michel Foucault, *Power / Knowledge: Selected Interviews and Other Writings 1972–1977*, trans. Colin Gordon, Leo Marshall, John Mepham, and Kate Soper; ed. Colin Gordon (New York: Pantheon Books,

1980), chaps. 5–8. I stress the "if" here; I am not sure how to interpret Foucault. For a helpful reading, see Sharon D. Welch, *Communities of Resistance and Solidarity: A Feminist Theology of Liberation* (Maryknoll, N.Y.: Orbis Books, 1985). For a searching critique, see Cornel West, *The American Evasion of Philosophy: A Genealogy of Pragmatism* (Madison: University of Wisconsin Press, 1989), pp. 223–26.

13. See Stout, *Ethics after Babel*, p. 201. MacIntyre (*Whose Justice?*, p. 360) allows a role for first principles that seem "necessary and evident" to those within a tradition, but such principles will have proved themselves "superior to their historical predecessors" in the "process of dialectical questioning" and "justification"; they are not "self-sufficient" or "self-justifying."

14. James M. Gustafson, *Ethics from a Theocentric Perspective*, vols. 1 and 2 (Chicago: University of Chicago Press, 1981, 1984). See John P. Reeder, Jr., "The Dependence of Ethics," in *Gustafson's Theocentric Ethics: Interpretation and Assessments*, ed. Harlan Beckley and Charles Sweezey (Macon, Ga.: Mercer University Press, 1988). See also Stout, *Ethics after Babel*, pp. 167–88.

15. Compare Daniels, "Wide Reflective Equilibrium," pp. 259–61, on the "independence constraint," and n. 8, p. 261 on background theory as "foundation."

16. On the one hand Rorty seems to allow appeals to the transcendent as part of the search for private perfection, but on the other hand he apparently interprets *any* appeal to transcendent reality as well as to human nature as such as an epistemological error, a search for security obtained through some purported link to noncontingent reality. With Timothy P. Jackson, I argue that a pragmatist epistemology cannot in principle rule out these sorts of appeals. Timothy P. Jackson, "Theory and Practice of Discomfort: Richard Rorty and Pragmatism," *The Thomist* 51, no. 2 (April 1987): 270–98.

17. Rorty, "Priority," p. 258. It does not seem to me that to deny a transcendental "I" settles the question of how to account for our sense of personal agency, i.e., whether we need to presuppose something that *has* interpretations, just as the loss of ahistorical "essences" does not settle metaphysical questions about whether there are natural kinds and if so, of what sort. On "decentering the subject," see Charles B. Guignon and David R. Hiley, "Biting the Bullet: Rorty on Private and Public Morality," in *Reading Rorty: Critical Responses to "Philosophy and the Mirror of Nature" (and Beyond)*, ed. Alan R. Malachowski (Oxford: Basil Blackwell, 1990), pp. 34ff. I do not intend here "to salvage a notion of a centered self after the demise of foundationalism" in the sense to which Guignon and Hiley refer as the "hermeneutic approach," namely, the attempt to combine antifoundationalism with the claim that there is nonetheless a formal structure of the self's "self-interpreting activity" that furnishes "conditions for the possibility of any interpretation whatever" (pp. 344–50). On these issues see also Martin Hollis, "The Poetics of Personhood," in *Reading Rorty*, pp. 244–56.

18. Rorty, "Priority," n. 22, p. 278. See also pp. 269, 271. At one point he contrasts the "liberal metaphysician" who wants a "common human essence" with the "liberal ironist" who insists only on a "shared ability to suffer humiliation": *Contingency, Irony, and Solidarity* (Cambridge: Cambridge University

Press, 1989), p. 91. See also, for example, "Freud and Moral Reflection," in Rorty, *Essays on Heidegger and Others* (Cambridge: Cambridge University Press, 1991), pp. 160–61; "Habermas and Lyotard on Postmodernity," in Rorty, *Essays on Heidegger and Others*, pp. 174–75; "On Ethnocentrism: A Reply to Clifford Geertz," in Rorty, *Objectivity, Relativism, and Truth* (Cambridge: Cambridge University Press, 1991), pp. 207–8. See Stout (*Ethics after Babel*, pp. 256–60) on how "modest pragmatists" can appeal to their view of human nature. On Stout's view, Rorty like Rawls allows for " 'common sense plus the social sciences' " (Stout, *Ethics after Babel*, n. 17, p. 324; n. 20, pp. 327–28; Rorty, "Priority," n. 17, p. 277). For Rorty, however, such appeals to common sense and the social sciences (a notion of "human nature" in this sense) do not amount to a view of the nature of persons as having a "natural center," as opposed to the view that we are "centerless networks of beliefs and desires" ("Priority," p. 269).

19. Thomas McCarthy distinguishes between "universal" and "transcendental" (i.e., foundationalist) claims and cogently asks where Rorty gets his certainty that there are no universals of various sorts. "Ironist Theory as a Vocation: A Response to Rorty's Reply," *Critical Inquiry* 16 (Spring 1990):645, 649, 650–51. McCarthy asks whether there are any "contingent universals" that even in the absence of a common human language would provide more common features than the capacities for pain and humiliation that Rorty acknowledges; such features "would be relevant if they began to spin a web of shared humanity" (p. 649). The sections on understanding and agreement in this chapter try to develop this suggestion.

20. See Joel Feinberg, "Abortion," in *Matters of Life and Death*, ed. Tom Regan (New York: Random House, 1980), p. 187. Feinberg treats the notion of common sense or descriptive personhood as a convention embodied in language.

21. Alan Gewirth, *Reason and Morality* (Chicago: University of Chicago Press, 1978).

22. For a substantive critique of Gewirth's argument, see MacIntyre, *After Virtue*.

23. David B. Wong, *Moral Relativity* (Berkeley and Los Angeles: University of California Press, 1984).

24. In *After Virtue* MacIntyre seemed to claim that in various cultures humans could recognize that their good is intersubjective. Different cultures would construe the good differently but this underlying feature of human nature and hence of human good was similar and commonly knowable. In *Whose Justice?*, MacIntyre suggests, I believe, that traditions that share this view could have different concepts of rationality and justice.

25. MacIntyre, *After Virtue*, p. 229; see also pp. 190–91, 195, 219, 220, 232, 250–51.

26. Wong, *Moral Relativity*, p. 158. See also Stout's analysis of Wong in *Ethics after Babel*, pp. 91–93, 95–96, 98–100.

27. Rorty himself wants to emphasize compassion. See Jo Burrows, "Conversational Politics: Rorty's Pragmatist Apology for Liberalism," in *Reading Rorty*, ed. Malachowski, pp. 326, 335 n. 14. See also Annette C. Baier, "Hume: The Women's Moral Theorist?" in *Women and Moral Theory*, ed. Eva Feder Kittay

and Diana T. Meyers (Totowa, N.J.: Rowman and Littlefield, 1987), pp. 37–55; Lawrence Thomas, "Trust, Affirmation, and Moral Character: A Critique of Kantian Morality," in *Identity, Character, and Morality: Essays in Moral Psychology*, ed. Owen Flanagan and Amélie Okensberg Rorty (Cambridge, Mass.: MIT Press, 1990), pp. 235–57. On moral content in conceptions of the person, see Norman Daniels, "Moral Theory and the Plasticity of Persons," *Monist* 62 (July 1979): 265–87; and compare Richard J. Bernstein, "One Step Forward, Two Steps Backward: Richard Rorty on Liberal Democracy and Philosophy," *Political Theory* 15 (November 1987): 557.

28. On the error of thinking that moral systems are "conceptual schemes" between which there exists no possibility of translation and understanding, see Stout, *Ethics after Babel*, pp. 160–68.

29. MacIntyre argues that by learning a "second first language" we can discover that "we are unable to translate what we are now able to say in our second first language into our first first language" (*Whose Justice?*, p. 387; see pp. 370–71ff.). MacIntyre wants to say that some vocabularies are untranslatable as such but that by learning a second first language we can enrich our first first language. See Stout (*Ethics after Babel*, pp. 64–65) for the point that because of the possibility of "hermeneutical innovation," diversity does not entail nontranslatability ("hermeneutically sealed" cultures). According to MacIntyre (*Whose Justice?*, pp. 364ff.), once understanding is established a tradition can see by its own "standards of rational justification" that another tradition has the conceptual resources it needs. Thus traditions can debate and even defeat one another. There is no guarantee, however, that this sort of persuasion will occur (*Whose Justice?*, pp. 366–67, cf. 370).

30. I am grateful to Thomas Lewis and Stephen Wilson for suggesting the idea that there is a "fusion of horizons" involved even in learning a second first language.

31. Carol C. Gould, "The Woman Question: Philosophy of Liberation and the Liberation of Philosophy," in Carol C. Gould and Marx W. Wartofsky, eds., *Women and Philosophy: Toward a Theory of Liberation* (New York: G. P. Putnam's Sons, 1976), pp. 26–27. Compare Stout, *Ethics after Babel*, pp. 63–64ff., on similarity of usage; Sumner B. Twiss, "On Truth and Justification in *Ethics after Babel*," *Annual of the Society of Christian Ethics* (1990): 45–46, on shared norms of rationality; and Yearley, *Mencius and Aquinas* (Albany, N.Y.: State University of New York Press, 1990), chap. 5, on analogical comparison. I have not intended to suggest that "concrete universals" require any particular linguistic theory of universals. I suggest concrete universals as a matter of social description; if they exist, they could be accounted for in various ways.

32. Welch, *Communities*, pp. 26, 43–44. I am grateful to Anne Mattis for discussion of these points.

33. See Michael Walzer's criticisms of Sartre's preface to Franz Fanon, *The Wretched of the Earth* (New York: Grove Press, 1968), in *Just and Unjust Wars* (New York: Basic Books, 1977), pp. 204–5. See also *Interpretation and Social Criticism* (Cambridge, Mass.: Harvard University Press, 1987) pp. 57–61.

34. See Gilbert Harman, *The Nature of Morality: An Introduction to Ethics* (New York: Oxford University Press, 1977). Cf. Stout on Harman, *Ethics after*

Babel, pp. 87–90. See also Harman, "Is There a Single True Morality?" in Copp and Zimmerman, eds., *Morality, Reason, and Truth*, pp. 27–48.

35. See Stout on Neurath's boat, *Ethics after Babel*, pp. 57–59; as Stout argues, our boat need not become a prison. Cf. the "wall" erected by the settlers on Anarres in LeGuin's *The Dispossessed: An Ambiguous Utopia* (New York: Avon Books, 1976) and the prisons, literal and figurative, in the course of the narrative.

36. See Marilyn Chapin Massey, *Feminine Soul: The Fate of an Ideal* (Boston: Beacon Press, 1985). On the issue of relations of the "feminine" to dominant masculine traditions, Massey is against a mere fusion or relation of complementarity (pp. 7, 9, 165). She affirms those who seek to identify what is radically different in women's experience, but she seeks, I believe, not mere fusion or separation but "a completely new, *transformative* ethic" (p. 183; italics mine).

37. Welch, *Communities*, pp. 44–47; chap. 5.

38. Ibid., pp. 8, 81–82.

39. Ibid., pp. 26–28, 74–75, 82. Welch opposes beginning the process of solidarity and resistance with *reflection* on the human as such, preferring to begin with practice, with concrete experiences of injustice and resistance. She also clearly opposes attributing to contingent moral notions the status of necessity as a priori, ahistorical "absolutes" (75, 79). While she suggests that using any "universal" such as human dignity, freedom, or justice is "all too often, and perhaps even necessarily, to elevate as universal and normative a particular aspect of human being" (51; cf. 81), her basic theme seems to be that communities of solidarity and resistance rely on "provisional" "definitions" (82), "'proleptic universals'" (74). Thus while she can say "It would be . . . the greatest folly for me to criticize sexism on the grounds of universally recognized values such as equality, the nature of moral persons, or any other determination of what characterizes the human, and thus women, as such" (79), she clearly wants to employ general and universally applicable conceptions of freedom and justice in her critique. She may seem at times to want to dispense with universals entirely, to speak in terms of "universal accountability *rather than* what is universally true about human being" (81; italics mine), to "express a concern for the well-being of all people" without running the risk of using false universals (81), but I think her considered view is that we must proceed with our experientially based concepts while acknowledging their finite and morally imperfect (sinful) character (86). Thus "A feminist theology of liberation operates within a paradoxical tension, making transcultural claims and normative judgments, yet always remaining open to challenge and modification" (91). Since moral universals are not given ahistorical status, their tendency to exclude and mask their limitations can be recognized; their imperfect character can be acknowledged in a process of dialogue and revision.

40. Ibid., pp. 13–14.

41. Stout, *Ethics after Babel*, p. 5.

42. In speaking of the "liberal" tradition, with Rawls, Gewirth, and others as examples, I mean, minimally, as Rawls puts it, a conception that "protects the familiar basic rights and assigns them a special priority; it also includes measures to ensure that all persons in society have sufficient means to make effective use of

those basic rights." Rawls, "The Idea of an Overlapping Consensus," *Oxford Journal of Legal Studies* 7 (1987):17.

43. Rorty, in "The Priority of Democracy to Philosophy," insists that Rawls is to be read as a pragmatist. Liberal perspectives and principles remain for Rorty intuitions or convictions justified by reflective equilibrium, not by views about persons as such.

44. This is a point made by Joseph Razza. See Seyla Benhabib on the "generalized" and the "concrete" Other: "The Generalized and the Concrete Other: The Kohlberg-Gilligan Controversy and Moral Theory," in *Women and Moral Theory*, ed. Kittay and Meyers, pp. 163ff. Benhabib attacks the Rawlsian veil of ignorance as incoherent, for it abstracts from what gives us identity (our ends and relations as "embodied, affective, suffering creatures"). The "self" behind the veil of ignorance, however, is only a way of modeling a basic moral commitment. (Note 32 on p. 176 attempts to reply to objections; the heart of the issue in my view is whether one wants to give normative priority to the "generalized Other." See pp. 168ff.) For a view supportive of Benhabib, see Welch, *A Feminist Ethic of Risk* (Minneapolis: Fortress Press, 1990), pp. 127–29, 137–40, and Iris Marion Young, "Impartiality and the Civic Public: Some Implications of Feminist Critiques of Moral and Political Theory," in *Feminism as Critique: On the Politics of Gender*, ed. Seyla Benhabib and Drucilla Cornell (Minneapolis: University of Minnesota Press, 1987), pp. 57–76, 171–74. See also MacIntyre, *Whose Justice?*, pp. 384, 396, 400–401, chap. 17. He emphasizes the particularity of traditions and resists the "forms of modern liberal culture" that deprive us, he says, "of the particularities of our histories."

45. See the first and last chapters of Massey, *Feminine Soul*.

46. See Stout on the idea of overlapping moral agreements and a "creole" (*Ethics after Babel*, chaps. 3, 9–11). An overlap might signify a looser set of partial agreements rather than a public consensus on principles of justice and considered judgments Rawls envisages. For Rawls and Stout the "overlap" seems to amount to more than a pattern of intersecting judgments; it is a common, i.e., a shared language. See Rawls, "Overlapping Consensus," pp. 1–25.

47. "Overlapping Consensus," p. 9.

48. Rawls's basic view of a consensus on justice seems to be that of an overlap of comprehensive and general views: "Since different premises may lead to the same conclusions, we may simply suppose that the essential elements of the political conception, its principles, standards and ideals, are theorems, as it were, at which the comprehensive doctrines in the consensus intersect or converge. . . . Since we assume each citizen to affirm some such view or other, we hope to make it possible for all to accept the political conception as true, or as reasonable, from the standpoint of their own comprehensive view, whatever it may be" (ibid., pp. 9, 13; cf. p. 11). Yet he outlines a "model case of an overlapping consensus" that "contains three views," only the first two of which involve overlapping comprehensive and general views (p. 9). The first is that of a religious faith that supports the public conception of justice including toleration, and the second is that of a comprehensive and general philosophical doctrine such as Kant's or Mill's (pp. 5–6). The third, however, does not proceed from a comprehensive and general

doctrine: "the third supports the political conception not as founded on any wider doctrine but rather as in itself sufficient to express values that . . . normally outweigh whatever other values may oppose them" (p. 9). (In all three views, the consensus itself once developed will furnish "valid and sufficient reasons singled out by that conception itself" [p. 6] for the purpose of reaching agreement in public debate.) The citizens who hold the third view "have, of course, other views as well, views that specify values and virtues belonging to other parts of life; they differ from citizens holding the two other views in our example of an overlapping consensus in having no fully (as opposed to partially) comprehensive doctrine within which they see all values and virtues as being ordered. They don't say such a doctrine is impossible, but rather practically speaking unnecessary" (p. 16). Indeed Rawls suggests that "many if not most citizens come to affirm their common political conceptions without seeing any particular connection, one way or the other, between it and their other views" (p. 19). The political conception may "gain an initial allegiance to itself" and subsequently reshape comprehensive religious and philosophical doctrines (p. 23; cf. p. 19). By the end of "Overlapping Consensus," indeed, the third view seems to have pride of place: "Political liberalism is represented in our model case of an overlapping consensus by the third view once we take the political conception in question as liberal" (p. 24). In any case, Rorty allows that in some cases comprehensive and general views cannot be bracketed, in particular, those upholding the consensus might have to "deny that the concern for salvation requires anything incompatible with [equal liberty of conscience]" (p. 14; cf. 15ff). See also "The Priority of Right and Ideas of the Good," *Philosophy and Public Affairs* 27 (Fall 1988): 251–76, especially section 8.

49. "Overlapping Consensus," pp. 1–2, 6. Rawls says: "Many religious and philosophical doctrines tend to be general and fully comprehensive."

50. Ibid., p. 3 n. 4; pp. 3–8. Rawls does not want to argue for a world government, but to suggest the possibility of principles to govern the relations of states (p. 3 n. 3).

51. Ibid., p. 9; pp. 16ff.

52. See Rorty, "Ethnocentrism," pp. 206, 209–10, and "Cosmopolitanism without Emancipation: A Response to Jean-François Lyotard," in Rorty, *Objectivity, Relativism, and Truth*, p. 212ff. McCarthy argues that Rorty assumes "the ideal of universal human solidarity as a regulative ideal," but he insists that we can only ex nihilo create solidarity step by step, for there is no common humanity for us to "recognize" ("Ironist Theory," pp. 649–51). Rorty wants to encourage "the imaginative ability to see strange people as fellow-sufferers" (*Contingency*, p. xvi). He notes that we begin with attachments to particular persons (ibid., pp. 30–31), but he also seems to endorse Nabokov's view that "the ability to shudder with shame and indignation at the unnecessary death of a child—a child with whom we have no connection of family, tribe, or class—is the highest form of emotion that humanity has attained while evolving modern social and political institutions" (p. 147). But Rorty insists: "Simply by being human we do not have a common bond" (p. 177; see also pp. 30–31, 184). It is hard to see, however, how the liberal ironist's increasingly broader identification with subjects of suffer-

ing can take place without some appeal to the capacity for suffering and related features of persons. Rorty will allow us to compare "self-images" ("Ethnocentrism," p. 208) but not to discover a common humanity.

53. See Wong, *Moral Relativity*, on the possible interplay of these types of appeals.

54. See also Nancy Fraser, "Solidarity or Singularity? Richard Rorty between Romanticism and Technology," in *Reading Rorty*, ed. Malachowski, pp. 311ff. Compare West's proposal of a "prophetic pragmatism"—a mode of "cultural criticism and political engagement"—which reaches both within and across communities whose comprehensive and general doctrines differ (*American Evasion*, especially pp. 208–14, 226–35), and also Jean Hampton, "Should Political Philosophy Be Done without Metaphysics?," *Ethics* 99 (July 1989): 791–814. On senses of the public-private distinction and related issues, see *Liberalism and the Moral Life*, ed. Nancy L. Rosenblum (Cambridge, Mass.: Harvard University Press, 1989). My suggestion here is that within national communities and even in relations between them we can perhaps find common motivational grounds in diverse comprehensive schemes; if so, we would not have to distinguish so sharply between a public conception of justice and the sphere of private belief. Compare Rawls, "The Domain of the Political and Overlapping Consensus," *New York University Law Review* 64 (1989): 233–54, especially n. 46, pp. 251–52.

Chapter 9

ON HAVING A MORALITY IN COMMON

JEFFREY STOUT

WHAT ARE THE PROSPECTS FOR A
COMMON MORALITY?

THE PLACE IS Northern Ireland, Jerusalem, Sri Lanka, or Chicago. Two or more groups are in conflict over some issue, and we would like to see the conflict resolved reasonably and peaceably. One thing we will want to know is the extent to which their moral vocabularies, principles, patterns of reasoning, and judgments about specific cases resemble or can be made to resemble one another. If the similarity is great, we say that the groups in question have a common morality. If high similarity can probably be brought about by acceptable means, and members of the groups are willing to employ such means, we say that the prospects for a common morality are good. In this context, a question about the prospects for a common morality expresses a practical concern.

The same question can express another sort of concern. We notice that not everyone thinks and talks about moral topics in precisely the same way, and we would like to explain the differences philosophically. No one doubts that there are differences. But if the differences extend too far, we may feel compelled to become nihilists, skeptics, or radical relativists. The nihilist abandons the idea that there are moral truths. The skeptic abandons the idea that we are justified in believing whatever moral truths there may be. The radical relativist abandons the idea that we can justifiably apply moral propositions to people, deeds, and practices outside our own culture. With these alternatives in view, good prospects for a common morality would offer consolation. If moral diversity occurs within a single framework globally shared, and the differences in how people think and talk about moral matters can be explained in terms of deeper similarities, then confidence might be restored in moral truth, in justified moral belief, and in the possibility of cross-cultural moral judgment.

Practical and philosophical concerns can arise independently, but they often become intertwined. Doubts about how to respond in practice to a specific instance of moral conflict can induce philosophical reflection on the nature of morality, and philosophical reflection can influence one's practical approach to the conflicts one faces in life. Yet it is worth distinguishing the two sorts of concern when we can. Otherwise we risk confusion over what ought to count, in a given context, as a common morality. Where we are concerned to resolve a conflict between two groups, we will mean one thing by the prospects for a common morality. Where we are concerned to assess nihilism or skepticism, we will usually mean something else.

Our question about the prospects for a common morality is a daunting one, too unwieldy to answer well. It needs deflation. What makes it so unwieldy? It is really a congeries of questions, each of which can be asked in the same words. It needs division. How should we proceed? By distinguishing various questions in the congeries, tracing each to the concern that makes it matter, and then seeing whether answers come more easily. We must proceed by means of analysis, but with pragmatic intent.

SIMILARITY AND THE RESOLUTION OF CONFLICT

It goes without saying that two groups would share a common morality if their ways of thinking and talking about moral topics were exactly similar in all respects. But there is obviously no such pair of groups to be found. In a trivial sense, each group's morality is unique, differing in some respect from others. No ethical theorist denies this. When we make comparisons among moralities, we count some respects of similarity and difference as relevant and others not. Which respects count as relevant in a given context depends on which concerns motivated the comparison. By the same token, we count varying degrees of similarity in relevant respects of comparison sufficient to establish that two or more groups hold a morality in common. Again, the relevant degree of similarity depends on the concern at hand.

Not everyone thinks and talks about moral topics. Newborns do not, nor do some of the insane or the comatose. Perhaps some societies do not. But it goes without saying that for any two people who think and talk about moral topics, their ways of doing so (in short, their moralities) will resemble each other in some respects. Anyone's morality resembles everyone else's in some respects. That all moralities are ways of thinking and talking is itself something they have in common, something that guarantees formal and functional similarities of various sorts. That all moralities are about the same kind of topic is also something they have in common, such that the substantive moral commitments of any two groups can be expected to resemble each other in some degree. Let us say that a uniformity is some respect in which all moralities resemble each other closely. Theorists differ on what the actual uniformities are, the closeness of the similarities in which they consist, and the relevance they have to various practical and explanatory concerns. They do not differ on whether there are any uniformities.

Moralities, as I use the term, are ways of thinking and talking about a particular kind of topic. Even if I could say precisely what a way of thinking and talking is, the term would still be vague, given the fuzzy boundaries of the topics we call moral. For the most part, the vagueness is tolerable, and for two reasons: first, because it rarely comes into play, since most cases we discuss are some distance from the fuzzy boundaries; and second, because when it does come into play, it is usually resolved by context. When we confront an alien group and its strange ways of thinking and talking, we take our initial cues from the habitual uses of the term *moral* that are embedded in our ordinary discourse at that time. If some of the topics that the strangers think and talk about exhibit overall similarity to the topics we habitually call moral, we can, for most purposes, safely designate their way of thinking and talking about those topics a morality. Overall similarity itself is a vague notion, consisting as it does "of innumerable similarities and differences in innumerable respects of comparison, balanced against each other according to the relative importances we attach to those respects of comparison."[1] The vagueness derives from the fluctuation of relative importance across contexts. We can resolve the vagueness, if need be, by specifying which respects of comparison are important to our current concerns.

Suppose our concern is practical and quite limited. We ask what the prospects are for a common morality in Belfast. We want to know, ultimately, whether the conflict among the Catholics and Protestants who live there can be settled and what can be done to achieve that end. The scope of the relevant comparison class is relatively narrow. We need not concern ourselves, in this context, with distant tribesmen, ancient Egyptians, or humanity as a whole. What respects of comparison matter? We must focus mainly on the differences most responsible for creating or sustaining the conflict and the similarities most likely to facilitate settlement.

Most of us are concerned about many different moral conflicts. It would be fortunate if the theorists could show that all such conflicts could be adjudicated in terms of one set of moral uniformities (presumably, either a very large set of truths about particulars together with some certain means of knowing them or a small set of principles together with some determinate means of subsuming cases under them). Then we could say that there is a common morality in a very strong sense—a sense relevant simultaneously to a wide range of practical and philosophical concerns. Many theorists have tried to prove the existence of a morality that possesses these powers of adjudication. But even if they have all failed, as I suspect they have, and even if they will all continue to fail, as I suspect they will, it remains possible to proceed piecemeal, taking each conflict as it comes and trying one's best to find the means of adjudication in whatever makes the moralities in question similar. The possibility of adjudication in a given case does not depend on a guarantee of adjudication in all cases. And it seems likely that adjudication will succeed in more cases if it allows itself to rely on local similarities, not merely on global uniformities. Of course, not all types of similarity will help, and some will hinder.

Some moralities are *akin* to each other. Kinship is a special kind of similarity, brought about by sharing a common history of development up to a certain point and then separating. Protestantism and Catholicism are members of the same ethical family. Their moralities branch off from the same stem. Their kinship helps determine the character of conflict in Belfast, both for good and for ill. It engrains many close similarities in vocabulary, attitude, and reasoning that could turn out to be useful in adjudication. It also means, however, that each group defines itself against the other, thus hardening whatever differences there are. In comparative ethics, as in folk genealogy, a family tree is especially rigid where branches diverge from the stem.

The moralities of two groups in conflict are *parallel* to each other in cases where they have developed along closely similar lines without branching from the same stem. Many rural societies have parallel moralities structured around a hierarchical system of roles. The moral world consists of fathers, mothers, eldest sons, younger sons, daughters, friends, neighbors, strangers, enemies, and so on. To know how to respond to others, you need to know what roles you occupy, what roles they occupy, and what relations obtain between your roles and theirs. Duties and entitlements are all specific to roles and pertain mainly to the distribution of honor, which is recognized as the dominant good. Conflicts between such groups often start with an insult, move through a cycle of violent vengeance, and end at times in a negotiated settlement designed to limit disproportionate bloodletting. Parallel distinctions between strangers and enemies, accompanied by parallel rules requiring hospitality for the former, can keep such groups out of conflict over prolonged periods. But parallel commitments to honor as the dominant good and to vengeance as a means of protecting it can perpetuate conflict.

Two groups with independent histories and relatively dissimilar moralities can come into conflict when one conquers or subjugates the other. If Antonio Gramsci and Michael Walzer are right about such cases, the dominant group virtually always tries to justify its dominance to the oppressed.[2] In the course of making its justificatory arguments, the dominant group introduces its victims to unfamiliar moral concepts, principles, and ideals that, when applied in new ways, may be used by the oppressed to justify rebellion. Let us say that when this happens, one morality acquires *Gramscian similarities* to another. Anticolonial and revolutionary struggles are nowadays defended mainly in terms of borrowed ideas, detached from one morality and grafted onto another. Gramscian similarities can increase rather than decrease the likelihood of conflict between two groups. They have also, however, significantly increased the overlap among existing moralities. One unwitting result of imperialism and capitalism is that nearly every emerging group in the Third World justifies itself in a language of liberation and self-determination—a modern European scion grafted onto many varieties of native stock. The moralities of these groups are to some extent parallel with each other, while each has Gramscian similarities with the moralities of the colonial powers.

Cases of moral conflict, then, come in kinds. I have mentioned only a few, but even this limited sample suffices to show that the task of adjudication takes very different forms from one kind of case to another. Anyone who really cares about resolving moral conflicts had better proceed on an ad hoc basis, keeping the scope of comparison as narrow as possible. This policy maximizes the similarities available for adjudicatory work on each occasion by minimizing the number of groups to be compared. If we knew the moral uniformities in advance, we would always be in a position to call on them, if they are relevant, no matter what the setting. That would be nice. But we can get by without such knowledge, for practical purposes, trusting that uniformities will necessarily turn up locally among the similarities obtaining in the case at hand. If we are unable to tell which are which, so what? In real life adjudication, it does not matter: the more similarities that help, the better.

JUSTIFICATION

Philosophers have their own reasons for wanting to tell which from which. One reason is that they would like to know what resources there are for responding to moral skepticism. Those resources would be very powerful indeed if there were a common morality in something like the "very strong sense" mentioned halfway through the previous section. Any set of uniformities among moralities able to adjudicate all moral conflicts should also be able to refute all moral skeptics. It would do so by showing skeptics not only that they are justified in holding moral beliefs but what some or all of those beliefs are. I reject moral skepticism. I affirm that many of us are justified in holding some of the moral beliefs we hold.

Whatever reasons make the skeptic feel compelled to deny this leave me unswayed. Yet affirming that many of us are justified in holding some of the (nontrivial) moral beliefs we hold is not the same thing as affirming that someone has established a set of (nontrivial) moral beliefs that any human being or rational agent, regardless of context, would be justified in accepting. Doubting the latter claim does not, therefore, make me a moral skeptic, as defined here. It only makes me skeptical of one especially grandiose attempt to refute moral skeptics.

Behind my doubt is the idea that being justified in believing something is a relation among a person, a proposition, and an epistemic context. Epistemic contexts obviously vary. Because one context differs from the next, not everyone is justified in believing the same propositions. This goes for nonmoral and moral propositions alike. Quine is justified in believing Gödel's Theorem that a complete deductive system is impossible for any fragment of mathematics that includes elementary number theory. Euclid believed no such thing, though through no fault of his own. Quine, unlike Euclid, was trained to think and talk in the language of twentieth-century logic, so he is able to entertain propositions Euclid did not have the conceptual wherewithal to entertain, including some that figure in the reasoning that led Gödel to his theorem. Quine also has the advantage of access to Gödel's proof itself, which was not worked out until 1931. The proof serves as Quine's evidence, justifying his acceptance of its conclusion. Once he had studied the proof and understood it, Quine would have been unjustified to disbelieve its result. If you could travel back in time to visit Euclid, and you induced him to entertain the conclusion of Gödel's proof without otherwise altering his epistemic context, he would not be justified in believing it. If he disbelieved it, you would not fault him by judging him unjustified, for you understand that two people can be justified in holding different beliefs, given the vocabularies, styles of reasoning, and evidence available to them in their respective contexts.

Now consider Ignazio Silone's novel *Bread and Wine*, which is set in Italy in the 1930s.[3] The novel's protagonist is Pietro Spina, a socialist who returns from exile, disguised as a priest, to live among the peasants of his native Abruzzi, whom he hopes to organize into a revolutionary movement. The Abruzzi peasants adhere to a morality of the type described briefly in my discussion of parallel moralities among rural groups. Despite its assimilation of certain Christian elements, their morality remains for the most part one of role-specific duties and one in which honor dominates other goods. Spina has traveled in circles the peasants have not. His epistemic context differs from theirs. He entertains propositions couched in moral vocabularies they do not know, his reasoning follows different patterns, and he therefore disbelieves much of what they believe.

Spina's time among the peasants changes him. It, too, contributes to his epistemic context. He therefore abandons some moral beliefs he held in exile, acquiring others in their place. But he does not simply convert to the peasant morality. Silone is no romantic. He is careful to show that someone with Spina's life history would be unjustified in accepting certain peasant beliefs—for example, about the causal efficacy of using ox horns to ward off evil, the moral consequences of resignation to fate, or the just treatment of unmarried pregnant women. Spina rejects such beliefs and is justified in rejecting them. He does not, however, fault the peasants for believing what they believe. They are justified in believing even many of the falsehoods they believe, given the limitations of their context.

It may be, of course, that Silone was giving an untrue picture of who was justified in believing what in Italy circa 1935. What matters, for my purposes, is simply that there are differences among moralities like the ones described in Silone's novel and that they make the kind of difference to our judgments about justified belief that I have been suggesting. Silone's novel illustrates that there are important differences in what moral beliefs people in various contexts can justifiably accept. Could it not still be, however, that there are *some* (nontrivial) moral propositions everyone is justified in believing—a common morality for epistemologists? For all I have said so far, it remains possible that there are, although I assign a low probability to the prospects of showing that there are.

I have been speaking of "everyone." It would seem that the scope of comparison could not be broader. Yet not every human being need be included. In this context, we may ignore the newborns, insane, and comatose mentioned earlier. To exclude them, let us say that we are confining our attention to rational human agents. Can we not, then, define rationality strictly, so that anyone who fails to accept certain moral propositions falls outside the comparison class? We can indeed. We can achieve a similar result by defining the term *moral* narrowly, so that human rights or respect for persons as ends in themselves are the only moral topics. Nothing prevents us from defining such terms as we please. But if the definitions are arbitrary, designed solely to exclude potentially relevant counterexamples to the theses we are testing, they accomplish nothing.

The only relevant notion of rationality would be one we could use in rendering defensible normative judgments about the various human beings who actually engage in moral reasoning, ourselves included. It is perfectly conceivable that we will someday be justified in deviating significantly from the beliefs we are currently justified in believing. It would therefore be foolish to define rationality in such a way that our future selves, with all their possibly good reasons for deviating from our path, would nonetheless be disqualified by definition from the class of rational agents. Our future selves deserve better treatment from us. So do Abruzzi peasants, distant tribesmen, and ancient Egyptians. Anyone—past, present, or future—might turn out to be less than fully rational, humans being what they are. But our normative verdict on someone's rationality cannot sensibly be settled by definition a priori, and it needs to proceed in any case by attending to details of context, with the burden of proof falling to the prosecution.

I see no way of telling what new moral vocabulary, style of reasoning, or form of evidence might turn up next, either in the findings of anthropologists and historians or in the handiwork of creative geniuses and moral reformers still to come. Nor do I see a way of telling in advance how such novelties will affect the list of propositions people are justified in believing. Euclid would have been very surprised to be told about Gödel's Theorem. Kant would have been very surprised to be shown the bearing of Einstein's theory of special relativity on the epistemic status of Euclidean propositions that he deemed universally justified. Neither Euclid nor Kant had any way of knowing how new developments would alter the relevant epistemic relations. We are in no better position in ethics. Our distant ancestors had no way of anticipating some of the considerations that make us troubled over sexism. Chances are that our distant descendants will discard some moral propositions that we find deeply intuitive or that a clever philosopher has proven to the satisfaction of his followers. Which propositions these may be, we cannot say. Humility is the best policy.

Humility, I say; not skepticism. Unlike moral skeptics, as defined here, I am not denying that we are justified in holding various moral beliefs. How can we claim to be justified in believing something and also suitably humble in matters epistemic? We can say that being justified is relative to context and that the relevant features of context might change in unexpected ways. Until they do change, we remain justified in believing certain things. The possibility of change is not yet a reason to abandon any particular belief. But it is a reason to consider our moral knowledge fallible. If being justified in believing something depends on context, and context can change, perhaps for the better, then we should do our best to remain open to that possibility.

The line of reasoning that counsels humility with respect to our own beliefs also counsels charity toward strangers. People from distant times or places are apt to believe some things we deem false, even if we and they are equally justified in holding our respective beliefs. That is what we should expect if being justified is a contextual affair. Unless we are prepared to give up our own beliefs at the points of conflict, we shall have to say, on pain of self-contradiction, that some of their beliefs are false. But unless we can show that they have acquired their beliefs improperly or through epistemic negligence, we had better count them as justified in believing as they do. And while we are at it, we had better consider the possibility that their context affords them better access than we enjoy to some truths.

Being justified in believing a proposition is not the same as being able to justify it or to justify believing it. There are many legitimate ways of acquiring beliefs. Accepting the conclusion of a sound justificatory argument is only one of them. Many beliefs are acquired through enculturation. I say, with Thomas Reid and others, that we are justified in holding such beliefs except in those cases where we have adequate reason to doubt or reject them or where for some other reason (like culpable neglect of evidence) we are not doing our best as inquiring minds.[4] I say, with Wittgenstein and others, that many of these beliefs we would not know how to justify in a noncircular and informative way even if we tried, and that life is too short for us to supply arguments in support of many of them. I say, with C. S. Peirce and others, that if we ceased to take the vast majority of them for granted, far from enhancing the capacity to think scrupulously, we would lose the capacity to think at all. It makes sense to say that we can be justified in accepting a belief acquired through enculturation even in the absence of a justifying argument. It is unreasonable to demand justifying arguments across the board. Skeptics have been wrong in making this demand, and their opponents have been wrong in trying to meet it.

Justifying a proposition, unlike being justified in believing one, is an activity. The result of the activity is a justification. Let us say that a justification of the proposition P is an answer to the question, Why believe that P?[5] If the answer is successful, we say that the proposition in question is justified. In what, then, does the success of a justification consist? It lies in eliminating relevant reasons for doubting P. What reasons for doubting P are relevant and what suffices for their elimination? That depends on context—in particular, to whom the justification is addressed. Call the class of such people the justification's *audience*. Reasons for doubting P are relevant if they prevent or might prevent someone in the audience from being justified in believing P. Relevant reasons for doubting P have been eliminated when everyone in the audience is justified in believing P.

We sometimes speak of justifying a proposition *to* someone, either oneself or someone else. In such cases, the audience of the justification is specified. I justify a proposition to myself when I construct or rehearse an argument that makes me justified in believing it. I justify a proposition to someone else, S, when I construct or rehearse an argument that makes S justified in believing it. More often, we speak simply of justifying a proposition, allowing context to specify the audience. Philosophers have long tried to discover, in abstraction from any context in particular, what conditions a successful justification of a moral proposition ought to satisfy. In doing so, they have usually attended exclusively to features of ethical justification qua argument, and they often ended in puzzles about the status of first principles or the logical transition from nonmoral premises to moral conclusions. We are now in a position to see why they have met with little success. If my analysis is correct, abstraction from context in a theory of justification is bound to end in frustration. Justifications are answers to why-questions of a certain sort. As such, they are dependent on context for three reasons: first, because conversational context determines the question to which a justification counts as an answer and thus the sort of information being requested; second, because conversational context determines a justification's audience; and third, because a justification's success can be appraised only in relation to the epistemic context of its audience, including its relevant reasons for doubting and the propositions its members are justified in believing.[6]

Now consider a bit of ethical fiction. Someone proposes a candidate for the title of supreme moral principle. Being newly minted, it is not already accepted currency, and we have our doubts. So the question arises, Why believe it? A brilliant philosopher constructs a justification. The justification consists of a relatively complicated argument, but not so complicated that the philosophically astute cannot follow it. Suppose that, after diligent study, we accept its premises as true. We find no mistakes in the proof, no reason to question its validity. We are prepared to say, as Gödel's fellow logicians were in the case of his theorem, that the justification is successful. We therefore come to accept the new proposal as the supreme moral principle, and we are justified in believing it true.

I do not deny that this could happen. I do want to insist, however, on the importance of considering the limits on who might plausibly be expected to look upon such a justification as a reason for accepting its conclusion. Otherwise, we shall be tempted to exaggerate what will have been shown by the justificatory argument. We must distinguish a justification's intended audience from its actual audience. Whatever a justification's intended audience may be, its actual audience cannot extend beyond the class of people who understand the vocabulary in which it is cast and who have mastered the patterns of reasoning required to follow it. The limits of an actual audience are not set; they can be expanded by pedagogical means or by missions to the heathens. But it is worth reminding ourselves that the actual audiences of all justifications produced so far in human history have been limited, the philosophical justifications especially so. Saying to ourselves that we are addressing our justifications to all rational agents does not by itself affect what other people are justified in believing. We can increase the membership of a justification's actual audience only up to a point.

The ethical analogue of Gödel's Theorem, even if it were justified to the satisfaction of all living philosophers, would not thereby become the common moral property of humankind. Many people, including Abruzzi peasants and (in all likelihood) members of the great philosopher's own family, would still have no real reason to accept it. The reasons for accepting it would be other people's reasons, not theirs. It would be uncharitable on our part to fault them for not accepting it, just as it would be uncharitable of Quine to fault Euclid for failing to anticipate Gödel or Kant for failing to anticipate Einstein. If Pietro Spina's favorite peasant or my nonphilosophical grandmother accepts a belief at odds with our newly justified supreme moral principle, they might still be justified in believing what they do. Our proof has no place in their epistemic context. They fall outside the actual audience of our justification. If we direct our argument prudently, they will fall outside its intended audience as well.

There is another sense in which our justifications ought to be addressed to a limited audience, a sense related to the policy of humility. Future generations will find themselves in epistemic contexts unlike ours. We do not know what the respects of dissimilarity will be, so we cannot know what their reasons for doubting will be or what they will be justified in believing. It follows that we cannot know how successful our justifications will be for them. So it would be foolish to address our justifications to the audience of *all* rational agents, regardless of time or place.[7] We would only make the success of our justifications impossible to determine, thereby making the question of success pointless. We know from experience that justifications are fallible. To require that they be infallible to count as successful is to misunderstand the indispensable role they play in our lives. Justifications are successful if they eliminate relevant reasons for doubting. The reasons future generations might have for doubting, being necessarily unknown to us, hardly count as relevant.

My grandmother's reasons for doubting the validity of a complicated ethical proof can be known: we need only ask her. But her reasons for doubting the proof's validity are not likely to give us pause, for my grandmother lacks the philosophical training to be a competent judge of such matters. No logician is tempted to reject Gödel's Theorem simply because there are some people who would dismiss Gödel's reasoning as gobbledygook. Yet many philosophers devote serious attention to the question of what one would say to the philosophically inclined Nazi. Their worry seems to be that if one cannot justify one's moral beliefs to the imaginary Nazi, then one is not justified in holding those beliefs. The worry might derive from either or both of two sources: a tendency to confuse being justified in believing something with being able to justify it; and the mistaken idea that successful justifications must be addressed to a universal audience. We are now concentrating on the latter, so perhaps we should ask whether any philosopher seriously intends to say that Nazis are morally competent. If not, why should a Nazi's reasons for doubting be considered relevant to the appraisal of our moral beliefs? People whose lives prove them unwise, and especially the extremely vicious, are obviously not good judges of moral truth. Nazis are extremely vicious. If *they* doubt our moral conclusions, we should expect to have trouble in persuading them by rational argument. Their reasons for doubting need not be eliminated before we consider ourselves justified in rejecting their beliefs as false.

My grandmother is no philosopher and no Nazi. She may not be a competent judge of sophisticated proofs, but she is a wise woman, a competent judge of moral truths of many kinds. So if she doubts the truth of a supposedly supreme moral principle because it obviously conflicts with her settled convictions about specific cases, her reasons for doubting may be relevant to the principle's epistemic status. If the principle conflicts with her view of the wrongfulness of murder, for example, the philosopher should take that into consideration. The task will be to explain how she could have come to believe a proposition incompatible with the truth of the proposed principle. Her competence as a judge makes her reasons for doubting relevant. When other people differ with us over the truth of matters they are competent to judge, we often need to justify our own view by explaining how they came to believe a falsehood. Failure to work out a good explanation of their apparent error sometimes leaves us unjustified in believing a proposition we would otherwise have adequate reason to accept. It may be more reasonable for us to change our minds on the disputed point than to assume that our disputants believe wrongly and let that go unexplained. Hence the place of authority in ethics.

TRUTH

The doctrine defended in the previous section may, for ease of reference, be called a contextualist account of justification. I have not tried to make the account precise or complete, for that would have taken us on a long detour into formal pragmatics and the logic of why-questions, but I have tried to present the account in enough detail to make it plausible and to suggest how it might be related to concerns about "a common morality" that arise in the area of moral epistemology. Keep in mind, however, that the epistemologist's interest in refuting or assessing skepticism is only one of the concerns that make philosophers debate the prospects of a common morality. It is one thing to ask whether there are moral propositions everyone is justified in believing or whether we need to seek a universal audience for our justificatory arguments; it is quite another thing to ask whether there are moral truths, whether in calling them true we can sensibly mean more than that they are true *for us*, or whether some moral propositions apply to everyone. The latter three questions have more to do with nihilism and relativism than with skepticism. In this final section, I hope to show that my contextualist view of justification does not require me to answer them negatively.

The first thing to be said is that I have used the notion of moral truth liberally throughout this paper. Far from denying it, I have been presupposing it. For example, when I said that Pietro Spina *disagreed* with the Abruzzi peasants on what constitutes just treatment of unwed pregnant women, I meant to imply that Spina and the peasants entertain the same proposition, that the proposition is either true or false, and that in disagreeing on the issue either he believes a falsehood or they do. So long as Spina remains committed to his view on that topic, he is logically committed to rejecting the conflicting peasant view on that topic as false. Nihilists (as defined in the second paragraph of this chapter) could not describe a case of moral conflict in this way. They would have to redescribe it without relying on the notion of moral truth, most likely construing Spina and the peasants as mistaken about the nature of their conflict. But I see no adequate reason for redescribing it in that way, least of all one that derives from my contextualist account of justification.

Someone might want to claim that the peasant view is true for them, just as Spina's is true for cosmopolitan Italian socialists. If this means only that the peasants accept their view as true and Spina accepts his as true, there is no point in discussing the claim, for it merely paraphrases what I have already granted. We do sometimes use the expression *P is true for S* as a synonym for the expression *S believes P* or *S accepts P as true*. What if the claim were intended to imply that we should understand *P is true* to mean *P is true relative to M*, where M names the morality of the speaker? This would make the claim more interesting, but it would also put it in conflict with my account of moral diversity. At no point have I introduced a relativist conception of truth in describing a moral conflict. Nor would I want to do so.[8]

A relativist conception of truth erases disagreement among groups rather than making it intelligible. To say that Spina's view is true relative to his group's morality and that the peasant's view is true relative to theirs would imply that both views could be right simultaneously and that neither party's view entails rejection of the other's. But Silone does not describe the relation between Spina's moral beliefs and the peasants' in this way. If he did, his novel would lack moral tension: Spina would be neither genuinely at odds with the peasants on the issues where he eventually holds his ground, nor able to learn from them on matters where he eventually changes his mind. I stand with Silone in holding that there are such cases of genuine moral conflict in life. Nazis and I differ in many respects. We belong to different groups, each with its own way of thinking and talking about moral topics. I also differ with Nazis in another respect: I reject various moral propositions they believe, including their view of what constitutes just treatment of Jews. The fact that we have different moralities should not be allowed to obscure the equally important fact that we disagree about the moral truth. If I am right about justice, then the Nazis are wrong. Using a relativist conception of truth to redescribe our differences would dissolve the conflict in which we take ourselves to be engaged.

Yet have I not been defending a version of relativism throughout the second and third sections of this essay? And if so, is it not too late for me to be distancing myself from a relativist conception of moral truth? The second section does imply that the prospects of adjudicating a moral conflict between two groups depend upon what their respective moralities are. Say, if you like, that this makes adjudication relative. The third section does argue that being justified in believing a moral proposition is a relation and that the success of a justificatory argument is a contextual affair. Say, if you like, that this makes justification relative. But do not assume that these doctrines commit me to a relativist conception of moral truth, for they do not.

Adjudication, justification, and truth are distinct concepts, requiring separate explications. The first two are very closely related, for the obvious reason that rational adjudication of a moral conflict typically involves offering justifications to people in the hope of changing what they are justified in believing. If justification is relative, it should not be surprising that adjudication is too. None of this implies, however, that every concept we encounter in ethics will exhibit a similar relativity. My claim is that the concept of truth does not. It would therefore be misleading to summarize my position as the claim that morals are relative. "The thesis of moral relativism," like "the thesis of a common morality," is not in fact a thesis at all, but an intersection in conceptual space where distinct ideas tend to be run together and need to be disentangled before thought can proceed.

When Spina believes that a given practice is unjust and the peasants disbelieve it, either he or they accept a falsehood. It is not possible for a proposition and its negation to be true simultaneously, in ethics or anywhere else. But when Spina believes the proposition and the peasants believe its negation, they can both be justified. Similarly, Spina can be justified in believing a moral proposition at one point in his life and justified in rejecting precisely the same proposition at a later point, whereas the truth-value of the proposition has remained the same all along. By considering these possibilities, we can see how differently the concepts of truth and justification behave. It is because they behave so differently that it makes sense to combine a contextualist account of justification with the traditional philosophical notion that moral truth, however vast and complicated it may be, is one.

Contextualist epistemology, in other words, is compatible with the idea that there is a common morality, in the sense of an infinitely large set consisting of all the true moral propositions but not a single falsehood or contradiction. Infinitely large and including propositions cast in myriad possible vocabularies we will never master, this common morality boggles the mind. We will never believe, let alone be justified in believing, more than a tiny fraction of the propositions it encompasses. If God exists, God believes them all and is justified in believing them all, but no one else could come close.[9] Notice that a common morality in this sense is not a morality in the sense discussed earlier. It is merely a set of propositions, not a way of thinking and talking.

To see the difference and why it matters, consider an idea Borges and others have played with, the fantasy of a universal library in which all propositions are transcribed. If we had access to the ethics collection housed in that library, it would not do us much good. There would be too much there, much of it false, irrelevant to us, or in languages we do not understand. Even if we found somewhere in the stacks a universal translation manual that allowed us to understand any sentence in the entire collection, we would still need our own way of thinking and talking. As beings with finite cognitive powers, we would still need some way to sort the true from the false, the relevant from the irrelevant.

Somewhere in that library there is a *Concise Encyclopedia of Ethical Truth*.[10] We do not know how long it is or how long it will take us to find it or even what it would be to know that we had found it, but it is there. It is written in some language we can learn (if we are lucky, a new and improved version of our own), and it includes only this: the ideal ethical deductive system, chosen according to God's standards of truthfulness and our standards of relevance, simplicity, and cognitive utility. There are many encyclopedias of ethics in the universal library—many deductively closed, axiomatizable sets of moral sentences. But most of them include falsehoods, and many of those including only truths are not ideal by our standards of relevance, simplicity, and cognitive utility. Our standards are vague and in tension with one another, so they may fail to select a uniquely ideal system. If several systems are equally ideal, it does not matter which we use. Any system second to none is good enough to count as the regulative ideal of ethical inquiry. For the contextualist, an ideal system can function as a goal, but not as a means we can use for discovering moral truth. It is not a way of thinking and talking about moral topics. If we did have access to the universal library and stumbled upon the *Concise Encyclopedia of Ethical Truth*, we would still have to think and talk about whether we had the right volume in our hands. You can't tell this book by its cover.

Let anything count as a genuine moral principle if it functions as an axiom in an ideal deductive system of moral truth.[11] Such principles constitute a common morality in yet another sense sometimes discussed in philosophy, for their formal generality guarantees that they *apply* to all of us. When combined with other truths, principles entail theorems, some of which are also universal in application. Here, I trust my readers will be good enough to grant, is one example of a moral truth that is universal in application without itself being an axiom: that no one, under any circumstances whatsoever at any point in human history, has a right to do what the Nazis did to the Jews. Whatever the genuine moral principles are, they must account for such truths as this. Countless moral truths—some known, others not known—have universal applicability. My kind of contextualist need not deny any of them.

I do deny that an ideal system or its axioms can function as our criterion of moral truth.[12] The point is epistemological. How could we ever know that the ideal system was the standard we were actually applying? To know this would be to know that there was no possibility of improvement in our cognitive capacities and epistemic context. Being finite and aware of the long history in which our fallibility makes itself manifest, even if we had achieved *the* ideal system, we could never be justified in believing that we had, in closing our minds to the possibility of further rational revision of our moral outlook. We have no way of knowing what it would be like to be at the end of ethical inquiry.[13] At any time, the ideal system might differ in some respect from what we justifiably believe.

This is just another way of saying that truth and justification are distinct, that the two concepts behave differently—in ethics, as elsewhere. To say that some of the moral propositions we are justified in believing might not be true is to remind ourselves that no matter how well we think and talk about moral topics, it remains possible to do better. To strive for moral truth as finite beings conscious of our finitude is to keep that possibility in view, to keep alive the struggle for this-worldly betterment, not to wish for a final revelatory moment, a moral philosopher's eschaton.

The *Concise Encyclopedia of Ethical Truth* is merely the philosophical imagination's variation on three themes: the notion that moral truth is one, the hope that the fraction of it we care about is not infinitely complicated, and the realization that it cannot be reduced to what we already know. It is not a handbook anyone can use, even at the end of inquiry. Our thinking and talking about moral topics will continue as long as we do. It will not be brought to conclusion by the discovery of an ideal moral system. Its structure is not that of an encyclopedia. It is a *Phenomenology of Spirit* no chapter of which is the last. In it the phrase "Absolute Knowledge" names an object of wishful thinking, not a common morality the philosopher could someday bestow upon humankind.

NOTES

I wish to thank David Lewis for his helpful comments on the first draft of this chapter.

1. David Lewis, *Counterfactuals* (Cambridge, Mass.: Harvard University Press, 1973), p. 91.

2. See especially Michael Walzer, *Interpretation and Social Criticism* (Cambridge, Mass.: Harvard University Press, 1987), pp. 41–43.

3. Ignazio Silone, *Bread and Wine*, trans. Eric Mosbacher (New York: Signet, 1986).

4. For a Reidian account of the related concept of being rational in one's believings, see Nicholas Wolterstorff, "Can Belief in God Be Rational If It Has No Foundations?" in *Faith and Rationality: Reason and Belief in God*, ed. Alvin Plantinga and Nicholas Wolterstorff (Notre Dame, Ind.: University of Notre Dame Press, 1983), pp. 135–86.

5. For a pragmatic account of explanations as answers to why-questions, see Bas C. van Fraassen, *The Scientific Image* (Oxford: Oxford University Press, 1980), chap. 5. If van Fraassen is right, explanations are answers to questions of the form, Why *P*? I am suggesting analogously that (epistemic) justifications are answers to questions of the form, Why believe that *P*?

6. See van Fraassen: "An explanation is not the same as a proposition, or an argument, or list of propositions; it is an *answer*. (Analogously, a son is not the same as a man, even if all sons are men, and every man is a son.) An explanation is an answer to a why-question. So, a theory of explanation must be a theory of why-questions" (ibid., p. 134, italics in original).

The discussion of explanation went wrong at the very beginning when explanation was conceived of as a relationship like description: a relation between theory and fact. Really it is a three-term relation, between theory, fact, and context. No wonder that no single relation between theory and fact ever managed to fit more than a few examples! Being an explanation is essentially relative, for an explanation is an *answer*. (In just that sense, being a daughter is something relative: every woman is a daughter, and every daughter is a woman, yet being a daughter is not the same as being a woman.) Since an explanation is an answer, it is evaluated *vis-à-vis* a question, which is a request for information. But exactly what is requested, by means of the question "Why is it the case that *P*?", differs from context to context. In addition, the background theory plus data relative to which the question is evaluated, as arising or not arising, depends on context. And even what part of that background information is to be used to evaluate how good the answer is, *qua* answer to that question, is a contextually determined factor. So to say that a given theory can be used to explain a certain fact, is always elliptic. (Ibid., p. 156, italics in original)

7. Thus Alasdair MacIntyre is right to claim that in ethics, as in science, "what we have to aspire to is not a perfect theory, one necessarily to be assented to by any rational being, because invulnerable or almost invulnerable to objections, but rather the best theory to emerge so far in the history of this class of theories." He continues: "The possibility has always to be left open that in any particular field . . . some new challenge to the established best theory so far will appear and will displace it." *After Virtue*, 2d ed. (Notre Dame, Ind.: University of Notre Dame Press, 1984), p. 270.

8. I qualify and expand upon this conclusion in *Ethics after Babel* (Boston: Beacon Press, 1988), chaps. 1–4.

9. God is omniscient by definition, which means that he knows every truth there is, including the moral ones. If he knows all the moral truths, he must be justified in believing them. On my account of being justified in believing something, this means (roughly) that God is epistemically without fault in believing the moral propositions he believes. It does not mean that God is able to justify his beliefs to himself. This is a good thing, for what would count as an omniscient being's relevant reasons for doubting? Of course, this does not prevent God from justifying a belief to someone else if he pleases, for an omniscient being would know everyone else's relevant reasons for doubting and also every possible way of eliminating those reasons by presenting justificatory arguments. See van Fraassen, p. 130.

10. In this paragraph and the next, I am drawing parallels from Lewis, *Counterfactuals*, pp. 73–74. In his discussion of F. P. Ramsey's theory of lawhood, Lewis invites us to imagine "that God has decided to provide mankind with a *Concise Encyclopedia of Unified Science*, chosen according to His standards of truthfulness and our standards of simplicity and strength."

11. This is a point about the logical structure of an ideal system, not about how we think and talk about moral topics. The latter is not a matter of simply applying a deductive system by deriving consequences from principles. It is often a matter of testing relatively uncertain principles by seeing how well they organize and explain relatively certain judgments about cases.

12. I also deny that we can explain what makes moral judgments true by saying that they correspond to the propositions included in or derivable from an ideal moral system. My reason is that we used the notion of moral truth in constructing our conception of an ideal moral system. Likewise, assuming that godhood is defined in part by the ability to know all truths, it would be circular to say that moral truths are true by virtue of correspondence to what God believes.

13. For this reason, there is no point in *defining* moral truth as what we would believe about moral topics at the end of ethical inquiry. See Richard Rorty, "Life at the End of Inquiry," *London Review of Books*, 2 August–6 September 1984, 6.

Chapter 10

CONFLICTS AMONG IDEALS OF
HUMAN FLOURISHING

Lee H. Yearley

IN THIS ESSAY I concentrate on conflicts about which ways of life reflect human flourishing. That is, I focus on those situations in which people disagree about matters that concern their understanding of the best kind of life, the most fully human way to be and behave. I am especially interested in conflicts between obviously good kinds of lives— for instance, conflicts between a life dedicated to pastoral simplicity and a life dedicated to public service, or between a life dedicated to perfectionist goals such as meditation or the retranslation of Wang Yang-ming and a life dedicated to teaching beginners about meditation or Wang Yang-ming.

I also, however, discuss conflicts where we believe one ideal is obviously better than another. This might include conflicts between a life dedicated to the pursuit of fame and a life dedicated to the cultivation of genuine friendships, or those between a life dedicated to acquiring a personal fortune to satisfy hedonistic desires and a life dedicated to sacrificing personal gain to help the poor. In these cases, an "extrinsic" but not an "intrinsic" conflict is present.

In an extrinsic conflict one disagrees with others but is sure who is right. In an intrinsic conflict, a conflict between obviously good lives, one is tempted by the point of view of another community or person; one confronts the possibility that the option presented is a better way of life than one's own. Discussing extrinsic conflicts, which surely are prevalent, is important in itself, and it helps to clarify one's general position on all conflicts, especially the role played by what I call the good person criterion.

Most rewarding, however, is discussing intrinsic conflicts among good people. That discussion illuminates what follows from the fact that each of us goes lopsided to the grave, that each of us is a limited specialist in human goodness. It also helps us to understand something crucial about the character of modern spiritual discipline—that it must embody an apparently odd combination of regret and joy, and that its mortal enemies are idolatry and envy. But more on that later.[1]

THE PREVALENCE OF THE IDEAL OF A SINGLE KIND OF HUMAN FLOURISHING

I begin with a brief historical note and an important point that emerges from it. I can claim some expertise in three traditions that, to my mind, contain remarkable similarities within differences: Aristotle and his ancient and modern nonreligious interpreters; Aristotelian Christianity, especially Aquinas and the Thomistic tradition; and Confucianism, especially the tradition represented by Mencius and Wang Yang-ming. In all of these traditions the notion that such a thing as human goodness exists cohabits with the idea that only a single, if somewhat variegated, kind of human flourishing exists. This position usually rests on the assumptions found within that developmental, biological model that underlies their ideas of human nature, although it is often reinforced by the notion of either an underlying Universal Mind or a creator God. But whatever its sources and exact formulation, the conception of human goodness allows for only small variations.[2]

The thinkers in these traditions have, then, embraced a particular ideal. To propose either a single, limited form of ideal human flourishing or a harmony among somewhat different forms of human flourishing is to affirm a particular notion of the character of human flourishing. Most important here, that affirmation involves rejecting the notion that conflicts among ideals of human flourishing can or even should exist.

Many moderns question the belief in a single ideal of human flourishing or a harmony among ideals of human flourishing. They think it fits uneasily with the facts they see and perhaps even with the religious ideals they treasure. Moreover, many moderns question specific assumptions that underlie the traditional belief. They query, for example, traditional claims about the character of the reality the best human lives reflect; claims about the accessibility of that reality to humans; and claims about the ability of people to identify it correctly and continuously to live in contact with it.

These traditional claims about singleness or harmony, and the assumptions on which they rest, are very problematic. Moreover, such claims usually reflect only one aspect of the traditions in which they are made and often contradict other important strands in their respective traditions. This situation suggests that in examining them we need to employ some form of the so-called hermeneutics of suspicion. That is, we must ask what unconscious needs or class privileges these ideas meet; we must inquire into how these notions aid social control and normalization. I do not, however, pursue these topics here, since any pursuit of them must be detailed and delicate if it is to produce other than crass results. I instead proceed with a more theoretical analysis of how we should think about evident conflicts among human ideals.

The Problem of Idolatry in Thinking about Human Flourishing

Focusing on the diversity of human flourishings makes clear an often painful and always chastening fact: a significant gap exists between whatever may be ultimately good and our grasp of it. This general notion can be put in stronger and weaker ways. I favor a form strong enough to make weak people like me tremble. That is, I think the reality we face, partially manifest, and sometimes affirm has a vaster and more densely harmonized arsenal of goods than we can grasp or even imagine, surely when we look at flourishing individuals and even when we look at groups of flourishing individuals. One obviously need not go that far. It is enough to maintain a healthy realism about the evident incompleteness of our normal ideas and actions when we use either our own or other people's best activities as the standard by which to judge. It is enough to be attentive to the distinctions among the ideals of excellence present in divergent cultures and traditions.

Maintaining such realism is difficult. The dangers of idolatry are always present in any thinking about human flourishing. (It even occurs when I think about people who pursue goals I think are wrong—that is, in my extrinsic conflicts—but those occurrences are not my concern here.) That is, we are all prone to an immoderate attachment to images that capture only part of the truth. Any good can, for us, become an idol. Indeed, the drive to knowledge that can turn into idolatry is as deep, powerful, and easily deformable as the drive to nourishment or sexual expression. Like those other two drives it serves a basic need; idolatry serves the need to understand and to control our environments. Like those other two drives, grave difficulties characterize any sustained attempt to control or form it appropriately, and constant vigilance is necessary.

In fact, the drive to idolatry may be even more difficult to manage than the other two drives. It utilizes higher and therefore more subtle and complex functions. It involves all the possible pitfalls and pratfalls that accompany any understanding of the self and the world that avoids self-deception and comically one-sided perception. Only the very greatest thinkers, at their most sensitive, seem able to deal adequately with it. The analyses found, for example, in the second chapter of the *Chuang Tzu* or in Aquinas's most skillful uses of analogical predication do avoid it.

Intellectuals who think seriously about ideas of human flourishing are also, of course, liable to idolatry. The grossest manifestations of such thinking match anything a less-tutored mind can produce even if its packaging is, to most of us at least, more becoming. Most important here is a subtle form of idolatry to which intellectuals are especially liable. It occurs when they hypostatize or reify ideals of life, when they make abstractions into subsistent entities or forget that an abstraction is not something concrete. Even the work of the most sophisticated thinkers in the most sophisticated traditions will occasionally, sometimes often, be marked by this. But their clumsier followers, a description that unfortunately fits most of us most of the time, are veritable adepts at it.

We need to keep continually in mind that the pictures of ideal human flourishing that sophisticated thinkers present are intellectual constructions. (Even the thicker concepts contained in such ideal portraits, the notions of a particular virtue, for example, present only general guidelines.) They are best seen, then, as necessarily abstract and bloodless ideas that function as targets or goals. Their vagueness is a saving grace, not a sign of failure.

Stressing the difference between an abstract ideal and its concrete instantiations is not to question the significance of the abstract ideal. The exact characters of the ideas of human flourishing are not unimportant. Indeed, they are often all-important. But they function as general goals or targets, as guideposts that help one to identify suspicious, incorrect, or appropriate directions for oneself and others.

Conflicts Between Good and Bad Abstract Ideals of Human Flourishing

It makes a good deal of difference, sometimes all the difference, if a person's character and actions reflect a pursuit of fame or of friendship; a pursuit of simple sense pleasure or of complex intellectual, spiritual, and aesthetic pleasures; a pursuit of personal material gain or of sacrificial action that aims to help others. How exactly these general goals acquire specific form will depend on idiosyncrasies introduced by culture, personal history, and individual temperament.

The variations and even conflicts due to such idiosyncrasies should be embraced, if the goals are good. Indeed, we ought (as I argue later) to relish them and to have the often-painful lessons they provide inform our pictures of our own lives. Fundamental conflict should occur only between those who aim at versions of praiseworthy goals and those who are attached to goals or targets that contrast with them, goals such as fame, simple sense pleasure, or personal material gain. That is, fundamental conflicts should occur only when conflicts are "extrinsic" rather than "intrinsic."

This means that differences between general, abstract, and vaguely defined goals are often crucial. They tell us whom we should be worried about, and they show us who is dangerous both to themselves and to others. They help us to answer the critical and often vexing question of whom we should confront. Once, then, we have identified the goal or goals someone seeks—often an admittedly difficult task—we can more truly evaluate others and ourselves. We can remain largely unaffected by what are (in almost all circumstances) adventitious characteristics, characteristics such as charm, literateness, or irascibleness. Such characteristics may lead us to ameliorate judgments, and they surely have a place, an important place, in the whole economy of life.[3]

But if identifying real enemies and true allies (as well as those who do not fit easily into either category) is important, then searching for people's general goals is critical. Such identifications are important, not just to win battles about policy or to stop the bad from hurting the good or the innocent. They are also crucial if we are to help change those who have errant goals. And, of course, those who have errant goals will usually include us. As Pogo, the comic strip sage, said: I have met the enemy and he is me.

Unfortunately, many of the most severe such conflicts among ideals of human excellence cannot be dealt with just by reasoning or rhetoric, and sometimes not even humanely. Those who most need to change cannot be changed, at least not by rational argument, skillful persuasion, or even those many powerful educational practices that occur at a relatively late stage in a person's life.

I discuss my rationale for this somber conclusion in the next section. Here, however, I want to make clear why this position is not just another version of what Bellah and others have called "expressive individualism"—or even of that "vulgar relativism" which (in self-contradictory fashion) counsels noninterference on relativistic grounds. To take this position on the difficulty or even impossibility of overcoming such conflicts is not to counsel silence, apathy, or a sophisticated version of "anything goes." One does not in the name of such realism have to become fatalistic or to descend to the intellectual and spiritual flabbiness of expressive individualism.

Assume, for example, that I am thrown in with people whose lives clearly manifest an ideal of human flourishing that leads them to sacrifice family and friends to the pursuit of reputation and money. I can and I will argue with them. I can and I will try to dilute their influence on other people and institutions. Indeed, my disagreement with them is of crucial importance, and I use all my intellectual resources to try to make them change their mind. If I fail, however, I continue to think they are wrong. The frustrating problem, the problem that can generate a state close to despair, is that I cannot convince them they are wrong. I then turn to the important practical task of trying to moderate the influence they have on others. Were I facing people whose actions more directly hurt others, such as slum lords, the practical task would be even more crucial, and the luxury of continuing discussion might have to be even more quickly curtailed.

The conflict with such people is an extrinsic one. I never seriously consider that their view is a correct one, or, if I do, I realize that such a consideration shows a disturbing weakness in me. They represent, then, no challenge to my own sense of human flourishing. Indeed, they may well reinforce my sense of the value of my own ideal. This is true even though I realize that like other people I have a propensity to idolatry, a capacity for self-deception, and an often-unconscious need to reinforce my own sense of what is most important.

The opportunity to see in action a life dedicated to such errant goals, the chance to inventory and reflect upon my reactions to it, serves to deepen the sense that my picture of human flourishing is better than their picture. Such an understanding arises not just from the chance to witness the effect such a life has on others. It also arises from the growing accumulation of evidence that a life that sacrifices friends and family for fame and financial profit fails to express an adequate understanding of human flourishing.

That understanding remains no matter how I may evaluate a person's culpability for choosing that life. Indeed, all too often what is most clear is that we lack the needed information to make any such evaluation in a nuanced way. That understanding also remains no matter what the person who lives that life may say about pleasures gained and triumphs won. Freud was more right than we often like to think when he argued that such triumphs are usually purchased at the price of deep, neurotic divisions or its cousin, the dulled consciousness of severe repression.

The Good Person Criterion and Conflicts among Good and Bad Ideals

I can, then, be sure that people seek goods that stunt their lives and yet also that I cannot convince them of their error. To accept this somber conclusion is to find myself in a situation that may seem indefensible and surely demands further explanation. My explanation rests on describing and defending what I call the good person criterion.

The good person criterion refers to the idea that the good or flourishing person provides us with the ultimate criterion for deciding what characterizes human flourishing. The good person shows us what state we should seek and what actions we should do. We possess neither precise rules, nor inherent capacities, nor clear procedures that will produce adequate answers to the question of what we should do or be when full human flourishing is the subject. Therefore, if we wish to discover what to do or be we must finally rely on the example and the judgments of good people. This does not mean that reasons cannot be produced and will not help to guide us. But it does mean that we must rely on the identification and understanding of good people.

Labeling complex positions is a precarious business, but versions of the criterion appear not only in the Aristotelian tradition and the Thomistic tradition, where it is linked to the idea of knowledge by connaturality, but also in the Confucian tradition's notions of model emulation, attention (*ssu*), and extension (usually *tui* or *ta*).[4] The idea is, of course, developed in different ways in the three traditions. Notable distinctions appear, for example, in the way they characterize a realm of injunctions, a realm of binding universal obligations, and relate it to the good person criterion. (The Thomistic tradition, from which I draw most, has the most robust sense of the scope and importance of injunctions, for instance.) Moreover, thinkers in these three traditions often fail to distinguish clearly between two aspects of the good person criterion. The first is that only good people possess the dispositions that allow them to think effectively about ethics. The second is that good people will turn to other good people (which may include oneself in one's best moments) to obtain guidance about what to do and be. Distinguishing these aspects is important. That consultation occurs highlights that even good people are imperfect. It also shows the significance of continuing reflection and thus of giving and evaluating reasons.

Whatever the variations in each tradition's formulations, the basis of the good person criterion is clear. We discover human excellences by referring to excellent humans and excellent humans by referring to human excellences. We use good people to identify what is good and we know those people are good because they manifest the goods we came to know from the examples of good people. The notion is clearly circular, but the circle is, I think, a benign or even virtuous one rather than a vicious one.

Two claims or ideas underlie the criterion. First, the conceptions we use when thinking about human flourishing will often be imprecise. Second, these conceptions will be fully understood by, and therefore compelling to, only those people who are inclined to accept them, to people who have a sympathetic grasp of them that arises from their present dispositions. These two ideas are closely related, but I examine them separately.

The first idea rests on the presumption that how one knows depends on what one knows. Kinds of knowing are differentiated sharply according to the subject matter being considered. We can be only as conceptually precise as the subject matter allows, and ethics is a subject that allows for little precision. We must, then, pursue and consider ideas about human flourishing in the proper way and with the appropriate spirit.

Accepting this notion involves affirming the ideas discussed earlier about the dangers of idolatry and the conceptual character, the necessary saving vagueness, of ideals of human flourishing. More controversially, it also involves affirming that the criteria we use to evaluate people and their actions resemble, in illuminating ways, the criteria we use to make aesthetic judgments, as when we say a novel is deft or clumsy, superficial or deep. The resemblance to other forms of aesthetic judgments is less clear, as when we call a novel banal or exciting, well constructed or badly formed, brilliantly inane or stolidly provocative.

Criteria like these are slippery; identifying and explaining exactly why one quality applies rather than another can be difficult. We do, however, use such criteria, and often with assurance; that is, we feel no intrinsic conflict when we are opposed. Most important here, we realize that the aptness of the judgments made from such criteria rests finally on the sensibilities of the observer.

We will finally discount the views of a person who thinks Shakespeare's late comedies are superficial or boring, even after an intense discussion of the plays. We will also discount the views of a person who makes, after intense conversation, similar comments about kinds of human excellence. A person can reject the late comedies on the grounds that illusion plays little role in love and that, when it does, it is rarely funny. He resembles the person who rejects the idea that family and friends are more valuable than wealth and fame and who thinks his posture is neither sad nor even, at times, one that leads to ridiculous behavior. Such judgments need not end the interchange; we may finally be persuaded that what seemed deep was superficial or vice versa. But the grounds for making such changes will remain our sense of how apt or true is someone's grasp of the human situation.

The resemblance between these kinds of judgments occurs because almost all judgments about the appropriateness of an action, and thus of the agent who acts, depend upon our grasping a multitude of factors about the agent, the world, and the particular situation faced. To judge correctly, for example, that someone in love is bewitched by an illusion and is behaving in a humorous way involves understanding a multitude of specific, contingent factors. Indeed, the very understanding of those factors involves a skillful appreciation of the salient characteristics of specific circumstances and of our own and others' intentions.

We must have, then, an overall view of life that enables us to identify abstractly what is important, and we must also have the sensitivity, the quality of attention, that allows us to see what is important in a concrete situation. The complexity of the processes involved in these judgments means that, save in a few instances, the only rules are economical summaries of the judgments of good people or vague, even mock, rules, such as "act courageously." These mock rules or economical summaries are important, although appreciating or following them depends, of course, on our predispositions. They provide us with needed stability when we either lack the time to make thoughtful decisions or realize that we need to protect ourselves against the distortion of our own bias or emotion.

Aristotelians, Thomists, and Confucians often present this picture of the ethical life in mild terms. We must note, however, the considerably more dramatic way in which David Wiggins, focusing on a distinctively modern position, states what is for us a crucial point about the character of this kind of thinking:

> I entertain the unfriendly suspicion that those who feel they *must* seek more than all this [the Aristotelian position] provides want a scientific theory of rationality not so much from a passion for science, even where there can be no science, but because they hope and desire, by some conceptual alchemy, to turn such a theory into a regulative or normative discipline, or into a system of rules by which to spare themselves some of the agony of thinking and all the torment of feeling and understanding that is actually involved in reasoned deliberation.[5]

Wiggins's observation makes clear what underlies (and therefore what is at stake in) arguments about the ability to resolve basic differences about appropriate human goals. It is nothing less than a general vision of the human condition and of people's ideal state.

The most extreme opponents of the good person criterion claim that humans can attain, whether by themselves or with supernatural help, a perspective that is disengaged from the vagaries of self-understanding and from much of the world's evident complexity. When humans attain that perspective, it is said, they manifest a new freedom, dignity, and power, whether they exercise it in clear-headed planning or in following evidently true rules that arise from reason or even revelation. We see here, then, a clash between both general pictures of the human situation and compelling spiritual ideals.[6]

The fundamental character of this clash is worth underlining. Doing so helps us to understand both the depth of the conflict and the difficulty of any attempt to adjudicate it. Proponents of the different positions may not even be able to recognize the integrity of their opponents' respective enterprises. An adherent of the good person criterion, for example, may think an opponent is asking questions to which no human can give sensible answers. Conversely, the opponent may believe the adherent is not even addressing the questions that need to be addressed.

The conflict rests finally on the second notion underlying the good person criterion, the notion that the pursuit of the best human goals depends upon people having specific dispositions that enable them to appreciate and desire those goals. Those dispositions arise largely from processes of habituation, whatever their source, that occur before people can—or even when they cannot—effectively cultivate themselves. (As discussed briefly later, the sources of the needed dispositions can be many, and identifying them is difficult, especially if transhuman sources are considered.) Human flourishing, then, depends upon people having a taste for activities and states that they can attain only by habituation and that they, usually, must be trained or moved to reach.

Correct and compelling judgments about appropriate kinds of human excellence rest, then, on a variety of personal attributes. A quantity of experience that has been absorbed and reflected on is one such attribute, and many will, in time, be able to possess some version of it. But people can do little about obtaining other attributes, except over long periods of time, through rigorous self-cultivation, and (perhaps) with the help of transcendent powers. Most important is the general habituation people receive, *mutatis mutandis*, from an upbringing in a good family or community or from the action of sacred forces. Such habituation alone enables people to incline toward, and to take pleasure in, actions and states that are good.

Put differently, judgments about human ideals and the pursuit of them rest finally on what people are disposed to love. A good person will, for example, be disposed to love sacrificial giving, complex intellectual achievements, and the equilibrium meditation produces. Those dispositions all arise largely from cultivation received before one can cultivate oneself or from powers that one cannot force to act.

If people completely lack such habituation they will find unwelcome, painful, or even absurd the states or acts that manifest true human excellences. If people have received proper habituation but are still young, or if they have received incomplete or conflicting kinds of habituation, those states or acts will have some appeal. Other powerful desires, however, will conflict with them. At the least, the pull of the best states will be too limited to form their actions consistently.

The sobering conclusion of this perspective is clear: those who most need to hear both about the characteristics of human flourishing and about why they should possess them cannot really hear the message. Reflection about the human good works well, then, only with those who are already inclined to live in good ways, only with those who have a taste for it. Reflection in this area is effective only if it generates greater self-understanding, only if it reinforces and solidifies already-present inclinations. Without such inclinations, reflection is impotent.

Reflection's role is limited, then, but it can bring significant changes within people who already have at least some orientations that are appropriate. People may not have recognized the full force or real values of their existing dispositions, or they may not have grasped the importance of those dispositions as constituent parts of a good life. I may come to realize, for example, that direct service to my community, not philosophy, is the life I really love or the life I must pursue in this particular situation. Similarly, I may come through reflection to grasp the daunting implications of my inclination to value personal friendship, family relationships, or complex aesthetic pleasures as basic human goods. Such reflections can, then, lead me to undertake that often long and difficult process of self-cultivation by which I attempt to remold my dispositions.

Some such changes arise from direct reflection on a subject. Others come from the more complicated forms of understanding that arise from reflective living through difficult circumstances. But all such changes, as well as all such actions and thinking, involve starting from and continually moving within the language, attitudes, and loves one has. It involves, then, all the lack of precision evident in any process of self-understanding in which one tries to grasp what one wants and why. And it presupposes that one wants appropriate things. We always see through the lens of what we are, of how we are disposed to love and be.

The good person criterion rests on the role of dispositions and the character of knowledge of human flourishings. Utilizing it explains, I hope, why one can be sure both that some people pursue errant goals and that one cannot convince them of their error. (I have, however, no ready answer to the empirical question of just how many people are disposed to pursue only errant human goals.) It helps to explain why talk with some of them is as likely to be productive as Xerxes' lashing of the Hellespont. Thomistic notions of invincible ignorance, the Confucian notion of "no man" [*pu jen*], and perhaps even Aristotelian notions of the "brute" all point to this category of people that our experience also reveals.

It is far more difficult to decide about the state of those seemingly great numbers of people who are not easily deemed depraved and yet who seem to pursue what are, at best, extremely problematic goals of human flourishing. Any adequate answer to this question would have to proceed case by case. Moreover, I think (or perhaps I just hope) that almost all of these cases exhibit more confusion than evil. Let us turn, then, to the more gratifying subject of how we ought to think about conflicts among what are clearly high human ideals.

REGRET AND THE CONFLICT AMONG JUSTIFIABLE IDEALS OF HUMAN FLOURISHING

These conflicts occur when I face, for example, a college friend who has chosen to teach high school in a slum (or perhaps in a wealthy suburb) or when I meet someone who has chosen to forgo the moderate, bourgeois comfort of an academic life to take a menial job that allows her to meditate and pursue a passionate interest in T'ang dynasty Buddhism. Heated discussion between us may occur about our choices of how to live, but I never question the significance of the other's chosen goals. My questions aim only to clarify if the life fits the person, to see if it accords or wars with cultural context, personal temperament, and individual history. Furthermore, I may well try to extend the possible influence such people have on other people or institutions.

Finally, lives like these produce an intrinsic challenge to my life. I may even change what I do, either in radical ways or in small but substantial ways. The depth of my response to the challenge those lives pose does not depend upon my evaluation of the abstract goal their lives represent—I accept that each represents an excellent kind of human flourishing. Rather, it depends on whether a particular life can fit with me. It depends, then, upon the consideration of a great variety of particular, personal matters, such as whether my personal history, cultural location, given responsibilities, and distinctive talents make it possible for me to live well that kind of life.

It may seem that to ask only these kinds of questions when considering such conflict is to adopt a preference theory of the good. With conflicts between good and bad ideals something resembling preference is involved only in the sense that one admits that all people cannot be rationally convinced about the real character of human flourishing. Emphasizing how a choice of goals must "fit" with particular personal characteristics does, of course, mean that a kind of personal preference is crucial.

But the notion of preference, like the notion of desire, can easily become so inflated that we end up with a notion that obscures critical distinctions and fails to reflect the fact that how we know depends on what we know. Such an inflation of the category of preference makes sense only if we mistakenly believe that two options exhaust all the possibilities— that is, either that all decisions arise from rational processes that are basically the same in all people, or that all decisions (or preferences) arise from individual characteristics that are by definition unique or at least distinctive.

I want, however, both to underline how qualities of character determine some choices of goals and yet to make a number of distinctions about how kinds of dispositions and forms of reason operate. Put briefly (or even telegraphically) I want to differentiate choices that arise from first-order desires and choices that arise from second-order desires or volitions and argue that only the former are best described as preferences. This distinction, in turn, rests on differences between the roles that general goals play in people's decisions. That is, I distinguish between weak and strong evaluations and call only the former simple preferences. Weak evaluations arise when I decide among a number of contingent desires, all of which I would like to fulfill if the desires themselves and circumstances allowed it. Strong evaluations arise from a decision about what kind of person I aim to be, a decision in which I use the contrastive terminology of worthy and unworthy when I think about my desires. Furthermore, as discussed earlier, I want to argue for the importance of reflection about one's dispositions and how they fit into one's general view of the good life. Finally, other important distinctions arise from one's formulation of the way in which history determines us, but that topic can best be treated by moving on to the role that regret should play in the life of good people.[7]

Severe limits—of history, temperament, and culture—clearly define us all. But they do not simply determine our choices even when, as surely happens in many cases, they define a context in which we have only a few real alternatives. A recognition of these limits produces another, distinctively modern, component in any flourishing life: the presence of regret.

When good people recognize that divergent varieties of human flourishing are possible, they must feel a kind of regret. This regret does not arise from their recognition that they did something they should not have done while having the power to do the appropriate thing. That is regret about one's own frailty or even wickedness. Nor is it the regret that arises when one does something one knows to be virtuous, such as refusing to browbeat a student to obtain information, even though it causes results one abhors—the possible destruction of a promising academic career that might have been prevented if one possessed the information. That is regret about a world that produces such impossible choices, a world that is, to use Christian terms, not just contingent but sinful, a world that is, to use Confucian terms, not just natural but distorted.

The regret referred to here differs from both of these all-too-common kinds of regret. I call it spiritual regret. It is the regret that results from having learned another lesson in the hard curriculum that our human finitude presses on us. This regret arises, then, from once again having seen how limits operate. Some of the limits are the result of distant past choices, some are the results of matters beyond one's control, and some are the result of that convoluted combination of choice and chance that so often sets who we are and what we do.

This regret can arise in different forms at different times in one's life. But it seems clearly to be linked to age, or better to maturity, to a well-understood fund of experience. Any full-blooded grasp of it depends upon understandings that only maturity can produce: the sense that possibilities are not unlimited; the sense that autonomy, while crucial, is not the only thing of worth; the sense that we must live with choices we made even if the reasons for them, or even the choices themselves, are hard to remember.

To recognize these things is sobering. It may even induce deep fear and sadness, or the anxiety, despair, and spiritual sloth (*acedia*) that they can generate. Part of us would like to believe some version of the deeply untrue advertising slogan that says we can have it all. The better part of us realizes, however, that in many of the areas that are most important to us a "no shopping" principle operates. To think we can pick and choose among ideals of human flourishing as we pick and choose among food, wines, or clothes is to be deeply mistaken.

The most revealing examples of this inability to shop occur in those painfully illuminating moments when you deeply appreciate something you know is an unacceptable option for you and will not, you hope, become an option for those you love most. Examples are many, especially if one studies either other cultures or Western history. Some strike especially close to home: Mencius's refusal to greet a bereaved person in order to honor ritual [*li*]; Aquinas's defenses of virginity; Chuang Tzu's powerful notion of compassion, which leads him to overlook evident wrongdoing. Others are more distant and yet they still bite: Confucius's validation of the heroism evident in a gamekeeper's refusal, at risk of death, to answer an improper summons so that proper rank and relations may be protected; the way that Indian villagers, responding to their sense of social and even cosmic harmony, find more objectionable a widow who eats fish three times a week than a doctor who refuses to treat a sick patient because that patient is poor. With these latter, more distant options we enter that vexing territory where, especially in cross-cultural contexts, conflicts among justifiable goods shade into conflicts between justifiable and unjustifiable goods. Here, however, I focus only on conflicts among justifiable ideals of human flourishing.[8]

For me, perhaps the most striking example of such a conflict occurred when I spent two hours very early one morning in Korea on a cliff above the South China Sea looking at the Sokkurum Buddha. The spiritual vision presented there was as powerful as I have ever seen. Yet I wanted it neither for myself nor for those about whom I care most. At such times, one realizes that Bernard Williams's influential distinction between notional and real confrontations fails to account for a very important range of confrontations that fall between those two poles.[9]

Williams's distinction helps us recognize that we cannot really choose some options that confront us. A notional confrontation does differ from a real one: the crucial difference is understanding that I cannot, without ceasing to be me, incarnate the excellences I face in a notional confrontation. I could choose to try to become a professor in Korea and therefore aim to acquire virtues I do not now have. But I cannot choose to manifest the virtues of a traditional Korean shaman without surrendering so many basic ideas and attitudes that I would cease to be me. A number of significant confrontations, however, fail to fit neatly in either category. I could imagine attempting to incarnate the excellences I saw in the Sokkurum Buddha that morning in Korea. I admired them, they tempted me, and I believe I could have chosen them and remained myself. But I did not want to choose them, and I hoped that those about whom I most care would not choose them.

Such a situation represents the clearest case of a regret that rests on the contingencies of where one was born and what one chose, even wisely chose, in the past. Those contingencies reflect the extraordinary power of community and thus tradition in human life. In a simple, direct sense, the possibility or impossibility of fully participating in a community establishes whether or not an option is a real one. Almost no Westerner can really become a Confucian because almost no Westerner can really join and live fully within a Confucian community. In a less direct, more complex sense, communities of memory define for us the real possibilities. They subconsciously, or unconsciously, form those sentiments and sensibilities, those general notions and specific ideals, that underlie any choice we make.

Recognizing the power of community and other related forces in people's lives does not also lead to affirming that people will rarely, if ever, change in substantial ways. Conversions do occur, whether from one community to another or from one general viewpoint to another. Reflection on one's dispositions as discussed earlier can generate such changes. Nevertheless, the fact that fundamental changes do occur and a view that stresses the significance of community and dispositions often underlie the ideas of those religious thinkers who emphasize the role of transhuman powers. Whether it is Chuang Tzu on the link of fate (*ming*) or the daemonic (*shen*) and true sagehood or Lonergan on the relation of conversion and grace, both the difficulty and possibility of fundamental transformations generate an account that turns to religious language and speaks of transhuman sources of human action. Indeed, it is this feature, among others, that can make regret "spiritual."[10]

To recapitulate, regret of a spiritual sort arises when one recognizes three things: first, that various, legitimate ideals of human flourishing exist; second, that conflict among them means that no single person can come close to exhibiting all of them; and third, that those states which one can possess will often be determined by forces either beyond one's immediate control or beyond anyone's control.

Such an understanding is sobering. But it must also be informed by a joy that arises from realizing the plethora of human goods that do exist in the world, and that exist as they do because no single person can possess them. To stress the role of joy may seem, to some, to bring with it the rancid odor of sentimentality. Sentimentality, however, lives uneasily with spiritual regret. Moreover, sentimentality is a problem only when it hinders us from seeing the hard edges of the world or when it forces us to demonize someone or something that has made pitiable the object of our sentiment. Chuang Tzu, the early Taoist, can serve well as a guide here. Few if any have looked at the world in as clear-eyed or unsentimental a fashion. And yet few if any have also taken as much joy in the presence of different kinds of goods in the world. In fact, Chuang Tzu reserves his most stinging irony for those, like the well frog, who cannot imagine the plethora of goods, or for those, like most Confucians, who fail to see them.[11]

Indeed, the fact that one cannot actualize many integral human goods will produce sadness only if one thinks one is the sole locus of value in the world, the only being worth considering. If one looks attentively at the larger world one will see others who manifest goods of human flourishing that one cannot. This is especially true if one attends to cultures whose context and history have led to irreversible developments (the results of what Charles Taylor calls the ratchet effect) that differ from our own, such as cultures in which an appreciation of nature or family is more central than in our own culture.

We cannot, for good reasons, enjoy the goods of human flourishing that others possess in the way we enjoy our own. But their presence will produce a real joy in us, unless we think we are the only beings of worth. One may or may not believe that the variations in human flourishing manifest some higher reality, whether the creator God many Christians depict or the Tao many Confucians celebrate. But any sensitive observer has to recognize that those flourishings are flourishings and that they exist as they do just because they conflict with one's own goods. The only question left, then, is whether one will not just honor but also derive joy from the goods evident in those conflicting kinds of human flourishing.

ENVY AND CONFLICTS AMONG JUSTIFIABLE IDEALS OF THE GOOD

I have dealt here with two kinds of conflict. First were conflicts in which abstract ideals of human flourishing differ, as between those of a person guided by an ideal of self-sacrifice for others and those of a person guided by an ideal of fame and material well-being. Severe extrinsic conflicts may arise, but not intrinsic conflict. Neither does spiritual regret nor a joy in divergent goods occur.

The second kind of conflict, of central concern here, concerns situations where the abstract ideals differ and one values two or more of them but cannot, in fact, incarnate or act on some of them. Indeed, one may not even be able to imagine acting on them, even though one realizes one could do so; that is, they fit between real and notional possibilities as they usually are defined. These kinds of conflicts can be more or less dramatic. On the one hand is the important but undramatic conflict present in the distinction between my life as a comfortable academic and my friend's life as a teacher in the slums. On the other hand is the dramatic distinction between most of what I value and much of what I saw in the Sokkurum Buddha.

These conflicts do and should produce regret as well as a joy in the plethora of goods. When they do not, or when someone says they cannot, it is because of two deformations to which we all are liable. The first is idolatry—the reifying of an abstract ideal into a concrete something—as discussed earlier. The second is envy.

Envy is one of the more disturbing and complicated human phenomena. La Rochefoucauld thought almost no one could easily admit to being envious, and he found especially terrifying the fact that the spectacle of a friend's misfortune can warm something in our hearts. Many have commented on how, unlike most vices, envy produces few evident or simple pleasures. Unlike lust or gluttony, for example, envy seems mainly to produce pain or perverse pleasures. It even seems, to use modern terms, to be linked to masochism and, perhaps, to sadism.

Envy, then, has many faces, most of them perplexing. It may, for example, animate a kind of emulation that positively feeds self-cultivation, but it may also animate a kind of belittlement that impedes self-cultivation. For our purposes, however, an excellent starting point is Aquinas's analysis of those aspects of envy that are present when it is understood as a deadly deformation of human life. Envy is, he thinks, a deep sin or deformation, a human tendency that manifests our fundamental corruption. When one is envious, one resents the goods that others possess or manifest. When envious, one wants to take from others those human goods that one either also has or that one fails to possess. Indeed, when most truly envious, one does not even necessarily want to possess another's good—one simply wants that person not to have it. One is happy to let an arid desert exist rather than let bloom those flowers one cannot possess.[12]

To use the terms of our previous discussions, the truly envious resent the goods they face in real, notional, and "in between" confrontations. They resent even the goods present in notional confrontations insofar as they know that people either appreciate and pursue such goods or have appreciated and pursued them. Perhaps even more striking, the truly envious resent the goods or apparent goods present in both intrinsic and extrinsic conflicts. Goods they see no reason to possess and feel no desire to choose are objects of their envy, if ones on which they focus less.

Envy, according to Aquinas, is a failure of charitable love, even a primitive offense against it. Indeed, it is the most likely place for hatred of God to appear, given that we know and love God through his effects. The envious fail to love others. But they also fail to love those kinds of goods that can and do exist, even if they do not possess them. Envy is, in the context of our analysis, a failure to see and honor the spiritual truth present in the fact that divergent human goods conflict. It is the failure to see that the fact of each person's finitude need not mean that the variety of possible goods is simply an expression of finitude.

Put differently, envy and the resultant failure to recognize conflicting kinds of human flourishing are a deformation that leads one to overlook one of the more crucial principles in both religion and ethics: the otherness of people. (That otherness manifests itself in and underlies the notion of individuality, although that notion will, of course, have different valences depending on the metaphysical context.) Envy is a, or even the, solipsistic sin. It can also express the most extreme form of distorted self-love and the kind of idolatry that recognizes only the goods the idolater possesses. It rests directly on pride and manifests clearly the primitive kind of self-assertion that the notion of pride tries to capture. Unwillingness to see differences, to comprehend others, is its product. That unwillingness can also, at times, even be its source, as when one sees others merely as threats and thus not as beings who differ from oneself.

We are and we must be specialists in the human good. We must always walk, stumble, or stride lopsided to the grave. Because that is all true we are necessarily involved in conflicts among goods. Hierarchies among those conflicting goods may exist. Most great teachers in most great traditions have surely thought so. But they also have recognized that hierarchies depend on criteria, and criteria shift, depending on what question is asked or what good is highlighted. Moreover, when they force themselves to think through the hardest cases, the great teachers recognize that time, place, and temperament undermine any notion of a stable, easily applicable hierarchy. Aquinas's delicately nuanced, even tortured analysis of the roles of the active and contemplative life exhibits this, for example, as does Wang Yang-ming's counsel to find one's spiritual task in whatever situation confronts one.

We as moderns have an even better sense than almost any past person could have of how fragile, how contingent, those hierarchies are for which one can argue. We therefore have the opportunity, I think, to appreciate more fully the crucial roles played by the ideal of conflicts among notions of human flourishing. These conflicts tell us how real is our goodness, how complete is our lack of goodness, and how striking is the plethora of goods that surround us.

Such conflicts also allow us to understand that idolatry and envy undermine our ability to affirm what we should. Moreover, recognizing the conflicts also leads us to live with that mixture of regret and joy that ought to characterize our own, distinctive kind of human flourishing. The message is clear; the reception of it is, as always, difficult.

NOTES

1. In what follows I presuppose that we all agree on the need to protect a very minimal set of abstract, universally binding injunctions; I recognize that for some what I presuppose constitutes the real subject of any discussion of a common morality. For more on the relationship of injunctions and ideals of human flourishing see Lee H. Yearley, *Mencius and Aquinas: Theories of Virtue and Conceptions of Courage* (Albany: State University of New York Press, 1990), pp. 6–13, 48–51. My approach there draws on Alan Donagan's defense of both the integrity and the limits of what he calls a rationalist morality; see especially Donagan, "Consistency in Rationalist Moral Systems," *Journal of Philosophy* 81, no. 6 (1984): 308–9.

Much can be said, of course, about different kinds of conflicts. For example, in some conflicts similar ideals are present but particular people's instantiations of the ideal are opposed. Others arise not just from hard choices but from genuine conundrums, situations (all too familiar at the level of public policy) in which sensible people cannot even agree on what the state of affairs is or what the consequences will be. Finally, in some situations differences are too important for normal conflicts to exist (the narrow realm of evidently outrageous wrongdoing), while in others differences are too unimportant for them to exist (the wide realm of taste).

2. An important difference among the three traditions concerns their respective understandings of human beings' "natural," unnurtured capacities to lead flourishing lives, or at least to see the rationale for very general moral judgments. I examine this and related issues in *Mencius and Aquinas*, pp. 44–51, 58–60, 72–78, 84–95.

3. The significance for people's character and action of general goals is not universally accepted, but I do not rehearse here the very powerful arguments for that notion. More difficult is the issue of just how aberrant are most people's goals; I discuss that briefly later.

4. Perhaps the classic Western statement of the "good person criterion" appears in Aristotle's *Nichomachean Ethics*: see 1176a10–29 for a clear formulation and note 1176b9–1177a10 for an indirect one; also note 1140b5. The idea rests on the procedure announced at 1094b13–1095a11 and 1095b1–14. For Aquinas's treatment of connatural knowledge see, *Summa Theologiae* 1.1.6.ad 3; 1.2.22.2; 2.2.27.4.ad 1. On extension and attention, see, for example, *Mencius* 1a7; 6a6, 13, 15; 7a15; 7b3. (In pursuing this and following references to Men-

cius, I recommend using *Mencius*, trans. D. C. Lau [Baltimore: Penguin Books, 1970]). For differences among these thinkers that influence their development of this criterion, see note 2 and Yearley, *Mencius and Aquinas*, pp. 6–13, 48–51, 84–95.

It is worth noting that virtually no one in these three traditions accepts the version of democratic liberalism that, following Shklar, can be called the liberalism of fear; see Judith Shklar, *Ordinary Vices* (Cambridge, Mass.: Belknap Press of Harvard University Press, 1984). I think such a notion follows from the good person criterion, however, because it allows us best both to guard against dangers to any kind to human flourishing and to protect the plethora of possible human fulfillments. Whether such liberalism can ever adequately nurture many important kinds of fulfillment is another, and very sobering, question.

5. David Wiggins, "Deliberation and Practical Reason," in A. Rorty, ed., *Essays on Aristotle's Ethics* (Berkeley and Los Angeles: University of California Press, 1980), p. 237; for others who develop similar positions, see Jonathan Lear, *Aristotle: The Desire to Understand* (Cambridge: Cambridge University Press, 1988), pp. 141–60; John MacDowell, "Virtue and Reason," *Monist* 62 (1979): 331–50; and Martha C. Nussbaum, *The Fragility of Goodness: Luck and Ethics in Greek Tragedy and Philosophy* (Cambridge: Cambridge University Press, 1986), pp. 290–312.

6. The general position outlined here has modern adherents among some decision theorists and neo-Kantians, but it also appears in the work of some Augustinians, Mohists, and Stoics. The vexing issue of how best to conceive the role of autonomy and responsiblity in versions of these two positions is discussed by Bernard Williams, *Ethics and the Limits of Philosophy* (Cambridge, Mass.: Harvard University Press, 1985), pp. 35–53, 110–19, 148–55, 174–96.

7. The general position I outline here, using various terms of art, is spelled out in Harry Frankfurt, "Freedom of the Will and the Concept of a Person," *Journal of Philosophy* 68, no. 1 (1971): 5–20; Gary Watson, "Free Agency," in G. Watson, ed., *Free Will* (New York: Oxford University Press, 1982), pp. 96–110; and Charles Taylor, *Human Agency and Language: Philosophical Papers 1* (Cambridge: Cambridge University Press, 1985), pp. 15–44. (I think, incidentally, that a person may make strong evaluations that clearly are bad, not good.) On the general issue of how history forms character see Stuart Hampshire, *Morality and Conflict* (Cambridge, Mass.: Harvard University Press, 1983), pp. 20–26, 32–43, 127–69, from whom the idea of a "no shopping principle" is drawn. Also note the discussion of various thinkers on this subject in my review essay on virtue, "Recent Work on Virtue," *Religious Studies Review* 16, no. 1 (1990): 1–9.

8. See, for example, *Mencius* 3b1, 4b27; *Summa Theologiae* 2.2.152; and *Chuang Tzu*, chap. five. (In this and following references to Chuang Tzu, I recommend using *Chuang-tzu: The Seven Inner Chapters and Other Writings from the Book Chuang-tzu*, trans. Angus Graham (London: George Allen and Unwin, 1981).

9. For Williams's distinction between notional and real confrontations, see *Ethics and the Limits of Philosophy*, pp. 160–67.

10. Many problems surround, of course, any examination of the sources for either dispositions or substantial changes in dispositions. For an examination of some of them see Yearley, *Mencius and Aquinas*, pp. 84–95, 106–11, 175–82.

11. See, for example, the Autumn Floods dialogue in chap. 17 of the *Chuang Tzu*. That this kind of "preference" also involves joy in other's goods shows yet another way in which it differs from more normal notions of preference.

12. Aquinas's main treatment of envy is found in *Summa Theologiae* 2.2.36. Those who doubt either that the more extreme forms of envy occur or that they reveal much about normal forms might want to examine, in addition to Aquinas's treatment, Melville's presentation of Claggart in *Billy Budd*. Melville was well aware that many readers might find Claggart an implausible character; see especially his comments in chapter 10.

Chapter 11

THE PRIORITY OF DEMOCRACY TO PHILOSOPHY

RICHARD RORTY

THOMAS JEFFERSON set the tone for American liberal politics when he said "it does me no injury for my neighbor to say that there are twenty Gods or no God."[1] His example helped make respectable the idea that politics can be separated from beliefs about matters of ultimate importance—that shared beliefs among citizens on such matters are not essential to a democratic society. Like many other figures of the Enlightenment, Jefferson assumed that a moral faculty common to the typical theist and the typical atheist suffices for civic virtue.

Many Enlightenment intellectuals were willing to go further and say that since religious beliefs turn out to be inessential for political cohesion, they should simply be discarded as mumbo jumbo—perhaps to be replaced (as in twentieth-century totalitarian Marxist states) with some sort of explicitly secular political faith that will form the moral consciousness of the citizen. Jefferson again set the tone when he refused to go that far. He thought it enough to privatize religion, to view it as irrelevant to social order but relevant to, and possibly essential for, individual perfection. Citizens of a Jeffersonian democracy can be as religious or irreligious as they please as long as they are not "fanatical." That is, they must abandon or modify opinions on matters of ultimate importance, the opinions that may hitherto have given sense and point to their lives, if these opinions entail public actions that cannot be justified to most of their fellow citizens.

This Jeffersonian compromise concerning the relation of spiritual perfection to public policy has two sides. Its absolutist side says that every human being, without the benefit of special revelation, has all the beliefs necessary for civic virtue. These beliefs spring from a universal human faculty, conscience—possession of which constitutes the specifically human essence of each human being. This is the faculty that gives the individual human dignity and rights. But there is also a pragmatic side. This side says that when the individual finds in her conscience beliefs that are relevant to public policy but incapable of defense on the basis of beliefs common to her fellow citizens, she must sacrifice her conscience on the altar of public expediency.

The tension between these two sides can be eliminated by a philosophical theory that identifies justifiability to humanity at large with truth. The Enlightenment idea of "reason" embodies such a theory: the theory that there is a relation between the ahistorical essence of the human soul and moral truth, a relation which ensures that free and open discussion will produce "one right answer" to moral as well as to scientific questions.[2] Such a theory guarantees that a moral belief that cannot be justified to the mass of mankind is "irrational," and thus is not really a product of our moral faculty at all. Rather, it is a "prejudice," a belief that comes from some other part of the soul than "reason." It does not share in the sanctity of conscience, for it is the product of a sort of pseudoconscience—something whose loss is no sacrifice, but a purgation.

In our century, this rationalist justification of the Enlightenment compromise has been discredited. Contemporary intellectuals have given up the Enlightenment assumption that religion, myth, and tradition can be opposed to something ahistorical, something common to all human beings qua human. Anthropologists and historians of science have blurred the distinction between innate rationality and the products of acculturation. Philosophers such as Heidegger and Gadamer have given us ways of seeing human beings as historical all the way through. Other philosophers, such as Quine and Davidson, have blurred the distinction between permanent truths of reason and temporary truths of fact. Psychoanalysis has blurred the distinction between conscience and the emotions of love, hate, and fear, and thus the distinction between morality and prudence. The result is to erase the picture of the self common to Greek metaphysics, Christian theology, and Enlightenment rationalism: the picture of an ahistorical natural center, the locus of human dignity, surrounded by an adventitious and inessential periphery.

The effect of erasing this picture is to break the link between truth and justifiability. This, in turn, breaks down the bridge between the two sides of the Enlightenment compromise. The effect is to polarize liberal social theory. If we stay on the absolutist side, we shall talk about inalienable "human rights" and about "one right answer" to moral and political dilemmas without trying to back up such talk with a theory of human nature. We shall abandon metaphysical accounts of what a right is while nevertheless insisting that everywhere, in all times and cultures, members of our species have had the same rights. But if we swing to the pragmatist side, and consider talk of "rights" an attempt to enjoy the benefits of metaphysics without assuming the appropriate responsibilities, we shall still need something to distinguish the sort of individual conscience we respect from the sort we condemn as "fanatical." This can only be something relatively local and ethnocentric—the tradition of a particular community, the consensus of a particular culture. According to this view, what counts as rational or as fanatical is relative to the group to which we think it necessary to justify ourselves—to the body of shared belief that determines the reference of the word "we." The Kantian identification with a central transcultural and ahistorical self is thus replaced by a quasi-Hegelian identification with our own community, thought of as a historical product. For pragmatist social theory, the question of whether justifiability to the community with which we identify entails truth is simply irrelevant.

Ronald Dworkin and others who take the notion of ahistorical human "rights" seriously serve as examples of the first, absolutist, pole. John Dewey and, as I shall shortly be arguing, John Rawls serve as examples of the second pole. But there is a third type of social theory—often dubbed "communitarianism"—which is less easy to place. Roughly speaking, the writers tagged with this label are those who reject both the individualistic rationalism of the Enlightenment and the idea of "rights," but, unlike the pragmatists, see this rejection as throwing doubt on the institutions and culture of the surviving democratic states. Such theorists include Robert Bellah, Alasdair MacIntyre, Michael Sandel, Charles Taylor, early Roberto Unger, and many others. These writers share some measure of agreement with a view found in an extreme form both in Heidegger and in Horkheimer and Adorno's *Dialectic of Enlightenment*. This is the view that liberal institutions and culture either should not or cannot survive the collapse of the philosophical justification that the Enlightenment provided for them.

There are three strands in communitarianism that need to be disentangled. First, there is the empirical prediction that no society that sets aside the idea of ahistorical moral truth in the insouciant way that Dewey recommended can survive. Horkheimer and Adorno, for example, suspect that you cannot have a moral community in a disenchanted world because toleration leads to pragmatism, and it is not clear how we can prevent "blindly pragmatized thought" from losing "its transcending quality and its relation to truth."[3] They think that pragmatism was the inevitable outcome of Enlightenment rationalism and that pragmatism is not a strong enough philosophy to make moral community possible.[4] Second, there is the moral judgment that the sort of human being who is produced by liberal institutions and culture is undesirable. MacIntyre, for example, thinks that our culture—a culture he says is dominated by "the Rich Aesthete, the Manager, and the Therapist"—is a *reductio ad absurdum* both of the philosophical views that helped create it and of those now invoked in its defense. Third, there is the claim that political institutions "presuppose" a doctrine about the nature of human beings and that such a doctrine must, unlike Enlightenment rationalism, make clear the essentially historical character of the self. So we find writers like Taylor and Sandel saying that we need a theory of the self that incorporates Hegel's and Heidegger's sense of the self's historicity.

The first claim is a straightforward empirical, sociological-historical one about the sort of glue that is required to hold a community together. The second is a straightforward moral judgment that the advantages of contemporary liberal democracy are outweighed by the disadvantages, by the ignoble and sordid character of the culture and the individual human beings that it produces. The third claim, however, is the most puzzling and complex. I shall concentrate on this third, most puzzling, claim, although toward the end I shall return briefly to the first two.

To evaluate this third claim, we need to ask two questions. The first is whether there is any sense in which liberal democracy "needs" philosophical justification at all. Those who share Dewey's pragmatism will say that although it may need philosophical articulation, it does not need philosophical backup. On this view, the philosopher of liberal democracy may wish to develop a theory of the human self that comports with the institutions he or she admires. But such a philosopher is not thereby justifying these institutions by reference to more fundamental premises, but the reverse: He or she is putting politics first and tailoring a philosophy to suit. Communitarians, by contrast, often speak as though political institutions were no better than their philosophical foundations.

The second question is one that we can ask even if we put the opposition between justification and articulation to one side. It is the question of whether a conception of the self that, as Taylor says, makes "the community constitutive of the individual"[5] does in fact comport better with liberal democracy than does the Enlightenment conception of the self. Taylor summarizes the latter as "an ideal of disengagement" that defines a "typically modern notion" of human dignity: "the ability to act on one's own, without outside interference or subordination to outside authority." On Taylor's view, as on Heidegger's, these Enlightenment notions are closely linked with characteristically modern ideas of "efficacy, power, unperturbability."[6] They are also closely linked with the contemporary form of the doctrine of the sacredness of the individual conscience— Dworkin's claim that appeals to rights "trump" all other appeals. Taylor, like Heidegger, would like to substitute a less individualistic conception of what it is to be properly human—one that makes less of autonomy and more of interdependence.

I can preview what is to come by saying that I shall answer "no" to the first question about the communitarians' third claim and "yes" to the second. I shall be arguing that Rawls, following up on Dewey, shows us how liberal democracy can get along without philosophical presuppositions. He has thus shown us how we can disregard the third communitarian claim. But I shall also argue that communitarians like Taylor are right in saying that a conception of the self that makes the community constitutive of the self does comport well with liberal democracy. That is, if we *want* to flesh out our self-image as citizens of such a democracy with a philosophical view of the self, Taylor gives us pretty much the right view. But this sort of philosophical fleshing-out does not have the importance that writers like Horkheimer and Adorno, or Heidegger, have attributed to it.

Without further preface, I turn now to Rawls. I shall begin by pointing out that both in *A Theory of Justice* and subsequently, he has linked his own position to the Jeffersonian ideal of religious toleration. In an article called "Justice as Fairness: Political not Metaphysical," he says that he is "going to apply the principle of toleration to philosophy itself," and goes on to say:

> The essential point is this: as a practical political matter no general moral conception can provide the basis for a public conception of justice in a modern democratic society. The social and historical conditions of such a society have their origins in the Wars of Religion following the Reformation and the development of the principle of toleration, and in the growth of constitutional government and the institutions of large market economies. These conditions profoundly affect the requirements of a workable conception of political justice: such a conception must allow for a diversity of doctrines and the plurality of conflicting, and indeed incommensurable conceptions of the good affirmed by the members of existing democratic societies.[7]

We can think of Rawls as saying that just as the principle of religious toleration and the social thought of the Enlightenment proposed to bracket many standard theological topics when deliberating about public policy and constructing political institutions, so we need to bracket many standard topics of philosophical inquiry. For purposes of social theory, we can put aside such topics as an ahistorical human nature, the nature of selfhood, the motive of moral behavior, and the meaning of human life. We treat these as irrelevant to politics as Jefferson thought questions about the Trinity and about transubstantiation.

Insofar as he adopts this stance, Rawls disarms many of the criticisms that, in the wake of Horkheimer and Adorno, have been directed at American liberalism. Rawls can agree that Jefferson and his circle shared a lot of dubious philosophical views, views that we might now wish to reject. He can even agree with Horkheimer and Adorno, as Dewey would have, that these views contained the seeds of their own destruction. But he thinks that the remedy may be not to formulate better philosophical views on the same topics, but (for purposes of political theory) benignly to neglect these topics. As he says:

since justice as fairness is intended as a political conception of justice for a democratic society, it tries to draw solely upon basic intuitive ideas that are embedded in the political institutions of a democratic society and the public traditions of their interpretation. Justice as fairness is a political conception in part because it starts from within a certain political tradition. We hope that this political conception of justice may be at least supported by what we may call "overlapping consensus," that is, by a consensus that includes all the opposing philosophical and religious doctrines likely to persist and gain adherents in a more or less just constitutional democratic society.[8]

Rawls thinks that "philosophy as the search for truth about an independent metaphysical and moral order cannot . . . provide a workable and shared basis for a political conception of justice in a democratic society."[9] So he suggests that we confine ourselves to collecting "such settled convictions as the belief in religious toleration and the rejection of slavery" and then "try to organize the basic intuitive ideas and principles implicit in these convictions into a coherent conception of justice."[10]

This attitude is thoroughly historicist and antiuniversalist.[11] Rawls can wholeheartedly agree with Hegel and Dewey against Kant and can say that the Enlightenment attempt to free oneself from tradition and history, to appeal to "Nature" or "Reason," was self-deceptive.[12] He can see such an appeal as a misguided attempt to make philosophy do what theology failed to do. Rawls's effort to, in his words, "stay on the surface, philosophically speaking" can be seen as taking Jefferson's avoidance of theology one step further.

On the Deweyan view I am attributing to Rawls, no such discipline as "philosophical anthropology" is required as a preface to politics, but only history and sociology. Further, it is misleading to think of his view as Dworkin does: as "rights-based" as opposed to "goal-based." For the notion of "basis" is not in point. It is not that we know, on antecedent philosophical grounds, that it is of the essence of human beings to have rights, and then proceed to ask how a society might preserve and protect these rights. On the question of priority, as on the question of the relativity of justice to historical situations, Rawls is closer to Walzer than to Dworkin.[13] Since Rawls does not believe that for purposes of political theory we need think of ourselves as having an essence that precedes and antedates history, he would not agree with Sandel that for these purposes we need have an account of "the nature of the moral subject," which is "in some sense necessary, non-contingent and prior to any particular experience."[14] Some of our ancestors may have required such an account, just as others of our ancestors required such an account of their relation to their putative Creator. But *we*—we heirs of the Enlightenment for whom justice has become the first virtue—need neither. As citizens and as social theorists, we can be as indifferent to philosophical disagreements about the nature of the self as Jefferson was to theological differences about the nature of God.

This last point suggests a way of sharpening up my claim that Rawls's advocacy of philosophical toleration is a plausible extension of Jefferson's advocacy of religious toleration. Both "religion" and "philosophy" are vague umbrella terms, and both are subject to persuasive redefinition. When these terms are broadly enough defined, everybody, even atheists, will be said to have a religious faith (in the Tillichian sense of a "symbol of ultimate concern"). Everybody, even those who shun metaphysics and epistemology, will be said to have "philosophical presuppositions."[15] But for purposes of interpreting Jefferson and Rawls, we must use narrower definitions. Let "religion" mean, for Jefferson's purposes, disputes about the nature and the true name of God—and even about his existence.[16] Let "philosophy" mean, for Rawls's purposes, disputes about the nature of human beings and even about whether there is such a thing as "human nature."[17] Using these definitions, we can say that Rawls wants views about man's nature and purpose to be detached from politics. As he says, he wants his conception of justice to "avoid . . . claims about the essential nature and identity of persons."[18] So, presumably, he wants questions about the point of human existence, or the meaning of human life, to be reserved for private life. A liberal democracy will not only exempt opinions on such matters from legal coercion, but also aim at disengaging discussions of such questions from discussions of social policy. Yet it will use force against the individual conscience, just insofar as conscience leads individuals to act so as to threaten democratic institutions. Unlike Jefferson's, Rawls's argument against fanaticism is not that it threatens truth about the characteristics of an antecedent metaphysical and moral order by threatening free discussion, but *simply* that it threatens freedom, and thus threatens justice. Truth about the existence or nature of that order drops out.

The definition of "philosophy" I have just suggested is not as artificial and ad hoc as it may appear. Intellectual historians commonly treat "the nature of the human subject" as the topic that gradually replaced "God" as European culture secularized itself. This has been the central topic of metaphysics and epistemology from the seventeenth century to the present, and, for better or worse, metaphysics and epistemology have been taken to be the "core" of philosophy.[19] Insofar as one thinks that political conclusions require extrapolitical grounding—that is, insofar as one thinks Rawls's method of reflective equilibrium[20] is not good enough—one will want an account of the "authority" of those general principles.

If one feels a need for such legitimation, one will want either a religious or a philosophical preface to politics.[21] One will be likely to share

Horkheimer and Adorno's fear that pragmatism is not strong enough to hold a free society together. But Rawls echoes Dewey in suggesting that insofar as justice becomes the first virtue of a society, the need for such legitimation may gradually cease to be felt. Such a society will become accustomed to the thought that social policy needs no more authority than successful accommodation among individuals, individuals who find themselves heir to the same historical traditions and faced with the same problems. It will be a society that encourages the "end of ideology," that takes reflective equilibrium as the only method needed in discussing social policy. When such a society deliberates, when it collects the principles and intuitions to be brought into equilibrium, it will tend to discard those drawn from philosophical accounts of the self or of rationality. For such a society will view such accounts not as the foundations of political institutions but as, at worst, philosophical mumbo jumbo or, at best, relevant to private searches for perfection, but not to social policy.[22]

In order to spell out the contrast between Rawls's attempt to "stay on the surface, philosophically speaking" and the traditional attempt to dig down to "philosophical foundations of democracy," I shall turn briefly to Sandel's *Liberalism and the Limits of Justice.* This clear and forceful book provides very elegant and cogent arguments against the attempt to use a certain conception of the self, a certain metaphysical view of what human beings are like, to legitimize liberal politics. Sandel attributes this attempt to Rawls. Many people, including myself, initially took Rawls's *A Theory of Justice* to be such an attempt. We read it as a continuation of the Enlightenment attempt to ground our moral intuitions on a conception of human nature (and, more specifically, as a neo-Kantian attempt to ground them on the notion of "rationality"). However, Rawls's writings subsequent to *A Theory of Justice* have helped us to realize that we were misinterpreting his book, that we had overemphasized the Kantian and underemphasized the Hegelian and Deweyan elements. These writings make more explicit than did his book Rawls's metaphilosophical doctrine that "what justifies a conception of justice is not its being true to an order antecedent to and given to us, but its congruence with our deeper understanding of ourselves and our aspirations, and our realization that, *given our history and the traditions embedded in our public life*, it is the most reasonable doctrine *for us*."[23]

When reread in the light of such passages, *A Theory of Justice* no longer seems committed to a philosophical account of the human self, but only to a historico-sociological description of the way we live now.

Sandel sees Rawls as offering us "deontology with a Humean face"— that is, a Kantian universalistic approach to social thought without the handicap of Kant's idealistic metaphysics. He thinks that this will not work, that a social theory of the sort that Rawls wants requires us to postulate the sort of self that Descartes and Kant invented to replace God—one that can be distinguished from the Kantian "empirical self" as choosing various "contingent desires, wants and ends," rather than being a mere concatenation of beliefs and desires. Since such a concatenation— what Sandel calls a "radically situated subject"[24]—is all that Hume offers us, Sandel thinks that Rawls's project is doomed.[25] On Sandel's account, Rawls's doctrine that "justice is the first virtue of social institutions" requires backup from the metaphysical claim that "teleology to the contrary, what is most essential to our personhood is not the ends we choose but our capacity to choose them. And this capacity is located in a self which must be prior to the ends it chooses."[26]

But reading *A Theory of Justice* as political rather than metaphysical, one can see that when Rawls says that "the self is prior to the ends which are affirmed by it,"[27] he need not mean that there is an entity called "the self" that is something distinct from the web of beliefs and desires that that self "has." When he says that "we should not attempt to give form to our life by first looking to the good independently defined,"[28] he is not basing this "should" on a claim about the nature of the self. "Should" is not to be glossed by "because of the intrinsic nature of morality"[29] or "because a capacity for choice is the essence of personhood," but by something like "because *we*—we modern inheritors of the traditions of religious tolerance and constitutional government—put liberty ahead of perfection."

This willingness to invoke what *we* do raises, as I have said, the specters of ethnocentrism and of relativism. Because Sandel is convinced that Rawls shares Kant's fear of these specters, he is convinced that Rawls is looking for an "'Archimedean point' from which to assess the basic structure of society"—a "standpoint neither compromised by its implication in the world nor dissociated and so disqualified bydetachment."[30] It is just this idea that a standpoint can be "compromised by its implication in the world" that Rawls rejects in his recent writings. Philosophically inclined communitarians like Sandel are unable to envisage a middle ground between relativism and a "theory of the moral subject"—a theory that is not about, for example, religious tolerance and large market economies, but about human beings as such, viewed ahistorically. Rawls is trying to stake out just such a middle ground.[31] When he speaks of an "Archimedean point," he does not mean a point outside history, but simply the kind of settled social habits that allow much latitude for further choices. He says, for example,

> The upshot of these considerations is that justice as fairness is not at the mercy, so to speak, of existing wants and interests. It sets up an Archimedean point for assessing the social system without invoking a priori considerations. The long

range aim of society is settled in its main lines irrespective of the particular
desires and needs of its present members. . . . There is no place for the question
whether men's desires to play the role of superior or inferior might not be so
great that autocratic institutions should be accepted, or whether men's perception of the religious practices of others might not be so upsetting that liberty of
conscience should not be allowed.[32]

To say that there is no place for the questions that Nietzsche or Loyola
would raise is not to say that the views of either are unintelligible (in the
sense of "logically incoherent" or "conceptually confused"). Nor is it to
say that they are based on an incorrect theory of the self. Nor is it *just* to
say that our preferences conflict with theirs.[33] It is to say that the conflict
between these men and us is so great that "preferences" is the wrong
word. It is appropriate to speak of gustatory or sexual preferences, for
these do not matter to anybody but yourself and your immediate circle.
But it is misleading to speak of a "preference" for liberal democracy.

Rather, we heirs of the Enlightenment think of enemies of liberal democracy like Nietzsche or Loyola as, to use Rawls's word, "mad." We
do so because there is no way to see them as fellow citizens of our constitutional democracy, people whose life plans might, given ingenuity
and good will, be fitted in with those of other citizens. They are not
crazy because they have mistaken the ahistorical nature of human beings.
They are crazy because the limits of sanity are set by what *we* can take
seriously. This, in turn, is determined by our upbringing, our historical
situation.[34]

If this short way of dealing with Nietzsche and Loyola seems shock-
ingly ethnocentric, it is because the philosophical tradition has accustomed us to the idea that anybody who is willing to listen to reason—to
hear out all the arguments—can be brought around to the truth. This
view, which Kierkegaard called "Socratism" and contrasted with the
claim that our point of departure may be simply a historical event, is
intertwined with the idea that the human self has a center (a divine spark,
or a truth-tracking faculty called "reason") and that argumentation will,
given time and patience, penetrate to this center. For Rawls's purposes,
we do not need this picture. We are free to see the self as centerless, as a
historical contingency all the way through. Rawls neither needs nor
wants to defend the priority of the right to the good as Kant defended it,
by invoking a theory of the self that makes it more than an "empirical
self," more than a "radically situated subject." He presumably thinks of
Kant as, although largely right about the nature of justice, largely wrong
about the nature and function of philosophy.

More specifically, he can reject Sandel's Kantian claim that there is a
"distance between subject and situation which is necessary to any measure of detachment, is essential to the ineliminably *possessive* aspect of

any coherent conception of the self."[35] Sandel defines this aspect by saying, "I can never fully be constituted by my attributes . . . there must always be some attributes I *have* rather than am." On the interpretation of Rawls I am offering, we do not need a categorical distinction between the self and its situation. We can dismiss the distinction between an attribute of the self and a constituent of the self, between the self's accidents and its essence, as "merely" metaphysical.[36] If we are inclined to philosophize, we shall want the vocabulary offered by Dewey, Heidegger, Davidson, and Derrida, with its built-in cautions against metaphysics, rather than that offered by Descartes, Hume, and Kant.[37] For if we use the former vocabulary, we shall be able to see moral progress as a history of making rather than finding, of poetic achievement by "radically situated" individuals and communities, rather than as the gradual unveiling, through the use of "reason," of "principles" or "rights" or "values."

Sandel's claim that "the concept of a subject given prior to and independent of its objects offers a foundation for the moral law that . . . powerfully completes the deontological vision" is true enough. But to suggest such a powerful completion to Rawls is to offer him a poisoned gift. It is like offering Jefferson an argument for religious tolerance based on exegesis of Christian Scriptures.[38] Rejecting the assumption that the moral law needs a "foundation" is just what distinguishes Rawls from Jefferson. It is just this that permits him to be a Deweyan naturalist who needs neither the distinction between will and intellect nor the distinction between the self's constituents and its attributes. He does not *want* a "complete deontological vision," one that would explain *why* we should give justice priority over our conception of the good. He is filling out the consequences of the claim that it is prior, not its presuppositions.[39] Rawls is not interested in conditions for the identity of the self, but only in conditions for citizenship in a liberal society.

Suppose one grants that Rawls is not attempting a transcendental deduction of American liberalism or supplying philosophical foundations for democratic institutions, but simply trying to systematize the principles and intuitions typical of American liberals. Still, it may seem that the important questions raised by the critics of liberalism have been begged. Consider the claim that we liberals can simply dismiss Nietzsche and Loyola as crazy. One imagines these two rejoining that they are quite aware that their views unfit them for citizenship in a constitutional democracy and that the typical inhabitant of such a democracy would regard them as crazy. But they take these facts as further counts against constitutional democracy. They think that the kind of person created by such a democracy is not what a human being should be.

In finding a dialectical stance to adopt toward Nietzsche or Loyola, we liberal democrats are faced with a dilemma. To refuse to argue about what human beings should be like seems to show a contempt for the spirit of accommodation and tolerance, which is essential to democracy. But it is not clear how to argue for the claim that human beings ought to be liberals rather than fanatics without being driven back on a theory of human nature, on philosophy. I think that we must grasp the first horn. We have to insist that not every argument needs to be met in the terms in which it is presented. Accommodation and tolerance must stop short of a willingness to work within any vocabulary that one's interlocutor wishes to use, to take seriously any topic that he puts forward for discussion. To take this view is of a piece with dropping the idea that a single moral vocabulary and a single set of moral beliefs are appropriate for every human community everywhere, and to grant that historical developments may lead us to simply *drop* questions and the vocabulary in which those questions are posed.

Just as Jefferson refused to let the Christian Scriptures set the terms in which to discuss alternative political institutions, so we either must refuse to answer the question "What sort of human being are you hoping to produce?" or, at least, must not let our answer to this question dictate our answer to the question "Is justice primary?"[40] It is no more evident that democratic institutions are to be measured by the sort of person they create than that they are to be measured against divine commands. It is not evident that they are to be measured by anything more specific than the moral intuitions of the particular historical community that has created those institutions. The idea that moral and political controversies should always be "brought back to first principles" is reasonable if it means merely that we should seek common ground in the hope of attaining agreement. But it is misleading if it is taken as the claim that there is a natural order of premises from which moral and political conclusions are to be inferred—not to mention the claim that some particular interlocutor (for example, Nietzsche or Loyola) has already discerned that order. The liberal response to the communitarians' second claim must be, therefore, that even if the typical character types of liberal democracies *are* bland, calculating, petty, and unheroic, the prevalence of such people may be a reasonable price to pay for political freedom.

The spirit of accommodation and tolerance certainly suggests that we should seek common ground with Nietzsche and Loyola, but there is no predicting where, or whether, such common ground will be found. The philosophical tradition has assumed that there are certain topics (for example, "What is God's will?," "What is man?," "What rights are intrinsic to the species?") on which everyone has, or should have, views and that these topics are prior in the order of justification to those at issue in political deliberation. This assumption goes along with the assumption that human beings have a natural center that philosophical inquiry can locate and illuminate. By contrast, the view that human beings are centerless networks of beliefs and desires and that their vocabularies and opinions are determined by historical circumstance allows for the possibility that there may not be enough overlap between two such networks to make possible agreement about political topics, or even profitable discussion of such topics.[41] We do not conclude that Nietzsche and Loyola are crazy because they hold unusual views on certain "fundamental" topics; rather, we conclude this only after extensive attempts at an exchange of political views have made us realize that we are not going to get anywhere.[42]

One can sum up this way of grasping the first horn of the dilemma I sketched earlier by saying that Rawls puts democratic politics first, and philosophy second. He retains the Socratic commitment to free exchange of views without the Platonic commitment to the possibility of universal agreement—a possibility underwritten by epistemological doctrines like Plato's Theory of Recollection[43] or Kant's theory of the relation between pure and empirical concepts. He disengages the question of whether we ought to be tolerant and Socratic from the question of whether this strategy will lead to truth. He is content that it should lead to whatever intersubjective reflective equilibrium may be obtainable, given the contingent make-up of the subjects in question. Truth, viewed in the Platonic way, as the grasp of what Rawls calls "an order antecedent to and given to us," is simply not relevant to democratic politics. So philosophy, as the explanation of the relation between such an order and human nature, is not relevant either. When the two come into conflict, democracy takes precedence over philosophy.

This conclusion may seem liable to an obvious objection. It may seem that I have been rejecting a concern with philosophical theories about the nature of men and women on the basis of just such a theory. But notice that although I have frequently said that Rawls *can be content* with a notion of the human self as a centerless web of historically conditioned beliefs and desires, I have not suggested that he *needs* such a theory. Such a theory does not offer liberal social theory a *basis*. If one *wants* a model of the human self, then this picture of a centerless web will fill the need. But for purposes of liberal social theory, one can do without such a model. One can get along with common sense and social science, areas of discourse in which the term "the self" rarely occurs.

If, however, one has a taste for philosophy—if one's vocation, one's private pursuit of perfection, entails constructing models of such entities as "the self," "knowledge," "language," "nature," "God," or "history" and then tinkering with them until they mesh with one another—one *will* want a picture of the self. Since my own vocation is of this sort, and the moral identity around which I wish to build such models is that of a citizen of a liberal democratic state, I commend the picture of the self as a centerless and contingent web to those with similar tastes and similar identities. But I would not commend it to those with a similar vocation but dissimilar moral identities—identities built, for example, around the love of God, Nietzschean self-overcoming, the accurate representation of reality as it is in itself, the quest for "one right answer" to moral questions, or the natural superiority of a given character type. Such persons need a more complex and interesting, less simple-minded model of the self—one that meshes in complex ways with complex models of such things as "nature" or "history." Nevertheless, such persons may, for pragmatic rather than moral reasons, be loyal citizens of a liberal democratic society. They may despise most of their fellow citizens but be prepared to grant that the prevalence of such despicable character types is a lesser evil than the loss of political freedom. They may be ruefully grateful that their private senses of moral identity and the models of the human self that they develop to articulate this sense—the ways in which they deal with their aloneness—are not the concern of such a state. Rawls and Dewey have shown how the liberal state can ignore the difference between the moral identities of Glaucon and of Thrasymachus, just as it ignores the difference between the religious identities of a Catholic archbishop and a Mormon prophet.

There is, however, a flavor of paradox in this attitude toward theories of the self. One might be inclined to say that I have evaded one sort of self-referential paradox only by falling into another sort. For I am presupposing that one is at liberty to rig up a model of the self to suit oneself, to tailor it to one's politics, one's religion, or one's private sense of the meaning of one's life. This, in turn, presupposes that there is no "objective truth" about what the human self is *really* like. That, in turn, seems a claim that could be justified only on the basis of a metaphysico-epistemological view of the traditional sort. For surely if anything is the province of such a view, it is the question of what there is and is not a "fact of the matter" about. So my argument must ultimately come back to philosophical first principles.

Here I can only say that if there were a discoverable fact of the matter about what there is a fact of the matter about, then it would doubtless be metaphysics and epistemology that would discover that meta-fact. But I think that the very idea of a "fact of the matter" is one we would be better off without. Philosophers like Davidson and Derrida have, I think, given us good reason to think that the *physis–nomos, in se–ad nos*, and objective–subjective distinctions were steps on a ladder that we can now safely throw away. The question of whether the reasons such philosophers have given for this claim are themselves metaphysico-epistemological reasons, and if not, what sort of reasons they are, strikes me as pointless and sterile. Once again, I fall back on the holist's strategy of insisting that reflective equilibrium is all we need try for—that there is no natural order of justification of beliefs, no predestined outline for argument to trace. Getting rid of the idea of such an outline seems to me one of the many benefits of a conception of the self as a centerless web. Another benefit is that questions about whom we need justify ourselves to—questions about who counts as a fanatic and who deserves an answer—can be treated as just further matters to be sorted out in the course of attaining reflective equilibrium.

I can, however, make one point to offset the air of light-minded aestheticism I am adopting toward traditional philosophical questions. This is that there is a moral purpose behind this light-mindedness. The encouragement of light-mindedness about traditional philosophical topics serves the same purposes as the encouragement of light-mindedness about traditional theological topics. Like the rise of large market economies, the increase in literacy, the proliferation of artistic genres, and the insouciant pluralism of contemporary culture, such philosophical superficiality and light-mindedness helps along the disenchantment of the world. It helps make the world's inhabitants more pragmatic, more tolerant, more liberal, more receptive to the appeal of instrumental rationality.

If one's moral identity consists in being a citizen of a liberal polity, then to encourage light-mindedness may serve one's moral purposes. Moral commitment, after all, does not require taking seriously all the matters that are, for moral reasons, taken seriously by one's fellow citizens. It may require just the opposite. It may require trying to josh them out of the habit of taking those topics so seriously. There may be serious reasons for so joshing them. More generally, we should not assume that the aesthetic is always the enemy of the moral. I should argue that in the recent history of liberal societies, the willingness to view matters aesthetically—to be content to indulge in what Schiller called "play" and to discard what Nietzsche called "the spirit of seriousness"—has been an important vehicle of moral progress.

I have now said everything I have to say about the third of the communitarian claims that I distinguished at the outset: the claim that the social theory of the liberal state rests on false philosophical presuppositions. I hope I have given reasons for thinking that insofar as the communitarian is a critic of liberalism, he should drop this claim and should instead develop either of the first two claims: the empirical claim that democratic institutions cannot be combined with the sense of common purpose predemocratic societies enjoyed, or the moral judgment that the products of the liberal state are too high a price to pay for the elimination of the evils that preceded it. If communitarian critics of liberalism stuck to these two claims, they would avoid the sort of terminal wistfulness with which their books typically end. Heidegger, for example, tells us that "we are too late for the gods, and too early for Being." Unger ends *Knowledge and Politics* with an appeal to a *Deus absconditus*. MacIntyre ends *After Virtue* by saying that we "are waiting not for a Godot, but for another—doubtless very different—St. Benedict."[44] Sandel ends his book by saying that liberalism "forgets the possibility that when politics goes well, we can know a good in common that we cannot know alone," but he does not suggest a candidate for this common good.

Instead of thus suggesting that philosophical reflection, or a return to religion, might enable us to re-enchant the world, I think that communitarians should stick to the question of whether disenchantment has, on balance, done us more harm than good, or created more dangers than it has evaded. For Dewey, communal and public disenchantment is the price we pay for individual and private spiritual liberation, the kind of liberation that Emerson thought characteristically American. Dewey was as well aware as Weber that there is a price to be paid, but he thought it well worth paying. He assumed that no good achieved by earlier societies would be worth recapturing if the price were a diminution in our ability to leave people alone, to let them try out their private visions of perfection in peace. He admired the American habit of giving democracy priority over philosophy by asking, about any vision of the meaning of life, "Would not acting out this vision interfere with the ability of others to work out their own salvation?" Giving priority to that question is no more "natural" than giving priority to, say, MacIntyre's question "What sorts of human beings emerge in the culture of liberalism?" or Sandel's question "Can a community of those who put justice first ever be more than a community of strangers?" The question of which of these questions is prior to which others is, necessarily, begged by *everybody*. Nobody is being any more arbitrary than anybody else. But that is to say that nobody is being arbitrary at all. Everybody is just insisting that the beliefs and desires they hold most dear should come first in the order of discussion. That is not arbitrariness, but sincerity.

The danger of re-enchanting the world, from a Deweyan point of view, is that it might interfere with the development of what Rawls calls "a social union of social unions,"[45] some of which may be (and in Emerson's view, should be) very small indeed. For it is hard to be both enchanted with one version of the world and tolerant of all the others. I have not tried to argue the question of whether Dewey was right in this judgment of relative danger and promise. I have merely argued that such a judgment neither presupposes nor supports a theory of the self. Nor have I tried to deal with Horkheimer and Adorno's prediction that the "dissolvent rationality" of the Enlightenment will eventually cause the liberal democracies to come unstuck.

The only thing I have to say about this prediction is that the collapse of the liberal democracies would not, in itself, provide much evidence for the claim that human societies cannot survive without widely shared opinions on matters of ultimate importance—shared conceptions of our place in the universe and our mission on earth. Perhaps they cannot survive under such conditions, but the eventual collapse of the democracies would not, in itself, show that this was the case—any more than it would show that human societies require kings or an established religion, or that political community cannot exist outside of small city-states.

Both Jefferson and Dewey described America as an "experiment." If the experiment fails, our descendants may learn something important. But they will not learn a philosophical truth, any more than they will learn a religious one. They will simply get some hints about what to watch out for when setting up their next experiment. Even if nothing else survives from the age of the democratic revolutions, perhaps our descendants will remember that social institutions *can* be viewed as experiments in cooperation rather than as attempts to embody a universal and ahistorical order. It is hard to believe that this memory would not be worth having.

NOTES

1. Thomas Jefferson, *Notes on the State of Virginia*, Query XVII, in *The Writings of Thomas Jefferson*, ed. A. A. Lipscomb and A. E. Bergh (Washington, D.C., 1905), 2:217.

2. Jefferson included a statement of this familiar scriptural claim (roughly in the form in which it had been restated by Milton in *Areopagitica*) in the preamble to the Virginia Statute for Religious Freedom: "truth is great and will prevail if left to herself, . . . she is the proper and sufficient antagonist to error, and has nothing to fear from the conflict, unless by human interposition disarmed of her natural weapons, free argument and debate, errors ceasing to be dangerous when it is permitted freely to contradict them" (ibid., 2:302).

3. Max Horkheimer and Theodor W. Adorno, *Dialectic of Enlightenment* (Seabury Press, New York, 1972), p. xiii.

4. "For the Enlightenment, whatever does not conform to the rule of computation and utility is suspect. So long as it can develop undisturbed by any outward repression, there is no holding it. In the process, it treats its own ideas of human rights exactly as it does the older universals . . . Enlightenment is totalitarian" (ibid., p. 6). This line of thought recurs repeatedly in communitarian accounts of the present state of the liberal democracies; see, for example, Robert Bellah, Richard Madsen, William Sullivan, Ann Swidler, and Steven Tipton,

Habits of the Heart: Individualism and Commitment in American Life (Berkeley: University of California Press, 1985): "There is a widespread feeling that the promise of the modern era is slipping away from us. A movement of enlightenment and the liberation that was to have freed us from superstition and tyranny has led in the twentieth century to a world in which ideological fanaticism and political oppression have reached extremes unknown in previous history" (p. 277).

5. Charles Taylor, *Philosophy and the Human Sciences*, vol. 2 of *Philosophical Papers* (Cambridge: Cambridge University Press, 1985), p. 8.

6. Ibid., p. 5.

7. John Rawls, "Justice as Fairness: Political not Metaphysical," *Philosophy and Public Affairs*, 14 (1985) 225. Religious toleration is a constantly recurring theme in Rawls's writing. Early in *A Theory of Justice* (Cambridge, Mass.: Harvard University Press, 1971), when giving examples of the sort of common opinions that a theory of justice must take into account and systematize, he cites our conviction that religious intolerance is unjust (p. 19). His example of the fact that "a well-ordered society tends to eliminate or at least to control men's inclinations to injustice" is that "warring and intolerant sects are much less likely to exist" (p. 247). Another relevant passage (which I shall discuss below) is his diagnosis of Ignatius Loyola's attempt to make the love of God the "dominant good": "Although to subordinate all our aims to one end does not strictly speaking violate the principles of rational choice . . . it still strikes us as irrational, or more likely as mad" (pp. 553–54).

8. Rawls, "Justice as Fairness," pp. 225–26. The suggestion that there are many philosophical views that will *not* survive in such conditions is analogous to the Enlightenment suggestion that the adoption of democratic institutions will cause 'superstitious' forms of religious belief gradually to die off.

9. Ibid., p. 230.

10. Ibid.

11. For Rawls's historicism see, for example, *Theory of Justice*, p. 547. There, Rawls says that the people in the original position are assumed to know "the general facts about society," including the fact that "institutions are not fixed but change over time, altered by natural circumstances and the activities and conflicts of social groups." He uses this point to rule out, as original choosers of principles of justice, those "in a feudal or a caste system," those who are unaware of events such as the French Revolution. This is one of many passages that make clear (at least read in the light of Rawls's later work) that a great deal of knowledge that came late to the mind of Europe is present to the minds of those behind the veil of ignorance. Or, to put it another way, such passages make clear that those original choosers behind the veil exemplify a certain modern type of human being, not an ahistorical human nature. See also p. 548, where Rawls says, "Of course in working out what the requisite principles [of justice] are, we must rely upon current knowledge as recognized by common sense and the existing scientific consensus. We have to concede that as established beliefs change, it is possible that the principles of justice which it seems rational to choose may likewise change."

12. See Bellah et al., *Habits of the Heart*, p. 141, for a recent restatement of this "counter-Enlightenment" line of thought. For the authors' view of the prob-

lems created by persistence in Enlightenment rhetoric and by the prevalence of the conception of human dignity that Taylor identifies as "distinctively modern," see p. 21: "For most of us, it is easier to think about how to get what we want than to know exactly what we should want. Thus Brian, Joe, Margaret and Wayne [some of the Americans interviewed by the authors] are each in his or her own way confused about how to define for themselves such things as the nature of success, the meaning of freedom, and the requirements of justice. Those difficulties are in an important way created by the limitations in the common tradition of moral discourse they—and we—share." Compare p. 290: "the language of individualism, the primary American language of self-understanding, limits the way in which people think."

To my mind, the authors of *Habits of the Heart* undermine their own conclusions in the passages where they point to actual moral progress being made in recent American history, notably in their discussion of the civil rights movement. There, they say that Martin Luther King, Jr., made the struggle for freedom "a practice of commitment within a vision of America as a community of memory" and that the response King elicited "came from the reawakened recognition by many Americans that their own sense of self was rooted in companionship with others who, though not necessarily like themselves, nevertheless shared with them a common history and whose appeals to justice and solidarity made powerful claims on our loyalty" (p. 252). These descriptions of King's achievement seem exactly right, but they can be read as evidence that the rhetoric of the Enlightenment offers at least as many opportunities as it does obstacles for the renewal of a sense of community. The civil rights movement combined, without much strain, the language of Christian fellowship and the "language of individualism," about which Bellah and his colleagues are dubious.

13. See Michael Walzer, *Spheres of Justice* (New York: Basic Books, 1983), pp. 312ff.

14. Michael Sandel, *Liberalism and the Limits of Justice* (Cambridge: Cambridge University Press, 1982), p. 49.

15. In a recent, as yet unpublished, paper, Sandel has urged that Rawls's claim that "philosophy in the classical sense as the search for truth about a prior and independent moral order cannot provide the shared basis for a political conception of justice" presupposes the controversial metaphysical claim that there is no such order. This seems to me like saying that Jefferson was presupposing the controversial theological claim that God is not interested in the name by which he is called by human beings. Both charges are accurate, but not really to the point. Both Jefferson and Rawls would have to reply, "I have no arguments for my dubious theological-metaphysical claim, because I do not know how to discuss such issues, and do not want to. My interest is in helping to preserve and create political institutions that will foster public indifference to such issues, while putting no restrictions on private discussion of them." This reply, of course, begs the "deeper" question that Sandel wants to raise, for the question of whether we *should* determine what issues to discuss on political or on "theoretical" (e.g., theological or philosophical) grounds remains unanswered. (At the end of this paper, I briefly discuss the need for philosophers to escape from the requirement to answer questions phrased in vocabularies they wish to replace, and in more

detail in "Beyond Realism and Anti-Realism," in *Wo steht die sprachanalytische Philosophie heute?*, ed. Ludwig Nagl and Richard Heinrich (Vienna: R. Oldenbourg, 1986).

16. Jefferson agreed with Luther that philosophers had muddied the clear waters of the gospels. See Jefferson's polemic against Plato's "foggy mind" and his claim that "the doctrines which flowed from the lips of Jesus himself are within the comprehension of a child; but thousands of volumes have not yet explained the Platonisms engrafted on them; and for this obvious reason, that nonsense can never be explained" (*Writings of Thomas Jefferson*, 14: 149).

17. I am here using the term "human nature" in the traditional philosophical sense in which Sartre denied that there was such a thing, rather than in the rather unusual one that Rawls gives it. Rawls distinguishes between a "conception of the person" and a "theory of human nature," where the former is a "moral ideal" and the latter is provided by, roughly, common sense plus the social sciences. To have a theory of human nature is to have "general facts that we take to be true enough, given the state of public knowledge in our society," facts that "limit the feasibility of the ideals of person and society embedded in that framework" ("Kantian Constructivism in Moral Theory," *Journal of Philosophy*, 77 [1980]: 534).

18. Rawls, "Justice as Fairness," p. 223.

19. In fact, it has been for the worse. A view that made politics more central to philosophy and subjectivity less would both permit more effective defenses of democracy than those that purport to supply it with "foundations" and permit liberals to meet Marxists on their own, political, ground. Dewey's explicit attempt to make the central philosophical question "What serves democracy?" rather than "What permits us to argue for democracy?" has been, unfortunately, neglected. I try to make this point in "Philosophy as Science, as Metaphor, and as Politics," in *The Institution of Philosophy*, ed. Avner Cohen and Marcello Dascal (LaSalle, Ill.: Open Court, 1989), pp. 3–11.

20. That is, give-and-take between intuitions about the desirability of particular consequences of particular actions and intuitions about general principles, with neither having the determining voice.

21. One will also, as I did on first reading Rawls, take him to be attempting to supply such legitimation by an appeal to the rationality of the choosers in the original position. Rawls warned his readers that the original position (the position of those who, behind a veil of ignorance that hides them from their life chances and their conceptions of the good, select from among alternative principles of justice) served simply "to make vivid . . . the restrictions that it seems reasonable to impose on arguments for principles of justice and therefore on those principles themselves" (*Theory of Justice*, p. 18).

But this warning went unheeded by myself and others, in part because of an ambiguity between "reasonable" as defined by ahistorical criteria and as meaning something like "in accord with the moral sentiments characteristic of the heirs of the Enlightenment." Rawls's later work has, as I have said, helped us come down on the historicist side of this ambiguity; see, for example, "Kantian Constructivism": "the original position is not an axiomatic (or deductive) basis from which principles are derived but a procedure for singling out principles most fitting to the conception of the person most likely to be held, at least implicitly, in a democratic society" (p. 572). It is tempting to suggest that one could eliminate all reference to the original position from *A Theory of Justice* without loss, but this is as daring a suggestion as that one might rewrite (as many have wished to do) Kant's *Critique of Pure Reason* without reference to the thing-in-itself. T. M. Scanlon has suggested that we can, at least, safely eliminate reference, in the description of the choosers in the original position, to an appeal to self-interest in describing the motives of those choosers. ("Contractualism and Utilitarianism," in *Utilitarianism and Beyond*, ed. Bernard Williams and Amartya Sen [Cambridge: Cambridge University Press, 1982].) Since justifiability is, more evidently than self-interest, relative to historical circumstance, Scanlon's proposal seems to be more faithful to Rawls's overall philosophical program than Rawls's own formulation.

22. In particular, there will be no principles or intuitions concerning the universal features of human psychology relevant to motivation. Sandel thinks that since assumptions about motivation are part of the description of the original position, "what issues at one end in a theory of justice must issue at the other in a theory of the person, or more precisely, a theory of the moral subject" (*Liberalism and the Limits of Justice*, p. 47). I would argue that if we follow Scanlon's lead (note 21) in dropping reference to self-interest in our description of the original choosers and replacing this with reference to their desire to justify their choices to their fellows, then the only "theory of the person" we get is a sociological description of the inhabitants of contemporary liberal democracies.

23. Rawls, "Kantian Constructivism," p. 519. Italics added.

24. Sandel, *Liberalism and the Limits of Justice*, p. 21. I have argued for the advantages of thinking of the self as just such a concatenation; see "Postmodernist Bourgeois Liberalism," *Journal of Philosophy*, 80 (1983), pp. 583–89 and "Freud and Moral Reflection," in *The Pragmatists' Freud*, ed. Joseph E. Smith and William Kerrigan (Baltimore: Johns Hopkins University Press, 1986). When Sandel quotes Robert Nozick and Daniel Bell as suggesting that Rawls "ends by dissolving the self in order to preserve it" (*Liberalism and the Limits of Justice*, p. 95), I should rejoin that it may be helpful to dissolve the metaphysical self in order to preserve the political one. Less obliquely stated: it may be helpful, for purposes of systematizing our intuitions about the priority of liberty, to treat the self as having no center, no essence, but *merely* as a concatenation of beliefs and desires.

25. "Deontology with a Humean face either fails as deontology or recreates in the original position the disembodied subject it resolves to avoid" (ibid., p. 14).

26. Ibid., p. 19.

27. Rawls, *Theory of Justice*, p. 560.

28. Ibid.

29. It is important to note that Rawls explicitly distances himself from the idea that he is analyzing the very idea of morality and from conceptual analysis as the method of social theory (ibid., p. 130). Some of his critics have suggested that Rawls is practicing "reductive logical analysis" of the sort characteristic of "analytic philosophy"; see, for example, William M. Sullivan, *Reconstructing Public Philosophy* (Berkeley: University of California Press, 1982), pp. 94ff. Sullivan says that "this ideal of reductive logical analysis lends legitimacy to the notion that moral philosophy is summed up in the task of discovering, through the anal-

ysis of moral rules, both primitive elements and governing principles that must apply to any rational moral system, *rational* here meaning 'logically coherent'" (p. 96). He goes on to grant that "Nozick and Rawls are more sensitive to the importance of history and social experience in human life than were the classic liberal thinkers" (p. 97). But this concession is too slight and is misleading. Rawls's willingness to adopt "reflective equilibrium" rather than "conceptual analysis" as a methodological watchword sets him apart from the epistemologically oriented moral philosophy that was dominant prior to the appearance of *A Theory of Justice*. Rawls represents a reaction against Kantian ideas of "morality" as having an ahistorical essence, the same sort of reaction found in Hegel and in Dewey.

30. Sandel, *Liberalism and the Limits of Justice*, p. 17.

31. "Liberty of conscience and freedom of thought should not be founded on philosophical or ethical skepticism, nor on indifference to religious and moral interests. The principles of justice define an appropriate path between dogmatism and intolerance on the one side, and a reductionism which regards religion and morality as mere preferences on the other" (Rawls, *Theory of Justice*, p. 243). I take it that Rawls is identifying "philosophical or ethical skepticism" with the idea that everything is just a matter of "preference," even religion, philosophy, and morals. So we should distinguish his suggestion that we "extend the principle of tolerance to philosophy itself" from the suggestion that we dismiss philosophy as epiphenomenal. That is the sort of suggestion that is backed up by reductionist accounts of philosophical doctrines as "preferences" or "wish fulfilments" or "expressions of emotion" (see Rawls's criticism of Freudian reductionism in ibid., pp. 539ff.). Neither psychology nor logic nor any other theoretical discipline can supply non-question-begging reasons why philosophy should be set aside, any more than philosophy can supply such reasons why theology should be set aside. But this is compatible with saying that the general course of historical experience may lead us to neglect theological topics and bring us to the point at which, like Jefferson, we find a theological vocabulary "meaningless" (or, more precisely, useless). I am suggesting that the course of historical experience since Jefferson's time has led us to a point at which we find much of the vocabulary of modern philosophy no longer useful.

32. Ibid., pp. 261–62.

33. The contrast between "mere preference" and something less "arbitrary," something more closely related to the very nature of man or of reason, is invoked by many writers who think of "human rights" as requiring a philosophical foundation of the traditional sort. Thus my colleague David Little, commenting on my "Solidarity or Objectivity?" (*Post-Analytic Philosophy*, ed. John Rajchman and Cornel West [New York: Columbia University Press, 1985]), says "Rorty appears to permit criticism and pressure against those societies [the ones we do not like] *if we happen to want to* criticize and pressure them in pursuit of some interest or belief we may (at the time) have, and for whatever ethnocentric reasons we may happen to hold those interests or beliefs" ("Natural Rights and Human Rights: The International Imperative," in *Natural Rights and Natural Law: The Legacy of George Mason*, ed. Robert P. Davidow, [Fairfax, Va.: George Mason University Press, 1986], pp. 67–122; italics in original). I would rejoin that Little's use

of "happen to want to" presupposes a dubious distinction between necessary, built-in, universal convictions (convictions that it would be "irrational" to reject) and accidental, culturally determined convictions. It also presupposes the existence of such faculties as reason, will, and emotion, all of which the pragmatist tradition in American philosophy and the so-called existentialist tradition in European philosophy try to undercut. Dewey's *Human Nature and Conduct* and Heidegger's *Being and Time* both offer a moral psychology that avoids oppositions between "preference" and "reason."

34. "Aristotle remarks that it is a peculiarity of men that they possess a sense of the just and the unjust and that their sharing a common understanding of justice makes a polis. Analogously one might say, in view of our discussion, that a common understanding of justice as fairness makes a constitutional democracy" (Rawls, *Theory of Justice*, p. 243). In the interpretations of Rawls I am offering, it is unrealistic to expect Aristotle to have developed a conception of justice as fairness, since he simply lacked the kind of historical experience that we have accumulated since his day. More generally, it is pointless to assume (with, for example, Leo Strauss) that the Greeks had already canvassed the alternatives available for social life and institutions. When we discuss justice, we cannot agree to bracket our knowledge of recent history.

35. Sandel, *Liberalism and the Limits of Justice*, p. 20.

36. We can dismiss other distinctions that Sandel draws in the same way. Examples are the distinction between a voluntarist and a cognitive account of the original position (ibid., p. 121), that between "the identity of the subject" as the "product" rather than the "premise" of its agency (ibid., p. 152), and that between the question "Who am I?" and its rival as "the paradigmatic moral question," "What shall I choose?" (ibid., p. 153). These distinctions are all to be analyzed away as products of the "Kantian dualisms" that Rawls praises Hegel and Dewey for having overcome.

37. For some similarities between Dewey and Heidegger with respect to anti-Cartesianism, see my "Overcoming the Tradition," in Richard Rorty, *Consequences of Pragmatism* (University of Minnesota Press, Minneapolis, 1982). For similarities between Davidson and Derrida, see Samuel Wheeler, "Indeterminacy of French Translation," in *Essays on "Inquiries into Truth and Interpretation,"* ed. Ernest LePore (Oxford: Basil Blackwell, 1986).

38. David Levin has pointed out to me that Jefferson was not above borrowing such arguments. I take this to show that Jefferson, like Kant, found himself in an untenable halfway position between theology and Deweyan social experimentalism.

39. Sandel takes "the primacy of the subject" to be not only a way of filling out the deontological picture, but also a necessary condition of its correctness: "If the claim for the primacy of justice is to succeed, if the right is to be prior to the good in the interlocking moral and foundational senses we have distinguished, then some version of the claim for the primacy of the subject must succeed as well" (*Liberalism and the Limits of Justice*, p. 7). Sandel quotes Rawls as saying that "the essential unity of the self is already provided by the conception of the right" and takes this passage as evidence that Rawls holds a doctrine of the "priority of the self" (ibid., p. 21). But consider the context of this sentence. Rawls says: "The

principles of justice and their realization in social forms define the bounds within which our deliberations take place. The essential unity of the self is already provided by the conception of right. Moreover, in a well-ordered society this unity is the same for all; everyone's conception of the good as given by his rational plan is a sub-plan of the larger comprehensive plan that regulates the community as a social union of social unions" (*Theory of Justice*, p. 563). The "essential unity of the self," which is in question here, is simply the system of moral sentiments, habits, and internalized traditions that is typical of the politically aware citizen of a constitutional democracy. This self is, once again, a historical product. It has nothing to do with the nonempirical self, which Kant had to postulate in the interests of Enlightenment universalism.

40. This is the kernel of truth in Dworkin's claim that Rawls rejects "goal-based" social theory, but this point should not lead us to think that he is thereby driven back on a "rights-based" theory.

41. But one should not press this point so far as to raise the specter of "untranslatable languages." As Donald Davidson has remarked, we would not recognize other organisms as actual or potential language users—or, therefore, as persons—unless there were enough overlap in belief and desire to make translation possible. The point is merely that efficient and frequent communication is only a necessary, not a sufficient, condition of agreement.

42. Further, such a conclusion is *restricted* to politics. It does not cast doubts on the ability of these men to follow the rules of logic or their ability to do many other things skilfully and well. It is thus not equivalent to the traditional philosophical charge of "irrationality." That charge presupposes that inability to "see" certain truths is evidence of the lack of an organ that is essential for human functioning generally.

43. In Kierkegaard's *Philosophical Fragments*, we find the Platonic Theory of Recollection treated as the archetypal justification of "Socratism" and thus as the symbol of all forms (especially Hegel's) of what Bernard Williams has recently called "the rationalist theory of rationality"—the idea that one is rational only if one can appeal to universally accepted criteria, criteria whose truth and applicability all human beings can find "in their hearts." This is the philosophical core of the scriptural idea that "truth is great, and will prevail," when that idea is dissociated from the Pauline idea of "a New Being" (in the way that Kierkegaard refused to dissociate it).

44. See Jeffrey Stout's discussion of the manifold ambiguities of this conclusion in "Virtue Among the Ruins: An Essay on MacIntyre," *Neue Zeitschrift für Systematische Theologie und Religionsphilosophie* 26 (1984), pp. 256–73, especially p. 269.

45. This is Rawls's description of "a well-ordered society (corresponding to justice as fairness)" (*Theory of Justice*, p. 527). Sandel finds these passages metaphorical and complains that "intersubjective and individualistic images appear in uneasy, sometimes unfelicitous combination, as if to betray the incompatible commitments contending within" (*Liberalism and the Limits of Justice*, pp. 150 ff.). He concludes that "the moral vocabulary of community in the strong sense cannot in all cases be captured by a conception that [as Rawls has said his is] 'in its theoretical basis is individualistic.'" I am claiming that these commit-

ments will look incompatible only if one attempts to define their philosophical presuppositions (which Rawls himself may occasionally have done too much of), and that this is a good reason for not making such attempts. Compare the Enlightenment view that attempts to sharpen up the theological presuppositions of social commitments had done more harm than good and that if theology cannot simply be discarded, it should at least be left as fuzzy (or, one might say, "liberal") as possible. Oakeshott has a point when he insists on the value of theoretical muddle for the health of the state.

Elsewhere Rawls has claimed that "there is no reason why a well-ordered society should encourage primarily individualistic values if this means ways of life that lead individuals to pursue their own way and to have no concern for the interests of others" ("Fairness to Goodness," *Philosophical Review*, 84 (1975), p. 550). Sandel's discussion of this passage says that it "suggests a deeper sense in which Rawls's conception is individualistic," but his argument that this suggestion is correct is, once again, the claim that "the Rawlsian self is not only a subject of possession, but an antecedently individuated subject" (*Liberalism and the Limits of Justice*, pp. 61ff.). This is just the claim I have been arguing against by arguing that there is no such thing as "the Rawlsian self" and that Rawls "takes for granted that every individual consists of one and only one system of desires" (ibid., p. 62), but it is hard to find evidence for this claim in the texts. At worst, Rawls simplifies his presentation by imagining each of his citizens as having only one such set, but this simplifying assumption does not seem central to his view.

Chapter 12

TRUTH AND FREEDOM: A REPLY TO

THOMAS MCCARTHY

RICHARD RORTY

THOMAS MCCARTHY is remarkably good at seeing the inter-connections between theorists' ideas, at explaining why they say the odd things they do, and at helping them out of the holes they dig themselves into. When I feel baffled by something Jürgen Habermas is saying, I read McCarthy on Habermas and things clear up. I am very flattered that he has taken the time to write about my stuff. I got the same benefits out of reading him on myself as I have gotten from reading him on Habermas and on Michel Foucault. He writes about me with great understanding and sympathy, and helps me understand my own twists, turns, and predicaments better than I had before.

As it happened, I started thinking about how to reply to McCarthy's article ("Private Irony and Public Decency: Richard Rorty's New Prag-matism," *Critical Inquiry* 16 [Winter 1990]: 355–70) shortly after writ-ing a brief criticism of Hilary Putnam's discussion of truth in his recent book *Representation and Reality*.[1] As McCarthy says, Putnam is one of those who, like Habermas, wants to develop concepts of "reason, truth, and justice, that, while no longer pretending to a God's-eye point of view, retain something of their transcendent, regulative, critical force" (p. 367). I criticize Putnam's treatment of truth on just this point. I argue that since Putnam has dropped the notion of a God's-eye point of view, a way the world is apart from our descriptions of it in language, he had better give up on the idea of true sentences as representations of reality, and give up trying to charge the idea of "truth" with what he calls "normative" mean-ing. He had better look elsewhere for regulation and criticism—away from traditional topics of philosophical reflection.

Generalizing from the case of Putnam, I would reply to McCarthy by urging that when we look for regulative ideals, we stick to freedom and forget about truth and rationality. We can safely do this because, what-ever else truth may be, it is something we are more likely to get as a result of free and open encounters than anything else. Whatever else rationality may be, it is something that obtains when persuasion is substituted for force. So what is really important to think about is what makes an encounter free from the influence of force. As I have urged elsewhere, if we take care of political and cultural freedom, truth and rationality will take care of themselves.[2] Since I regard modern philosophy as having centered around a discussion of truth, I regard philosophy as not very useful in the pursuit of such freedoms, as having become largely a distraction from that pursuit. That is why I say things that surprise and distress McCarthy—for instance, that philosophers should not expect to be the avant-garde of political movements.

McCarthy thinks truth more important than I do. Specifically, he thinks that "'truth' . . . functions as an 'idea of reason' with respect to which we can criticize not only particular claims within our language but the very standards of truth we have inherited" (p. 369). By contrast, I think that what enables us to make such criticisms is concrete alternative suggestions—suggestions about how to redescribe what we are talking about. Some examples are Galileo's suggestions about how to redescribe the Aristotelian universe, Marx's suggestions about how to redescribe the nineteenth century, Heidegger's suggestions about how to describe the West as a whole, Dickens's suggestions about how to redescribe chancery law, Rabelais's suggestions about how to redescribe monasteries, and Virginia Woolf's suggestions about how to redescribe women writing.

Such fresh descriptions, such new suggestions of things to say, sentences to consider, vocabularies to employ, are what do the work. All that the idea of truth does is to say, "Bethink yourself that you might be mistaken; remember that your beliefs may be justified by your other beliefs in the area, but that the whole kit and kaboodle might be misguided, and in particular that you might be using the wrong *words* for your purpose." But this admonition is empty and powerless without some concrete suggestion of an alternative set of beliefs, or of words. Moreover, if you have such a suggestion, you do not need the admonition. The *only* cash value of this regulative idea is to commend fallibilism, to remind us that lots of people have been as certain of, and as justified in believing, things that turned out to be false as we are certain of, and justified in holding, our present views. It is not, as McCarthy says, a "moment of unconditionality that opens us up to criticism from other points of view" (p. 370). It is the particular attractions of those other points of view.

For example: my awareness that my beliefs "'may turn out to be false after all'" (p. 369) does not open me up to criticism from the poor lost souls who write me abusive twelve-page single-spaced letters, replete with diagrams exhibiting the nature of the universe. I *am* opened up to criticism by critics like Habermas, McCarthy, Nancy Fraser, and others, because they are able to redescribe my own position in terms that make me say, "Gee, there might be something to that; when so described, I *do* look pretty bad." The "moment of unconditionality" is, in Ludwig Wittgenstein's phrase, "a wheel that can be turned though nothing else moves with it, . . . not part of the mechanism."[3] "Idealizing elements" do *nothing* to help me sort out the nut cases from the people to whom it pays to listen.

Concrete suggestions are a necessary condition of intellectual and moral progress, but not, of course, sufficient. Good luck is another necessary condition, and political and cultural freedom are others. Here is another area of disagreement between McCarthy and myself. McCarthy thinks that the ideals of political and cultural freedom are linked, in our culture, to "transcultural notions of validity." He says that our culture is "everywhere structured around" such notions (p. 361). Maybe so, but maybe the temptation to believe that it is so structured is just a professional deformation of us philosophy professors. My own hunch, or at least hope, is that our culture is gradually coming to be structured around the idea of freedom—of leaving people alone to dream and think and live as they please, so long as they do not hurt other people—and that this idea provides as viscous a social glue as that of unconditional validity.[4]

McCarthy, however, thinks that the question "Is the proposition 'freedom is a good thing' true in an unconditional sense?" is still one our culture is moved to ask. By contrast, I argue against Putnam that when we gave up on God, we tacitly and gradually began giving up on "true in an unconditional sense." I think that we may have moved on, or may at least be in the process of moving on, to a culture in which freedom can stand on its own feet. By contrast, McCarthy and Jacques Derrida are at one in believing that the entire culture of the West, right down to our own day, is permeated and structured by Greek metaphysics—by an aspiration toward something transcendent, beyond historical and cultural change, toward what Derrida calls "a reassuring certitude, which is itself beyond the reach of play."[5]

I have to admit that this claim has some plausibility. Perhaps the best evidence for it is that we philosophers are still called on to "answer Hitler," and abused if we confess our inability to do so. We are supposed to prove Hitler wrong by finding something beyond him and us—something unconditional—that agrees with us and not with him. It might well be said that a culture in which such demands are incessant is still structured by metaphysical ways of thinking, and that in such a culture one cannot responsibly decline the task McCarthy assigns the philosopher—the task of "recogniz[ing] the idealizing elements intrinsic to social practices and build[ing] on them" (p. 370).

Like Habermas and Karl-Otto Apel, McCarthy sees my refusal to take on the job of answering Hitler as a sign of irresponsible "decisionism" or "relativism."[6] But I have always (well, not always, but for the last twenty years or so) been puzzled about what was supposed to count as a knockdown answer to Hitler. Would it answer him to tell him that there was a God in Heaven who was on our side? How do we reply to him when he asks for evidence for this claim? Would it answer him to say that his views are incompatible with the construction of a society in which communication is undistorted, and that his refusal of a voice to his opponents contradicts the presupposition of his own communicative acts? What if Hitler rejoins that to interpret truth as a product of free and open encounters rather than as what emerges from the genius of a destined leader begs the question against him? (What if, in other words, he goes Heideggerian on us?) Richard Hare's view that there is no way to "refute" a sophisticated, consistent, passionate psychopath—for example, a Nazi who would favor his own elimination if he himself turned out to be Jewish—seems to me right, but to show more about the idea of "refutation" than about Nazism.[7]

If I were assigned the task not of refuting or answering but of *converting* a Nazi (one a bit more sane and conversable than Hitler himself), I would have some idea of how to set to work. I could show him how nice things can be in free societies, how horrible things are in the Nazi camps, how his Führer can plausibly be redescribed as an ignorant paranoid rather than as an inspired prophet, how the Treaty of Versailles can be redescribed as a reasonable compromise rather than as a vendetta, and so on. These tactics might or might not work, but at least they would not be an intellectual exercise in what Apel calls *Letztbegründung*.[8] They would be the sort of thing that sometimes actually changes people's minds. By contrast, attempts at showing the philosophically sophisticated Nazi that he is caught in a logical or pragmatic self-contradiction will simply impel him to construct invidious redescriptions of the presuppositions of the charge of contradiction (the sort of redescriptions Heidegger put at the Nazis' disposal).

Like a lot of other people who wind up teaching philosophy, I, too, got into the business because, having read some Plato, I thought I could use my budding dialectical talents to *demonstrate* that the bad guys were bad and the good guys good—to do to contemporary bad guys (for example, the bullies who used to beat me up in high school) what Socrates thought he was doing to Thrasymachus, Gorgias, and others. But, some twenty years back, I finally decided that this project was not going to pan out—that "demonstration" was just not available in this area, that a theoretically sophisticated bully and I would always reach an argumentative standoff. McCarthy, Apel, and Habermas still see some hope for the Socratic project. Since I do not, I decline the assignment McCarthy offers the philosopher and try to redescribe my own job. I redescribe it as picking and choosing among the elements in our culture, playing up some and playing down others.

In the light of this redescription, I can formulate the gist of my reply to McCarthy by saying: there are traditions within our culture that stand over and against the one you take as central, and these are the ones I want to encourage. I am not caught in the trap you describe, of being unable to "appeal to peer agreement, established norms, or anything of the sort" because I do not, in fact, find myself in a culture "everywhere structured around transcultural notions of validity" (p. 361). It is, fortunately, not so structured *everywhere*, just in some places. So I can appeal to things that are said and done in the other places. I can play off some elements in our culture against others (thus doing, I think, the same thing that Socrates and Plato did, no matter what they described themselves as doing). We live in a culture that has been nurtured not just on "the Bible, on Socrates and Plato, on the Enlightenment" (p. 365), but on, for example, Rabelais, Montaigne, Sterne, Hogarth, and Mark Twain.

The novel is just one of the elements in our culture that I should argue is *not* structured around transcultural notions of validity. But it is perhaps the clearest case, so I happily join Milan Kundera in appealing to the novel against philosophy. In his *Art of the Novel*, currently one of my favorite books, Kundera says:

> As God slowly departed from the seat whence he had directed the universe and its order of values, distinguished good from evil, and endowed each thing with meaning, Don Quixote set forth from his house into a world he could no longer recognize. In the absence of the Supreme Judge, the world suddenly appeared in its fearsome ambiguity; the single divine Truth decomposed into myriad relative truths parceled out by men. Thus was born the world of the Modern Era, and with it the novel, the image and model of that world. . . .
>
> Man desires a world where good and evil can be clearly distinguished, for he has an innate and irrepressible desire to judge before he understands. Religions and ideologies are founded on this desire. They can cope with the novel only by translating its language of relativity and ambiguity into their own apodictic and dogmatic discourse. They require that someone be right: either Anna Karenina is the victim of a narrow-minded tyrant, or Karenin is the victim of an immoral woman; either K. is an innocent man crushed by an unjust Court, or the Court represents divine justice and K. is guilty.[9]

Focusing more closely on the opposition between the "idealizing elements" in our culture and the elements that represent what he calls "the wisdom of the novel," Kundera says:

> Rabelais' erudition, great as it is, has another meaning than Descartes'. The novel's wisdom is different from that of philosophy. The novel is born not of the theoretical spirit but of the spirit of humor. One of Europe's major failures is that it never understood the most European of the arts—the novel; neither its

spirit, nor its great knowledge and discoveries, nor the autonomy of its history. The art inspired by God's laughter does not by nature serve ideological certitudes, it contradicts them. Like Penelope, it undoes each night the tapestry that the theologians, philosophers, and learned men have woven the day before.[10]

This undoing is effected by redescription, by proffering a vocabulary for talking about some particular person, situation, or event that cuts across the vocabulary we have so far used in our moral and political deliberations. The novel does not offer an argument within the same dialectical space we have previously been occupying, but rather the glimpse of other such spaces. The urge to redescribe, cultivated by reading novels, is different from the urge to demonstrate, cultivated by reading metaphysics. Kundera's "wisdom of the novel" has no use for McCarthy's "moment of unconditionality." The closest it can come to this is the regulative ideal of All Possible Novels—every redescription from every possible angle, all available at once. But this is not very close. For the realm of possibility is not something with fixed limits; rather, it expands continually, as ingenious new redescriptions suggest even more ingenious re-redescriptions. Every purported glimpse of the boundaries of this realm is in fact an expansion of those boundaries.

Does this mean that the wisdom of the novel encompasses a sense of how Hitler might be seen as in the right and the Jews in the wrong? Yes, I am afraid that it does. Someday somebody will write a novel about Hitler that will portray him as he saw himself, one that will, momentarily, make its readers feel that the poor man was much misunderstood. (A.J.P. Taylor's *Origins of the Second World War* can be viewed as a sketch for certain chapters of that novel.)[11] Someday somebody will write a novel about Stalin as Good Old Uncle Joe. I hope nobody writes either very soon, because reading such a novel seems too much for the remaining victims of either murderer to have to bear. But such novels will someday be written. If we are to be faithful to the wisdom of the novel, they *must* be written.

This ability to adopt every possible point of view is the aspect of the novel that is hardest for us to take, the ability that made Plato turn away in revulsion from the poets and attempt to invent a less flexible genre, one that had more in common with geometry. But, as I suggested above, the poet's flexibility turned out to be matched by the ability of Plato's heirs to formulate axioms from which to deduce, and vocabularies in which to phrase, an apologia for anything you please (slavery, the Inquisition, bourgeois democracy, the Nazis, the Cultural Revolution). This is the aspect of philosophy that is hardest for us to take, and that has, in recent times, made many poets and novelists turn from it in revulsion.

The impulse that leads us to reject instruments (the philosophical system, the novel) that can be turned to any and every purpose is that we *know* that we are the good guys and the Nazis are the bad guys. We should like to find some way of making this knowledge as clear to *everyone* as it is to us—to exhibit what McCarthy calls its "transcultural . . . validity" (p. 361). The trouble is, of course, that this same sort of knowledge-claim is made, in all sincerity, by the bad guys, and that we shall never have any resources available that will not be equally available to them. Talk of a "moment of unconditionality" does nothing, as far as I can see, to get us out of this predicament. That is why I can only suggest we cease to feel it as a predicament—that we cease to want something we have learned we cannot have, that we give up on "transcultural validity." This amounts to giving up on what so-called postmodernists call "logocentrism." That renunciation seems to me what pragmatism and "postmodernism" have in common. Where the latter goes off the rails is, as McCarthy nicely puts it, in "inflating the overcoming of metaphysics into a substitute for politics" (p. 363). So I do not see myself as, in McCarthy's words, "attempt[ing] to neutralize the political implications" of postmodernist theorizing (p. 367). What's to neutralize? I do not see that there are any such implications.[12]

As long as one thinks of "reason" as the name for a faculty capable of attaining transcultural validity, one will want a theory of the nature of rationality. But if one gives up on transcultural validity, then one will suspect that we have said enough about rationality when we say that any fool thing can be made to seem rational by being set in an appropriate context, surrounded by a set of beliefs and desires with which it coheres. The interesting question is not whether a claim can be "rationally defended" but whether it can be made to cohere with a sufficient number of *our* beliefs and desires.[13] My suspicion of theories of rationality, and of grand social theory generally, is not, however, offered as a result of a philosophical demonstration. That would, indeed, be self-referentially inconsistent in just the way McCarthy suspects I am inconsistent. I would defend this suspicion, instead, by pointing to the track record of the journalists, novelists, and anthropologists—the people who bring lots of sordid details to our attention—and arguing that the utility of their contributions has been much greater than that of the theorists. They seem to me to be the people who lately have been most efficient at doing social good, in regulating and criticizing our political activities. My attitude is not "theory is dead," but rather "as things have been going, it looks as if we could use a bit less theory and a bit more reportage." I am not saying that the idea of truth is "invalid" or "untenable," nor that it "deconstructs itself," but simply that for our present purposes there are more useful ideas (for example, freedom).

I hope this account of my views explains, if it does not excuse, my perhaps overblown rhetoric in Guadalajara (quoted by McCarthy at the beginning of his essay [p. 355]). What I was trying, pretty awkwardly, to say at the InterAmerican Congress of Philosophy was something like this: Don't assume that because we are philosophers we can be of any special use, in our professional capacity, to struggles against imperialism, or racism. Don't assume, because Lenin wrote about Berkeley and Mach, that all revolutionaries need to be briefed on such topics. Don't assume that the Marxists were right that a correct theoretical analysis of the situation will be indispensable for getting rid of the local oligarch, or the CIA, or the KGB. Don't assume that, because the leader of Sendero Luminoso wrote his dissertation on Kant, he has a clearer view of Peru's problems, or a clearer vision of a possible future for his country, than the relatively uneducated woman trying to organize a food cooperative in the shantytowns outside of Lima.

McCarthy finds it ironic that an "absolute split between a depoliticized theory and a detheorized politics should be the final outcome of a project that understands itself as a pragmatic attempt to overcome the dichotomy between theory and practice" (pp. 366–67). But the only reason I speak of "depoliticized theory" is to take note of the fact that the most original theorists of recent times (for example, Heidegger, Derrida) do not give liberals like McCarthy and me any useful new tools.[14] As to "the dichotomy between theory and practice," this seems to me overcome as soon as we follow Alexander Bain and C. S. Peirce in thinking of our beliefs as rules for action—tools for getting what we want—rather than as accurate or inaccurate representations of reality, or as candidates for unconditional validity. Thinking of belief in this way, as McCarthy rightly says, "amounts to flattening out our notions of reason and truth by removing any air of transcendence from them" (p. 360). But once this flattening is accomplished, the question of which tools are best suited to achieve which ends remains as salient as ever. That question can only be answered experimentally—by reference to local conditions, the situation in which alternative tools are proffered. A fortiori, the question of how much theorizing political deliberation needs at any given point can only be answered in this way. This is what I meant by saying that "we should think of politics as one of the experimental rather than of the theoretical disciplines."[15]

So when McCarthy says that my view prevents us "from even thinking, in any theoretically informed way, the thought that the basic structures of society might be inherently unjust in some way, that they might work to the systematic disadvantage of certain social groups" (p. 367), all the burden falls on "basic" and on "in any theoretically informed way." There is nothing in my view that hinders our noticing the misery and hopelessness of inner-city American blacks or Latin American slum-dwellers or Cambodian peasants. Nor is there anything that suggests such misery and hopelessness is irremediable. There is only the suggestion that we already have as much theory as we need, and that what we need now are concrete utopias, and concrete proposals about how to get to those utopias from where we are now.

That the middle class of the United States, as of South Africa, is unwilling to pay the taxes necessary to give poor blacks a decent education and a chance in life seems to me a fact we need no fancier theoretical notions than "greed," "selfishness," and "racial prejudice" to explain. That successive American presidents have ordered or allowed the CIA to make it as difficult as possible to depose Latin American oligarchies seems another such well-known fact, whose explanation is to be found on the level of details about the activities of, for example, the United Fruit Company and Anaconda Copper in Washington's corridors of power. When I am told that to appreciate the significance of these facts I need a deeper understanding of, for example, the discourses of power characteristic of late capitalism, I am incredulous.

Maybe I have not been reading the right theorists, but I really have no clear idea what it means to say that "the basic structures of society" (capitalist society, presumably) are responsible for these facts, any more than to say that other "basic structures" (those of noncapitalist societies) are responsible for the plight of the Romanians or the Tibetans. I am not sure what a "theoretically informed way" to think about these matters would be, as opposed to a historically and journalistically informed way. I can happily agree that philosophers and social theorists have, in the past, done a lot of good by giving us ways to put in words our vague sense that something has gone terribly wrong. Notions like "the rights of man," "surplus value," "the new class," and the like have been indispensable for moral and political progress. But I am not convinced that we are currently in need of new notions of this sort. A lot of social theory nowadays seems to me just putting overelaborate icing on cakes historians, journalists, economic statisticians, anthropologists, and others have already baked.

It seems to me that people who believe in "a moment of unconditionality" and in intercultural validity are still prone to think that there is an activity called "radical reconceptualization" that might tear the scales from our eyes and let us see what is *really* going on—see things as God sees them. Even though McCarthy and Putnam claim to have renounced the idea of a God's-eye point of view, their faith in theory and for the idea of truth seems to me to reflect a nostalgia for the logocentrist's unveiling-reality model of inquiry as opposed to the pragmatist's invention-of-new-tools model. For if one uses the latter model, the notion "basic structure of society" will fade out in favor of notions like "malleable social structure," "pressure point for initiating structural change." The question "What is the truth about our society?" fades out in favor of questions like "What would let more people in this society get more freedom?" "What will it take to elect a left-wing Democratic (Labor, SPD) government?" and "Is there anything except coca paste that Peru could produce and export in quantities sufficient to significantly raise the Peruvian standard of living?" The question "Is this value interculturally valid?" fades out in favor of questions like "Do you have any better values to suggest?" The question "How can you be sure your values are unconditionally valid?" fades out in favor of the question "How can we be sure that discussion of alternative values is as free, open, and imaginative as possible?" Social theorists and philosophers deserve a hearing in such discussion, for, like everybody else, they may have something imaginative to say. But there is no guarantee that they will, and no reason to view them as indispensable.

NOTES

1. See Richard Rorty, "Putnam on Truth," *Philosophy and Phenomenological Research* vol. 52/2 (June 1992) 415–18.

2. See Rorty, "The Priority of Democracy to Philosophy," in *The Virginia Statute for Religious Freedom: Its Evolution and Consequences in American History*, ed. Merrill D. Peterson and Robert C. Vaughn, Cambridge Studies in Religion and American Public Life (Cambridge: Cambridge University Press, 1988), pp. 257–82. Reprinted in this volume as chap. 11.

3. Ludwig Wittgenstein, *Philosophical Investigations*, 3d ed., trans. G.E.M. Anscombe (New York: Macmillan, 1958), no. 271.

4. I discuss the question of the strength of this social glue in my *Contingency, Irony, and Solidarity* (Cambridge: Cambridge University Press, 1989), pp. 82–88.

5. Jacques Derrida, *Writing and Difference*, trans. Alan Bass (Chicago: University of Chicago Press, 1978), p. 279. I have previously criticized Derrida's claim that this characteristically metaphysical urge is central to our culture, particularly in my "Deconstruction and Circumvention," *Critical Inquiry* 11 (September 1984):1–23, especially pp. 19–21.

6. See Karl-Otto Apel, *Diskurs und Verantwortung: Das Problem des Übergangs zur postkonventionellen Moral* (Frankfurt am Main: Suhrkamp, 1988), especially pp. 399–425.

7. See R. M. Hare, "Toleration and Fanaticism," *Freedom and Reason* (Oxford: Oxford University Press, 1963), pp. 157–85.

8. See Apel, *Diskurs und Verantwortung*, pp. 406ff.

9. Milan Kundera, *The Art of the Novel*, trans. Linda Asher (New York: Grove Press, 1988), pp. 6–7.

10. Ibid., p. 160.

11. See A.J.P. Taylor, *The Origins of the Second World War* (1963; Harmondsworth: Penguin Books, 1977).

12. See, on this point, my "Two Cheers for the Cultural Left," *South Atlantic Quarterly* 89 (Winter 1990): 227–34. McCarthy shares some of my doubts on this point, as when he criticizes Derrida's attempt to "be postmetaphysical in thinking about ethics, law, and politics" and says that "a better way of being postmetaphysical in ethics, law, and politics is to stop doing metaphysics, even of

a negative sort, when thinking about them" (McCarthy, "On the Margins of Politics," *Journal of Philosophy* 85 [November 1988]: 645, 648). More generally, McCarthy tends to agree with Jürgen Habermas's criticisms of the political utility of Derrida and Foucault in Habermas, *The Philosophical Discourse of Modernity: Twelve Lectures*, trans. Frederick Lawrence (Cambridge, Mass.: Harvard University Press, 1987); I do as well, with the reservations expressed in my *Contingency, Irony, and Solidarity*, pp. 61–69.

13. For a defense of this brand of ethnocentrism, see my "Solidarity or Objectivity," in *Post-Analytic Philosophy*, ed. John Rajchman and Cornel West (New York: Columbia University Press, 1985), pp. 3–19, and my "On Ethnocentrism: A Reply to Clifford Geertz," *Michigan Quarterly Review* 25 (Summer 1986): 525–34.

14. On this point see my *Contingency, Irony, and Solidarity*, pp. 91–95.

15. Rorty, "From Logic to Language to Play: A Plenary Address to the Inter-American Congress," *Proceedings and Addresses of the American Philosophical Association* 59 (1986): pp. 752–53.

CONTRIBUTORS

ROBERT MERRIHEW ADAMS, Professor of Philosophy, University of California, Los Angeles

ANNETTE C. BAIER, Professor of Philosophy, University of Pittsburgh

ALAN DONAGAN (deceased), Doris and Henry Dreyfuss Professor of Philosophy, California Institute of Technology

MARGARET A. FARLEY, Gilbert L. Stark Professor of Christian Ethics, Yale University

ALAN GEWIRTH, Edward Carson Waller Distinguished Service Professor of Philosophy, University of Chicago

DAVID LITTLE, Senior Scholar, United States Institute of Peace, Washington, D.C.

GENE OUTKA, Dwight Professor of Philosophy and Christian Ethics, Yale University

JOHN P. REEDER, JR., Professor of Religious Studies, Brown University

RICHARD RORTY, University Professor of Humanities, University of Virginia

JEFFREY STOUT, Professor of Religion, Princeton University

LEE H. YEARLEY, Professor of Religious Studies, Stanford University

INDEX